SPECTACULAR SPECULATION

SPECTACULAR SPECULATION

THRILLS, THE ECONOMY, AND POPULAR DISCOURSE

URS STÄHELI

Translated by Eric Savoth

STANFORD UNIVERSITY PRESS

STANFORD, CALIFORNIA

Stanford University Press
Stanford, California

Spectacular Speculation: Thrills, the Economy, and Popular Discourse was originally published in German under the title *Spektakuläre Spekulation: Das Populäre der Ökonomie* © Suhrkamp Verlag Frankfurt am Main 2007.

Library of Congress Cataloging-in-Publication Data

Stäheli, Urs, 1966– author.

[Spektakuläre Spekulation. English]

Spectacular speculation : thrills, the economy, and popular discourse / Urs Stäheli ; translated by Eric Savoth.

pages cm

Translation of: Spektakuläre Spekulation : das Populäre der Ökonomie.

Includes bibliographical references and index.

ISBN 978-0-8047-7131-3 (cloth : alk. paper)

ISBN 978-0-8047-7132-0 (pbk. : alk. paper)

1. Speculation—United States—History. 2. Speculation—History. 3. Finance—Social aspects—United States—History. 4. Finance—Social aspects—History. I. Title.

HG4910.S628 2013

332.64'5—dc23

2012020652

CONTENTS

ILLUSTRATIONS

ACKNOWLEDGMENTS

This book has profited from many discussions at different locations. I would like to thank Rudolf Stichweh of the Faculty of Sociology at Bielefeld University for supporting the project, and Ute Tellmann for many discussions about poststructuralism and economics. A large part of the book was researched and written during a study visit to the Department of Comparative Literature at Stanford University, made possible by a research fellowship from the Swiss National Science Foundation. My conversations at Stanford with Hans-Ulrich Gumbrecht and Nico Pethes were more than inspiring, not least in sensitizing me to how speculation generates effects of presence. During regular visits to the research group on public and political management at the Copenhagen Business School, I discussed the various stages of the book across disciplinary and theoretical boundaries. In particular, I am grateful to Niels Andersen Aakerstroem, Allan Dreyer Hansen, Christian Frankel, and Christian Borch for enthusiastic discussions. I owe much to Dirk Verdicchio for the conversations we had in Bern and Basel about the interface of popular culture and economics, and in conversations with Jens Ruchatz, Torsten Hahn, and Christina Bartz at the Medien und kulturelle Kommunikation (Media and Cultural Communication) research school in Cologne, I discovered that the subject by no means resists theorization. I am grateful to Christian Wymann and the Suhrkamp editorial office for their patient, close reading of the manuscript of the German edition of this book, and I thank Eric Savoth for translating it and for always responding very constructively to my comments. Thanks also to Emily-Jane Cohen at Stanford University Press for having supported this English edition. Finally, I thank Viola Weigel for her many suggestions, aesthetic judgment, and constant encouragement of this speculative undertaking.

SPECTACULAR SPECULATION

INTRODUCTION

Speculation has for a long time had the reputation of being an exceptionally unpopular field of study. As early as the eighteenth century, authors eager to win readers were strongly advised against tackling this curious subject and the disgraceful moral squalor embodied in its dry economic transactions.[1] Nevertheless, the Scottish man of letters and journalist Charles Mackay (1814–89) decidedly rejected the notion that accounts of speculation would inevitably bore readers because of their coldness. In his famous book *Extraordinary Popular Delusions and the Madness of Crowds*, Mackay looks at speculation in the context of exceptional outbreaks of speculatory fever, which are of interest precisely because of the moral collapse, deception, and rapid fluctuations in fortune they involved:

> [T]he subject is capable of inspiring as much interest as even a novelist can desire. Is there no warmth in the despair of plundered people? no life and animation in the picture which might be drawn of the woes of hundreds of impoverished and ruined families? of the wealthy of yesterday become the beggars of to-day? . . . of the powerful and influential changed into exiles and outcasts, and the voice of self-reproach and imprecation resounding from every corner of the land? Is it a dull or uninstructive picture to see a whole people shaking suddenly off the trammels of reason, and running wild after a golden vision, refusing obstinately to believe that it is not real, till, like a deluded hind running after an ignis fatuus, they are plunged into a quagmire? (Mackay 1980 [1841–52], 74)

Speculative manias aroused reader interest precisely because they displayed instances of moral collapse, delusion, and rapid fluctuations of fortune. With a pleasant shudder, the reader of *Extraordinary Popular Delusions* observes entire nations making ludicrous speculative spectacles of themselves. Like the British cultural studies demanding a history of the "people" and their culture over a hundred years later, Mackay foregrounds the "people" and their fate—though with a serious gaze, not meant to glorify them.[2]

The spectacularity of speculation captured the attention of popular writers earlier than that of academics. Economics struggled, even at the end of the nineteenth century, to find a vocabulary for speculation that would be properly economic. Speculation itself, however, was already established as a popular economic practice. Not only did trading in securities on the streets overlap with forms of entertainment such as gambling, but a prolific everyday literature devoted to speculation sprang up, variously taking the form of moral treatises warning about the social and psychic consequences of speculation, plays and stories unfolding its melodramatic potential, and stock exchange handbooks explaining this wondrous economic phenomenon.[3]

Financial speculation is situated in a singular network of economic abstraction and popular spectacularity. Not until the nineteenth century was it possible to establish the fledging new modes of speculation as legitimate economic practice (Goux 1997, 2000).[4] It thus became necessary to come up with new economic self-descriptions and external descriptions no longer exclusively based on the discourse of production, exchange, and labor. What was unique was that stock speculation, which converts its economic referents into a play of self-generated signs, abstracts from the "real" values previously considered to underwrite the substance of economic operations. Moreover, it lacks the "warmth" and link to the "people" self-evident in other modes of economic practice, such as work or consumption. The popular enthusiasm displayed for this abstract mode of the economy almost everywhere is thus somewhat astonishing.

This popularity was from the outset by no means unproblematic, since it could impede speculation from establishing itself as a new economic practice. Even where speculation was established, its popularity proved to be simultaneously an opportunity and a hindrance. For with its success, speculation came to occupy a representative function in economic self-descriptions. Speculation represented synecdochically, as it were, the entire economy. This mode of representation became possible because speculation—in its abstractness—came close to economic idealizations of the perfect market. What did it mean, however, when this abstractness itself became a spectacle? The theoretical and historical interest of this book is linked to this relation between abstraction and spectacularity. How was this tension represented discursively at the time? What conceptual struggles arose as a result of it? What discursive techniques were developed to be able to control this tension and perhaps even use it to establish speculation as a field? The "popular" of the economy is read, in this sense, as the terrain on which the "essence" of the economy is decided—a terrain marked by undecidability and boundary conflicts.

These questions have led me to a sociological-historical analysis of the discourse of speculation between 1870 and 1930, primarily in the United States. In the first half of the nineteenth century, speculation occupied a position of little significance in popular culture.[5] However, by the end of the 1920s, it became a constant object of public debates. In this period, an important reconfiguration of economic discourse that challenged the production-centered neoclassical paradigm also took place. At the end of the nineteenth century, stock market speculation was not yet established, and its articulation was heavily contested. Precisely for this reason, a historical-sociological analysis can show how speculation emerged amid fierce debates. Indeed, speculation is still contested today, although contemporary challenges seem like a restaging of earlier critiques.[6] In the America of the late nineteenth and early twentieth centuries, speculation provoked a veritable discursive explosion because it was seen as a form both of economic and noneconomic practice.

However, the chronology of American discourses of speculation cannot be precisely delimited. A number of terminologies, stereotypes, and argumentative strategies emerged long before the period under consideration. For example, criticisms of speculation as deception and fiction are already to be found in Daniel Defoe's writings, in the seventeenth century, and similar arguments surfaced again in American investment magazines after the decline of the so-called new economy of the 1990s. The period investigated here is distinguished from earlier centuries based on how speculation sought to establish itself as a legitimate form of communication. Only at the end of the nineteenth century did theories arise attempting to constitute speculation as economic. Around this time, the issue of the ethics of speculation was supplemented—and even partly replaced—by the question of its "economicity" [Ökonomizität]. This discursive economization intensified the tensions between exclusive speculation on Wall Street and popular speculation on Main Street. In the period considered here, speculation came to be seen as the "temper of the age" rather than as a pathology.

After the introduction of the stock ticker machine in 1867, traders no longer had to be physically present on the floor of the stock exchange—a development that allowed stock speculation to greatly expand its scope—and there was a dramatic inclusionary impulse in stock trading after 1900. Although figures from the time are hardly reliable, they suggest how rapidly the number of shareholders grew. The number of direct and indirect shareholders rose from an estimated 4.4 million in 1900 to 26 million in 1932.[7] Following the euphoric speculative boosterism of the 1920s, this growth then came to a temporary stop with the stock market crash in 1929.

Discourses of speculation in America around 1900 invite analysis because of their privileged position in the history of speculation. European and American observers consistently saw the United States as the land of speculation, something that was criticized on both moral and political grounds. This criticism did not, however, change the privileged position of speculation. Risk taking was considered to be intrinsic to a democratic economy, in which anyone prepared to take on risk could eventually become a winner.

This book does not solely restrict itself to the discourse of speculation that developed in the United States. Speculative rationales were not constituted along national lines. Interdiscursive networks ignored national borders, even if discourses of speculation were articulated differently according to region. There were various theories and concepts about American speculation. No single concept of it dominated, but America was seen by all of them as the "nation of speculation."

The popularity of speculation makes it necessary to expand classical scholarly conceptualizations with material from mass culture, conceived of in the widest sense.[8] It is of interest to see how everyday manuals speak of stock market speculation, define financial limits, and articulate economic fears and hopes. The corpus examined here consists of the most important American stock handbooks and introductions, accounts in popular periodicals of how the market functions,[9] and the work of advisers and early psychologists of speculation aiming to depict the ideal speculator.[10] This material makes it possible to identify the challenges to economic inclusion that arose when speculation was established as a legitimate form of economic practice.[11]

This book does not analyze current discourses of speculation, but nonetheless seeks to contribute to a "sociology of the present" through historical analysis. In the Foucauldian sense of a "history of the present," historical material will be confronted with present-day questions, placing this material within a genealogy of *homo oeconomicus* (Vogl 2002) that has seen a particularly striking elaboration of the notion of the "neoliberal" subject.[12] This genealogical perspective aims at providing insight into the complex discursive conditions that allowed the ideal speculator to emerge as a central model of economic subjectivity. Unlike moral critiques directed at economic models of subjectivity, this analysis does not seek to "humanize" the calculating economic subject.[13] Rather, it enquires into the disparate, disputed discursive conditions that go to make up the ideal speculator, who in many respects approximates *homo oeconomicus* and is just as popular and contested a figure.

This line of questioning has far-reaching methodological consequences. Entirely in accord with analyses oriented by conceptual history, I am interested in how distinctions are created and stabilized in thinking and writing about speculation. My interest also extends to the paradoxes such distinctions entail—and to how these paradoxes are neutralized.[14] This approach demands a stronger consideration of textual microstructures than Niklas Luhmann's analysis of semantics does. Representative overviews will be combined with case analyses that focus on passages exemplifying the "popular" of the economy (drawing from and rearticulating the concept of the popular as used by cultural studies, as I explain later). Here, a deconstructive reading is important. Rather than (often prematurely) accepting a hegemonic and preferred meaning as given, I examine the fissures in specific texts where the contingency of governing distinctions becomes clear.[15] From a sociological perspective, such passages are of interest. The complex and often contradictory premises on which apparently "clear" distinctions rest can now be analyzed. While Derridean deconstruction often celebrates such aporias, I try to show how they function in financial apparatuses of inclusion.[16] This effort requires that I not only speak of semantic key distinctions (as Luhmann does), but also of discourses. Luhmannian semantic analyses are best suited for examining how distinctions are established, but the concept of discourse locates them in comprehensive strategies, understood in the sense of "strategies without strategists," which arise as the structural effects of discursive modes of organization that lack an underlying intention.[17]

How to theorize the popular attraction that speculation exerted? It is here that the concept of the popular becomes crucial. One possible conception of the popular—simply along empirical lines—would be based on the number of speculators. Quantitatively measurable growth would then become a criterion for the popularity of speculation. Such a notion, however, would not address the discursive and affective appeal of speculation, and how the figure of the speculator is being made and represented as popular figure. As an alternative to quantitative approaches to the subject of speculation, the concept of the popular is important, since it is interested in representational and communicative strategies.[18] Although this concept has proved to be very useful for analyzing the political construction of social and cultural identities, in its original version, it was not seen as appropriate for analyzing economic processes. In cultural studies, the popular is portrayed as a critical response to the capitalist social order, hence the economy cannot be popular.[19] Cultural studies has always kept the issue of the economy at arm's length. This distancing is expressed either in the form of simple disinterest or, more commonly, in a false respect for the economy. The analytical approaches of cultural studies often perpetuate oversimplified conceptions of capitalism as hegemonic and focus on subversive micropractices directed against capitalist macro-power.[20]

Moreover, these approaches obscure cultural studies' rare engagements with forms of popular capitalism that have not always already decided in favor of the "people," such as Thatcherism. "[T]he left has never understood the capacity of the market to become identified in the minds of the mass of ordinary people, not as fair and decent and socially responsible (that it never was), but as an expansive popular system," Stuart Hall writes (1988, 215).[21] As an "expansive popular system," the market is not opposed to the logic of the popular. The success of Thatcherism, according to Hall, lay in connecting the people to the market, that is, creating a popular attraction of the market: "[Its] strategy has been to align the positive aspiration of people *with* the market and the restoration of the capitalist ethic" (218). In the Thatcherite inclusive apparatus, the idea of freedom was translated from politics into economics in order to appeal to the "little" people.[22]

Of course, the conjunction of the popular and the market have not been limited to Thatcherism. Thomas Frank (2000) coined the term "market populism" to analyze American discourses at the end of the nineteenth century that already saw a mystical force for national unification at work in the market. This market populism reached a high point in the discourses of the so-called new economy in the 1990s. In opposition to political institutions, often seen as corrupt and untransparent, the market was seen as speaking for "the people." It was treated virtually as a grassroots entity, since it was not dependent on the mediating authority of representative democracy. Rather, "the people" could directly express themselves in the language of price, based on what they decided to buy and sell: "Markets expressed the popular will more articulately and more meaningfully than did mere elections. Markets conferred democratic legitimacy; markets were a friend of the little guy; markets brought down the pompous and the snooty; markets gave us what we wanted; markets looked out for our interests" (Frank 2000, xiv). Or, to put it succinctly: "Markets ® Us."

It is not surprising that an analysis of the popularity of the market—or of market populism—has been sharply criticized, and even accused of trivializing the forces of the capitalist market.[23] For some representatives of cultural studies, consolidating the "hegemonic" economic order with popular capitalism can only be provocative. One appears to ennoble the market by granting it a privileged relation to the people. Why should the market be fought against if it has already conquered the hearts and minds of the people and become their voice?

Stuart Hall sees the popularity of the market as a peculiar—and exceptional—conjunction (as, in a certain sense, does Thomas Frank). However, I shall suppose that economic inclusion, like all forms of inclusion, has to use popular strategies and modes of representation. This popular logic often falls out of view when economic inclusion is understood as exclusively led by specific interests or needs. The stock market—a place where one hopes to get "something for nothing"—thus stands for the popular of the economy despite being unintelligibly abstract to laypeople.

The concept of the popular used here should not automatically be seen as subversive. It instead refers to how modes of inclusion in the economic system have been configured—particularly in America around 1900. Around this time, inclusion was deeply contested in emerging forms of the stock market. My approach presupposes that economic inclusion is not accomplished simply through rational calculation. As John Maynard Keynes argued (1973 [1935]), the decision to speculate ultimately cannot be economic, but belongs to an irrational "animal instinct." I would like to take seriously Keynes's suggestion that there is a noneconomic aspect to structuring economic processes of inclusion.

My concept of the popular draws on Luhmann's theory of inclusion. Processes of inclusion are organized in all functional systems through the establishment of the roles of the public and the professionals (Stichweh 1988). For example, it is possible to be included in economic systems as a consumer or producer. Since the concept of inclusion under consideration cannot be reduced to role-theoretical expectations, I address figures of inclusion rather than the public role alone. These figures of inclusion not only represent the universalism of a system but also construct actors as universalistic fictions (cf. Hutter and Teubner 1994).

The speculator is precisely such a figure of inclusion. These figures are—at least in the self-descriptions of functional systems—disposed toward universalism. Each system is, in principle, open to all who have the necessary functional competencies: everyone can become a speculator! The universalism of a specific system is founded on specific functional references and competence profiles. Systems-theoretical analyses often presuppose that this specification derives automatically from the societal function of a particular system. However, the discourses, narratives, and images that flesh out the figure of the speculator can be highly contested. A specific profile of the speculator did not automatically emerge from the function of finance. At a minimum, this profile required that financial resources be available to the speculator: only creditworthiness opened access to finance. In both the United States and Europe, however, intense conceptual struggles arose over the articulation of this minimal profile. The figure of the speculator fluctuated between conflicting modes of inclusion. On the one hand, speculation demanded special competence and thus excluded those who were "unfit" or not educated to speculate. On the other hand, since, on a formal level, speculation required nothing more than access to money, potentially anyone could be included—regardless of his or her professional skills. These fluctuating requirements created standards of professional competence and knowledge for speculation, but also established a disciplinary mechanism that shaped the identity of the speculator. To discuss speculation is to discuss the popularity of speculation. Because nearly anyone can participate in speculation, it threatens to produce an uncontrollable universalism of undisciplined economic subjects.

European discourses of speculation provide many critical examples of excessive inclusivity that invoke a "minimal profile." For example, Max Weber took aim at small speculators "armed with practically nothing beyond good lungs, a little notebook, and a pencil,"[24] whom he portrays unsuited for stock trading, since they lack the fundamental prerequisites, including the capital needed to survive a crisis and knowledge of the market. Stock trading, Weber argued, was above all *not* a profession for small speculators, and he called for competent, well-trained market participants socialized within the strict boundaries of professional speculation. This contrasts with the belief that the participation of numerous small speculators—regardless of their competence—increases the liquidity of the market, expressed in the slogan of the online broker Instinet: "The bigger the crowd, the better the performance" (*Business Week*, 8 January, 2001).

This tension between disciplinary and popular forms of inclusion was already being debated energetically at the beginning of the twentieth century, when border conflicts arose about the definition of a system-specific universality. How far did participant roles have to extend before they compromised the "competence profile" of actors in a given structure, such as the speculator occupying the role of *homo oeconomicus*? To put it another way, what prevented the economicity of speculation from being lost in financial gaming?

Such an analysis of the popular of the economy is interested in how the borders between the stock market audience and its outside are organized—and in how this outside is described. The outside is not arranged in an arbitrary and empirically contingent relation to a particular construction of the audience, but assumes a constitutive function. Since the audience and its figures cannot be fully universalized, the outside articulates the boundaries but also the aim of existing "universalities." In turn, these boundaries identify sites where such universalities can be expanded. My thesis is that the popular can be specified precisely in relation to its outside. The popular (e.g., "market populism" [Frank 2000]), can be formally defined as *the communicative process that distinguishes between the professional audience and its outside*. This process makes it possible to understand better how the popularity of the market can be grasped conceptually. The popular is not simply constituted by specific economic promises (e.g., the promise of equal opportunity), but by excessive universalistic arguments of inclusion. The popular thus plays a central role in constructing a financial audience whose legitimate borders are repeatedly contested. To speak about the popular means to examine the role the noneconomic outside public plays in "audience making" (Ettema and Whitney 1994) for the economy. A discussion of the popular of the economy thus has to analyze how a given universalism is related to its outside. This relation takes different forms. On the one hand, (a) imaginary conceptualizations of the outside serve as a delimiting barrier, and what is external to the audience becomes a *threat scenario* that makes plausible the need to delineate a specific system of universalisms. On the other hand, (b) the external is identified as *potential for inclusion*, and thus as a way to extend universal modes of inclusion.

(a) *The nonaudience as excluded*: The nonaudience initially represents the other that absolutely cannot be included in functional systems. In our case, this other is the "crowd" that cannot be reduced to individual speculators, even through refined technologies of inclusion. Self-descriptions are often fascinated with the nonaudience as imaginaries of their outside. These imaginaries include rhetorics of the crowd, particularly descriptions of female speculators as the virtual embodiment of an impossible subject position (see chapter 6). In a fundamental sense, the outside is understood as unincludable. The nonaudience is not simply another audience subject to inclusionary and disciplinary procedures, but escapes all boundaries (Kristeva 1982, 4). As outside, the nonaudience resists individualization and thus threatens the rationality of a system. This outside circumvents the structure underlying constructs of the audience. An audience distinguishes itself by the individuality of its members—and by the capacity of these members to make individual decisions. In this way, microdiversity is created (Luhmann 1997b). Market fluctuations that become the basis for investment arise only because investors do not make the same decisions about buying and selling. Imaginary conceptualizations of the outside are thus concerned with how deindividualization threatens the structure of the audience. For example, discussion of panic thematizes how individuality dissolves into reciprocal imitation (see chapter 4).

(b) *The potential of the nonaudience for inclusion:* When the nonaudience is designated as potentially includable, it is subordinated to the processes of universalization in a given functional system. These processes expand not only the size of the audience but also its force as a universal figure of inclusion. The audience is understood as expandable by future speculators. In principle, the unincluded can also be included when subject to system-specific criteria of individualization. With the details of the audience yet to come embedded in governmental technologies, in the Foucauldian sense of governmentality, inclusion can be designated as a *problem* requiring treatment by techniques that first allow for the distinction between audience and nonaudience.[25] Communicative attempts to convert the audience yet to come into an audience arise precisely because the outside can be discussed as a problem of inclusion.

This problem arises in particular for the establishment of new figures of inclusion like that of the speculator. Thus, the gambler is identified as a potential speculator—but as a speculator who has not yet been formed as an economic subject through techniques of discipline and knowledge (see chapter 1).

These two ways to construct the outside of an audience appear mutually to exclude each other. The "outside as rejected" contrasts with the "outside as potential." However, in both cases similar problems of representation emerge. Something has to be represented that exceeds—and delimits—its own universalism. Thus, the same vocabulary (e.g., the discourse of crowds) is often deployed for both representational demands. The crowd becomes material for a utopia of education and inclusion, but also provides the occasion for imaginaries of miscarried inclusionary efforts.

Both cases thus require forms of communication that address an unspecified outside—an outside conceived of either as the potential for or the threat of inclusion. Functional systems cannot rely on their specialized languages alone to this end, but have to adopt forms of communication that make inclusion attractive. This demand comes to the foreground in one of the earliest accounts of popular capitalism—the account Raymond Williams gives, but admittedly does not follow, in *Culture and Society, 1780–1950* (1962).[26]

In a pamphlet titled *A Short View of the Immorality and Profaneness of the English Stage* (1698), Jeremy Collier criticized popularity as "courting the favour of the people by undue practices" (cited in Williams 1986 [1976]). Although Collier disparaged the popular, his conception is more interesting from a communications-theoretical perspective than the essentialization of "the people" prevalent in cultural studies today. Collier offered inclusion not only as an abstract possibility but also as a *seduction*. One could be seduced to inclusion by means of "undue practices"—forms of communication that do not belong to the universalizing tendency of a given system but enable it to expand.

Communication-theoretical analysis of the popular has to engage the "undue practices" extending modes of inclusion in functional systems without corresponding to the "logic" of a given system. Since what is external to the audience (from the perspective of a given functional system) is not adequately individualized, functionally specified modes of communication have to be transgressed. The nonspeculator can only become a speculator by being addressed as a nonspeculator. Otherwise, inclusion can only include the speculator who is already a subject. The advertising slogan "Make your first winning investment now . . . by investing in yourself" embodies the tautology that one already has to be an investor to become an investor, which can only function in the process of inclusion by introducing additional presuppositions.[27] Everyone is presupposed to be a speculator from birth, and life itself is treated as a permanent practice of risk.

Popular means of communication are deployed without satisfying a functional system's claims to differentiation. Two forms of communication allowing the construction of a function-specific audience are *hyperconnectivity* and *affectivity*. Hyperconnectivity means the ability to connect to a large number of different contexts (Stäheli 2000a). In opposition to symbolically generalized media, hyperconnective forms become more connective when they lose specificity. Such forms include the entire ensemble of media relating to theater and staging, as well as techniques of popularization distinguishing between audience and nonaudience in functional systems. Examples include the ways fireworks and mass demonstrations are used in politics, science is staged and popularized in experiments, miracles are used in religion, and mechanisms of suspense are adopted from gambling in the stock market.

In contrast to dramatic assertions that we live in a "simulation society" (Baudrillard), my claim here is not that hyperconnective media have become the dominant form of communication (e.g., the term "casino capitalism" presumes that the potential of the economy is exhausted by gambling). Such exaggeration fails to see how hyperconnective forms *overlap* with communication specific to functional systems. For example, how are moments of gambling embedded in speculation without automatically transforming the economy into a game? Hyperconnective media certainly appear in all functional systems. However, this appearance should be cause neither to celebrate nor to criticize the dissolution of system boundaries. How hyperconnectivity relates to forms of differentiation in a system is ultimately an empirical question. Undoubtedly, popular communication in "unpopular" systems is not free of risk and often leads to boundary conflicts—whether they be about how to determine the legitimate boundaries for a universalistic conception of the audience or about how popular communication relates to a given symbolically generalized medium. The economic character of speculation is left open to attack when finance is transformed into spectacular entertainment—even if liquidity is thus increased (see chapter 1). Popular communication facilitates processes of inclusion and the functioning of a system, but can also produce boundary conflicts. These contradictory effects of popular communication elude theorists of the simulation society, who always dissolve boundary conflicts in favor of an omnipresent logic of staging.

Popular communication is distinguished, not only by hyperconnectivity, but also by *affectivity*.[28] It is important not to reduce the concept of affectivity to a theory of action. Max Weber and Talcott Parsons—whose theories inform much sociological thinking on emotion—conceptualize affectivity as an intentional orientation-guiding action. However, this intentionality is of less interest than the way affect opens up connective forms of communication. The greed of the speculator as a motive is less relevant than the function of "greedy" communication. Affectivity helps to structure communications processes but cannot be reduced to communication.

Like Gilles Deleuze, the Australian media theorist Moira Gatens (1996) regards affectivity as a relational concept that avoids defining affects as properties. Rather, she emphasizes the capacity of affects to move and be moved. Affects like greed, fascination, or overconfidence facilitate—and sometimes even frustrate—inclusion through nonrational processes. Like hyperconnectivity, affectivity can produce boundary conflicts. However, affectivity does not test the boundaries of a determined communication system, but of communication itself. Affectivity can support processes of communication through the activation of bodily resources, in the sense of "symbiotic mechanisms" (Luhmann 1974). However, it can also develop an autonomy that communication can no longer control.[29]

In its supportive role, affective communication may remove the pressures of rational understanding,[30] thus increasing the connectivity of speculative transactions. This effect can be observed in stock market discussion of the experiences of a novice entering the exchange for the first time (Stäheli 2003a). The exchange environment is experienced as pleasurable visual and auditory activity—an experience that increases the probability of connective operations: it is possible to enjoy the traders' cries as exotic precisely because they are not understandable. In turn, one is invited to acquire the techniques that will decode those cries. The production of affectivity is not primarily linked to informational content, but rather to the media that disseminate communication. Thus, for analyzing universal figures like *homo oeconomicus*, one has to take an interest in the "affective media" (Parisi and Terranova 2001, 125) employed in processes of inclusion. These media display a curious power to fascinate.

Fascination has scarcely been elaborated on a theoretical level as a social and cultural category, aside from some observations by Maurice Blanchot (1982).[31] This is not the place to rectify that shortcoming. Nonetheless, I do not want to abandon the category, since it captures a layer of events that eludes models of inclusion exclusively fixed on processes of meaning. What fascinates is not determined information, but rather communicative media exerting their own attractive force. For example, the ticker tape, on which the latest stock prices were printed in nearly real-time, and the ticker-tape machine themselves became objects of fascination (see chapter 7). A fusion of medium and individual takes place here, while the subjectivity of the latter is temporarily suspended. The pleasure of the popular can be grasped in this singular process of desubjectification: "Pleasure can just as well be linked to the destruction of identification and objectification, to the undermining of subjective stability" (Shaviro 1993, 43). Contrary to psychoanalytic doctrines of identification and sociological role theories, the popular unfolds its force, not only through the identification with a popular figure, but rather through desubjectification—through the experience of difference. The affectivity excluded from successfully constructed audiences remains present as desubjectified outside. Speculation feeds on this desubjectification—for example, in gambling—by making it enjoyable.

The tension that interests us here comes into view if we conceive of the popular as a category that surpasses—but always refers to—specific modes of communication within functional systems. For the popularity belonging to speculation is now neither quantitatively dissolved nor exposed as ideological deception, but rather analyzable as an ambivalence produced in the economy. Thus, it is necessary, not simply to relativize the seriousness and the spectacle of speculation as arbitrary perspectives, but to think of their specific interplay. The relation of the economy to the popular is anything but simply an empirical coincidence. The popular is inscribed deeply in the functioning of the economic system. My starting point is that the economy must produce its own popular side in order to function, but simultaneously acquires a number of problems that it must endlessly engage. As the border conflicts and processes of inclusion in popular capitalism indicate, its role cannot be determined by an economic analysis of popular culture. Nor will the representation of speculation in popular culture be foregrounded here. Representations of the economy in popular media like newspapers and stories will indeed be of interest. However, this interest will always concern the functioning of the economy—the question of what representational forms the conflicts and dramas of the popular assume and how these forms are intertwined with modes of inclusion in the economic system. The popular in the economy, then, is not an external force that directs itself as an anti-capitalist movement against hegemonic economic structures. Rather, the popular is a constitutive element of and for the functioning of the financial system.[32]

The popular is conceptualized as excessive and thereby becomes a border concept producing its own outside—whether by exceeding universalist discourse, thereby losing the ability to distinguish between the economically oriented speculator and the gambler, by inflating speculative communication, or by celebrating monetary contingency transformed into an object of entertainment. In all these cases, the popular does not stem from the outside, but works as if it had an external position: as the gambler who must be excluded, as affectivity to be controlled and extinguished, or as "artificial" contingency that must be separated from "real" economic contingency. In order to think this internal outside of functional systems, the popular will be deployed here as a distinction that plays a central role in regulating apparatuses of inclusion.

My analysis of discourses of speculation is divided into three thematic constellations: *game and speculation, crowds,* and *media.* The three parts do not follow a strict chronology, but present the popular of the economy from different perspectives. The communication-theoretical perspective emphasizes the struggles to divide "serious" economic and "popular" gambling communication. The inclusion-theoretical perspective focuses on the relation between the individual speculator and the market as described in terms of crowds. The media-theoretical perspective deals with the ambivalence of the ticker as a medium of dissemination.

The first part (*gambling and speculation*) traces the vehement struggles surrounding the distinction—indiscernible to the layperson at the time—between speculative operations and games of chance. The conflicts examined in this part are not internal to the economy, but what makes speculation economic is at stake. My interest is in how speculation handles its own entertaining nature—that is, in both the means it uses to become a "serious" economic operation and the ways in which economic contingency becomes entertainment.

The second part (*crowds*) is likewise dedicated to conceptual struggles, in particular those arising over the construction of an ideal audience for speculation. As an object of representation, speculation may have lacked interest for some authors; but it nonetheless developed a peculiar allure that threatened established notions of an economic audience. To observers, speculation was not only economic communication in a narrow sense but a spectacle that could powerfully affect an audience—whether through a "culture of contingency" or the pleasure of feverish imagination. This allure led to the objection, in self-descriptions of finance, that many speculators lacked competence. Starting in the second half of the nineteenth century, the discourse of the crowd was thus increasingly employed to describe market participants. Around 1900, this trajectory reached a high point in discussion of speculation informed by crowd psychology—a debate that the contrarian school transformed into a philosophy of investment. I seek to discover how the language of inclusion was shaped by disciplinary mechanisms and processes of individualization.

The final part (*media*) examines the media driving inclusionary processes, which are seldom discussed, although only they can account for the affective force exerted by modes of inclusion. The stock market ticker—whose history has long been neglected—serves as the nexus of two narratives. On the one hand, the ticker was a successful medium of dissemination. Anyone with access to a ticker could receive stock prices in nearly real time. In this sense, access to stock market communication was expanded to a hitherto unimagined degree. On the other hand, as an object of wonder, the ticker itself became an affectively charged medium. I discuss how these two developments supplemented—but also impeded—each other.

In all three parts, I am interested in cases in which the popular has operated as both a challenge and a threat, whether the popular of the economy was seen as problematic or even as something that it was impossible fully to get rid of in speculation. "Spectacular speculation" was spoken of long ago as the curious procedure making "serious" speculation primarily a popular and entertaining phenomenon. Along with the concept of the popular, this spectacle of speculation is taken seriously in this book. This implies two aspects: the popular of the financial economy is certainly not simply a contingent empirical exteriority that could have been avoided. At the same time, the spectacularity of speculation is not generalized as a placeholder for a lost reality. In both cases, the very difference to be developed here in the concept of the popular would be lost.

Part I

Gambling and Speculation

CHAPTER I

GAMBLING AND SPECULATION

ENTERTAINING CONTINGENCY?

What's your game? . . . Speculation I believe.

—Jane Austen, "The Watsons"

"The Watsons" is the surviving fragment of an unfinished novel by Jane Austen, who refers here to a card game called "speculation," which was popular in the nineteenth century.[1] The term also alludes, of course, to stock speculation. Reflecting on the pleasures remaining for a modernity that had become monotonous, the behavioral psychologist John B. Watson immediately thought of speculation: "Sex is so free and abundant that it hardly comes any more in the realm of excitement. . . . We all get bored. Stock gambling is about the only thing that offers the same kind of *thrill* that big game hunting does, and you can play the market right at your desk" (Watson in Fred C. Kelly 1962 [1930], xiv; emphasis added).

Watson was thinking of stock speculation, not as an economic activity, but as a first-class form of entertainment—the last thrill left to moderns for whom routine and boredom stifled any form of excitement.[2] The French economic historian Robert Lacour-Gayet also noted the fact that thrill seeking was a distinguishing feature of American speculation. A few months before the stock market crash in 1929, Lacour-Gayet referred to Americans' having indulged over the past five years in the "luxury of a permanent thrill" (1929, 159). For the French, the English word "thrill" became the term that best fitted American culture.

The euphoric affirmation of the thrill of the stock market is logically (and not historically) the suspension of the distinction between speculation and gambling. Terms like "stock gambling" and, later, "the money game" may have appeared to create a self-evident link between gambling and speculation.

However, these terms owed less to polemics against the stock market than to an enthusiastic plea for speculation by figures like Watson and Lacour-Gayet. This articulation of gambling and speculation proved to be based on complex pre-suppositions and conflicts. In order to be combined with gambling as a thrill, speculation had first to be separated from gambling as a "serious" economic operation and only later to be reunited. This re-articulation of gambling and speculation did not simply form a cyclical pattern based on their division and recombination. Rather, the figure of the speculator arose from their dialectic. The speculator was born as a privileged figure of economic subjectivity in the conflict between gambling and speculation—a figure that had to assert itself in the tension between diverting thrill and economic communication.

The intense conflicts surrounding this distinction can be better understood in light of the provocation behind the gambling metaphor. Gambling con-trasted with the stock exchange, often represented as the perfect market. No other form of economic communication seemed as appropriate to embody the neoclassical ideal of an efficient market. The stock trader was always supplied with current information on transactions, something that had to be pains-takingly determined in other markets.[3] Moreover, the stock trader was also spared the elaborate procedure of acquiring products and could devote all his attention to observing and producing prices. The French economist Léon Wal-ras (1834–1910) saw the stock market as a quintessential market model, since it combined perfect competition and ideal pricing—which, moreover, took place with minimal delay (Walras 2005 [1880]; Goux 1997, 162; Walker 2000). A similar belief in the stock exchange as the perfect market can be found in contemporary American discourses on speculation. William C. Van Antwerp (1867–1938) of E. F. Hutton & Co. wrote, for example: "Buyers seek the larg-est market they can get in order to obtain the lowest prices; sellers in order to obtain the highest prices . . . and so it was learned long ago that economy of time and labor, as well as a theoretically perfect market, could be best secured by an organization under one roof of as many dealers in a commodity as could be found." The stock exchange produced a fair price under "ideal conditions" by temporally and spatially condensing the communication of prices.[4] Hence, the stock exchange became the domain of *homo oeconomicus*—the central fiction of economic rationality—embodied in speculators who found scope to pursue their calculated self-interest in its institutionalized economic freedom.[5]

The stock exchange constituted the economic imaginary through a pro-cess of rigorous self-referential abstraction. Precisely because the stock market bracketed customary economic external references, it figured as a self-referential system par excellence. To a large extent, this notion of the stock exchange replaced external references with instances of payment continuously linked to each other: "The financial market exists, so to speak, as the proper market of the economic system. . . . The operations of this market are, to the highest degree, determined self-referentially, that is, are oriented toward the self-reference of the economic system, and towards the reflexivity of its medium: money" (Luhmann 1988, 116).

Speculation did not have to relate either to the labor process or to a business's fundamental data. Products also played a reduced role as interchangeable signs that, in the best case, served as points of reference for the speculative imagination of traders. Speculation acquired its communicative criteria only from itself. The productivity or the earning potential of a business could be monitored, but primarily to see how other observers monitored these economic references. Stock market speculation was a classic instance of second-order observation, being simultaneously an operation and an observation. Payments—the basic operation of the economic system—were observed as observations in a process that grounded further payments.[6]

Because of this dissociation from economic references, stock market speculation has been read as a self-sufficient "stock exchange paradigm" (Goux 1997, 2000). By abandoning external references, speculation set free an arbitrary play of signifiers grounded in the desire of economic subjects (Bigelow 1998). Even if one does not want to follow Goux's euphoric poststructuralist reading, it nonetheless emphatically foregrounds the self-referentiality of stock market communication. This heightened self-reference made the stock market the "market of markets" for many observers.[7] As the American economist Henry Crosby Emery (1872–1924) pointed out, socialists like Pierre-Joseph Proudhon (1809–65) had first discovered this new meaning of the stock market, whereas many "capital friendly" authors had overlooked it. According to Emery, Proudhon understood the stock exchange as "the symbol of modern commerce . . . the center of the vast industrial system which he denounces" (Emery 1969 [1896], 158). Evidently, some critics of capitalism better understood the symbolic power of the stock exchange than many economists and moralists.

Given the privileged position of the stock exchange in the economic imaginary, it might seem surprising that speculation also functioned as entertainment. One would not expect a cool-headed character like *homo oeconomicus* to pursue the thrill of speculation. Yet speculation was both celebrated and criticized as *popular communication* before the first stock exchanges were founded. The intense conflicts over the distinction between gambling and speculation were centered on this aspect of entertainment. It is striking that speculation and gambling intersected, and that stock speculation, an economic practice confined primarily to second-order observations, became so popular. How did the exclusive circuit of communication in stock speculation stay connected to the "people" who served as the fictive popular actor? The stock market would seem to be a particularly good example of "elite" communication, because it was organized like a club.[8] The peculiar logic of the stock market would also seem to be indifferent to the normative criteria of the "moral economy," based on ideals of equivalence and fairness. With these tensions, stock speculation presented itself as an ambivalent form of communication. On the one hand, it was a highly exclusive and self-referential field. On the other hand, it was a popular amusement almost as disreputable as gambling. My concept of the popular analyzes the tension between these two aspects of speculation. The thrill of speculation uncovers the popular in stock market communication, indicating that, along with its economic "seriousness," speculation is also a form of entertainment.

A brief comparison with other functional systems shows how unusual it is for entertainment to be joined to a second-order economic observation. In the academic system, epistemological papers are hardly comprehensible to laypeople interested in popular science. Procedural conflicts in the legal system are often seen as a complicated and often unnecessary postponement of the legal drama that is actually of interest. "Art for art's sake" is likewise often a reliable means of excluding a wide audience. However, finance operates differently. The self-observation of the economy in finance appears to create a thrill that is to a large extent missing in second-order observation in other functional systems.

This thrill seeking goes well beyond professional traders. It includes laypeople who often do not possess basic financial knowledge. Second-order observations demand the high degree of competence specific to a functional system, and speculation is no different in this regard. However, despite this required competence, speculation exerts a peculiar attraction on the uninitiated—even if (or precisely because) it has to remain incomprehensible to them. The contingency generated by the self-referential play of speculation is highly entertaining.[9] This thrill could thus also threaten the economic legitimacy of speculation, whether by threatening to make speculation incalculable or by invoking its exterior as a source of contamination. The challenge facing a communications-theoretical analysis of finance arises in understanding market populism not merely as a psychological phenomenon but as something intrinsic to the stock market. The speculator may certainly be driven to get rich, but this does not explain how speculation simultaneously processes economic and entertainment contingencies.

Semantic conflicts distinguishing gambling and speculation address the *problem of the noneconomic in the economic*. In gambling and speculation, the boundaries of economic communication are specified, displaced, and once again fixed. The distinction between gambling and speculation is an essentially contested distinction.[10] Moreover, it is not simply one element among others, but constitutes what Philippe Desan (1993) calls an *imaginaire économique,* or "economic imaginary," within which not only the legitimacy of particular morally dubious practices but also the boundaries of the economic can be contested.[11]

Following William Connolly (1983), concepts are contested in three ways. First, their internal complexity leads to disputes over their definition. Second, how these distinctions are to be applied remains unclear. Third, the normative evaluation of these concepts is also contested. These conflicts are not settled by an "improved" definition or other theoretical efforts, but emerge precisely because there is no overriding logic to resolve them.[12] The distinction between gambling and speculation has been contested in all of these ways. Controversy arose as to whether speculation could be distinguished from gambling as an economic operation. Likewise, how to apply this distinction was often intensely debated, particularly in the discussion about futures trading. Normatively, a wide spectrum of irreconcilable positions on speculation arose—ranging from those that condemned its moral abjectness to those that celebrated it as the "most economic" of economic operations.

In what follows, I track thematic "spots" in which templates for these efforts to distinguish gambling and speculation were articulated. Following a brief communications-theoretical discussion of gambling and speculation (1), my analysis begins with a prehistory of this distinction in the seventeenth and eighteenth centuries. At this time, gambling and speculation were equated with each other. From this point of view, the novel form of "wild contingency" proved to be fascinating and dismaying (2). Discussions of the argumentative strategies deployed by opponents of speculation and gambling also took an interest in how the two forms were equated (3). Precisely because these criticisms strengthened each other, they posed a challenge to positions friendly to speculation. I trace efforts to separate speculation from gambling, and to observe speculation as a legitimate form of economic communication (4). This expulsion of gambling from speculation took shape as an extremely demanding process that led to a "paradox of purification" with far-reaching consequences (5). The last section of this chapter discusses how a popularized version of neoclassical economics was the first to connect gambling and speculation from a perspective friendly to the latter. With this connection, such arguments also destabilized the presuppositions underlying their own calculations (6).

I. Gambling and Speculation as a Theoretical Problem: The Provocation of Contingency

Before we can analyze conflicts over the distinction between gambling and speculation, we need to situate them within the coordinates of social theory. To do so, it is necessary to outline the mode of communication at stake in gambling and speculation. Only then can we see how this mode of communication is fraught with assumptions and accompanying zones of indeterminacy. In these zones of indeterminacy, conflicts over the distinction between gambling and speculation are put into play.

Gambling includes all the forms of communication in which payment depends exclusively on a contingent future event—an event often specifically produced for this very purpose.[13] Gambling is a form of communication that—like economic communication—uses money as its medium of payment. However, this similarity by no means ensures its economic nature. For example, as will be discussed later, moralistic monetary discourses see gambling as a noneconomic and illegitimate use of money. Critics argue that profits and losses in gambling are detached from effort and knowledge. However, these criteria are not persuasive from a systems-theoretical standpoint, which determines whether an operation belongs to a given system based on its capacity for communicative connection, rather than on individual motives, intentions, and competences.

Yet systems theory also has difficulties mapping gambling socially. Gambling may appear to be economic because it operates with a payoff: "The economy consists of endless new payments" (Luhmann 1988, 52). In this sense, a successful payoff in roulette or in a card game likewise contributes to the autopoiesis of the economic system. An analysis restricted to money as an

economic medium would have to identify gambling as economic communication. However, it becomes more difficult to determine the economic character of gambling when one follows Luhmann's functional conception of the
economy. Luhmann emphasizes that the economy is not formed by the arbitrary use of money, but by *scarcity*. Money is a means by which the scarcity of
goods is reproduced, translating it into prices. The economy is oriented by the
scarcities it generates, and produces corresponding programs to handle them:
"In the modern economy, *all* economic operations must comply with both
languages of scarcity *together*, so the overall code of the economy applies, and
this code alone—namely, to *pay* for *services*," Luhmann asserts.[14]

Only this double economy of scarcity (of goods and money) makes the
explosive theoretical consequences of gambling clear. Gambling utilizes
money as a medium (and payment as a unit of communication) like any economic operation. However, the problematics of gambling differ from those
found in economic communication oriented toward the sale of goods. Gambling presupposes a scarcity of money (by promising a future and contingent
payoff) but discards the "language of scarcity" of goods.[15] In contrast to speculation with futures, gambling does not negotiate fictive goods or services.
Rather, gambling entirely dispenses with staging sales transactions.[16]

For Luhmann, the modern economy orientates itself toward two problems
of scarcity: the scarcity of goods and of money. Gambling caricatures—and
thereby inverts—the premodern economy that was confronted only with a
scarcity of goods. In gambling, the double scarcity of money and goods is
abandoned for an exclusive orientation toward the scarcity of money. Gambling is provocative because although it uses money as a medium, it is exclusively interested in the scarcity of money. The gambler buys neither a real nor
fictive good. As a result, the gambler begins to deal with the medium of money
itself and becomes fascinated with its possibilities. The use of money itself
becomes a thrill. Detaching money from the twin discourses of economic
scarcity opens up the possibility of border conflicts and is even regarded as
something shocking.

How can the thrill of gambling be grasped conceptually? Gambling
involves a particularly interesting mutation in the function of payment. Not
only does gambling break with the dual language of scarcity, but it also introduces a suspense mechanism modifying how payments operate.[17] In a typical
payment, clear roles are assigned to the giver and receiver. If I buy a choco-
late bar in a store, everyone taking part in the transaction will assume that

the salesperson receives the money I tender in exchange for it. Gambling differs in an important way from sales on precisely this point. The gambler does not know in advance who will receive the money at stake.[18] If lucky, she will win back, not only her own ante, but also the antes of other players. Part of the thrill of gambling arises in this temporary indeterminacy of address. I know who sits with me at the table but not who will pay up. Gambling introduces an aspect of uncertainty into a money-based practice—an uncertainty that money actually reduces. The gambler waits impatiently for the decisive moment—the moment that resolves the unbearable, yet extremely pleasurable, uncertainty. She enters a delimited time frame in which "normal" monetary operations are suspended. The near future will determine what roles are to be assumed in the payoff. The introduction of this uncertainty is an enormous strain, and it is hardly surprising that the language of gambling is highly moral. Games of chance have to fall back on morality as a means of ensuring future normalcy despite the introduced improbability. Sayings like "Gambling debts are debts of honor" refer precisely to this. In such sayings, morality makes it acceptable to postpone determining the roles of payer and payee.

Walter Benjamin underscores this experience of contingency in gambling (1973 [1937]). For Benjamin, gambling has a shock character, since I shall *suddenly* know whether I have won or lost. This shock is not possible when order collapses, but only when the distinct rules of a game are followed. Thus, gambling is characterized as much by the successful resolution of contingency as by this contingency itself. Everything can begin again as if nothing had happened: "Starting all over again is the regulative idea of the game" (Benjamin 1973, 137). The experience of contingency in gambling ends, at least in terms of how roles are divided, with the same clarity to be found in other payment operations. Clear rules ensure a fair procedure after the wager. No doubt arises as to who the winner is.

Gambling makes it possible to experience contingency as a ritualized form of presence.[19] During the moments when the roles of winner and loser are uncertain, the gambler displays a wide range of affects. It was characteristic to describe the gambler—in opposition to the classic *homo oeconomicus*—as lacking will and self-control: "What particularly characterizes gamblers is their *lack of any character.* Their *tumultuous and contrary feelings* reciprocally destroy each other and leave only confused traces. They have the faces of lost men with no distinct physiognomy" (Dusaulx cited in Kavanagh 1993, 36).

In the eighteenth century, gambling provided the conditions for the gambler to become a distinct figure characterized by affective intensity—and thus a figure of pure presence. The pleasure of desubjectification transformed the gambler into an affective site. The gambler paradoxically subjectivized this suspense by extending the presence of a monetary operation. In this form of presence, traditional modes of being an economic subject reached their limits and produced the pleasure of desubjectification so typical of the popular.

These brief comments are not intended to formulate a systems theory of gambling. Nonetheless, they should indicate how the thrill of gambling can be described in terms of communications theory. Such description makes it possible to recognize how gambling "plays" with the structure of common economic operations by introducing a moment of shock and suspense in payment operations. In gambling, well-structured zones of indeterminacy are allowed to enter monetary operations, but with the guarantee that order will be restored in the end. The money will be given to a receiver, and the game will begin again with equal chances for its players.

Gambling thus functions as a mutant form of "normal" economic communication.[20] As monetary communication, gambling takes the form of a payment operation without orienting itself toward the societal function of the economy. A strange proximity between money as a medium and gambling thus arises—a proximity that can also be found in speculation. Speculation is difficult to determine conceptually, because it is also a mutant form of "normal" economic communication. Until recently, systems theory had hardly considered financial markets and speculation (but see Baecker 1999; Piel 2003). This oversight is surprising. Financial markets are based on the reciprocal observation of their participants and are thus highly self-referential. It might be expected that a social theory focusing on the problem of self-reference would take particular interest in speculation. Speculation is distinguished from other economic operations in the way its "self-referentiality [is] raised to an extreme level."[21] In contrast to other forms of economic communication, speculation finds no "point of contact in the system's environment" (Luhmann 1988, 116). Like gambling, speculation threatens to escape from the problem of scarcity that Luhmann sees as constituting economics: "By recursively networking with other observations, markets do not refer to reality on the basis of objects of observation. Rather, markets find this reference to reality in the facticity of their own operation" (Piel 2003, 28). How, though, does this "operative facticity" function?

In an ideal typology, operating speculatively means being concerned with producing difference: "What the dealer desires is not to own, but to 'make a difference'" (Goux 1997, 72). The speculator does not want to own or exchange products, but exclusively to observe and produce differences in price. Max Weber's efforts to elaborate this loss of reference indicate the extent to which definitions of stock exchange communication can be circuitous:

> [O]n the exchanges, a deal is struck over a set of goods that are not present, and often "in transit" somewhere, or often yet-to-be produced; and it takes place between a buyer who usually does not himself wish to "own" those goods (in any regular fashion) but who wishes—if possible before he receives them and pays for them—to pass them along for a profit, and a seller, who usually does not yet have those goods, usually has not produced them, but wishes to furnish them for some earnings of his own. (Weber 2000c [1894], 309–10)

With speculation, a vocabulary oriented toward commodity exchange and the materiality of goods encounters its limits. Neither goods (like wheat) nor enterprises are the products of speculation. Rather, the only product of speculation are the prices it independently creates—and creates precisely where the economy leaves "price gaps."[22] Prices assume a double function in the way speculation operates. Speculation observes how prices are formed and realizes prices in businesses. A similar doubling can be found in other economic operations. However, speculation prioritizes observation of prices over obtaining them: "It allows for observation of price formation in transactions before a price is locked in. It turns observing price formation into a business" (Baecker 1999, 296). At this point, it becomes evident that time structures how speculation operates. The "before" of price observation can be separated from the "after" of price realization, but only to allow the typical form of retroactive observation to take place.[23] The temporal basis of speculation also shapes the conceptual history of the term. The speculator scouts unknown territory.[24] Even if the speculator operates individually, a counterpart is still needed. The speculator is an observer who profits by observing other observers in order to see what they cannot see on the horizon.

These brief remarks have to remain vague. Nonetheless it already becomes clear that speculation and gambling occupy a precarious position in relation to "normal" economic practices. Both abandon reference to preceding values. Neither gambling nor speculation is oriented toward products or the problem of scarce goods. Rather, both develop highly self-referential forms of economic

processes. This development leads, however, to diverging theoretical consequences. For Luhmann and many others, the stock market is representative
of the economic system because it exemplifies pure self-reference. However,
gambling, although close to this radical self-reference, threatens to depart
from what is socially understood as the economy. Gambling and speculation
thus occupy different positions in economic self-description.[25]

The economic status of speculation remained indeterminate during a long
period when, like gambling, it was detached from the problem of scarcity.
Gambling and speculation occupy an uncertain position even within a systems theory of economics, suggesting that studies are needed to examine how
such boundaries are determined. If the monetary nature of an operation cannot definitively decide whether it belongs to the economic system, additional
criteria to handle this undecidability become important.[26]

2. The Prehistory of Gambling and Speculation: Gambling Epidemics in England and the United States—or, the Allure of Contingency

Distinguishing gambling from speculation revolved around the contingency
produced by money in this border region and the question how to establish
it as economic character. Here different understandings of it intersected. On
the one hand, this contingency was seen as in some sense a socially "useful"
way of understanding economic risk; on the other, pursuing it was regarded as
"useless" thrill seeking purely for the sake of entertainment. How were these
understandings of contingency separated? What strategies were deployed to
handle this entertaining and spectacular "surplus" in finance?

Until the nineteenth century, gambling and speculation were not seen
as separate in either Europe or the United States, but rather as a somewhat
disreputable congeries located in popular culture (Nicholson 1994, 58). The
popularity of games of chance—whether card or dice games, early forms of
the lottery, or the most varied kinds of sweepstakes (such as horse racing)—
largely helped make speculation an activity that referred only to itself. Before
examining how the distinction between gambling and speculation was established in the United States, I would like to consider its European prehistory,
which clearly points to the connection between gambling and the introduction of paper money.

In the seventeenth century, England fell under the spell of a widespread
enthusiasm for gambling. "In the seventeenth century, the phenomenon of

gambling appeared suddenly to burst upon a startled society, which continued to reel from the shock of its almost epidemic proportions for the next hundred years," Gerda Reith writes.[27] Gambling began to thrive with the establishment of paper money, which abandoned referentiality to become a flexible medium of representation (cf. Shell 1999). The status of money as medium changed in England during the eighteenth century; it became "a demiurgic force thriving in its own movement" (Kavanagh 1993, 87), independent of other values (e.g., the gold or silver standard).

Enthusiasm for gambling was directly linked with the logic peculiar to money. In gambling, money created new money without labor or exchange of products. This creation of money itself became fascinating. Gambling experimented with the new potential of money by testing the boundaries of the latter, and thus exploring ever-new ways to produce contingency. Gambling was concerned with the way money itself functioned as a medium. Fascination with the generalizability of money led to practically everything becoming the potential object of a bet: "The universal equivalent in a capitalist economy became the universal wager in games of chance" (Reith 1999, 59). The advent of banknotes as a medium of speculation went hand in hand with fascination with the self-referentiality of money that was concerned with neither "intrinsic" moral values nor economic values. Without this new logic of money, English and American gambling culture is as unthinkable as the "epidemic" of stock speculation. Paper money and gambling culture co-evolved, so to speak. A desire for self-reference could be found in both the infectious delirium of gambling and the captivating dynamic of speculation. In light of this tight interpenetration of gambling and speculation, historians have noted a serious shortcoming in Weber's thesis on Protestantism. Modern capitalism required not only Protestant techniques of self-discipline but also the Dionysian spirit of the gambling table: "Rather than being antithetical to capitalism as Weber suggested, greed and the irrational gambling impulse actually helped to advance its institutions" (Chancellor 1999, 44).

Gambling served as the background against which different early forms of speculation emerged. For Daniel Defoe, gambling and speculation were contingent: "Stock-Jobbing is a Play; a Box and Dice may be less dangerous, the Nature of them are alike, a Hazard."[28] Defoe did not deal with the productive activity of speculation, but rather juxtaposed a logically constructed *transparent world* of necessity with a world of deceptive and irrational contingency. Stock traders, who disregarded the rule of causality and produced intransparency, were "unaccountable people"; fluctuating market prices that could no longer be explained by rational argument had nothing to do with "intrinsick value" (Defoe 2000c [1701], 37). Defoe saw in speculation a danger based on lack of reference and ground that had to be resisted. He compared stock speculators to criminals, since both employed fictions, deceptions, and manipulations: "[Stock-jobbing is] founded in Fraud, born of Deceit, and nourished by Trick, Cheat, Wheedle, Forgeries, Falsehoods, and all sorts of Delusions; Coining false News, this way good, that way bad; whispering imaginary Terrors, Frights, Hopes, Expectations, and then preying upon the Weakness of those, whose Imagination they have wrought upon, whom they have either elevated or depress'd" (Defoe 2000a [1719], 130).

The distinction between gambling and speculation that would become significant in the nineteenth century was not yet relevant for Defoe. Such a comparison would have appeared to be too harmless and self-evident. Defoe wanted to reveal speculation as a form of activity that made not only gambling, but also highway robbery, appear harmless by comparison (Defoe 2000a, 132).

Many of Defoe's contemporaries equated speculation with robbery. This equation became common in criticism of speculation after the nineteenth century. It is striking that Defoe did not entirely collapse speculation with monetary media (especially paper money) and credit. Rather, he sought to delimit a legitimate form of credit from gambling and speculation. Money gained legitimacy by being subordinated to trade, as did credit.[29] Money and credit supported trade, and, as a rule, existed in a harmonious relationship: "Money raises Credit, and Credit in its turn is an Equivalent to Money" (Defoe 2000c [1701], 35). With this relationship, Defoe initiated a notable critique of speculation—a critique that accepted money and credit as necessary elements of modern international trade.[30] In this way, Defoe anticipated the subsequent separation of speculation as economically useful from gambling as deceitful.

Contingency, rather than the distinction between productivity and parasitism, played a primary role in how Defoe distinguished the illegitimate speculation by stock traders from trade and credit. Money and credit were situated in a well-ordered system that related them as complementary and rational. In contrast, speculation was an uncontrolled contingency that threatened established ideas of order. Fluctuating stock prices followed no rational pattern. They could not be explained economically, but were groundless (Defoe 2000c, 37). This lack of ground served as a provocation for Defoe's economic thought—a provocation he could only counter by introducing a new ground. Ultimately, stocks fluctuated according to the will of stock traders, whose self-interest thus supplanted the grounds provided by reason. In response to the unease caused by this noncausal form of contingency, Defoe thus deployed conspiracy theory.[31]

The attention Defoe gave to handling contingency in his rejection of stock jobbing indicates the discursive challenges confronting theories of speculation. Gambling and speculation were a new form of contingency that could not simply be incorporated into the existing economic paradigms. This form of contingency also made it necessary to revise the dominant conception of *homo oeconomicus*. The economic subject defined by ownership (ideally, land-ownership) in a stratified society had to be rearticulated, or at least complemented, by a second figure of inclusion (cf. Pocock 1975). This second subject was neither a landowner who had to protect his estate nor a manufacturer. Speculative "moneyed interests" substituted love of risk for real property.[32]

Beginning in the seventeenth century, gambling was also an important part of American culture. It often connoted a specific class in Europe, but it was less socially differentiated in the United States. We may distinguish between two attitudes to gambling imported from Europe. The Puritans strictly criticized gambling. In Massachusetts, this attitude led to a wider prohibition of a range of recreational activities. Not only was the possession of cards and dice punished, but even singing and dancing in private rooms was forbidden (Dunstan 1997, 8). In contrast, New Englanders saw some forms of gaming as a welcome pastime. The frontier spirit was characterized by daring and openness to risk, and love of gambling was especially noted in the American West—above all, in California: "Like bettors, pioneers have repeatedly grasped the chance to get something for nothing—to claim free land, to pick up nuggets of gold, to speculate on western real estate. Like bettors, frontiersmen have cherished risks in order to get ahead and establish identity. Like bettors, migrants to new territories have sought to begin again in a setting that made all participants equal at the start" (Findlay 1986, 4; cf. Dunstan 1997, 8).

The frontiersman united the figures of the gambler, speculator, and migrant. All three exemplify how processes of subjectivization were used to deal with modern contingency. The unpredictability of the future was articulated, not as a danger, but as a chance—a chance offered to anyone prepared to take a risk, but a chance that also broke with the way economics conceived of equivalence.

American ideas about gambling combined the Jacksonian notion of democratic equality with a celebration of contingency. This successful articulation of gambling was later adopted with respect to speculation. Whereas Defoe understood speculative contingency as a threat to rational coherence, Americans euphorically emphasized that the inequalities developed in speculation could be overcome. In gambling everyone had the same chances. The roles of winner and loser were not determined in advance, but were established accidentally—even if skill and competence were factors in some games.[33] Pure forms of gambling, such as the lottery or roulette, at least momentarily promised equal chances for everyone.

The American sociologist Edward Devereux (1912–2002) speculated that games of chance serve as a corrective to the inequalities of capitalist society. "We find a number of pleasing ironies, and more than a measure of truth, in Devereux's image of a capitalistic system founded by antigambling Puritans held hostage to a roulette wheel," Vicki Abt et al. write (1985, 23). Gambling contrasted with labor and production: "*Alea* [i.e., the dice] is total disgrace or absolute favor. . . . It seems an insolent and sovereign insult to merit," because games based on luck put everyone "on an absolutely equal footing to await the blind verdict of chance" (Caillois 1961, 17–18). This form of equality is disconnected from individual knowledge and ability, as well as social circumstances. Equality and contingency are articulated in relation to monetary operations that have no external reference. Gambling involves an idea of money detached from representation and equivalence, making it possible "to get something for nothing." The idea of undermining the principle of equivalency was alluring to many, but it was simultaneously seen as a threat. In the nineteenth century, many American novels expressed anxiety about gamblers or speculators acquiring a fortune without labor (Weyler 1996, 208), something that called the foundations of the economy and society into question.

I have focused on the role contingency played in the prehistory of gambling and speculation in England and America. Defoe delimited legitimate trade by distinguishing it from gambling and speculation as irrational. His position was striking, because it did not introduce a general critique of paper money and credit, but saw them as necessary economic tools—a form of reasoning that would also be used in attempts to legitimate speculation during the nineteenth century. For Defoe, speculation and gambling upset economic rationality. Early European Americans distinguished between gambling and speculation as little as Defoe. In the United States, two attitudes developed toward the amalgam of gambling and speculation. The first was a critique of speculation influenced by Puritanism. The next section examines this attitude in greater detail. The second attitude celebrated contingency as a form of democratic equality. This attitude linked contingency to an all-inclusive "common culture" constituted by the popular—a culture distinguished for its "equality of being" (Williams 1962, 317). Everybody has his or her chance—the frontiersmen exemplified this equality of opportunity. They tested *their own* fortunes by taking risks. Similarly, gambling and speculation presupposed a radical form of equality. Yet this equality was constructed in a radically individualistic way. Anyone capable of observing contingency started from the same point. However, the individual determined whether risk was converted into opportunity. This fundamentally positive attitude toward speculation subsequently became more differentiated. The speculator was increasingly subject to disciplinary constraints intended to resist the allure of contingency. In the second part of this chapter, I shall return to this nexus of contingency and discipline.

3. Gambling and Speculation in Criticism:
Contingency as Threat

The intoxication of contingency and fascination with self-reference played a substantial role in the general acceptance of paper money as an economic medium. However, the operative closure of the economic system did not successfully contain and normalize this celebration of contingency in the early phase of financial speculation and gambling. Rather, the reflexivity of paper money allowed a "wild contingency" (Fuchs 1992) to emerge—a contingency so excessive that it resisted systematic programming. The compulsion to gamble and the thrill of speculation, the alarming images of desubjectivized speculators,[34] the carnivalesque and burlesque representation of gambling and speculation—all indicated that the medium of money was no longer subject to rational controls and functional borders. Anxious witnesses observed the entire English nation hypnotized by speculation. In the United States, Thomas Jefferson complained that rather than serving the nation's well-being, capital and labor were being subordinated to an uncontrollable gambling compulsion (Warshow 1929).

The contingency produced by the abstract medium of money underwent a process of normalization that led to the reinscription of established economic categories. Only when detached from a paradigm of labor and production could speculation be seen as anything more than an insidious form of gambling. With speculation, ideas of equivalence and fairness were replaced by positive understandings of individual economic daring and risk-consciousness, and material goods vanished into stocks and shares. Labor no longer required physical exertion, but focused on knowledge and the pleasure of the speculator. In order to be established as a legitimate form of communication, speculation had to fight on many fronts.

Thus the peculiar connection between equality and contingency in speculation was subjected to criticism—particularly because this connection challenged the basic principles of hegemonic economic discourses. At the end of the eighteenth century, criticism of gambling in America reached a high point (Weyler 1996, 217). It was condemned as a depraved and pathological form of behavior and was treated like a disease requiring legal regulation. Gambling cultures of the seventeenth and eighteenth centuries may have facilitated—or even made possible—the emergence of speculation. However, well-established moral criticism of gambling also provided a discursive template easily applied to speculation. In an effort to establish boundaries between gambling and speculation, an already well-tested vocabulary was deployed. Clergy, farmers' representatives, and social reformers in particular saw combating speculation as necessary to preserve the integrity of economy and society. In the 1870s, in the wake of the Civil War, criticism of gambling reached an even higher point, thanks in part to the increasingly virtual character [*Virtualisierung*] of stock market trading. At this point, a large proportion of the annual grain production was traded on the stock exchange—a process in which the fictionality of speculation was experienced as particularly scandalous (Goede 2004, 201). Five kinds of criticism of gambling and speculation can be distinguished.

First, as seen in Defoe, gambling and speculation were criticized as the highest expression of *irrationality*. On this point, the American discussion of gambling coincided with criticism in Europe. Gambling was described as a fall into barbarism. Civilization regressed with gambling by surrendering every form of rational control (MacDougall 1936, 1). "The essence of gambling consists in an abandonment of reason, an inhibition of the factors of human control" (Hobson 1906, 3). "Wild" passions returned in undisguised form, and belief in luck replaced rational calculation—in short, gambling produced "derationalising influences" (4). Proponents of speculation thus felt a stronger need to separate speculation from gambling: "Gambling has only the evils and none of the virtues of speculation. . . . [I]t fascinates those who engage in it by an unending series of shallow uncertainties and thoughtless surprises fit to tickle the feeble wits of savages and degenerate types of the human family" (Jones 1900, 165–66). Criticism of gambling focused on how the thrill of speculation—when freed from its economic function—made the gambler easily excitable. For the British writer J. A. Hobson it was inconceivable that a rational person would be involved in gambling. The cool-headed northern European could only be enticed to gamble under the influence of alcohol. These perceptions of irrationality can be traced back to the Enlightenment in France. For Jean Dusaulx, gamblers represented the Enlightenment's blind spot. They were an "empty space within the triumphant discourse of reason" (Dusaulx 1779, cited in Kavanagh 1993, 36). Sharp criticism of gambling as irrational was not based only on the gambler being "wild" or "barbarian." The gambler also had to opt rationally to be irrational (Reith 1999, 83).

Second, gambling and speculation were described as *compulsions* that destroyed an individual's body and spirit. The gambler experienced a loss of identity (Crump 2003 [1874], 13)—a phenomenon registered in images of ruined bodies. In particular, women obsessed with gambling exemplified how it could cause moral and physical decay: "Nothing is more frightful in its vulgarity and general demoralization than a woman, turned gambler. . . . This means not only loss of character, but loss of youth and beauty; it means nervous exhaustion and kindred physical ills" (Anon. 1901, 106). It is hardly surprising that gambling addiction was compared to opium addiction. However, gambling was ultimately more damaging, because it was contagious. The compulsion to gamble was regarded as a dangerous epidemic that could not be reduced to a private pathology, but challenged the social order and dissolved communities. Eighteenth-century American republican writers were especially anxious about the harm gambling did the commonwealth (Weyler 1996, 216).

Critics of speculation similarly identified a number of psychic and bodily symptoms of addiction. The typical speculator struggled with sleeplessness resulting from constant fear that he or she would miss important information and opportunities.[35] Speculation was described in terms of nervous compulsion (Link-Heer 1999). "It is stimulating in an unhealthy way that induces restlessness and calls for exciting pleasure" (Martin 1998, 248). Speculators lived fast—and might age even faster—when exposed to "fast capitalism" (Agger 1989).[36] "They live high, drink deep, and the excitement in stocks during the day is exchanged for gaming at night," with visible physical effects:

"Bald heads on young men, premature gray hairs, nervous debility, paralysis and untimely decay, which mark so many of the business men of New York, with ruined fortunes and characters, show how perilous and unsatisfactory is life in Wall Street."[37] Speculators not only experienced a physical breakdown. Tensions and passions were also inscribed on their faces. Following a stock market crash, speculators' faces were "pitiful studies in the tragic and grotesque" (Anon. 1882, 715).

It was particularly alarming that those infected by gambling, as it were, seduced others to gamble. The logic of vampirism made the process of inclusion in gambling into a threat. Elsewhere I have described vampirism as exemplifying how the popular functions (Stäheli 2002b). Infection crosses boundaries that are functionally defined as well as stratified. It exerts a pull that operates beyond—but nonetheless draws on—established modes of inclusion.[38]

Third, gambler and speculator were designated as *parasitic* on a community that relied on mutual exchange. In gambling, it was possible to win without labor or exchange of products. Gambling ignored the principle of economic equivalence and the ethics of responsibility and effort. For the philanthropic reformer at the beginning of the nineteenth century, enthusiasm for gambling eroded economic stability by disregarding economic categories like credit and trust (Fabian 1990, 2). Although the gambler produced nothing, with a little luck, he benefited from the general good. Gambling thus became an "insult" to the ethic of labor, since one could profit without exchange or return services (Frothingham 1882, 162). For the stock market commentator Frederic Bond, the gambler was an idler who lived at society's expense (1928, 35). The speculator likewise profited from the economic well-being of others (see, e.g., Martin 1908, 243; Madison in McCoy 1980, 158; Cowing 1965, 5). Since the speculator neither produced nor traded goods, he was considered a frivolous parasite who accomplished nothing for the community: "For it is plain to see that honest industry and honest commerce are suffering from a parasitic growth which is sapping both their physical strength and moral energy."[39] The charge of parasitism ensured that the speculator would be seen as an unproductive person undermining the principle of exchange.[40]

However, it was not only the parasitic character of gambling that was shocking. The fourth argument against gambling was that the gambler used money for *noneconomic purposes*. Gambling was criticized for its disregard for and misuse of money, which it merged together and circulated in such a way that it eluded representation—an unparalleled process of dereferential-ization [*Entreferentialisierung*]. "It [gambling] has no respect for the money it so carelessly passes from hand to hand," O. B. Frothingham wrote disgust-edly. "The pieces of coin . . . were but so many counters, representing no moral or aesthetic quality; neither beauty nor power; neither knowledge, character nor goodness; neither comfort nor elegance; neither public nor private good-will; neither utility nor grace" (Frothingham 1882, 162). Moreover, the gam-bler's disdain for the economic function of money went beyond indifference to its representational function. The gambler saw money as a *pure medium* lacking in reference. Winnings were not used to buy anything, but to raise the stakes in the next game. The logic of gambling foregrounded the thrill of self-reference, in which money was used to create more money: "What money purchased they did not really care for" (162). It was this indifference to ref-erentiality—more than lack of economic productivity—that constituted the gambler's unscrupulousness: "The gambler does not value money, does not understand its worth, attaches no significance to it; does not keep it; flings it recklessly about. . . . Of the true significance of money he has no inkling of an idea" (168).

For Frothingham, the gambler's fascination with money as a medium was equivalent to contempt for the economy. The gambler used an economic medium—and did so masterfully—for noneconomic purposes. With this use of money, we encounter the paradox of gambling in its ideal form. When used beyond its economic function, the medium of money set in motion a peculiar dynamic. Only when this medium lacked reference did its particular—and enthralling—structure appear. In gambling, money was exclusively a medium. It had no other value and was not reduced to buying power. However, rather than serving as economic self-fulfillment, fascination with the reflexivity of money threatened the way the economy functioned. In response to this threat, equivalent disciplinary and exclusionary measures were required.

Many contemporaries saw the economy as constituted by an exchange of services, and speculation was condemned for eroding the very heart of the economy. For example, the Progressive Congregational pastor Washing-ton Gladden (1836–1918) saw speculation, which he equated with gambling, as lacking any form of referentiality of the kind found in social forms of exchange. "If 'society' is 'produced' . . . 'by an exchange of services', gam-bling is the antithesis of society," Gladden wrote. He deplored the fact that speculation was removed from any social reference such as possession: "Men who never own any of these kinds of property spend their lives in gambling in them, or rather *about* them" (Gladden 1884, 625; emphasis added). The trouble with speculation can be found in this "about," which no longer made exchange possible. Like Defoe, Gladden could thus conceive speculation as a criminal zero-sum game—that is, as theft in which one person loses what the other wins.

Speculation was a temptation that innocent amateurs—the "lambs" and "suckers"—could not resist: "But it is a delusion which appeals seductively to the popular ambition to get rich easily and quickly" (Anon. 1884, 627). This delusion arose as a desire for easy money already apparent in how speculation breached the principle of equivalence. The Christian magazine *Outlook* accused the speculator of producing "something for nothing." The speculator demanded other people's possessions without being able to offer an equivalent for them: "[S]omething for nothing—is the badge for all the gambling tribe" (Anon. 1901, 202). Speculation had a seductive power because it *promised an immediacy* that disabled the classical logic of equivalence. Isabelle Rieusset-Lemarié has indicated how criticism of speculation helped revive notions of paradise—notions influenced by the immediacy of consumption (1992, 158). As mentioned, American criticism of speculation attacked this form of immediacy—whether as the idea that one could get something for nothing or that one could be included in economic processes without being subject to their standards of competence or disciplinary techniques.

Not only could anyone speculate. Anyone could immediately satisfy his or her wishes by speculating. This "paradisiacal" mode of inclusion was regulated by a principle of the noneconomic. The notion of an inexhaustible plenitude transformed the economic problem of scarcity by abolishing "the distance established between . . . objects and subject" (Simmel 2004 [1901], 78). What makes the economy economic was once again at stake, but now in relation to subjects to be included.[41] The speculator was driven by an "unhuman intensity" (Anon. 1901, 106), and speculation was criticized in these terms. Speculation became too attractive and included too many small speculators, and thus was seen as epidemic and vampiric. At the same time, it was affectively laden. Parallels to speculation extended beyond the notion of paradise. They also applied to the infectious character of temptation. In this way, the taboo against immediacy simultaneously functioned as a taboo against infection: "Temptation was seen as the quintessential contagious force—a force that contaminated simply by contact" (Rieusset-Lemarié 1992, 158).

Perhaps the greatest challenge of gambling concerned—and this is the fifth criticism—the position of *contingency*. In gambling, chance played a central role. Winners and losers were only determined by chance. The gambler hoped for an entirely random event to happen (see, e.g., Meeker 1922, 396)—an event that eluded all calculation and thus was simply "blind chance."[42] For the American Puritans, playing with fate in this way was near blasphemy: "[Gambling] prostituted divine providence to unworthy ends. . . . God determines the cast of the dice or the shuffle of the cards, and we are not to implicate His providence in frivolity" (Miller 1982 cited in Findlay 1986, 20–21). Gambling was a provocation because it freed contingency from an external cause and rationale. Rather, contingency was to be enjoyed for itself. Subsequent efforts to distinguish between speculator and gambler seized on precisely this point. For the gambler, contingency was an end in itself. Chance was "final," and served as a thrilling means of amusement. The speculator, however, attempted to read the enigma of contingency (Jones 1900, 166). Gambling thus celebrated an "empty" contingency whose foundation interested no one and whose ideal medium was money. Around 1900, criticism of speculative risk also attacked this "empty" contingency. In these attacks, a semantic differentiation of gambling and speculation began to emerge. Rev. C. H. Hamlin criticized speculation only in cases where it became gambling. He used the criterion of *pure risk* in order to separate speculation from gambling: "A risk that was all risk and no work was gambling" (Charles S. Hamlin, cited in Cowing 1965, 25; cf. Goede 2004). This criticism left open the possibility of a legitimate form of speculation—namely, a speculation that subordinated risk to economic function.

Denouncing the irrationality and damaging effects of gambling also gave rise to an early critique of culture and media. Criticism of gambling was not least criticism of entertainment as mere "nervous excitement." Condemnations of speculation focused on the somatic immediacy of the thrill linked to gambling: "To excite the nerves is a surer way of gaining wealth and reputation than to strengthen the mind. To this extent are we still barbarians; to this extent has civilization failed to lift men and women above their instincts" (Frothingham 1882, 163). Such a criticism implied a dualism of body and soul. Physical enjoyment of contingency was considered a relapse into barbaric, irrational times. In contrast, it became the privilege of speculation to deal rationally with contingency. Gambling was scandalous, not only because it posed a threat to official order, but also because the gambler *enjoyed* the fascination of chaos produced in contingency. This "empty" contingency lacking premise and intention constituted the thrill of gambling.

Georg Simmel places this gambler enthralled by the self-reference of gambling next to the adventurer:

> Just as the game itself—not the winning of money—is the decisive motive for the true gambler; just as for him, what is important is the violence of feeling as it alternates between joy and despair, the almost touchable nearness of the demonic powers which decide between both—so the fascination of the adventure is again and again not the substance which it offers us and which, if it were offered in another form, perhaps would receive little heed, but rather the adventurous form of experiencing it, the intensity and excitement with which it lets us feel life in just this instance.[43]

The gambler is not interested in winnings, or what can be bought with them, but is fascinated solely by the intensity of gambling. Lost in the game, the gambler enjoys the feeling of tension and sudden changes in circumstance,[44] experiencing an immediate presence (Gumbrecht 2004) at the temporary cost of identity. Gambling makes it possible to experience contingency in an entertaining form. In contrast to ways of celebrating contingency established later (e.g., avant-garde art), gambling is fun. Its unique alliance of *contingency* and *entertainment* necessarily eradicates religious notions of fate, so that fears of contingency can be experienced as groundless, and provides a new home for money, whose status as a self-reflexive medium fuses with the pleasure of contingency.[45]

Criticism of gambling and speculation followed similar lines of argumentation. This similarity is hardly surprising, given that speculation and gambling could be represented as noneconomic forms of communication by being equated with each other. Nonetheless, the distinction between gambling and speculation also surfaced in such criticism. For Washington Gladden, the element of chance remained hidden in speculation—a fact that made it more threatening than gambling. Speculation was "gambling which wears the mask of business," Gladden wrote in *The Century* (1884, 624).[46] At the end of the nineteenth century, gambling had not been thoroughly defeated, but largely domesticated (Fabian 1990, 3). By this time, gambling was strongly regulated by law. Yet precisely when gambling seemed past its prime, it was revived under another guise. Critics saw one of the greatest dangers precisely in the way speculation wore the mask of serious business. Gambling was undoubtedly morally reprehensible. However, its harmful effects were at least on display and could serve as a deterrent. Many critics thus wished that speculation had simply remained a game of chance: "To play it as a game is more tolerable than to make serious work of it, but it is a game that is apt to run away with its players, and absorb more thought, if not more money, than they can spare" (Martin 1908, 248). The disguise of economic responsibility, it was feared, would aggravate the pathological effects of gambling. With this disguise, the moral boundaries that prevented the respectable public from gambling disappeared. Nothing more stood in the way of hyperinclusion in speculation. From the perspective of critics, speculation abused the functional differentiation at work in the economy by masking a noneconomic form of communication as economic, thus producing a highly problematic connectivity.

CHAPTER 2

THE NORMALIZATION
OF "WILD CONTINGENCY"

STABILIZING THE DISTINCTION BETWEEN
GAMBLING AND SPECULATION

> Something is contingent insofar as it is neither necessary nor
> impossible; it is just what it is (or was or will be), though it
> could also be otherwise. The concept thus describes something
> given (something experienced, expected, remembered,
> fantasized) in the light of its possibility being otherwise; it
> describes objects within the horizon of possible variations.
> —Niklas Luhmann, *Social Systems*

A clear distinction between gambling and speculation was created when it
became possible to redefine the contingency of speculation as economic. This
chapter analyzes examples, drawn primarily from constellations of American
discourse on speculation, of the way in which this distinction was stabilized
and the speculator rendered fit for inclusion in the financial system.

The growing field of finance had to differentiate between gambling and
speculation for both internal and external reasons. The chief external threat
was intervention by another system—for example, rulings by the judiciary
on what financial operations were permissible. Clearly detaching speculation
from gambling signaled that the financial system was capable of policing its
own boundaries; there was thus no need for the courts to intervene.

The internal problem facing the financial system was that large numbers
of incompetent amateur speculators confused gambling and speculation.
This called into question the rationality of economic operations, once again

making them vulnerable to external critique. Two complementary strategies of differentiation were developed in response: *functionalization* and *inclusion and exclusion*. The strategy of *functionalization* addressed the problem of speculation's economic legitimacy, seeking to articulate it as a valid form of economic practice. In contrast, responding to the epidemic character of speculation, the strategy of *inclusion and exclusion* began with the problem of financial access and aimed to show that speculation was inclusive.

The relation between the ideal speculator and speculation only becomes clear in this difference between the strategies of functionalization and inclusion. Rather than presume that these two approaches can automatically be derived from each other, I shall examine their historically specific modes of articulation.

1. The Functionalization of Speculation

Discursive positions friendly to speculation tried to distinguish it as sharply as possible from gambling. These efforts responded to criticism that speculation was nothing but the demon of gambling wearing a "mask of business." Proponents of speculation did not entirely oppose opponents' moral criticism, but rearticulated the distinction between gambling and speculation on the same discursive terrain.[1] Two perspectives on the distinction between speculation and gambling had to be addressed: "The ministers have condemned them both as gambling: the public continues to do them both, calling it all speculation" (Anon. 1920, 231). The confused knot of gambling and speculation had to be untangled. A starting point for this task could even be found in the moral criticism of gambling by opponents of speculation. Proponents of speculation adopted such criticism to the extent of representing gambling as morally reprehensible and economically destructive.[2] Gambling wasted potential labor and time. This discursive strategy condemning gambling was not without risk. Failure to differentiate between gambling and speculation also made it impossible to problematize the premises on which criticism of gambling was based.

The inclusion of speculation required that it be represented as an important—even indispensable—component of the modern economy. Claims that speculation was unproductive and parasitic had to be refuted. Speculation had to be shown to be the "market of markets," not only integral to the economy but at its core. It thus also had to develop a justification on the basis of *function*. This justification was primarily economic, providing the discursive foundation for any moral justification, and not vice versa!

Typically, external observers discussed the "(im)morality of speculation," but financial self-observation was interested in the economic function speculation might fulfill. In contrast to a purely functionalist conception of finance, I am interested in how the function of finance is produced.[3] Inventing a function is crucial for the construction of a system, but is not its ontological basis, since the "grounds for the existence of particular institutions never reside in their functions" (Luhmann 2000, 138). It is thus important to distinguish between the ontology that grounds a system and the foundational discourses and myths of its function.[4] Only the second are of interest for my analysis. I shall examine three ways in which discourses on the functionalization of speculation were constructed. All three dimensions deal with the question of how to guarantee the economic viability of speculation.

1.1 The Product of Speculation (Factual Dimension)

To a large extent, criticism of speculation derived its force from the concept of the economy as the production and exchange of goods. The question of productivity was often raised as a basis for arguing that speculation was unproductive. The stock market was disparaged as a "bottomless pit," and the trader as a "low wretch." Stock traders, who created nothing of economic value and benefited from the labor of others, were the dregs of society. Van Antwerp indignantly combatted such charges in his defense of the stock exchange (1914, 226). He found the claim that stock speculators were "non-producers and parasites" particularly distressing. It overlooked the ways in which speculation was socially useful, he argued.

Defenders of speculation could respond in two ways. They could either attack the production model of the economy or attempt to show the productivity of speculation. The first strategy required turning away from the notion that the economy was based on labor and value—a move requiring a fundamental rearrangement of economic thought. Such a position could only be successfully defended by resorting to neoclassical arguments that resonated badly with the public at large and the critics of speculation. They spoke a different language and did not understand this defense, so they questioned the productivity of speculation. Instead, the proponents of speculation proposed a product unique to the stock market. What kind of product was created by Wall Street's abstract operations, processes entirely lacking physical existence? For the defenders of stock speculation, the answer was clear: the stock market was distinguished by its "power to form prices" (C. J. Fuchs 1891 cited in Emery 1969 [1896], 116). The stock market thus produced *prices*. As was the case with every other product, price encompassed qualitative differences. The reliability of this product made the stock market distinctive. As a quality, price ultimately provided a measure of the usefulness of the stock market.

It is difficult to overstate how deeply the discursive order was rearranged by the argument that stock exchanges primarily fulfilled the function of forming prices. The well-established physiocratic discussions about fair price took an exciting turn, since the criterion of determining fair price by labor was displaced. While the notion of fair price was still rooted in a representative discursive order, it now became clear that *natural* prices did not exist; they had to be *produced*. The determination of prices on the exchange was improved not by lengthy negotiation or struggle over the correct price, but instead because price became reliable economic information. The quality of prices was exclusively measured by how they came into existence: "The more *free* the competition between buyers and sellers, the more *minutely is price* regulated by demand and supply, and nowhere is competition more *free* than on the exchange" (Emery 1969 [1896], 113; emphasis added). In writings friendly to speculation, the stock market was seen as the stage for free competition—a status that made it an ideal location for prices to be formed. The prices produced on the stock market were rarely surpassed in exactness, since they were created on the basis of an ideal economic procedure. The metaphysics of fair price was replaced by the metaphysics of a free price that came into existence based on the laws of supply and demand. Rather than starting from a nearly ideal representation of price, this new metaphysics sought a procedure that was almost entirely internal. The *procedure* by which prices came into existence determined their exactness, and, in turn, the quality of the good produced by stock speculation. A *procedural* model of free price formation thus displaced the representational model of price.

Moreover, the quality of prices was measured by their *global* validity. Previously, prices negotiated on local markets had been subject to great fluctuation. Modern speculation, however, led to prices that were valid *worldwide*. The modern speculator and stock exchange thus became prototypical figures in the global society. Precisely because local differences could be ignored by being assimilated into speculation, "irrational" and "unfair" fluctuations in price connected to a specific local context were increasingly excluded. Supporters of the stock market claimed that the homogenization and globalization of prices was good for the very producers who most strongly criticized trading in grain futures or short-selling. These producers no longer had to depend on prices offered by untrustworthy grain traders in local markets, since the current worldwide price for grain was immediately available. The availability of prices also created greater security for investors; the Chicago Board of Trade was described as a "price insurance center" (Dies 1925, 24) protecting against unnecessary fluctuations in price by means of free speculation.

Speculators thus produced knowledge by presenting economic information in the clearly arranged and comparable form of prices (Emery 1969 [1896], 116). When rearticulated as a productive activity, speculation could be separated from gambling. Unlike speculators, gamblers never produced prices.[5] Critics of speculation did not fail to notice how stock speculation was translated into a paradigm of production. The writer and publicist Edward Sanford Martin admired the way defenders of speculation transformed it into a "work of fast usefulness," but attacked a weakness in the way speculators understood price: "[T]hough speculators do make prices, they are very apt to make them wrong" (Martin 1908, 243–44). The quality of self-organization in a functional system, he believed, could only be ensured by the quality of those included: only competent speculators could produce good prices.[6]

I.2 Speculation as the "Eye of Business"
(the Temporal Dimension)

The knowledge that crystallized in prices not only resulted from a nearly ideal model of free market competition, but was also oriented toward the future. Prices already included conjectures about probable future events (Emery 1969[1896], 117; cf. Van Antwerp 1914, 23). Speculation operated not with fixed values, but with possibilities—or, as a critic of speculation remarked, with "unknown and unknowable chances" (Anon. 1901, 201). Critics opposed this uncertainty to economic behavior that tried to avoid unnecessary risks. How could an orientation toward *future contingencies* be understood as genuinely economic?

The answer depended largely on how this relation to the future was constituted. Speculation existed in close proximity to gambling as long as both embraced an uncertain future. At the same time, this relation to the future gave speculation the opportunity to create an economic function not covered in other economic domains. With this function, speculation could find a place in the economy. Handbooks on speculation expressed an awareness of the opportunities that this difficult position could bring. Stock speculation was introduced as an *art of the future*, an art that made speculators the "eyes of business" (Meeker 1922, 424). In speculation, unrecognized future possibilities became visible, which would have otherwise remained closed to the economic gaze—an oversight that amounted to wastefulness. In the nineteenth century, a discourse began to form around the relation to the future opened up by speculation, whose primary function was predicting the way the market would develop (Holway 1992, 104).

In the 1850s, Pierre-Joseph Proudhon had already observed this prominent function of speculation in a way that set him apart from other theorists. Subsequently, he was well received by American theorists of speculation such as Henry Emery.[7] For Proudhon, speculation was an essential part of the economy. Speculation not only supplemented the other three constitutive dimensions of the economy (capital, labor, and trade), but was their driving force. Only speculation regulated the unique powers of innovation: "Speculation is thus, properly speaking, the spirit of discovery. It is speculation that invents, innovates, provides, resolves, and, like the infinite mind, *creates from nothing* all things. Speculation is the essential faculty of the economy" (Proudhon 1857 [1854], 5). Speculation was the brain that steered the capitalist economy and assigned the role of implementation to the other three economic dimensions (8). Proudhon no longer assumed that the forces of production automatically grew, only to be revolutionized from time to time by relations of production. He replaced this imperative of the philosophy of history with the dynamic of speculation.[8] Speculation became a visionary power, entirely in the sense of the Latin root of the verb *speculare*. By allowing calculations to be performed with future quantities, speculation anticipated developments in labor, capital, and trade.

A similar thought can be found in the English novelist Ralph Hale Mottram's history of speculation (Mottram 1929, 40), according to which, human beings resemble a donkey enticed by a dangling carrot: "[The carrot] is not merely nutritious, satisfying necessity; it is tasty, satisfying the donkey's aesthetic sense. Unless it dangles, he will not pull the barrow.... He must sniff and gaze, and trot after that ever-receding benefit. His eye gleams, his nostrils twitch—this is his speculative faculty at work" (11).

Without the dangling carrot, the donkey would remain immobile, and the economy behaves in precisely the same way. Only speculation ensures that innovations and discoveries take place. It guarantees the economy a future, which it observes in a way that makes current economic activity possible.

Through speculation, the future influences the present. The present can be adapted to "actual" future events. However, the donkey metaphor that Mottram introduces to persuade readers that speculation is useful remains ambivalent. Questions were raised about how speculation could function as the "eye of business." Like a donkey, the speculator could not see through the simple apparatus governing his or her activity. The speculator allured by the aesthetics of the dangling carrot could hardly be thought of as a rational economic actor. Economic rationality and irrationality were found to be in close proximity. Without speculation, the donkey simply would not move, and would perhaps fall asleep. With the capacity for speculation, the donkey begins to trot. However, the donkey remains unaware that it comes no closer to its object of desire.

To avoid this unproductive approach, another argumentative strategy about the speculative relation to the future was developed. Speculation was posited, not only as a driving force behind the economy, but as a *self-correcting* economic mechanism. Like a barometer that made it possible to predict the weather, speculation was always a step ahead of the market. While barometric readings had no influence on the weather, speculative prognoses could affect the economy. Using the language of probability, Supreme Court Justice Oliver Wendell Holmes Jr. expressed the economic effects of speculation in a particularly memorable way: "Speculation . . . by competent men is the *self-adjustment of society to the probable.* Its value is well known as a means of avoiding catastrophes, equalizing prices, and providing for periods of want" (198 US 236 [1905] cited following Dies 1925, 20; emphasis added). Rather than organizing and recording present needs, speculation represented *the future as present probability.* This representation was already fulfilled in what it represented. Representations of the future reinforced their own likelihood by bringing current economic activity into conformity with speculative prediction. Speculation blurred the boundaries between past, present, and future: "[Speculation brings] into the closest relations the economic past and future with the present" (Jones 1900, 195). In these probabilistic terms, speculation served normalization, which has always included comparison with others. By being compared with the capacities of others, one's accomplishments are brought into conformity with an imaginary mean. With the notion of probability, the future—and the risks of the future—became normalizing factors. Precisely at this point, speculation acquired its function. As a way of normalizing temporal contingencies, speculation was to be included in the arsenal of practices increasingly dominated in the nineteenth and twentieth centuries by statistics (cf. Hacking 1990).

The speculator thus became an agent of economic risk, and speculation gained a place in the social division of labor.[9] At the end of the nineteenth century, in fact, the speculator became a specialist in risk. The task of the speculator was to assume risks that could have disastrous consequences for others—for example, farmers or tradespeople (Cowing 1965, 10; Goede 2004). Risks were to be reduced by being redistributed and gradually discharged. This process took place within a framework of specialized understandings of risk. According to the stockbroker Edward Meeker, speculation functioned with the "assumption of those *necessary risks* which always exist during the process of distributing any kind of property" (Meeker 1922, 402; emphasis added). The speculator handled only socially necessary risks accompanying economic modes of organization. In contrast, the gambler engaged in self-created risks, "based upon future events without any necessary relation to ownership or property" (399–400).[10] "Necessary" risks were thus opposed to "excess" risks classified as artificial. The common ground between gambling and speculation identified by Emery could be extended to include the way these forms of risk depended on a future event (Emery 1969[1896], 98; Martin 1919, 76). This common dependence, however, only emphasized that the future event stood in an entirely different relation to the object of speculation. Speculative risks were not created by a fixed system of rules external to the goods acquired—as was the case in gambling. Rather, these risks were directly connected to the speculator's property. For example, speculation changed the demand for—and, in turn, the price of—wheat. Precisely this function distinguished speculation from gambling. The gambler took a similar, or perhaps greater, risk than the speculator. Gambler and speculator were driven by a profit motive. However, gambling had no influence on supply and demand (Conant 1904, 89). Betting that the price of wheat would drop influenced its future price as little as betting on a winner influenced the outcome of a horse race. The gambler was exclusively interested in risk, and even enjoyed the exposure to risk. The enjoyment of risk now became suspicious. Whoever enjoyed speculation primarily for the risk was a gambler who had strayed into the stock market (Dice 1926, 8). The gambler was defined as someone who took a risk for the sake of risk, and enjoyed the "pleasure of the *thrill*" (Mottram 1929, 20). The entertainment value of speculation became a contested site at which the boundaries between economy and noneconomy were drawn.

The ideal speculator outlined in the discourse of function did not love risk. In fact, this speculator was entirely risk averse. Brayton Ives (1888), a former president of the New York Stock Exchange, described the speculator as thoroughly conservative. The speculator wanted to reduce risks, rather than enjoy them.[11] Speculation thus paradoxically functioned to destroy its very reason for existing: "Risk and uncertainty are the two qualities essential to speculative transactions, and just so fast and so far as they are eliminated, just so fast and so far they cease to invite speculation" (Gibson 1889, 6). Edward D. Jones also emphasized this aspect of speculation: "The effect of true speculation is to eliminate itself" (Jones 1900, 168).

1.3 Speculation as Lubricant of the Market (the Social Dimension)

Speculation was given the social function of determining relationships between market participants. Product markets existed without speculation in the narrow sense and posed a challenge to the evidence that speculation was socially necessary. It thus became necessary to join "normal" market logic to the social dimension of speculation. Like the parasite, the speculator became a mediator—but a mediator regulating the law of supply and demand (Mottram 1929, 14). Speculation perfected the market by bringing buyer and seller into close proximity in the narrow space of the stock exchange (Hill 1975 [1904], 369). Through this social compression, speculation "lubricated" the law of supply and demand. The American economist Edwin Seligman emphasized the "indispensable function" of speculation as an escalation and intensification of "normal" economic processes: "Speculation tends to equalize demand and supply, and by concentrating in the present the influences of the future it intensifies the normal factors and minimizes the market fluctuation" (E. Seligman 1905 cited by Van Antwerp 1914, 42). The equalizing function of speculation ensured that the market acted "correctly," and that opportunities for profit could be distinguished from blind waste: "In this fashion the speculator is the advance agent of the investor, seeking always to bring market prices into line with investment values, opening new reservoirs of capital to the growing enterprise, shutting off the supply from enterprises which have not profitably used that which they already possessed."[12]

Speculation assumed the function of *bringing the market into agreement with itself.* Prices had to correspond to investment values—a correspondence that guaranteed order in the market.[13] The ideal market was not only represented, but also performatively generated, by speculation. Speculation functioned as a mechanism for selection that could, for example, separate profitable from unprofitable activity. In this way, representation and selection complemented each other. Unlike gambling, speculation was no longer criticized as the collapse of market rationality, but was seen instead as a mechanism that held the market together, and prevented prices and values from drifting apart. Put in other terms, *only speculation made the market what the market always should have been*: a rationally functioning structure requiring no external intervention.

Unlike legal or political measures that intervened from outside, speculation regulated the market from within. For Proudhon, speculation not only normalized financial markets, but also regulated product markets. This regulatory function is surprising, given that supply and demand was often hailed as a quasi-automatic law requiring no external intervention. The law of supply and demand was a natural force that could not be challenged by human beings: "The great law of supply and demand regulates everything and is no more to be resisted than the tides of the ocean. . . . Any reasonable man must concede that supply and demand regulate values, and that individual effort against this great law means destruction to the individual" (Hill 1975 [1904], 429–30).

John Hill allowed no room for the individuality of the speculator, who either complied with the iron law of supply and demand or was destroyed resisting it. This argument was repeated by crowd psychology in theorizing the destruction of the economic subject (see chapter 4). Nonetheless, the "positive" task of the individual speculator to perfect an already perfect law remained precarious. By reason of its visionary power, speculation supplemented the economy—as an addition that was deemed unnecessary, but without which the economy would not function:

> But through the stock market it is determined *almost automatically*, with as much *nicety* as anything can be determined which depends on human judgment, where further production is needed and where capital is needed. Upon that market is concentrated, in a sense, the *judgment of every human being in the world* having an interest in production either as consumer or producer. . . . That delicate register of values, that sensitive governor of production, that *accurate barometer of the people's needs*, could not be replaced by any process that any State socialist has devised or suggested.[14]

As a supplement, speculation had to function like a machine removed from individual irrationality. Speculation made possible encounters between buyers and sellers on a global level. The virtual, global congregation of speculators led the economy to rapidly and harmoniously adjust to probability. Speculation became a democratic barometer constituted by the collective intelligence of market participants, rather than an economy managed externally by the socialist state. This speculative rhetoric served as an early example of "market populism" (Frank 2000), in which the market became the mouthpiece of the people. The supplement was supposed to make the law of supply and demand agree with itself, and acted as a figure of self-observation closed to external influence. At the same time, the supplementary character of speculation was based on isolated individuals who stood to lose their individuality should they rise against the law they represented and perfected.

Discourses of functionalization were designed, as it were, to economize speculation—that is, to conceive and observe speculation as a genuine economic activity, and thus to clearly distinguish it from gambling. In the three dimensions discussed above, strategies were deployed to secure the economic character of speculation.

Factually, speculation was inscribed in a paradigm of production, and thus became a producer of *prices*. This process was not supposed to determine speculation as, on principle, another form of economic communication. Instead, speculation was described with the vocabulary of production in order to be separated from the unproductive activity represented by gambling. If prices were understood as products, it was possible to emphasize the self-referentiality of speculation. Prices arose in relation to other prices rather than to material goods. This strategy was not without risk, since questions could be raised about the quality of the product and the competence of the producers.

The product of speculation was not only distinguished from other goods because it lacked materiality, but also because it already contained the *future* of the economy. Temporally, speculation became the global, democratic "eye of business" capable of recognizing future risks and opportunities. The focus on handling risk placed speculation in a classical economic vocabulary. Speculation only worked with risks in order to reduce them, and thus to do a service to the rest of the economy. In this sense, speculation constantly progressed toward its own end. By successfully reducing economic risks, speculation threatened the basis of its own existence. While gambling was reproached for creating artificial risks for pure entertainment, speculation was seen as undoing itself.

Socially, speculation was thus understood as a necessary *supplement to the market*. Of course, markets could also function without speculation. However, only speculation created a genuine market by eliminating gaps and deficiencies in the "normal" market. Speculation lubricated a market that was—at least according to self-descriptions of the economy—itself already supposed to be perfect. Speculation was transformed into an economic activity by the notion that it could *perfect the market*. Communication by means of speculative prices was certainly self-referential and abstract, but it was wondrously connected to the rest of the economy. By contrast, gambling had broken away from, and become indifferent to, economic laws.

2. Strategies of Exclusion and Inclusion

The discourse of functionalization was accompanied by strategies of inclusion and exclusion that adapted to the discourse of functionalization, but that also followed their own logic. This dynamic has been implied several times. As we have seen, Justice Holmes famously defined speculation as the self-adjustment to the probable of society, a process personified in "competent men" (Dies 1925, 20). Competence prevented the speculator from being allured by the spectacle of pure contingency. Speculation not only had to assume an economic function, but the seriousness of the speculator had to be guaranteed. Only in this way could the speculator rise to the higher function of market supplement. Inclusion and exclusion were meant to combine a form of functional differentiation in the economy with an adequate mode of inclusion. This proved hard to achieve, since the mass of future speculators in no way met the theoretical ideal of the knowledgeable speculator.

2.1 The Exclusion of "Suckers"?

Objections to the way stock market speculation was presented to the public surfaced early on. The potential public of speculators, it was asserted, had a "false" impression of speculation. Debates ultimately arose as to whether it was even possible to talk about a public with regard to the stock market. The problems of self-presentation confronting speculation were related to strategies of functionalization. The argument that speculation fulfilled a necessary economic function was convincing in an academic context, but the fact remained that the functionality of speculation was hard to demonstrate. This functionality remained invisible to the public at large. The public saw speculation as little more than "the *sensational* feature of trade" (Hill 1975

[1904], 369; emphasis added). Speculation was easily confused with gambling. According to many functionalization advocates, close observers could hardly distinguish between the two. The alluring resemblance also included the idea—drawn from stereotypes of gambling—that on the stock market anyone could become rich with a little luck. This misconception that even the most ignorant could speculate was criticized in handbooks on speculation and the psychology of the stock market: "Many a man or woman who would not expect to be successful as a circus clown, opera singer, or grocer, without some kind of preparation or talent, nevertheless expects to be successful right off in the stock market—probably the most difficult game on earth" (Kelly 1962 [1930], 163). The speculating public consisted "of all classes of people with all degrees of mental power and knowledge . . . the group is relatively able and well informed on its main activity in life such as business, yachting, or dentistry, but the same cannot be said regarding the evaluation of securities or the art of speculating. In fact, as regards the stock market the public is amateurish in all respects except in speech" (J. A. Ross 1938, 58–59). "I wish you would leave this off the records. Well, to be perfectly frank with you, it is a pathetic basis on which the average man buys stocks," the professional speculator M. C. Brush told a hearing (59).

The notion that with enough money even "the ordinary man, without special training" could speculate was equivalent to the hubris of self-representation in a court of law (Clews 1973 [1908], 23). This notion again brought to the surface a tension in views of speculation. In principle, anyone with enough money should have access to the market and be able to speculate. However, this accessibility was seen as a threat to economic rationality.

Such arguments were in no way limited to the United States around 1900. During debates in France shortly following the 1987 stock market crash, amateur speculators were quickly identified as the source of market confusion and condemned, not only for erratic speculation, but for "contagious mimicry" (Rieusset-Lemarié 1992, 150). An article in Le Monde titled "Faut-il éliminer les petits porteurs?" (Should Small Shareholders Be Eliminated?) asserted, for example, that small shareholders "cost a lot and interfere with the impressive flow of information on the stock exchange. . . . it is necessary to e-lim-in-ate them. We have to do away with the hundreds of thousands of small transactions that 'scandalously' slow down the market."[15] Financial markets in the United States around 1900 and in France during the 1980s were said to suffer from "indiscriminate" openness. Incompetent individuals who confused speculation with gambling not only hurt themselves but also damaged the reputation—or even the function—of speculation. The democratic ideal of speculation thus had a downside. On the popular level, speculation loosened inclusionary restraints so effectively that it nearly lost function-specific criteria for inclusion. The seductive all-inclusiveness of popular stock market participation outpaced financial competence and functionality.

A similar argument can also be found in Max Weber's writings on the stock market, which are oriented toward the German context. Weber lamented the fact that too many "incompetent" speculators were included in market activity. In contrast to the conservative stock market criticism widespread in German aristocratic, labor, and agrarian circles, Weber took a "friendly" position toward the influence of the stock market on conditions in Europe. He saw the stock market as necessary for a complex modern economy. Only the stock market allowed for fast, reliable price formation (Weber 2000b [1894], 366). Nonetheless, even he regarded the large number of "unprofessional" speculators who did not understand the stock exchange as problematic: "The small speculator who seeks to make earnings out of small differences in prices, and who makes the exchange into a place where for the first time he goes chasing after the sort of wealth that he does not possess, is not fulfilling any aim of the national economy as a whole. Whatever might fall to him as earnings, the national economy also pays, in wholly unnecessary fashion, to a superfluous parasite" (Weber 2000c [1894], 333).

Weber explicitly criticizes the *"misleading behavior . . .* leading to economically irrational and dangerous 'gambling on the exchanges'" and argues against the "participation of unprofessional individuals who are ignorant of what goes on in exchange trading" (Weber 2000c, 331; trans. slightly modified). He speaks disparagingly of the "whole horde of small speculators, armed with practically nothing beyond good lungs, a little notebook, and a pencil" (Weber 2000b, 367):

> The widening of the market through bringing in the public, as it is made easier by futures trading, is drawing persons into commerce on the exchange—and this is beyond all doubt—who in fact must dispense with any professional knowledge of the exchange, as well as with any impulse to feel themselves *responsible* for financial gains and losses—whereby they would *independently* verify the proceedings that take place on the exchange. (Weber 2000b, 363; emphasis added)

The ideal market subject was responsible for his or her own decisions, and assumed this responsibility based on specific economic knowledge. For Weber, these decisions had to be reached, not by imitation, but by independent economic calculations.

Only qualified professional speculators would be found in an ideal financial market capable of forming optimal prices. Only the necessary capital ensured that market fluctuations would not interfere with speculators' decisions. Rather than the lack of reason displayed by small speculators, the market needed the "strong hands" of "large-scale capital-holders" (Weber 2000c, 333). In principle, Weber advocated the exclusion of small speculators. However, he proved to be skeptical about the exclusionary measures taken against them.[16] Weber saw dangers in an exchange investigation commission's proposal to compile a register of speculators in commodity futures to help create a "separation between 'qualified' and 'unqualified' speculators," arguing that it might stigmatize speculation by, as it were, forcing speculators to confess their identity.[17] Even qualified speculators would thus be scared away, and the exchange would suffer in its ability to form prices.

Furthermore, such measures would also have no regulatory effect on unprofessional speculators. During a "gambling epidemic," a register of speculators would not deter speculation (Weber 2000a, 574). The limited usefulness of exclusionary measures was implicitly grounded in the vocabulary of mass psychology. The behavior of the small speculator was seen as *epidemic*, and thus could not be controlled by rational means. Measures to protect the small investor had a limited effect. It was impossible "that the *essential* viewpoint from which one views the exchanges . . . be that of those customers who want their possessions to be guaranteed to them under all circumstances, who do not wish 'to be big shots' and yet who nonetheless wish to gamble all of their wealth on the exchange" (Weber 2000c. 332).

The United States differed from Germany in that a "right to speculation" was assumed there. Nonetheless, New York Governor Charles Evans Hughes's Committee on Speculation in Securities and Commodities, established in 1909 to investigate trading in futures, recommended that unqualified speculators be kept out of the market (Cowing 1965, 107; New York [State] Committee on Speculation in Securities and Commodities 1910). Carl Parker of Columbia University asserted in 1911 that "to meet the evil of speculation what is required is the elimination . . . of . . . those who are unfitted by nature, financial circumstances, or training to engage in it." Parker's

recommendation would have made it possible to remove undesired gamblers, but it violated the principle of universal rights to the market. Parker
thus qualified it by saying: "[T]o make such a law would strike at the roots
of personal liberty. The right to buy and sell is a fundamental one."[18] No law
could resolve the problem of inclusion. All that remained, Parker thought,
was to encourage better training for speculators. The ideal financial market
was an impossibility. On the one hand, markets had to be deregulated. On
the other hand, markets had to be regulated in order to scare away—or even
"eliminate"—small speculators. Since legal regulation would interfere with
deregulation, the call either for training or for moral barriers to unqualified
speculators became louder.

2.2 Inclusion: Counting the Public, Training Speculators

Severe disapproval was not the only position taken on speculation. Alongside
calls simply to exclude "unprofessional" speculators, a more nuanced regulation
of inclusion in accordance with the discourse of functionalization was called
for. The latter position produced two very different arguments. On the one
hand, the relation between the stock-trading public and finance was assumed to
be unproblematic. On the other hand, it was objected that the public needed to
be taught how to speculate competently before being allowed to do so.

The first argument viewed the public—apart from its specific constitu-
ents—as economically relevant. This argument for popular speculation is
nicely exemplified by the advertising slogan used by the online broker Instinet cited in the Introduction to this book: "The bigger the crowd, the better
the performance." The claim that increasing numbers of speculators raise the
liquidity of the market goes back to arguments put forward around 1900. Of
course, there was no unified "American" position on whether incompetent
small speculators damaged or contributed to the economy. Henry Emery, for
example, approached the problem of amateur speculators in contradictory
ways. These speculators were pure gamblers, and thus lacked the intelligence
and competence necessary to speculate. At the same time, Emery emphasized
that a great *number* of speculators could have a stabilizing influence on the
market. The public now had its own value: "The participation of the public,
however, does increase *numbers*, and in normal times numbers themselves
are a steadying influence in the market" (Emery 1969 [1896], 190; emphasis
added). The public was thus to be characterized, not by competent individuals, but by size.

Van Antwerp similarly defined the utility of popular speculation, quoting the German economic theorist Wilhelm Lexis (1837–1914): "Even though the market-place is largely filled with speculators, it is plain that the greater number of traders in securities, the greater will be the facility for buying and selling any quantity of securities" (Lexis 1896–97 cited in Van Antwerp 1914, 21). For Van Antwerp, economic performance depended to a large extent on a large public: "[C]apital must be enlisted, which is another way of saying that speculators must be attracted" (40). Only large numbers created equilibrium. The mass of speculators increased collective economic judgment and fixed prices at their proper level: "Ten thousand competitors in this business of bringing price and value together are of course better than one thousand: a hundred thousand would be better still" (41).[19] To be sure, Van Antwerp also observed that margin trading allowed poorly informed small speculators access to the financial market (50). However, he dismissed the idea of legally regulating the stock exchange. This regulation would have disastrous consequences:

> Whatever it may lose in the way of business from ignorant and silly people who are driven out of blind speculative undertakings leading to losses which they can ill afford, it will gain tenfold in imparting sound information through candor and publicity. . . . Prudence, thrift, and foresight are not to be eliminated, merely because the proletariat below stairs sometimes indulges in speculation and suffers the consequences of its folly. (Van Antwerp 1914, 60)

The inclusion of unprofessional speculators was not seen as a threat to economic rationality. Rather, Van Antwerp trusted the *rationality of quantity.* Unqualified speculators did not compromise the information produced by speculation, but raised market liquidity.

Access to the stock exchange was to be restricted neither by laws nor by exclusive clublike organizations. Rather, access to the exchange should be purely regulated by money and creditworthiness, that is, by purely economic criteria. Richard Lewinsohn and Franz Pick also argued for this minimal condition in their 1933 book *Der Sinn und Unsinn der Börse* (The Sense and Nonsense of the Stock Exchange). Almost anyone could trade in stocks: "The only prerequisite: money. Whoever wants to participate in the stock exchange has to have money."[20] Lewinsohn and Pick were also skeptical about attempts to regulate the stock exchange. Regulation might spare a few careless speculators misfortune, but made no sense in economic terms:

> In principle, the exchange, particularly the equity market, is a field for every-
> one. Restricting the trading floor to a small circle of professional traders is
> certainly possible, as happens on most stock exchanges, but no one can be pre-
> vented from buying stocks, and thus from playing the stock market. Gambling
> on the stock exchange is even more accessible than gambling in Monte Carlo,
> where it is at least necessary to legitimate oneself by giving one's true name.
> The only condition for admission to gambling on the stock market is having
> one's own money. (Lewinsohn and Pick 1933, 63–64)

The popularity of speculation was no longer directly linked with the stock
exchange as an *organization* whose accessibility was governed by rules. This
popularity could only be understood by distinguishing between organizations
and functional systems. The stock exchange as an organization could in no
way be governed according to the same regulations as the functional system
of the economy. Systems theory tends to see inclusion and exclusion specific
to a functional system as established through organizations. However, stock
speculation points to a striking divergence between membership in an organization and inclusion in a specific functional system. Lewinsohn and Pick
argued entirely on the level of functional systems. Participation in the economy could only be regulated by the value of stocks. Lower stock values made
amateur speculation easier.[21] Organizational rules thus lacked the power to
regulate access to—and, in turn, the potential popularity of—speculation.
Access to speculation was instead regulated by offering small shares accessible
even for the small man. Access to the market thus depended on how money as
medium was divided into uniform amounts. This shows that the inclusionary
regime relied in that respect not so much on competence as on the nominal
value of shares.[22]

The rhetoric of market populism celebrating speculation on the stock
exchange as a near-magical realization of democratic ideals came into being
around 1900. American economists saw "evidence of the successful 'democratic' distribution of national wealth" in the wide ownership of shares
(Lewinsohn and Pick 1933, 65). With this rhetoric, the idea of "market populism" (Frank 2000) came into being. The inclusion of large numbers of speculators was seen, not only as a trap for incompetent "suckers," but as democracy
in action. Politics thus ideally complemented economics. As a democratic site,
the stock exchange was not a product of political intervention; rather, it followed a logic that could always be measured in terms of economic efficiency.

For Van Antwerp (1914, 23), market prices represented democratically shared knowledge, a knowledge that not only unified the intelligence of all speculators, but also contributed to assessments of the future.[23] Each speculator was viewed as an entirely autonomous individual who was capable of responsible decisions, based on "superior knowledge thus freely given to him" (22).

Early accounts of the stock exchange already emphasize the democratic nature of speculative information equally accessible to a broad range of class, gender, and occupational identities. These social differences were formulated in stereotypical terms, representing the novel and unsettling aspects of speculation. The Anglo-American financier Henry Clews (1836–1923) made an especially strong plea for equality on the stock exchange, dismissing the idea of class distinctions as "semi-barbarous in its character and unworthy of a people professing advanced civilization" (Clews 1968 [1900], 206). U.S. citizens did not deserve to be subjected to a system of class distinctions, which failed to comprehend the fundamental equality of all American speculators and would only stir up jealousy: "There are no classes in this country as opposed to the masses, and we are all one mass, at least all citizens are, and that mass is composed of an aggregate of sovereign citizens in this great Republic" (10). The discriminatory vocabulary of class had to be replaced with a more unifying discourse of mass.

Not all proponents of nearly universal inclusion in the stock market reacted with such euphoria. Emery, for instance, criticized the fact that the public followed all kinds of rumor: "Every possible occurrence is seized upon as an excuse to stimulate a new movement on the part of the public" (Emery 1969 [1896], 177). For Emery, speculation was also fundamentally a problem of inclusion rather than of economic function. The greatest harm done by speculation came from "the *moral evil* of a reckless participation in the market by a wide outside public" (187; emphasis added). However, Emery opposed arguments about competence that appeared in handbooks on speculation. From a macroeconomic perspective (99), he regarded as implausible the notion that only a knowledgeable speculator could produce valid information—something suggested by Philip Carret (1896–98) and many others (e.g., by John R. McCulloch in the nineteenth and Arthur Twining Hadley at the beginning of the twentieth century). With luck, investors could make decisions in line with the "visionary function" of the stock market even without careful consideration. Emery was also opposed to putting moral pressure on the use of "speculative knowledge," no matter if difficult to distinguish from gambling.

The gambler was not to be underestimated. Decisions made by gamblers were often based on elaborately devised systems that were rational in their own way (99).

For Emery, then, the speculator could not be distinguished from the gambler on the basis of knowledge. By abandoning this distinction, he lost the initial criterion of competence that was so important to the idea of disciplining the speculator. However, he also questioned whether the inclusion of a large public would necessarily produce valuable collective knowledge (Emery 1969 [1896], 190). Yet Emery maintained that more speculators increased liquidity and reduced fluctuations in market rates. How did Emery reconcile this optimistic assumption with his views on the evils of speculation? He speaks not of a general evil but of a *moral* one (187), and this distinction is important. By separating morality from the economy, Emery was able to criticize the universalization of speculation. This distinction also allowed him to highlight the usefulness of speculation: "The widening market is simultaneously the cure of some evils and the cause of others. The former are mainly economic, the latter moral" (191). W. I. Thomas made a similar distinction when he separated the economic and psychological functions of the economy. Economically, speculation helped fix prices. Psychologically, speculation was just gambling and thus could be problematic—but not for the economy.

From this perspective, it was not necessary to exclude unprofessional speculators. This would only prevent the largest possible number of speculators from being included in the market. On a theoretical level, the problem of hyperinclusion was resolved by distinguishing between two perspectives. Speculation might be disastrous for speculators who unknowingly put everything they possessed—and thus their economic existence—on the line. However, these disasters did not interfere with the workings of the financial system. Emery argued strictly from the second perspective. Ruined speculators were only a problem to the extent that they could no longer speculate. Individual loss meant a loss of future business for the stock market.

With this purely functional approach to speculation, irrational behavior could be reformulated as a moral or psychological problem entirely outside the economy. However, many observers saw undesirable consequences in the strict application of this distinction. Taken to the extreme, the functional approach justified the wildest individual passions and illusions. Ultimately, all that mattered was the effect these passions and illusions had on the economy. Morality and psychology thus served as good outlets for ridding speculation of perceived flaws. Elements of speculation resembling gambling could be made into exclusively psychological questions. Economic problems arising in this resemblance subsequently disappeared. Pathologies and irrationalities were no longer part of the economy. In other words, the strategy of functionalization imagined overcoming the popular of the economy. Functional systems had to operate without hyperconnective mechanisms of communication such as suspense and thrill, which were largely seen as problematic.

However, Emery occupied an isolated position in popular theorizing about speculation. For critics of speculation, his strategy of distinguishing between the economy and psychology remained unacceptable. Emery displayed a lack of democratic sentiment by justifying speculation in purely economic terms—terms that also justified immoral behavior. For proponents of speculation, Emery's position was too risky. It complicated the strategically necessary distinction from gambling and misrepresented the role speculators played in forming knowledge. Emery did not exclude the possibility that greedy or incompetent speculators contributed to speculation. In this way, he subordinated arguments of inclusion or exclusion to a functional argument in favor of market equilibrium.

Arguments that emphasized the number of speculators, celebrated the effects and possibilities opened up by democratic inclusion, and psychologized gambling stood in contrast to descriptions emphasizing the disciplining of speculators. Such a view questioned whether inclusion in the stock market could be entirely regulated according to a speculator's financial resources. Instead, speculators had to be subjected to a strict disciplinary regime. This emphasis on disciplinary regimes was often complemented by arguments for inclusion of large numbers, thus trying to articulate two very different logics. The two arguments complemented each other, in that the individual speculator and the stock-trading public as a whole were seen as two faces of the same phenomenon, but if one of these was privileged, they clashed. If overextended, the argument of liquidity in large numbers led to a loss of interest in the behavior and ethics of the individual speculator. Yet it was also possible to exaggerate disciplinary techniques and demands for competence. Such exaggeration threatened the democratic ideal of inclusion and the liquidity of the market.

The link between the "visionary" rationality of the market and individual reason was established by the argument that only trained speculators could properly anticipate future events. Effective speculators had to be in a position to calculate the advantages and disadvantages of an investment. They also had to be able to distinguish companies with a promising future and industrial giants (e.g., the railroad companies) from passing trends. Uninformed speculators caused unnecessary market activity (see, e.g., Angas 1936, 12; McVey 1901, 138). "If universities were not the worst teachers in the world I should like to see professorships of speculation established at Oxford and Cambridge," Samuel Butler suggests in his novel *The Way of All Flesh*, but goes on to speculate that, given the dismal record of the universities, this would likely "end in teaching young men neither how to speculate, nor how not to speculate, but would simply turn them out as bad speculators" (Butler 1903, chap. 78; cited in Jackson 1995, 389).

The education of the speculator was the basis for a large body of literature, including autobiographies and handbooks. The public image of speculation had to be changed from one of parasitic activity to that of a rational profession: "People forget that the business of speculation requires special training, and every fool who has got a few hundred dollars cannot begin to deal in stocks and make a fortune" (Clews 1973, 35). Each new speculator had to be rigorously trained. No one was born a speculator. The best traders "have 'gone through the mill'" (36). With drastic metaphors, Clews emphasized that a good deal of effort was required to train speculators (37). Would-be speculators should have "some sledgehammer blows applied to their heads to temper them, like the conversion of iron into steel." The manufacture of trained speculators was endorsed with an industrial metaphor of production, thus translating financial inclusion into the language of labor and goods.

In his often-reprinted investment handbook *The Art of Speculation*, Philip Carret distinguishes speculators from gamblers in less drastic terms: "The speculators are those who use brains as well as ink in writing the order slips for their brokers." The speculator had to have prior knowledge and perform exact calculations, while the gambler left transactions entirely to chance. Crucial to this distinction was the question of whether profits were forecast *rationally*. The speculator always had "a logical ground for expecting so happy an event."[24]

However, intelligence and knowledge did not guarantee that a speculator would act rationally. The stock market psychologist Henry Harper maintained that men with considerable analytical skills and professional success sometimes failed as speculators because they lacked the self-discipline required to deploy their knowledge effectively. The losing speculator was not only oblivious, but also overconfident. Typical losing speculators could be characterized in the following ways: "a) no knowledge, only rumors and advice of friends; b) think they have learned everything; c) good knowledge, but bad temperament" (Harper 1966 [1926], 67). The speculator not only had to be competent, but also capable of keeping his or her *distance* from the market through disciplinary techniques (cf. Simmel 2004 [1901], 78): "[T]he hardest thing to learn in stock trading is to keep the eye *off* the market, hold firmly and patiently to good resolutions, *and not try to get rich too quickly*" (94–95). The lure of the promise of "something for nothing, much for little" had to be overcome. An autonomous economic subject could only be formed in the absence of such magical solutions.

Thus, speculation also suffered from its popularity: "This is one reason why the movies are so popular. It is this mental laziness that leads the public into error marketwise" (Moore 1921, 114). Through this comparison with film, the *popularity* of speculation was cast in a critical light. The properly trained speculator learned to renounce immediate enjoyment as economically unproductive, precisely the promise which was the basis of the popular dream of univseral inclusion.

The emphasis on knowledge and disciplined conduct of the speculator pointed to a preexisting rationality in the speculator. From this perspective, rationality lay with the speculator rather than with speculative knowledge about the future seen, for example, in forecasts of prices. The preexisting rationality of the speculator served two purposes. First, it ensured the rationality of the market. In simplified form, the argument ran as follows: only *external* reinforcement guaranteed the rationality of market forces that appeared to lack reason. Depending on which variety of this argument was used, market rationality was either founded on or, at least, reinforced by the speculator. The speculator held in reserve a separate rationality for cases of market failure. This complementary rationality external to the market also served a second purpose. The speculator could be constructed as a hard worker, entirely in the sense this term took from the vocabulary of productive labor. While gambling connoted effortless pleasure, speculation was redefined as a *labor* of knowledge. "If the speculator imagines that he can operate successfully without *preliminary hard work* to fit him for the business in hand he is grossly mistaken," Thomas Gibson insisted. The speculator could not rely on tips, but had to use "deductive and inductive reasoning."[25] In addition to guaranteeing the rationality of irrational markets, the speculator worked hard to produce knowledge. These two aspects of the speculator's rationality provided the foundation for specific disciplinary techniques.

Strategies of functionalization and inclusion were thus combined to "purify" speculation, making it more boring and less popular. The functionalization of speculation constrained the "wild contingency" of gambling. An economic purpose now existed for engaging with contingency. The thrill of speculation became a side effect, private or moral, to the "actual" goal of speculation. However, the discourse of functionalization did not resolve the problems of inclusion that arose when speculation began to attract a large public. Proponents of speculation such as Emery assumed that even incompetent speculators increased the liquidity of the market. For Emery, it was ultimately useful from a macroeconomic perspective to include these speculators. More common, though, were positions that viewed speculation neither as an end in itself nor as entertainment. Instead, the contingencies of the market posed a challenge that only a speculator with economic competence could address. The disciplined and professional speculator guaranteed that market rates were best described as "collective intelligence." The thrill of the popular remained unavoidable, but could be defused as a pathology "foreign" to speculation. The speculator might find pleasure in the entertaining contingency of the market, but such pleasure did not belong to the "essence" of speculation. The pleasure of speculation was handled in two ways. On the one hand, it was seen as an individual or psychological problem with potentially grave social consequences. On the other hand, it became the object of disciplinary techniques that formed qualified speculators only through the process of inclusion.

3. The Fictive Economy

Strategies of functionalization proved to be quite successful when assisted by a politics of inclusion. On the one hand, these strategies were attached to a language taken from the paradigm of production (prices as products, or price formation as a labor of knowledge). On the other hand, these strategies also sketched an image of speculation as a highly referential form of communication. By emphasizing this self-referentiality, speculation could be more readily distinguished from gambling. Prices "produced" by speculation relate to other speculatively formed prices. Furthermore, present futures (i.e., speculative predictions) influenced the future of the market. Speculation served as a way of adapting to the probable. Socially, the self-referentiality of speculation was again tied back to the economy. In this way, speculation turned into a supplement to the economy, a supplement that refined and perfected the laws of the market. The history of "functionalization" is thus also based on the discursive means by which speculation was described as self-referential communication.

What did these attempts at providing an economic function to speculation mean for critics of speculation? Did they, now deprived of their arguments, have to admit defeat? A few may have. However, a majority of critics seized on the effects of successful functionalization. The British economist William Stanley Jevons (1835–82) was disappointed by the fact that critics of speculation particularly mistrusted the notion of the perfect market: "It is a singular fact that markets have been the subject of popular prejudice and moral objection, almost in proportion to the perfection with which they economize time, transportation and effort, and equalize prices" (Jevons 1871 cited in Fayant 1909, 37). How did this "prejudice" against the "pure market" and speculation arise, even though discourses of functionalization seemed to have successfully economized speculation? This economization came at the cost of fictionalizing finance. Fictionalization counteracted efforts to translate the discourse of speculation into a language of production and reality. It was only with such efforts that the contrast between a classical economy of production and a financial economy became clear. Prices stood for "fictitious goods" that lacked the material reality of classical products.

Critics found the fictionality of speculation especially provocative. By the beginning of the nineteenth century, the fictionality of speculation had become a popular target of criticism.[26] The American political economist Henry Vethake (1791–1866) argued that speculation could exceed the real needs of a society and had to be strongly condemned when it became detached from reality—that is, fictive—in this way (Vethake 1838; cf. Harding 1993, 215). Nebraska senator Algernon Paddock (1830–97) maintained that the unreality of speculation was pathological, and that "speculation had become removed from the *realities of economic life*, that speculators, like victims of *schizophrenia*, were content to live in their own world of rumor and secrecy, trying to anticipate each other instead of promoting the nation's business" (Paddock cited in Cowing 1965, 20; emphasis added).

Charles Dudley Warner—who, together with Mark Twain, wrote *The Gilded Age* (Twain and Warner 1915 [1873])—masterfully presented this aspect of speculation in his novel *A Little Journey in the World* (1969 [1889]). Warner did not follow the typical critical strategy of equating gambling and speculation. Rather, he accepted this distinction and used it as a starting point to criticize speculation. Warner established the boundary between gambling and speculation by underlining the increased *fictionality* of speculation:

> This is business of the higher and almost immaterial sort, and has an element of faith in it, and, as one may say, belief in the unseen, whence it is character-ized by an expression dealing in futures. It is not gambling, for there are no chips used, and there is no roulette table in sight, and there are no piles of money or piles of anything else. . . . the man who buys and the man who sells can do something, either in the newspapers or elsewhere, to affect the worth of the investment, whereas in a lottery everything depends upon the turn of the blind wheel.[27]

Warner emphasized two features of speculation. First, he argued that specula-tion functioned as an entirely fictive realm. The economy transformed from a space of material exchange into an absolutely immaterial space, a space of pure fiction: "the young man sold what he did not have, and the other young man bought what he will never get."[28] This fictionalization was not without functional consequences for defining the boundaries of the economy. Unable to rely on referential values and goods, the most advanced sector of the econ-omy moved into close proximity with religion, both guided by faith in a hid-den power.

As a fiction, speculation came to be a symbol of economic self-reference, and, in turn, to introduce an element of unreality into the economy: "It is in its artificial nature that the evil of speculation consists, and whenever this artificial element enters into trade its effect is evil and only evil. It is not a question of legitimate and excessive speculation. Whether little or much, speculation is always injurious in proportion to its extent" (Hubbard 1888, 7).

An economic discourse relying on the vocabulary of exchange was thrown into confusion and provoked by economic practices such as futures trading, which "bypasses physical conditions of production and even the fundamental laws of identity" (Michaels 1987, 67). At stake, then, was the principle of iden-tity itself.[29] Even gambling was rooted more strongly in the real world, since it preserved "remainders of reality," such as the roulette table and chips. Specu-lation had given up these remainders to work only with differences in price. The devices used to produce contingency were virtualized in speculation. For the gambler, equipment such as cards, die, or the roulette wheel served to gen-erate chance events.[30] For the speculator, this equipment was replaced by a media apparatus. The lack of "real" objects led to a widespread suspicion that speculation was open to manipulation. The cunning speculator could exert a good deal of control over a market whose workings were closed to view.

This heightened fictionality proved to be highly ambivalent for processes of inclusion. This ambivalence becomes evident when we consider the way the self-referentiality of inclusionary events is typically conceived. An increase in self-referentiality often can be expected to result in a high degree of exclusivity. As seen at the beginning of this chapter, increased self-referentiality runs counter to modes of popular inclusion. Speculation, however, is an unusual case. As it becomes increasingly self-referential, it attracts a greater number of people who have little understanding of how the economy works. With this dynamic, we return to an initial point in the relation between gambling and speculation. In order to expel the popular thrill of speculation, a discourse of functionalization had to be developed. In this way, speculation was transformed into a self-referential economic activity.

The popular did not cling to speculation like a remnant of the past, but served as a remainder that helped perfect the function of speculation. At the same time, speculation also continued to resemble gambling as a form of entertainment. In the nineteenth century, successful stock traders—the "Leviathan financiers"—were described in a way similar to the previously mentioned figure of Simmel's gambler. In an 1870 article suggestively titled "The Romance of Business," successful traders were believed to speculate primarily for exhilaration rather than for profit. In a way, speculation became increasingly self-referential as it became increasingly attractive. The self-referentiality of speculation became a pleasure—and at the same time, a privilege. The true speculator was not driven by the petty desire to "get rich quick," but took pleasure only in speculation's self-referential activity. The pleasure taken in self-generating money could only be disturbed by external reference to goods or the consumption of profits. Circulation itself became pleasurable. Even the accumulation of wealth was of secondary importance. Self-reference was attractive precisely because speculators no longer had to address the problem of limited goods. A good example of this attraction can be found in Theodore Dreiser's (1912) novel *The Financier*. The main character is a successful financier who has lost all interest in the "real" goods with which he speculates. As Walter Benn Michaels (1987) has shown in an impressive study, goods are not abstract enough for Dreiser's financier. His craving for speculation cannot readily be confused with the spirit of gambling, but is sustained by the increasing self-reference that results from a process of economic purification. The financier's speculation is exclusively abstract, far removed from the world of production and use values, and thus also enjoyable. It is only when speculation loses its referential values that the very process of fictionalization can be experienced as a joyful and miraculous disappearance of goods.[31]

Fascination with the self-referential and fictional aspects of speculation was not restricted to professional speculators. The Englishman Arthur Crump (2003 [1874]) maintained that speculation was also pleasurable for people who did not speculate themselves, but observed speculators. For Crump, speculation was inherently spectacular and voyeuristic. As soon as speculation was observed, it became an "irresistible attraction as mere amusement" (Crump cited in Thomas 1901, 758). Speculation was not only fiction, but also performed its own fictionality. Architecturally, the stock exchange was organized like a theater. Anyone who entered the exchange could witness this theatrical apparatus. Activity on the floor was visible from the balcony. This view from the balcony surfaced in many descriptions of the stock market. For the novice, the balcony served as the first point of contact with the exchange. From the balcony of the Chicago wheat exchange, the "great world drama of wheat" could be enjoyed (Dies 1925, 5). For European observers, the view from the balcony conjured a sacred and secret experience: "One visits the stock market as one would visit a cathedral in which a service is being celebrated a little too loudly. . . . Without understanding much, visitors sense that they are in the presence of a mysterious power that simultaneously attracts and frightens them" (Lacour-Gayet 1929, 163–64). In contrast to this European allusion to sacrality, Dies viewed speculation from the perspective of the emerging culture industry. He compared the floor of the exchange to a film studio. The recording clerks were like "camera men preparing to film some spectacular event" (Dies 1925, 5). The exchange was at its most spectacular during a panic: "[N]ow, the spectator rejoices. . . . In stark fascination the spectators stare into the strained faces below" (6). No longer a private thrill for a potentially pathological gambler who dabbled in the stock market, speculation now staged its own contingency.

Initially, gambling led to a tragic loss of individuality for the gambler. Speculation opened the private struggle of the gambler to an audience. This struggle was driven from back rooms and gambling dens onto the grand stage of the stock exchange, "a theatre in which these primal passions battle as gladiators in the arena without concealment or pretence" (Nelson 1964 [1903], 26). *Homo oeconomicus* embodying calculated self-interest came to be represented by "spectacular speculators" (Wood 1966, 90). For critics, the stock exchange presented an indecent spectacle. A Christian publication lamented the sight offered to a young woman in the gallery: "There is something profoundly sad-dening in the spectacle of the mad rush and whirl of a great speculative move-ment, when men seem to part with their sanity and rush at prospective profits with a kind of inhuman intensity" (Anon. 1901, 106).

Efforts to separate speculation from gambling gave rise to a paradox of purification with important consequences.[32] Speculation and gambling were often confused with each other, which set in motion a dynamic of purification and normalization. Since, from the perspective of the speculating or gambling subject, no distinction between the two operations could be established, this distinction had to be secured by an intricate discourse of functionalization. However, the strategies for purifying speculation had an ambivalent effect, since they functioned too well. As a result, they produced an imaginary of pure self-reference. Speculation was fascinating precisely because it was so abstract. Once functionalized, speculation gained distance from gambling, however, at the cost of a heightened fictionality. Speculation, which referred only to itself, found in abstraction the basis on which to construct fictional goods, and thus became a stage for primal economic affects.[33]

Efforts to purify speculation made it into a spectacle. In *La société du spectacle*, Guy Debord lamented the fact that real life, and immediacy of whatever kind, had been replaced by images without reference (Debord 2006 [1967]). As a merely passive consumer, the spectator had been permanently detached from events. For Debord, an economic process of abstraction also led to the dominance of the spectacle. This process of abstraction penetrated to the core of social relations to make them spectacular. Economic abstrac-tion lent a spectacular character to speculation. Debord mourned the loss of a genuine way of life—a way of life replaced by dislocated social relations. However, the spectacular did not arise when a formerly genuine economy based on use value was replaced by an economy of exchange value. Rather, speculation became a spectacle around 1900 as a *process* of abstraction, the spectacularity of which was to be found precisely in those moments that Debord and other theorists of the simulation society [*Simulationsgesell-schaft*] see as permanently lost. On the stage of the stock exchange, it was possible to observe the simultaneous existence and disintegration of ratio-nal economic subjectivity. A process of abstraction was required to fash-ion the speculator into *homo oeconomicus*. At the same time, this process released a host of affects and intensities that brought about the destruction of an idealized economic subjectivity.

The spectacle of speculation was thus to be located in the conflict between ideal economic subjectivity and the intense affective displays on the trading floor. In a slightly different form, the stock market presents us with the "mass publicity" characterized by a tension between disembodied abstraction and physical, affective remainders that is discussed by Michael Warner (1992). Precisely these remainders pervaded speculation as a mass of bodies, voices, and ticker tape (and its contemporary media equivalents such as the electronic ticker). Disciplinary strategies were needed to purge speculation of uneconomic popular elements. However, purifying speculation only created a more intense fictionalization of the economy. This process allowed a latent moment of popularity to resurface. Struggles over the lacking in economic function of speculation were thus by no means entirely resolved. Self-descriptions of speculation now faced pressure to find a meaningful role for economic fictions. The heightened self-reference and fictionality of finance thus gave rise to new problems. Although finance may have understood its own fictionality as a successful second-order economic observation, this fictionality was often seen by other functional systems as operating outside the economy.

4. External Attacks on the Fictionality of Speculation:
Legal Struggles Against the Fictive Economy
Observers external to the economy by no means viewed the fictionality of speculation as given. Rather, speculation posed the problem of representing financial markets to an outside public. From a perspective internal to the economy, speculation could be given a meaningful function. However, the economic legitimacy of this function was both internally contested and a source of conflict in functional systems outside the economic system. The legal system reacted to the fictionality of futures trading in a particularly interesting way, since this system not only observed, but also intervened in the economy. Defining fictionality as a genuine economic mode of communication also raised the question of whether legal intervention was necessary, and, if so, in what form.

Even until recently, the relationship between speculation and law has been strained. The legal theorist Lynn Stout appropriately titled a 1999 essay on contemporary speculation in the United States "Why the Law Hates Speculators." Stout identifies a large discrepancy in the ways the economy was understood from legal and economic perspectives during the 1990s. On the one hand, nineteenth-century critiques of speculation as unproductive and harmful have been resurrected in recent legal debates. On the other hand, recent economic theories—echoing Emery—have emphasized that speculation leads to an increase in the efficiency of the economy. We cannot address the question of whether this comparison does justice to current debates in economic theory. More relevant to our concerns is the fact that legal observations of the economy can be clearly distinguished from economic self-descriptions, and that a number of topoi from traditional critiques of speculation have been adopted in recent legislation: "The public disapproves of speculation. So, traditionally, does the law" (Stout 1999, 707).

At the end of the nineteenth century, important Supreme Court decisions confirmed anti-speculation legislation directed especially against so-called bucket shops and futures transactions of certain kinds. This legislation primarily attacked the "irreal" and "fictional" character of speculative transactions. Speculation threatened to destroy rather than generate prices. Differential transactions led to inflation, and thus falsified "real" prices. As a result, speculation was seen as damaging to the economy: "[V]entures upon prices invite men of small means to enter into transactions far beyond their capital, which they do not intend to fulfill, and thus the apparent business in the particular trade is inflated and unreal, and like a bubble needs only to be pricked to disappear, often carrying down the bona fide dealer in its collapse."[34] The justices warned that unreal, incalculable stock prices would leave the small speculator at the mercy of a fluctuating market. In this way, the fictionalization of stock exchange communication was formulated as a problem of inclusion. As a fiction, the stock exchange was open to greater participation than otherwise would have been possible.

Pure wagers on price differences were seen as parasitical, like gambling, and in 1889, partly in response to unreal forms of futures trading in which "fictitious" transactions took place, the Supreme Court ruled to restrict futures trading and to prohibit pure differential transactions.[35] This ruling was confirmed in a 1901 decision, which held that futures trading as such was not uneconomic unless used as an occasion to gamble on price differences.[36] It was not easy, however, to find a criterion for distinguishing between an exclusively fictive operation and a real one.[37] The Court approached this problem by providing an external reference for the economy, rather than by accepting the notion that the economy was a self-referential fiction. The Court did not want to forbid all forms of futures trading, and thus avoided using material goods as a referential criterion. Instead, the "intention to deliver" became a criterion for legitimate futures trading. Futures were only valid "when the parties *really intend* and agree that the goods are to be delivered by the seller . . . if under the guise of such a contract, the *real intent* be merely to speculate (gamble) in the rise or fall of prices, and the goods are not to be delivered . . . , then the whole transaction constitutes nothing more than a wager, and is null and void."[38]

According to the Court, only intent guaranteed economic communication. From a legal perspective, *real intentions* became an essential feature. Psychological intentions provided a final refuge from the volatile realities of the economy. Legitimate and legal speculation was defined in relation to the intentions of the parties involved. This definition proved to be quite flexible, since intent only had to exist at the beginning of a transaction. A Canadian newspaper sympathetic to speculation published an article emphasizing that although, initially, "intention to receive or to deliver" had to exist, "subsequent events may render delivery unnecessary and settlement before the maturity of the contract desirable" (cited in Hill 1975 [1904], 378).

With legal regulation, the border conflict between gambling and speculation took an extremely threatening turn for the financial economy. Rather than the economic system regulating itself, legislation determined which transactions were valid and which were "null and void."[39] This intervention referred to no specific economic program, but to the form of permissible *operations*. For precisely this reason, legal intervention poses a radical challenge to financial economy. Legal decisions were decisions about whether an economic transaction could connect to another transaction. These decisions thus intervened in the very connectivity of the financial economy. Legal regulation of speculation presented the unusual case where operative connectivity was defined and narrowed according to the criteria provided by another system. This becomes an even more threatening challenge, since the legal system employed precisely the psychological criteria that economic discourse about speculation had sought to reject as legitimate argument—namely, a trader's intentions. From such an intentionalist perspective, that which was seen as economically legitimate did not depend on the delivery of goods, but on the intention to deliver them. By psychologizing an economic operation, the legal system inverted arguments made by some of those who sought to exclude the uneconomic from speculation by using the disciplinary and psychological strategies mentioned earlier. The fictionality of the economy thus created far-reaching effects. This fictionality was ultimately a serious provocation to external observers who tried to regain economic referentiality by means no longer considered as economic.

5. Internal Attacks on the Fictionality of Speculation: The Fiction of Fiction—Bucket Shops

Charges of excessive fictionality came not only from outside finance. Within finance itself, certain speculative practices were criticized as too fictional. In self-descriptions of finance, a distinction was made between "proper" and "improper" forms of economic fictionality. This struggle to define economic fictionality reached a high point in the conflict over so-called bucket shops.[40]

The term "bucket shop" is said to have referred originally to the practice of collecting beer dregs in a bucket to be shared among paupers who could not afford to drink at a bar. Financial bucket shops stood in for conventional brokerages rather than pubs.

In bucket shops, bets could be made on market trends. Stocks could also be fictively purchased without an actual transaction taking place on the stock market. A minimal amount of money was required to speculate in bucket shops. For precisely this reason, they became the favorites of novice speculators and opportunists. In the United States, the first financial bucket shops seem to have come into being around or before 1880. Soon they could be found not only in large American cities but also in small towns and rural areas with no immediate access to the stock exchange. Critics of gambling estimated the number of bucket shops in the United States to be as high as 5,000 in 1890 (Hochfelder n.d., 2). By conservative estimates, there were between 800 and 1,000 by 1900 (Fabian 1990, 191).

Notwithstanding that they were "fake exchanges" (Boyle 1921, 91) and resorted to luring potential clients with the offer of a "free lunch" or cigars (Fabian 1990, 192), bucket shops were deceptively similar to "legitimate" brokerages. Imitations of entire stock exchanges were especially impressive. The Consolidated Produce and Stock Exchange of Chicago founded in 1896 functioned like a bucket shop, but was in many respects more perfect than the actual stock exchange. This exchange operated by stricter rules than other exchanges. It even used actors to play the part of traders (Hill 1975 [1904], 76), leading bucket-shop clients who did not know the difference between stock market speculation and the gambling on prices that took place in the bucket shop to "imagine that they are speculating in the same manner as is their more fortunate neighbour" (21). Bucket shops attracted people "who would not 'dream of entering a room where faro or roulette is played' or of being caught in a 'poker room.'"[41] They thus became serious economic competition for the stock exchange.

Most infuriating to representatives of the stock exchange was the fact that bucket shops used "real" stock prices. Bucket shops no longer relied on a gambling apparatus to produce contingency, as was the case in gambling. Each bucket shop prominently featured a stock ticker for reporting stock quotes virtually in real time.[42] "Procuring a blackboard, a 'ticker', a few chairs and a sheet of paper, the bucketshop-keeper invites the public to his office for the purpose of betting with him as to the future prices that may appear on the 'ticker' tape" (Hill 1975 [1904], 441). "They buy from the telegraph companies, or steal by tapping wires, the quotations of the leading exchanges. . . . Quotations are the one thing absolutely essential to the existence of a bucketshop. The moment quotations cease coming in, betting stops and the bucketshop is out of business" (21).

The bucket shop was centered entirely on media, and this presence of media created the sense of mystery and attraction—a sense to which the real-time transmission of current stock prices contributed. One bucket shop, in the basement of a hotel, for example, was described as containing "a roll-top desk, a blackboard where they might study figures which they could not understand, a desk for telegraph instruments, a typewriter, and some other paraphernalia that added a touch of mystery to the situation" (MacDougall 1936, 81). Apart from a few rigged tickers, the stock quotations appearing in bucket shops were the same as in legitimate brokerages. With these quotations, bucket shops used the stock exchange itself as a device to produce contingency. Bucket shops needed the very same fluctuating prices whose rhythm attracted popular speculators.

In fact, bucket shops came closer than the stock exchange to the ideal market in at least one respect: business could be conducted more quickly in bucket shops than on the exchange.[43] In comparison to traditional brokerages, bucket shops processed orders with astonishing speed. These bucket-shop orders were pure wagers. The shop owner did not actually invest the money he was given on the market. In this way, bucket shops bypassed the time required to complete orders. The shop owner "speculated" that most people would be too optimistic, and thus take too many risks. At times, bucket-shop clients—who were often called "suckers"—nonetheless had been given a good tip. In such cases, the shop owner could manipulate prices in a number of ways, or, should it become necessary, flee.

For representatives of the stock exchange, the success of bucket shops was perplexing. James Boyle observes, for example, that "it is almost incredible the uncanny strength and vitality possessed by these *bastard institutions*" (1921, 91; emphasis added). Bucket shops presented an immediate danger to the stock exchanges. On the one hand, they competed in attracting capital. On the other hand, they hurt the reputation of the stock exchanges.[44] The Chicago Board of Trade fought for years to restrict the bucket shops' ability to access stock quotations. Inasmuch as the exchange produced, and thus also owned, these quotations, the Board of Trade argued, their use by bucket shops was no different from theft. Bucket shops had to be deprived of their sustenance—the actual quotations. The telegraph industry, however, was interested in having bucket-shop owners as clients. Moreover, according to an 1889 court decision, stock quotations were still considered open to the public. These considerations make the interest stock exchanges displayed in the telegraph industry understandable. By controlling the telegraph industry, the stock exchanges could also gain control over stock quotations. In 1905, the first legal decision appeared stating that the Chicago Board of Trade owned its quotations (Boyle 1921, 92ff.; Hochfelder n.d.).

Efforts were made in the struggle over stock quotations to define a legitimate form of *economic fictionality* that could be separated from mere copies. At over 400 pages, John Hill's book on bucket shops provides a wealth of information on efforts to define economic fictionality. In his indictment of bucket shops, Hill calls for a more precise use of distinctions between

> the *real* and the *unreal* in speculation; between the legitimate broker and exchange member, and the conscienceless bucket-shop shark; and between the bona fide broker's office, from which the orders given by customers of the office are *sent* to the great exchanges of the country to be executed in a legitimate manner, and the pretended broker's office where a notation on a sheet of paper *records* the bet of the customer with the proprietor. (Hill 1975 [1904], 19; emphasis added)

For Hill, nothing more than a fictive economy of "unreal speculation" took place in bucket shops. It is worth noting that Hill admitted an element of unreality into speculation. Hill borrowed a standard argument from critics of speculation, particularly agrarian populists. These critics saw speculation as having lost all relation to reality (Harding 1993, 217).

Endorsements of speculation thus had to find a way to emphasize its "reality" without being too restrictive (e.g., by excluding futures), which could not be done by citing fictive material goods. Precisely such goods were criticized in polemics directed against speculation. On the stock exchange, parties traded fictive goods that could not actually be exchanged. Goods became half-glimpsed specters such as "wind wheat," subject to "fictitious sales" (Cowing 1965, 9). The typical business practice of delivering goods or services no longer took place. In fact, this practice would have shut down the entire system of futures trading (Hill 1975 [1904], 373). Delivering goods to be immediately resold would have been much too expensive and slow to keep up with the dynamic of speculation. Speculation thus threatened the entire "referential" model on the basis of which economic transactions were conceived.

For Hill and many others, the most important foundation for the reality of speculation was not to be found in a "real" product, but in speculative communication itself. This reality arose from the legal status of speculation. Gamblers and speculators might handle fictive assets. However, speculation entailed a legal change in *property relations*. Henry Emery accordingly proposed a definition of speculation that contrasted with the Supreme Court decision on futures trading. Rather than viewing futures trading in light of the psychological motives or interests of speculators, Emery was satisfied with the "positivistic" criterion of whether property rights were acquired. Regardless of intent, the speculator bought or acquired a good:

> Gambling is a transaction in which one party pays over a sum of money from his own wealth because of the occurrence of a chance event. Speculation is a transaction which one acquires by purchase of the *right to a certain property* (not specifically designated perhaps), and gains (or loses) for himself the difference between the value of the property at the time of the sale and its value at the time of the purchase. (Emery 1969 [1896], 100; emphasis added)

For Emery, this criterion neither tested the moral desirability of certain economic operations, nor presumed the existence of unobservable psychic intentions. Rather, the criterion introduced by Emery made it possible to observe the way a transaction came to be counted as an economic operation. Emery's criterion was based on arguments provided by the legal system. Property rights determined whether an economic operation could be said to exist. With this criterion, Emery entered dangerous territory. The legal understanding of the economy closely resembled public criticism of speculation. The legal system created measures to distinguish between gambling and speculation by relying on a typical model of buying and selling. This model lacked classical economic elements such as the exchange of goods. Still, it was not only the uneconomic moments of pure fiction and arbitrariness that remained. Property rights compensated for the shortfall by confirming the economic nature of an operation, and they did not have to be invoked in order to do so. Property rights grounded the fiction of speculation, as it were. Speculation turned out to be only a temporary reduction of economic complexity. An exchange could actually take place if one of the parties insisted on it. For Emery, this argument based on property rights was more attractive than the psychological intentionalism adopted by the courts, because it did not require a new reference, such as ultimately inaccessible intentions. The economic nature of speculation was underwritten by the fact that a path could be traced from speculative fiction to economic reality. The law no longer had to rely on an external category in order to intervene in the economy. Instead, the law secured the basis of the economy, and could intervene if the speculation went too far astray. Ultimately, the law protected economic logic from itself.

Such legal intervention, which presented itself as protection of the economy against itself, relied, however, on a specific view of the economy firmly grounded in its referentiality. Traded goods became an essential part of "genuine" economic transactions, since property rights could not otherwise be acquired. Legal intervention may have seemed elegant and cautious, but it nevertheless remained under the influence of a classical exchange paradigm whose unreal reality was considered indispensable.

While legal discourse cautiously tried to find a reference for speculation (if only in the psychological reality of an intention), bucket shops remained able to fascinate clients with the power of economic fictionality. Like arguments for functionalization, the criterion of property exchange did not convince the speculating public. For this public, the fictionality of the stock exchange could hardly be distinguished from the fictionality of bucket shops. The two forms of communication were too similar from the perspective of an external observer. It was already difficult enough to distinguish games like roulette or poker from speculation. Bucket shops only made such distinctions more difficult. Bucket shops were "bastard institutions." They imitated stockbrokerages by using the same stock quotations as legitimate brokers. Their owners were now, however, accused of masking their gambling operations as stock trading by proponents of speculation who were themselves accused of wearing the "mask of business." Stock exchanges deflected the charge of charlatanism onto the bucket shops. As was already the case in general critiques of gambling, writers friendly to speculation made some of the most vehement attacks on bucket shops, which were accused of misusing the mask worn by stock exchanges.

This misuse was less important than the popular appeal of economic contingency. Bucket shops could, of course, easily be mistaken for stock exchanges. More provocative, however, was the way in which the contingency found deeply unsettling in legal terms became a pastime in bucket shops. These institutions fed on the contingency produced by "actual" stock exchanges, but no longer subordinated it to any economic function, showing that stock exchange trading could be sustained without a narrative of functionalization. Though often described as "parasites" of speculation, bucket shops depended on the parasite of the popular already residing in the financial economy. Economic contingency served as an undisguised source of entertainment in bucket shops, which required only a minimal amount of wealth for speculation, and thus were even far more inclusive than the stock exchange.

Bucket shops may have freed the popular of the economy from its economic functionality, but their popular appeal was not entirely detached from the economy. The first speculatory ventures of the financier Jesse Livermore (1877–1940) occurred in a bucket shop. Livermore failed in his first efforts at speculation on the stock exchange, which was further removed from the model of the efficient market, because he forgot to account for the delays required to complete his orders: "The tape always talked ancient history to me" (Lefèvre 1982 [1923], 24). To a greater extent than the stock exchange, the bucket shop thus measured up to the ideal of the efficient market—a market based especially on real-time communication.

Speculation was thus either overseen by the law or mimetically conducted by bucket shops. In both cases, concerns were raised about the reference of economic fictions. In the first case, popular criticism and the legal system used intentionality as a way of regulating economic activity. The reality of economic operations were understood to be guaranteed by the intentions of buyers and sellers. From a legal perspective, the absence of such intentions resulted in a mere economic fiction. In the second case, stock market trading had to stress its own referentiality to avoid unwanted competition from—or at least confusion with—bucket shops. For economists like Emery, however, the criterion of intentionality was not suited to the purpose of guaranteeing economic reality. Intentions could not be empirically verified. Yet the reality of the economy—and, in turn, the fictionality of the bucket-shop economy—still lacked a purely economic criterion. Rather, it was ensured by the legal principle of property exchange. Property exchange was designed to prevent the economy from losing touch with reality in the way already found to be immensely entertaining in bucket shops. The law performed an economic service, but the ultimately noneconomic foundation of the economy was forgotten in the process.

In both cases, then, noneconomic criteria underpinned the economy. The law relied on psychological intentions. The stock exchanges relied on the legal criterion of property exchange to fight bucket shops. However, excessive economic fictionality could only temporarily be overcome by criteria borrowed from other social realms. As both cases show, the fictionality intrinsic to stock trading—even when seen in different ways—was highly attractive to external observers. Both cases also reveal strategies for "containing" excessive fictionality, strategies that operated by separating economic fictions from para-economic fictions.

6. Speculation as Gambling: Pleasure and Disciplinary Mechanisms

Efforts to purify speculation unleashed processes of abstraction and fictionalization that themselves became a spectacle. In response, strategies had to be introduced to provide a reference for speculation. External observers had an increasingly difficult time distinguishing between gambling and speculation. The conflicts between stock exchanges and bucket shops made these difficulties particularly evident. The layperson could hardly differentiate between stockbrokers and bucket-shop operators wearing the "mask of business."

In the early twentieth century, the marginal utility school offered another strategy to address gambling and speculation. This problematized, and eventually abandoned, efforts to distinguish between gambling and speculation, as well as the language of production used to justify speculation. As a result, the pleasure derived from contingency came to occupy a new position. Critics influenced by neoclassical economics reassessed the role of pleasure in speculation, which was seen as serving to reduce contingency—for instance, by providing insight into the future. Notably, the economist Arthur Twining Hadley (1856–1930), president of Yale University, sought to reconcile the marginal utility school with criticism of gambling, and the Polish sociologist Leon Petrażycki (1867–1931), who regarded the logic of "something for nothing" as genuinely economic, theorized a psychology of speculation.

Under the influence of the marginal utility school, views of the functional role of speculation changed greatly. The individual (and genuinely isolated) economic subject replaced the collective and the nation as the standard by which the functionality of speculation was measured. Hadley (1897), who claimed to follow John Stuart Mill's thinking on speculation but was also influenced by earlier thinkers, assumed that subjects involved in *any kind* of exchange were rational. Even the gambler had to be seen as an economic subject capable of rational calculations. The gambler ultimately made a rational decision to gamble. As had already been observed with respect to the eighteenth century, however, this decision was paradoxical. The gambler made a rational decision to be irrational.

Hadley began with a hypothetical argument defending gambling as an economic operation. He agreed with this argument on systematic grounds, but refused to accept it entirely. Hadley posited a gambler who had set aside enough money to live and was content to gamble for reasonable stakes. Under these conditions, even losses could be useful to him. The gambler had a good time gambling, and lost only a small sum of money. Hadley was clearly dissatisfied with this line of reasoning. His objections sound a familiar moral note: "[T]he losses represent losses of comfort and self-respect, while the gains are spent in luxury and carousal" (1897, 98). Hadley argued in a way typical of middle-class criticisms of gambling. He saw luxury as morally bankrupt. The gambler showed a lack of self-respect. These criticisms of gambling were implicitly linked to a universal model of *homo oeconomicus*.

Hadley failed to consider how rationality could suddenly turn into irrationality. He criticized gambling in moral terms immediately after having justified it in economic terms. This sudden change in position obscured the point at which rational action began to corrupt *homo oeconomicus*, who ceased to be a sovereign subject capable of weighing losses and gains. The security of rational calculation quickly gave way to the vertigo of uncontrollable gambling. What drama had transpired between these two moments? Hadley only provides a hint. A single game was never enough. The gambler quickly caught gambling fever, and became *addicted* to gambling. The initial calculations designed to optimize the pleasure of gambling spun out of control. The gambler became *infected* by an excessive desire to gamble, and could no longer rationally decide to stop.

Hadley implicitly touches on a question that would be particularly important in disciplining the speculator. How to construct a rational subject immune to the infection represented by addiction to gambling, and perhaps also to speculation? How can the speculator avoid becoming an irrational "parasite" by means of fundamentally rational decisions? At stake was the fate of the speculator as a figure of inclusion. Hadley tried to save the speculator by precariously combining discourses of neoclassical economics and morality. He confined legitimate cost-benefit analysis within moral boundaries. From a theoretical and practical perspective, Hadley's solution is hardly convincing. Yet this solution indicates that, in order to function, neoclassical rationality also required the disciplinary mechanisms provided by morality. *Homo oeconomicus* had to be subject to disciplinary and moral guidance. Whereas Emery saw the overlap between speculation and gambling as a moral problem, Hadley hesitantly admitted that the enjoyment of contingency could play an economic role. However, morality had to be invoked to protect *homo oeconomicus* from the risks accompanying pleasure.

The Economic Logic of "Something for Nothing":
Leon Petrażycki

The Polish philosopher, sociologist, and legal scholar Leon Petrażycki (1906) showed what a thorough—and radical—formulation of economic rationality could mean for speculation. By using eclectic arguments, Arthur Hadley had tried to avoid condemning traditional critiques of speculation in a directly neoclassical way. However, Petrażycki made such a critique in radically psychological terms. As we have seen, critics of speculation traditionally accused speculators of wanting to have something for nothing. The speculator was described as a "lazy parasite" who lived off the products made by others. Speculators were accused of living better than those making the products.

For Petrażycki, such a critique was problematic. He saw the wish for easy gratification with minimal effort as a "general commercial postulate," a postulate that was "not only natural from the standpoint of private interests, but also necessary for the national economy in the current system of economic decentralization" (1906, 57). Petrażycki undermined conventional moral criticism by making an anthropological point about deeply rooted human laziness. Just as new tools were invented to reduce the strain of human labor, speculation was designed to increase profit by means of a well-placed investment. If economic rationality was defined by minimal effort for maximal gain, speculation was no different from other forms of economic practice: "The usual doctrine on the causes of speculation has become dubious by the fact that it employs a thesis and principle essential to social well-being in order to explain a particular category of social ills, and by the fact that, in order to hide the contradictions and leaps in logic, it employs unsympathetic turns of phrase that cast this principle in a negative light, and even slightly stigmatize it."[45]

The *gambler* now even mutated into a *paradigmatic economic figure*. The form of speculation that had been most sharply criticized suddenly came to represent an ideal of economic rationality defined by the minimal use of effort for attaining a particular effect. Too much effort was made by the speculator who took time to research the market and carefully evaluate his chances. Minimal effort was made only by the speculator who, with a light touch and a little luck, sensed the right moment to buy and sell. This kind of speculator showed what it meant to radicalize the notion of rational calculation when the referential certainties of premodern economic thought no longer existed. A speculator only had to choose, with little to no effort, the right stock at the right time. For Petrażycki, the logic of "something for nothing" was genuinely economic. He did not want to hold this logic accountable for causing speculation to lapse into insanity.

It was thus not irrational for the speculator to seek the most efficient way to make a profit, and, in doing so, to undermine the notion of fair exchange. Irrational speculation instead arose when the speculator overestimated his chances of making a profit.[46] Petrażycki also argued for a form of rationality that went beyond the individual speculator. In times of economic prosperity, crowd dynamics increased already existing optimism about the chances of making a profit at speculation: "The ever-present sight of wealth gained by those who invest money in stocks serves as an example, contagious in its effects, that draws in an increasing number of participants" (62). We again see the intersecting discourses already encountered in Hadley. For both Hadley and Petrażycki, the notion of contagion threatened to undermine rational self-interest, and thus the individuality of the speculator. Because Petrażycki wanted to defend speculation, he could not make its irrational elements an essential part of the "rationality of commerce." Rather, he had to locate these irrational elements in the supplementary affective mechanism of overconfidence.

In the United States, Hadley's reluctant view of speculation as rational economic action was separated from more radical defenses of speculation resembling the position taken by Petražycki. The distinction between gambling and speculation lost significance precisely because individual pleasure was fundamental to neoclassical economic theory. Shortly before the stock market crash of 1929, there appeared a "most extravagant piece of special pleading for special interests that one could hope to see" (MacDougall 1936, 123). Joseph Stagg Lawrence, an economist teaching at Princeton, took the notion of maximizing personal gratification so seriously that he ended up defending gambling as well as speculation: "The immorality of gambling is by no means self-evident. . . . If a man derives pleasure from a game of poker he is as much entitled to it as are other people who derive pleasure from attempts to improve the morals of their neighbours. . . . Pleasure is a legitimate end. . . . If it yields pleasure and enables a man to take his mind from other matters, it is productive in the highest sense" (Lawrence 1929, 144).

As for Petražycki, grounds for moral critique of speculation disappeared. The usefulness of pleasure surpassed any specific moral code: "Many economists today define ultimate income as that stream of pleasurable sensations which accrues to us within a period of time" (Lawrence 1929, 145). Efforts were no longer made to distinguish between genuine and false risks. Economic communication was based simply on readiness for risk—a readiness that was now seen in a positive light: "Christ himself took a chance" (139). The fact that risk could be found everywhere led Lawrence—after having dispensed with classical criteria used by critics of gambling, such as natural and artificial risk, knowledge, change in property, and morality—to render the distinction between gambling and speculation null and void.

The potential explosiveness of economic rationality became evident in Lawrence's provocative assumption that pleasure was, in itself, a legitimate aim. Hadley's moral critique of the speculator who used profits on luxury and carousing was no longer possible. Such behavior now represented an almost ideal form of economic rationality. Economic activity was no longer deemed useful by objective criteria, but by the subjective pleasure gained. According to Lawrence (1929, 144), material gain ultimately meant nothing if it could not be translated into pleasure. Economic rationality was no longer measured against collective results, but was individualized.

The economy was now based on an individual cost-benefit analysis that took into account material and psychic satisfaction. Discourses of functionalization had shifted reference. Speculation no longer had a function for the economy as a whole, but for the individual speculator. In this way, the economic rationality of speculation came to be so radically individualized that even problems distinguishing between gambling and speculation vanished, or at least became less dramatic. The now legitimate proximity of gambling and speculation returned to an implicit democratic ideal already found in discourse about gambling. Gambling found justification in the principle of "always beginning anew"—that is, in the impersonality that guaranteed everyone the same chances in the next round. Gambling embodied the democratic and economic ideal of equal opportunity envisioned for speculation. Speculation was seen as "one of the fairest and most open games ever played; a game in which every participant, man or woman, rich or poor, old or young, has an equal chance."[47] Popular speculation thus connected the entertainment value of thrills to a utopian vision of inclusion offering everyone a fair start.

In 1967, under the pseudonym "Adam Smith," the former broker and financial journalist George J. W. Goodman published *The Money Game*, a book that would become a best seller and be reprinted many times. As its title suggests, it was not written to uphold a distinction between gambling and speculation. Instead, the gambling metaphor—even if polemical in part—is used to enthusiastically affirm speculation.[48] Smith contends that the distinction between gambling and speculation is no longer necessary, basing this on the aspects of the economy that resemble gambling. To back up his argument that the distinction between gambling and speculation has collapsed, Smith cites the American economist and game-theory analyst Thomas Schelling: "The greatest gambling enterprise in the United States has not been significantly touched by organized crime. That is the stock market. . . . The reason is that the market works too well. Federal control over the stock market, designed mainly to keep it honest and informative . . . makes it a hard market to tamper with."[49]

Schelling's observations represent a striking shift in the distinction between gambling and speculation. Opponents of speculation still often criticized Wall Street for disguising gambling with the "mask of business." However, the mask of business had become unnecessary. Speculation was not only a game, but the *game of all games*. Other games could be manipulated, but speculation had the power to redeem itself. *Only gambling could make the market into an ideal market.* It was no longer necessary painstakingly to distinguish gambling from the market. Rather, the market came into its own through gambling. Even the pleasure of speculation no longer had to be concealed or psychologized. Pleasure instead became one of the most important factors in speculation, the factor most capable of making speculation more useful. The speculator experienced individual satisfaction that would otherwise have been too expensive to buy.

For Smith, this view of speculation has clear consequences for the speculator. Discussion aiming to stabilize the distinction between gambling and speculation always emphasized the speculator's objective "vision" of the future. Smith attributes an entirely subjective standpoint to the individual speculator. He implicitly follows the marginal utility school by aiming to explain the game of speculation by means of individual motivation. Emery granted that it was entirely possible for an individual speculator to be motivated by the fact that speculation is like gambling, but maintained that such motivation was to be ignored from a functional perspective. However, Smith defines speculation precisely by its resemblance to gambling. In order to truly play at speculation and become a "real speculator," it is not enough to have money in mutual funds or with financial consultants. If your money is managed by another person, "then you are not really interested, or at least the Game element . . . does not attract you" (Smith 1967, 13). Neither is it the goal of speculation to make as much money as possible.[50] "If you are a successful Game player, it can be a fascinating, consuming, totally absorbing experience, in fact it has to be. . . . But the real object of the Game is not money, it is the playing of the Game itself. For the true players, you could take all the trophies away and substitute plastic beads or whale's teeth; as long as there is a way to keep score, they will play" (13–14).

The speculator imagined by Smith incorporates figures such as Simmel's adventurer and gambler, and fulfills the worst fears expressed by critics of speculation. The modes of inclusion particular to speculation are openly linked to those of gambling. Speculation cannot be done on the side, but requires a nearly frenzied state of full inclusion. The goal of such inclusion is primarily the pleasure that accompanies speculation: "The Game is more fun" (Smith 1967, 14).

The criterion of individual pleasure used by Smith no longer requires a foundation. Those who derive no pleasure from speculation are not only bad speculators, but *not speculators at all*, since they do not allow themselves to be infected by a desire to play the game. This perspective led to an important change in a well-established code of conduct. For decades, handbooks on investment and the stock exchange had advised speculators to manage their money with as little emotion as possible. Now, speculation was characterized by the passion required for "total absorption," and the fun that resulted from such absorption. Smith by no means advocates a kind of "undisciplined emotionality." On a theoretical level, he connects rationality and pleasure in a way similar to the marginal utility school. For Smith, conceiving of speculation as gambling is also not without risk. It is threatened for him, as for Hadley, Petrażycki, and Lawrence, not by its similarity to gambling, but by the risk of the speculator being merged into the herd and hence becoming vulnerable to being stampeded with it. In *The Money Game*, Smith outlines a crowd psychology of the stock exchange to help the individual speculator avoid this and to maintain his individual identity even in difficult times. Still, even individual calculations were not exempt from becoming infected by the logic of the crowd and of absorbing the speculator into an almost formless crowd.

Finance had to struggle with problems of self-representation from the moment it began to emerge as a distinct system in the seventeenth century. Speculative operations could hardly be distinguished from gambling. The unsettling similarities between the two began with the fact that the people who worked as speculators could often be found gambling in basements, back rooms, or even openly on the streets. However, this fact was only the most obvious parallel and did not imply that gambling and speculation were identical. They could be functionally differentiated, and corresponding roles could be assigned to gambler and speculator. Of greater consequence for the confusion between speculation and gambling was the fact that even a careful observer had difficulties distinguishing between them. Anyone who played the role of ethnographer and sat in a coffeehouse where gambling and speculation took place would only be able to separate the two activities on the basis of the securities traded and the material infrastructure (e.g., dice and card games). If this ethnographer happened to be a systems theorist who ventured a formal analysis of the communications processes observed, he or she would quickly notice that in both cases payments were made, but no goods or services were received. Instead, a contingent future event would decide who left the coffeehouse with gains or losses. Confusion of gambling and speculation reached a high point in bucket shops, which created a setting in which speculation was indistinguishable from gambling.

Nonetheless, gambling took place in bucket shops, while speculation took place in stockbrokerages and on the exchange—at least according to proponents of speculation. Was the activity in bucket shops simply a sham worthy of condemnation? Did the bucket shops mimic speculation with the aim of duping the small speculator? The criminal activity surrounding bucket shops should not be ignored. However, I have approached bucket shops in a different way. I have taken the mimicry of speculation seriously, and treated this mimicry as a guidepost for my readings. Why did the mimicry of speculation have such a powerful discursive effect? Put another way, an explanation is needed for the way bucket shops—whose clients often did not recognize them as illegitimate copies of speculation—became popular, and, in turn, made the popularity of legitimate speculation legible.

The mimicry of speculation taking place in bucket shops made the fraught relationship between gambling and speculation particularly clear. Initially, gambling and speculation appeared to be indistinguishable. The only identifiable difference had to be established in terms of inclusion and exclusion. While gambling in bucket shops was open to anyone, only a small minority could invest directly on the stock exchange or through a broker. In the celebratory terms of cultural studies, speculation by the "people" was opposed to speculation by the financial elite. However, I have proposed using another conception of the popular, whose essence is not the "people," but that nonetheless accounts for the dynamic of universal communication. The popular cannot be reduced to the crowds in front of exchange doors or in bucket shops, but has to be seen as proper to finance itself.

Gambling and speculation do not represent two realms always already separated. Rather, the possibility that these realms can be confused—or even mimicked—points to the fact that gambling includes speculation, and speculation includes gambling. A permanent "labor of division" is required to keep gambling and speculation apart (cf. Munro 1997, 9ff.). Speculation owes a large part of its popularity to this resemblance to gambling. Moreover, it requires an element of gambling in order to function. No economic subject would choose to gamble on rational economic grounds (cf. Keynes 1973 [1935], 170).

The confusion of gambling and speculation on display in conflicts between the bucket shops and stock exchanges, or in the regulation of futures trading, did not leave the notion of speculation untouched. Speculation was characterized by the displaced ideals of gambling. Like gambling, speculation was affectively structured by a suspense mechanism. Speculation also had its own ideal of all-inclusiveness, an ideal corresponding to the possibility of beginning again on equal terms. Affect and democratic all-inclusiveness were not external to speculation. The fact that both types of communication were intricately entangled helps explain why they led to such heated conflicts. Speculation saw a threat to its seriousness in gambling—a threat that weighed all the more heavily because finance was a relatively new form of economic communication. As a fledgling form of communication, speculation had to prove its "seriousness," not least by establishing a discourse of "serious" speculation. Only in this way could speculation continue to exist in the face of internal and external attacks.

A broad discourse of functionalization that originated in economic theories of the late nineteenth century proved to be the most successful means of stabilizing the distinction between speculation and gambling, and thus of defending speculation against the accusation that it was no different from gambling. The discussion was not entirely academic. Debates outside academic circles had a great impact on how speculation and gambling were understood. These debates made their way into economics textbooks, popular articles and tracts, and books. I have emphasized the importance of the fact that the function of speculation was established as a discursive strategy.

This strategy of functionalization was intended to expel gambling from speculation by producing and displaying the function of speculation. Nonetheless, efforts to represent speculation were plagued by difficulties that, in turn, affected the modes of inclusion to which it was linked. Speculation produced prices whose quality could no longer be measured by referential criteria. This function had become incomprehensible to the external observer, a fact that was not only a PR problem for the stock exchange. Above all, speculation was self-referential, and had to provide the prices that would allow the economy to observe and, subsequently, steer itself. The functionalization of speculation thus entailed an increase in self-referentiality, which appeared to ensure that speculation would remain distinct from gambling, since gambling always had to rely on outside mechanisms to produce contingency. Radical self-reference brought the distinction between gambling and speculation into being. Gambling was relegated to dependence on external contingency—that is, gambling was said to lack the feedback mechanisms that would make contingency into self-produced contingency.

From the perspective of my notion of the popular, the self-referentiality of speculation imposed, or at least strongly emphasized, by the discourse of functionalization implies its own failure. Due to the increased self-referentiality of speculation, a process of fictionalization was released to which popular descriptions of speculation were particularly drawn. Since material referents no longer existed, the speculator had to treat speculation as an imaginative activity. However, it was not only the individual speculator who had to deal in fictive values and speculative fantasies. The process of fictionalization also became a spectacle on display in speculation itself. The spectacularity of speculation was based on external observations describing speculation as a process of fictionalization, and on the internal fictionalization confronting the individual speculator. This spectacularity was also one of the most important differences between speculation and gambling. Gambling often took place in hidden rooms, or in partly open and legal spaces. The gambler did not want to be observed by nongamblers. A particular form of gambling may have produced suspense, but rarely became a spectacle. For example, the spectacle of horse racing provided the contingencies required by a game of chance. However, the race rather than the bettors stood in the foreground. By contrast, speculation put on display the abstraction and subsequent fictionalization of the "real" economy. As was the case in gambling, the processes of abstraction and fictionalization at work in speculation pushed the boundaries of currently existing subjectivity. For this reason, gambling and speculation were described as experiences of presence, experiences the subject could no longer rationally contain and regulate. The economic subject reached its own limits in this process of fictionalization. Only speculation had an intrinsically voyeuristic structure that celebrated the temporary dissolution of economic subjectivity, and that staged the public spectacle of clashing affects—a spectacle whose pleasure was, for the most part, denied women. In response to the triumph of spectacle, efforts were made to find a referent for speculation. A referent such as "real intentions" or property rights guaranteed that the fictions produced by speculation maintained an economic dimension.

The argumentative terrain fundamentally shifted only when theories of the marginal utility school were popularized. Any hope of clearly distinguishing gambling from speculation was abandoned. Individual pleasure became a legitimate measure of economic rationality. Gambling and speculation now both counted as rational forms of economic communication. This notion, inspired by neoclassical economic thought, nonetheless remained under the sway of nineteenth-century discourses on gambling and speculation. Only popular accounts of the economy made evident a fact that could not be found in academic accounts of *homo oeconomicus*: the individuality of *homo oeconomicus* was under threat, a loss that would also mean the end of rational economic calculation.

Part II
Crowds

INTRODUCTION

Two problems emerged in the struggles over articulating gambling and speculation. On the one hand, speculation was subject in the nineteenth century to
a process of fictionalization in which all references, and even fictions of reference, were abandoned. Without these, it was no longer possible to establish
stable boundaries in an economy oriented toward production. In the face of
uncertainty about the "object" or "product" being traded, the issue arose of
whether transactions were economic or "mere" gambling. On the other hand,
the unstable distinction between gambling and speculation encouraged a
politics of inclusion. Discourses both friendly and hostile to speculation regularly questioned the professional competence of speculators. Toward 1900,
concerns were voiced—mostly in Europe, but also in the United States—that
this had gone much too far. Speculation no longer followed the principles
required to produce an individualized and competent audience: "When beggars and shoeshine boys, barbers and beauticians can tell you how to get rich
it is time to remind yourself that there is no more dangerous illusion than the
belief that one can get something for nothing," the famous stock speculator
Bernard Baruch mused.[1] A stable articulation of the distinction between the
financial profession and its *nonprofessional periphery* was needed. At the turn
of the twentieth century, this outside was seen as an irrational mass of speculators entirely lacking in financial competence, but nonetheless participating
in the market. The ideal of the competent, rational speculator gave way to the
nightmare image of irrational crowds of gamblers flooding the market. This

gave rise, on the one hand, to predictions of the collapse of inclusion and the requirement of specific functional competencies for speculation, and, on the other hand, made the peripheral mass of speculators the target of new techniques aiming to control and regulate finance.

Theories about crowd psychology were not specific to the economy, but were taken from already established self-descriptions of other functional systems. Politicians in particular invoked the crowd mentality to describe and strategically manage problems of inclusion.[2] The establishment of democratic governments in many European countries, notably after World War I, provided an impetus for universal political inclusion, raising questions about how to manage a political audience that had suddenly and drastically increased in size. How could the sound political judgment of rapidly growing electorates be guaranteed, avoiding interference with the functional logic of the political system? Precisely this problem arose in finance as well, in an intensified, but also displaced, form.

How did the concept of the crowd found mainly in politics become an economic concept able to regulate inclusion in the economic system? To answer this question, I first turn to Charles Mackay, who studied historical cases of money mania that arose before the emergence of a modern speculating audience. His understanding of crowd psychology was remarkably modern, and he draws significant analogies between the "madness of crowds" and financial speculation, but he does not yet regard crowds as constitutive of speculation.

In contrast to Mackay, who saw speculation as an exceptional, and spectacular, case, a different view of speculation is to be found in the nineteenth-century United States, which both self- and external descriptions perceived as a nation that owed its existence to the spirit of speculation. A discursive normalization of speculation thus took place. The analogy between speculation and crowds, characteristic of Mackay, lost its foundation. As a norm, speculation was now confronted with the abnormality of crowds. It is all the more astonishing, then, that not only critics of speculation, but also its proponents, describe speculation in America in terms of crowd psychology.

The distinction between the financial profession and the crowds of incompetent speculators that emerged in the nineteenth century proved to be very fragile. In Europe, crowd psychology arose in two seemingly irreconcilable forms. Gustave Le Bon spoke of an "age of crowds" (1903 [1895], 15), while Gabriel Tarde observed symptoms of an "age of the audience *(public)*" (1989 [1898]). These two diagnoses were connected in the American reception of crowd psychology, particularly in the writings of the Ukrainian American psychologist Boris Sidis.

The concept of suggestion was promoted in America around 1900 in order to describe stock speculation. The distinction between the professional public and the crowd is especially unstable in this model, even in the absence of apocalyptic scenarios such as those found in Le Bon's crowd psychology. The rise of the contrarian school of investment in the 1920s indicates, moreover, that the stock market was not only seen as ruled by suggestion. Now techniques of the self had to be developed in order to survive adverse market conditions.

CHAPTER 3

CHARLES MACKAY

THE SPECTACLE OF EQUALITY

Charles Mackay did not aim primarily for historical accuracy in his monumental study *Extraordinary Popular Delusions and the Madness of Crowds* (1980 [1841–52]), which presents examples of mass hysteria from diverse historical periods and social realms, ranging from financial speculation, alchemy, magnetism, fashions in facial hair, and witch hunts to haunted houses and the popular fascination with infamous criminals. Mackay limited his systematic considerations to a brief introduction and a few comments. His approach differed greatly from that of Gustave Le Bon, who fifty years later would explore the psychological laws of crowds. Rather than developing a theory or cultural critique, Mackay presented popular delusions in an entertaining way. The classical vocabulary of crowd psychology—for example, terms such as "hypnosis," "imitation," and "suggestion"—was not available to Mackay, and he relied primarily on the dramatic and spectacular character of his examples.

Mackay's book is not only of historical interest, but remains a regular best seller on speculation and investment.[1] In the 1930s, the financier Bernard Baruch wrote a foreword claiming to have saved himself millions of dollars by having read Mackay's book. For Baruch, the irrationality of the market was best explained in terms of the psychology of the crowd: "[a]ll economic movements, by their very nature, are motivated by crowd psychology. . . . Without due recognition of crowd-thinking (which often seems crowd-madness) our theories of economics leave much to be desired" (Baruch cited in Menschel 2002, 37). In his introduction to a recent edition of *Extraordinary Popular*

Delusions, the investment specialist Andrew Tobias recalls his first encounter with the book during his student years at Harvard Business School: "I subsequently learned that *any* business professor worth his salt would have had this book at tongue's tip; and that it had to do with the madness of crowds" (Tobias in Mackay 1980, ix). The many new editions of Mackay's book can be attributed less to historical nostalgia than to the hope that practical insights on contemporary financial markets can be gained from it.[2] Mackay's book is seen as a guide for better understanding today's market.[3] The billionaire financial manager Ron Baron is reported to have distributed *Extraordinary Popular Delusions* to his employees, hoping that it would serve them as a guide.

However, Mackay should not be too quickly understood as having written a guide to speculation. In *Extraordinary Popular Delusions,* the mass mentality simply serves as a provisional explanation for curious and seemingly irrational social phenomena; it does not provide an explanation for, or critique of, financial markets. The latter view of Mackay's book only emerged in its reception in the twentieth and twenty-first centuries.

I. Mackay's Crowd Psychology

Focusing on how Mackay narrates three different events involving economic crowds allows me to identify common semantic and argumentative features in descriptions of these crowds. These cases are the Mississippi scheme carried out by John Law in Paris,[4] the South Sea Bubble in England,[5] and the Tulipomania originating in the Netherlands during the seventeenth century, which is often considered to be the first speculation bubble.[6] Mackay's compendium does not develop a linear narrative reaching from early mass phenomena to the mass phenomena of the nineteenth century, and its later success has in part been due to his ahistorical approach. Precisely because it is believed that stock speculation has not changed in the past three hundred years, investment advisors still see his descriptions as valid—and as an implicit guide to proper speculation. This understanding of Mackay is of less interest to me than his description of speculation as mass hysteria.

A frequently cited passage from the foreword to the 1852 edition of *Extraordinary Popular Delusions* introduces key categories Mackay uses to describe crowds:

> We find that whole communities suddenly fix their minds upon one object, and go mad in its pursuit; that millions of people become simultaneously impressed with one delusion, and run after it, till their attention is caught by

some new folly more captivating than the first. We see one nation suddenly seized, from its highest to its lowest members, with a fierce desire of military glory; another as suddenly becoming crazed upon religious scruple.[7]

Mackay describes speculative crowds from the perspective of a political and journalistic observer, and thus from a point of observation not internal to the economic system. Crowds are thus not seen as a pathology within the economy, but as an illness that infects the nation from without by means of money. For Mackay, crowds are brought into existence by a collective blindness that ultimately leads to irrationality. Apart from this critique, he was also fascinated by a phenomenon that could arise suddenly and without reason, and could take hold of anyone. This fascination already indicates that crowds not only constituted a regression into barbarism, but that irrationality intermingled with contingency in a peculiar way. Mackay's account of crowds opened up an experimental field for testing the impact of increasing contingency on the many possible forms of modern collectivity—or of that which will replace established forms of collectivity. By reading the discourse of crowds as an effort to conceive of *the connection between increased contingency and sociality, I hope to avoid an essentialist reading of crowds;* the discourse of crowds neither celebrates a rebellious culture belonging to the people (even if such a description certainly applies to an extent) nor simply condemns the "popular" from an elitist point of view, as some representatives of cultural studies have claimed (e.g., Carey 1992).

Drawing on Luhmann's theory of meaning, discussion of crowds will be analyzed in three meaning dimensions.[8] In the fact dimension, crowds will be defined according to the way their expectations are structured by a *fictional object* (1.1). In the social dimension, crowds will be described as an indifferent, *classless*, and *hysterical collective* (1.2). In the temporal dimension, crowds will be characterized by their *suddenness* (1.3).

1.1 The Fictionality of the Collective Fixation (Fact Dimension)

As a theme, financial crowds were defined by fantasies of speculation as boundless wealth removed from temporal and/or spatial constraints.[9] For Mackay, this theme could only be fictional and imaginary, since it to a great extent created the delusion of equality. The indeterminacy and boundlessness of financially motivated crowds had the power to fascinate. Mackay writes in an almost formulaic way of a "boundless wealth" (Mackay 1980 [1841–52], 15, 52, 75) shared by all members of a crowd. In colonial projects such as the South Sea Bubble, this fantasy of boundlessness was linked to the hope of inexhaustible wealth in

an unknown land—a land that came to represent unexplored economic possibilities. Imagined wealth was a shared quasi-object (Serres 2007 [1980]) creating an individualized hope of success. This individualizing effect distinguished
speculative crowds sharply from political crowds. Although the illusion of
boundless wealth provided a common ground, such wealth ultimately did not
benefit the nation, or crowds of speculators. Instead, this illusion hid the goal of
creating individual wealth from the collective.[10] Paradoxically, shared illusion
served as a means of deindividualization through collective intoxication, *and* as
a means of individualization through hope for profit.[11]

Mackay emphasized at different points that this hope was highly unstable
and could collapse under the pressure of reality. The collapse of shared delusion
was described as a sobering return to reality, in which the fictional object dissolved. Particularly striking is a description of the South Sea Bubble in a parlia-
mentary history cited by Mackay. Speculation in the South Sea Company is represented as "a mighty fabric, which, being wound up by mysterious springs to a
wonderful height, had fixed the eyes and expectations of all Europe, but whose
foundations, being fraud, illusion, credulity, and infatuation, fell to the ground
as soon as the artful management of its directors was discovered" (Mackay 1980
[1841–52], 73). Implicitly, this model of delusion assumed that the instability of
collective illusion was connected to lack of reference. Like many of his contemporaries, Mackay expressed skepticism about an economy that lacked reference
and instead relied on paper money, stocks, and shares. In this sense, Mackay
was a typical observer of finance in its early days (cf. Pocock 1975).

Illusions lacked a real basis, and they could thus collapse at any moment.
Mackay makes this fact particularly clear with an allegory. He compares
speculation to a palace of ice built by Catherine the Great's minister Grigory
Potemkin (1739–91). In both cases, people are deceived by a fictive object that
is initially considered impressive. The illusion eventually comes undone. A
warm breeze melts the palace Potemkin has built for his mistress, and "none
were able even to gather up the fragments." In this case, too, a real object is
contrasted with a fictive object. While a real object can at least break into
pieces, the fictive object vanishes without a trace (Mackay 1980 [1841–52], 29).

Discourses of the crowd and of speculation can readily be connected, since
they both address the possibility and consequences of losing hold on reality.
Crowds can only be constituted by fictions ("popular delusions"). This concept guides Mackay's book. Fictions have also played a crucial role in other
cases, such as witch mania and the crusades. It is no accident that in the first

hundred pages of his compendium on crowds, Mackay uses examples from finance, a newly emerging social sphere that, like crowds, was preoccupied exclusively with fictive values. This fictionality was the precarious foundation on which a "boundless" and "inexhaustible" object (e.g., the endless wealth of the colonies) could be built. Crowds and speculation became illusory. They were marked by a loss of reality, represented either by the lost material reference provided by economic goods or by the lost economic rationality and sense of reality on the part of crowds.

Imaginary fixation is also characterized by its *exclusivity*. The speculator becomes addicted to speculation and, paralyzed by the "enchantment" of collective fiction, can do nothing else.[12] This communicative effect exerted such a strong pull that even the economy experienced harm, since aside from speculation, all economic activities were neglected. Robert Walpole warned Parliament during the South Sea Bubble that "the dangerous practice of stock-jobbing . . . would divert the genius of the nation from trade and industry. It would hold out a dangerous lure to decoy the unwary to their ruin, by making them part with the earnings of their labour for a prospect of imaginary wealth" (Walpole cited in Mackay 1980 [1841–52], 53). The "real" economic factors of trade and industry were neglected for the enticement of "imaginary wealth."[13] Efforts to get rich quick, also attacked by critics of speculation in America, harmed an economy that was based on production and relied on diligent labor. The "useless" preoccupation with fictive objects conflicted with the idea of productive labor that could alone create real values.

1.2 The Hysterical, Classless "Collective": The Social Dimension of Crowds

Emphasizing the limitations of class and social status as models of identity, discourses about crowds derived their power in the social dimension.[14] They tentatively described a communicative type lacking a strongly defined identity. It was not necessary to have a specific class, gender, or ethnicity in order to become a member of a crowd. Ideas of the crowd offered the advantage of a vocabulary for grasping phenomena that could not be reduced to specific social strata or to identity politics. Thus, "crowds" pointed to a transformation characteristic of modernity—namely, the fact that the alter ego has become anonymous.

Existing hierarchies, whether of gender or class, were erased when the other became radically anonymous, because these hierarchies were irrelevant to the functioning of crowds. Financially driven crowds, in their structure and in the motivation of their members, demonstrated this indifference to gender and class distinctions. Mackay describes the wish to become part of a crowd as a hope to make otherwise fixed hierarchies changeable or contingent: "Every fool aspired to be a knave" (Mackay 1980 [1841–52], 55). A characteristic of speculative crowds was that individual wealth could be gained by means of good fortune, which, in principle, was open to anyone. The prospect of sudden wealth was not limited to a particular group, but became universal in a quite literal sense. The indifference to established hierarchies made speculative crowds appear, at first glance, to be a heterogeneous mass. Crowds of speculators are often described as a chaotic mixture of people of greatly varied backgrounds. Mackay emphasizes that *everyone* was susceptible to speculation mania: young and old (15), men and women (55, 59), cooks and footmen (21). "Nobles, citizens, farmers, mechanics, seamen, maid-servants, even chimney-sweeps and old clotheswomen, dabbled in tulips" during the Tulipomania in the Netherlands, he notes (97). Walter Bagehot describes the flattening effect of speculative mania in Great Britain in similar terms: "The frenzy, I can call nothing less . . . descended to persons in the humblest circumstances, and the farthest removed by their pursuits from commercial cares. . . . Not only clerks and labourers, but menial servants, engaged the little sums they had been laying up for a provision against old age and sickness."[15]

Normal social distinctions collapsed. Speculation could infect even the most unlikely social groups, groups from which it was supposed to be the most distant.[16] It is no coincidence that Mackay uses the *list* as a mode of representing crowds. The list allows him to inscribe different kinds of identities as members of the crowd without providing a unifying principle.

Mackay does not limit himself to listing crowds, even if it helps him represent their heterogeneity. The social dynamic of crowds could only be fully developed when their members lost any distinctive identity. Crowds exerted a strong pull and were capable of making their members equal. Anyone who approached financially driven crowds could easily be attracted to and join them. Although crowd psychology had not yet been developed, Mackay describes this social logic of crowds as a *contagious process*. In doing so, he uses a vocabulary of psychopathology, including terms such as "frenzy" (1, 12, 54), "mania" (1, 94, 97), "panic" (72, 91), "contagion,"[17] and, already in the title of the book, "delusions." These terms, which later became important for crowd psychology, had primarily a descriptive function for Mackay, or pointed to illnesses that could not be explained, whose origin was unknown, and for which no cure existed. These illnesses were stand-ins for a process of collectively going mad (xviii), a process that made individuals lose their will and even their individuality. Certainly, crowds created a strange form of equality between individuals of heterogeneous backgrounds, but at the high price of shared madness. In this radically new discourse, equality no longer arose when a hierarchical society was overcome from within, but instead became synonymous with a pathological state of the social.

The psychopathological terms used to describe crowds were combined with a vocabulary of carnival still more deeply based in class society.[18] During a speculative *frenzy*, as during a carnival, class distinctions and fixed status were temporarily suspended.[19] Discourses of crowds tried to represent a mode of communication detached from stratification. This mode of communication was seen as a radical and, in part, scandalous shift to a new form of differentiation that lacked a referent. For Mackay, the new form of differentiation could not yet be named. The indifference of speculation to stratification was closely linked to the problem of regulating a new inclusionary regime. Control threatened to break down and become "carnivalesque" when speculation could no longer be regulated by class, status, and gender. Mackay describes the "tents and pavilions" set up in the gardens of the Hôtel de Soissons to help sell stocks in the following way: "Their various colours, the gay ribands and banners which floated from them, the busy crowds which passed continually in and out—the incessant hum of voices, the noise, the music, and the strange mixture of business and pleasure on the countenance of the throng, all combined to give the place an air of enchantment that quite enraptured the Parisians" (17).

Mackay contrasts the fictionality of shared illusion with the material reality of crowds. Even if held together by a chimera, crowds themselves were by no means an illusion. A fictional object could produce crowds whose sensuous reality was fascinating. The power of fictionality proved to be quite real. Financial crowds were not only a construct, but also gathered at defined locations such as in front of Law's house, where they applied for shares. According to Mackay, the scenes on the Rue de Quincampoix, where John Law's house stood, resembled a fair, in which business, roulette, and refreshments blended together.

Powerfully infatuated with themselves, crowds became the object of their own admiration. The fact dimension became the social dimension. A "fashionable lounge of the idle as well as the general rendezvous of the busy," the mass generated enthusiasm for more than imaginary goals—as Michel Serres (2007 [1980]) puts it; wealth became a quasi-object in the circulating and self-referential hopes of the crowd.[20] Mackay did not develop a concept for this phenomenon, which subsequently became important for crowd psychology. However, precisely because he lacked a concept, Mackay described the phenomenon more rigorously. The loss of differentiation that took place in crowds could be experienced as a crush of bodies, voices, and sounds. It was possible to learn about crowds with the senses. Crowds enchanted themselves by means of their own perceptible effects. The noise of crowds was not simply an unpleasant intrusion to be reduced as soon as possible. Parisians flocked, enraptured, to the Hôtel de Soissons in order to hear the crowds there.[21] Crowds increased in size when they became a fixed point of reference for the senses. A state of normalcy not only turned into hysteria but also became an enormous spectacle that took pleasure in its own existence (Mackay 1980 [1841–52], 75). This desire, not only to invert, but to dissolve established hierarchies finds its closest analogy in the popular celebrated by cultural studies.

Discourses of crowds thus undermined established notions of social differentiation. The rules governing stratification were suspended by hysterical fixations, but not replaced by new models of differentiation. Crowds thus represent in a spectacular, but also apocalyptic, way what could happen if existing forms of inclusion were dissolved.

1.3 Suddenness and Simultaneity: The Temporal Dimension

Part of what made crowds improbable was their unusual temporal structure. Unlike "traditional" collectives, crowds did not evolve from a distant origin, but appeared suddenly. As the passage cited at the beginning of this section makes particularly clear, crowds lacked a history: "We find that whole communities *suddenly* fix their minds upon one object, and go mad in its pursuit; that millions of people become *simultaneously* impressed with one delusion" (Mackay 1980 [1841–52], xvii; emphasis added). Emphasizing suddenness also meant that causal models of explanation were abandoned. Crowds ultimately came into existence for no reason. Their autocatalytic formation took place suddenly and spontaneously. An essential feature of crowds was that they could abruptly transform a state of normalcy into delusion or hysteria. This process was not analogue, but digital. Gradual progression gave way to temporal discontinuity.

The process of crowd formation could only be reversed with great difficulty. Mackay emphasizes that it would take a while for people to recover from the madness to which they quickly surrendered as part of the herd:

"[T]hey only recover their senses one by one" (xviii). The temporal categories used to describe crowds were also taken from discourses of illness.[22] Crowds formed with the suddenness of an epidemic—and, as in an epidemic, contagion took significantly more time than recovery. Contagion and recovery took place with different speeds on social and individual levels. The collective was marked by the logic of suddenness, while the individual was conceived of as part of a longer process. Once members of the crowd had lost their individuality, elaborate techniques of individualization were required to change the herd back into a public consisting of individuals.

These aspects of crowds centered on the present were supplemented by an orientation toward the future (particularly in the description of crowds that were financially or religiously motivated). The prospect of imaginary wealth was created spatially and temporally (Mackay 1980 [1841–52], 54). Wealth was waiting to be found in locations not yet known. In this way, the imaginary object can be linked to the colonial idea of discovery. Many of the companies involved in speculation also had colonial ambitions, such as the Mississippi Company, the South Sea Company, and the East India Company. This connection between speculative and colonial fantasies can be clearly seen in an eighteenth-century Dutch caricature of Law's Mississippi Scheme (fig. 1).[23]

Hysterical speculation is visualized topographically in figure 1 as the map of an island shaped like the head of a fool, on which are locations such as "Leugenburg" (Castle of Lies) and "Bedriegers Stadt" (Cheat Town). This is not the place for a thorough interpretation of its many allegories (see de Bruyn 2000), but one point should be noted: the fool's eyes represent an estuary linking the "R. de Bubbel"—the river named after the speculation bubble—to the ocean. As we saw in the previous chapter, the *eye* was articulated with speculation. The notion of speculation as foresight is caricatured by the location on the map at which speculative bubbles arose.

The relation to the future suggested by the fool's eyes is also very important for Mackay's discourse on financially obsessed crowds. Crowds are described as a phenomenon that almost entirely lacks a past, and that can infect a large number of people at the same time. The imaginary object that impresses crowds is likewise not related to the present, but to the future. Wealth was not primarily seen as already existing and ready for redistribution, but as an undreamed of possibility existing in the future. The colonies represented a similar possibility. They existed somewhere, but only as *the promise of future wealth*. The promise of wealth lacked a specific structure and aroused the speculative imagination

Fig. 1. Anonymous, *Afbeeldinge van't zeer vermaarde eiland Geks-Kop* (Depiction of the Famous Island of Fool's-Head), a Dutch caricature of John Law's Mississippi scheme, from *Het groote tafereel der dwaasheid* (The Great Mirror of Folly) (Amsterdam, 1720). 160 × 225 mm.

for precisely this reason. The *fictive* structure of the collective object was connected in an exemplary way to a literally utopian structure of the future. The imaginary object, situated "elsewhere," was uncertain because it stood for possibilities realized neither in the past nor in the present. Speculation relied on fictions of the future, fictions that could be derailed by investors with speculative fantasies. Precisely this articulation of fictionality as a mode for imagining the future became a central site of conflict in discourses of speculation at the end of the nineteenth and beginning of the twentieth century. Educating the speculator required producing an individual by means of disciplinary mechanisms, and thus also required normalizing the speculative imagination.[24]

2. Celebrating Inclusion Without Rules

Mackay's representations of money mania proved to be surprisingly modern. Of course, he did not aim to reconstruct his case histories precisely or to develop a theory of the market and crowds. The modernity of his observations can rather be found in the connection between two discourses. On the one hand, Mackay represents a new universal mode of inclusion. On the other, he emphasizes that finance is a fictive realm.[25] The discourse of the crowd allowed Mackay to outline a new mode of inclusion that appeared entirely to lack rules. Inclusion in financially motivated crowds no longer followed the classical criteria for a stratified society. Anyone could become part of such a crowd, even before consciously deciding to join it. Without rules of inclusion, it was impossible to specify the professional competence required to speculate. The absence of arguments for competence is striking in light of efforts to distinguish speculation from gambling as a legitimate form of communication. Mackay did not try to distinguish between competent and incompetent speculators, even if doing so would have allowed him to distinguish between a rational audience for speculation and an incompetent crowd. The fact that Mackay did not make such a distinction reveals the conditions of possibility for his argument. Thus, he had to presuppose that finance did not yet have its own audience and figures of inclusion. In turn, adequately functioning processes of individualization did not yet exist, processes necessary for any audience to be constituted. In this interstice, Mackay tested the imaginative potential offered by his case studies of crowds. Because these case histories existed at such an unusual interstice, Mackay could not rely on an already established logic of the popular in a functionally differentiated society. The popular would at the least presuppose an effort to distinguish between a *professional financial class* and its *outside*. For Mackay, such a distinction could not yet arise, as is evident in the fact that he treats the nation as a political public rather than a public specific to speculation. Nations, not speculators, were deluded and even driven to madness by finance.

This suction of inclusion can be explained by the way in which *popular delusions* characterized by *fictionality* functioned. For Mackay, speculation was a popular fiction that had to explain why inclusion could exert a strong pull. To explain this pull, Mackay again used the image of boundlessness. Boundless inclusion corresponded to boundless profit. The old social order had collapsed. The criteria provided by estates no longer limited access to functional realms, and profit was no longer bound to labor. Mackay saw fictionality and popular inclusion as benefitting from each other. Without seductive fictions, inclusion would not have such a strong pull, and without carnivalesque scenes of inclusion, fictions would lose their spectacularity.

Mackay tended to understand the connection between speculation and crowds by *analogy*. The discourse of crowds was well established, and could be used to describe a new phenomenon: both speculation and crowds were characterized by contingency and fictionality. These common characteristics prepared the way for the success of crowd psychology. Nonetheless, the relation between crowds and speculation remained coincidental in Mackay's descriptions—even if this relation hinted at being more thoroughly articulated. It was this status as *exception* that made Mackay's case histories appear to be only curiosities and spectacles. In contrast to later developments in crowd psychology, these exceptions had no constitutive relation with their "normal" other. Crowds came from the outside to plague "healthy" collectives, and the "real" economy was at times infected by a mania for speculation that acted like a disease.

CHAPTER 4

SPECULATIVE VISTAS

CROWDS AND SPECULATION IN THE UNITED STATES
DURING THE NINETEENTH CENTURY

> I shall use the words America and democracy as convertible terms.
> —Walt Whitman, *Democratic Vistas*

Crowd psychology was an established political discourse in America during the nineteenth century, and *Extraordinary Popular Delusions* found a ready audience there. Mackay had already been published in American periodicals during his lifetime, and he was even called "a gentleman well known in New York" by a reviewer in *Scribner's*.[1] In the twentieth century, too, he was respectfully consulted in the debate about speculation in the United States, as the work of Boris Sidis and the contrarian investment school show.

Though many elements are similar, clear distinctions exist between Mackay's narratives and accounts of the situation in nineteenth-century America. Mackay conceived of both fictive economy and crowd mania as *exceptions*, but a process of conceptual *normalization* took place in the United States. This is particularly evident in the altered New World notion of speculation, which was no longer treated as an economic curiosity, but as a positive feature of America as a nation. The perception of crowds was also rearticulated. In American discourse, crowds stood in a complex relationship to democracy, which cannot be reduced to the often oversimplified critiques found in European theories of crowds.

I. Crowds and Democracy

Political preconceptions about crowds in the United States differed greatly from those in Europe. Whereas the debate about crowds served in Europe to address the crisis of feudal structures (Ginneken 1992), the United States mostly lacked feudal traditions, and there was thus much less emphatic skepticism about democracy there than in Europe (Leach 1986, 100). From the outset, then, the debate over crowd psychology was less dramatized in the United States, and the classic dichotomous perception of crowds as both threatening and fascinating was less prevalent. Unlike in Europe, where equality was staged as a threat, no overarching struggle against democratic principles took place in America.

Crowds, and even mobs, were often still seen in the eighteenth century as legitimate forms of rural and democratic protest. In the nineteenth century, this changed (Leach 1992, 7). The increasingly frequent emergence of political crowds, often in the context of struggles over economic distribution, was seen as a threat to social order. However, in contrast to European mobs, American crowds did not threaten feudal power structures, but *democracy* itself.[2] A writer in the *New England Magazine* observed that the "ungovernable spirit" of the mob, "if it not be checked, will work certain destruction to our constitution and liberties" (W. 1834, 471). The greatest danger of mobs was that they could harm democratic institutions: fear of "popular excitement" would make a free exchange of opinions impossible. Mobs were also seen as consisting mostly of immigrants, the "Irish mob" in particular. It is striking that, despite national stereotypes, racist arguments were not used against mobs. Rather, immigrants were seen as lacking proper democratic education. Foreigners were often "ignorant and poor, without a knowledge of our institutions," and thus readily became proverbial "creatures of passion" (473).

This relationship between American democracy and perceptions of crowds and mobs helped to crystallize the distinction between democratic public (the people, the nation) and crowds. This distinction "between the *people* and the *mob* or *populace*" is basic to the popular, and it eventually became a central idea for constructing a political public during the nineteenth century (newspaper editorial from 1805 cited in Leach 1992, 7). From the 1830s on, crowds were considered separately from the nation and from public opinion. As a result, the notion of a modern public could be established. However, the separation between democratic public and mob proved to be quite unstable.[3] Democratic publics were often criticized as lacking a stable identity, and thus as being prone to turn into mobs. Crowds were the constitutive exterior to modern democratic publics, albeit an exterior lurking in public opinion.

This instability led to articulations of democracy along a spectrum bounded by two positions. One position was the idea of an *all-inclusive democracy*, as seen in Walt Whitman. The other position was *forcefully to control* the distinction between crowds and democratic public. In his political texts, Whitman articulates a radically democratic imaginary in a remarkable way; for example, in *Democratic Vistas*, he argues euphorically for a democracy of the crowd, a democracy in which individualism and crowds are reconciled: "But the mass, or lump character, for imperative reasons, is to be ever carefully weigh'd, borne in mind, and provided for. Only from it, and from its proper regulation and potency, comes the other, comes the chance of individualism. The two are contradictory, but our task is to reconcile them" (Whitman 1982 [1971], 940–41).

For Whitman, crowds were an essential foundation for a democracy, and thus should not be excluded from political processes. The "crowds" pointed to a suspension of the classical rules for exclusion that embodied the ideal of an all-inclusive democracy. Whitman saw democracy as far more than a governmental procedure. For him, it was a political form that could not be reduced to the liberal notion of rights. Rather than by conflicting opinions, it was characterized by an all-encompassing affect, or "universal physiological affection," that was a model of "sentimental democracy" (Esteve 2003, 27). Equality became equality of affect. Whitman outlines the ideal of an all-inclusive democratic audience, an audience defined, not by excluding crowds, but by *synthesizing* crowd and individual on the controlled basis of a collective affect.

This sentimental view of political crowds as an essential substrate of democracy can be contrasted with efforts to control, and at times violently suppress, urban crowds and mobs—efforts often supported by the use of police force (Bush 1991, 14). The second half of the nineteenth century saw a number of violent uprisings, which were portrayed by the press as dangerous, criminal mass movements. In a history titled *The Great Riots of New York*, Joel Headley (1873) characterized the participants in the election riots of the 1830s as crowds that could not be included in a democracy: "[A] mass of material wholly unfit for any political structure . . . men the greater part of whom could neither read nor write, who were ignorant of the first principles of true civil liberty" (cited in Esteve 2003, 39). In contrast to Whitman, who saw crowds as an essential foundation for democracy, Headley drew a clear boundary between a democratic public and externals unfit for democracy. This outside, reduced to its corporal materiality, was seen as impossible to include. Though police were used to control crowds, the connection between crowds and democracy remained more ambivalent in the United States than in Europe. Le Bon's (1903 [1895]) crowd psychology readily dismissed democracy as a crowd phenomenon, but in the United States, crowds were seen even by critics in the context of a positive understanding of democracy.

Despite these differing positions on democracy, important elements of the vocabulary used to represent crowds in America were borrowed from Europe—whether in the interest of controlling them or as an emphasis on affectivity and irrationality, contingency and instability. Crowds were not only described with the help of terminology originating in Europe, but were seen to result from the influx of European immigrants—especially immigrants from Ireland and Germany (Leach 1992, 10–11). They were composed of "[t]he Un-Americanized Element, . . . the worst elements of the Socialistic, atheistic, alcoholic European classes," the *Chicago Tribune* wrote in 1886.[4] The state of ferment in which such crowds could be found was often expressed in violent uprisings. Not only did "uncivilized" immigrants lead crowds to be seen as a *European phenomenon*, but American crowds were considered to be imitating political events in Europe. For example, the events of the Paris Commune were followed closely by the American press and seen as a threat to the United States (Leach 1994, 195–96). During the 1870s, a time prior to the development of crowd psychology, the threat of mobs was described in uneasy terms as a threat of *contagion*. As in Europe, a language of pathology was developed during this "era of fear and fantasy" (Bush 1991, 2) to describe crowds as contagious and morally decayed (14). Crowds were increasingly constituted by more than just the "lower classes," and thus posed a greater threat to democracy. This threat could have been contained, so the thinking ran, had crowds been exclusively formed of immigrants and the lower classes. However, mobs now spread like an epidemic and included even respectable citizens and honest workers (Leach 1994, 197).

The social conflicts over the distinction between crowds and audience were also reflected in sociology. The accounts the sociologist Edward Alsworth Ross (1866–1951) wrote of his trips to Europe exemplify perceptions of the connection between crowds and Europeanization.[5] Along with the philosopher and psychologist James Mark Baldwin (1861–1934), Ross was one of the American academics who most admired the work of Gabriel Tarde, and who relied on the theories developed by Tarde (particularly theories of imitation and of crowds). Ross also took an interest in crowds in order to describe the danger of Europeanization in the United States. Following a period of study in Berlin, he expressed disappointment with the decadence of old Europe at the end of the nineteenth century. Ross feared that the United States was threatened by a similar fate. The free land in the West had nearly disappeared, and the pioneer spirit of the United States might now surrender to the temptations of decadence. Ross believed that the idyllic American community—which he saw as possible in his day only in the Midwest—was being destroyed by floods of new immigrants, who constituted an explosive "folk-mass" in the cities of the United States.

American thinking about crowds thus belonged to a discourse of democracy that contained a wide spectrum of political positions. At one end of this spectrum, Whitman envisioned an all-inclusive democracy in which crowd and individual were united. At the other end, critics such as Ross saw crowds as a contamination of already established democratic institutions, and thus as having to be excluded. In both cases, the crowd referred to the new political institutions of a democratic society (in contrast to the conservative crowd discourse in Europe). The boundaries between the democratic public and the crowd became flexible. To preserve a distinct democratic public, the boundaries between it and its exterior had to be constantly redrawn. The fact that Whitman called Thomas Carlyle's critique of crowds feudalistic points to this important shift toward a genuine modern understanding of crowds. In the United States, crowds were already understood in reference to a functionally defined public, while in Europe they were seen (e.g., in the writings of Carlyle and Mackay) as threatening the feudal structures of a stratified society. This had the effect of making democracy quintessentially American. The fact that mobs were often composed of European immigrants threatened American democracy, not only for racial psychological reasons, but because their individual members had been raised in other societies and were thus not yet "fit" for democracy. They represented an anachronistic model of society—a society that had not yet learned to be democratic. Inclusion in the body of U.S. citizens thus implied functional competence, in this case, political education.

2. The United States as a Nation of Speculators

Walt Whitman called the United States synonymous with democracy, but his rhetoric was challenged by another kind of self-description, which drew on the nation's founding myth. Columbus's voyage was "the most colossal speculation in the annals of human enterprise," the economist George Gibson wrote. The English writer Ralph Hale Mottram (1883–1971) declared that the United States "might be described as born in credit."[6] This narrative of foundation created great discursive pressure to continue to the primary speculation begun by Columbus, since, were speculation to stop, the withering of the speculative spirit would also imply a national crisis. "I hope the day will never come when the speculative instinct is not at least latent in an American's mind. . . . *When speculation is dead, this country will be dead also,*" wrote William P. Hamilton, an early editor of the *Wall Street Journal,* who championed the celebrated Dow Theory (cited in Wilson 1963, 3; emphasis added). Speculation had not fulfilled its purpose with Columbus's discovery of America; it had to be constantly renewed in order not to atrophy and eventually die.

European observers were especially struck by this identification of America with the speculative spirit.[7] The French consul Patrice Dillon emphasized that speculation was natural for an American: "[The] Yankee is a stock-jobber by nature; no one understands the 'puff' better than he" (Dillon 1849, cited in Findlay 1986, 102).[8] "[T]he United States are, after all, the *stage of dramatic business par excellence.* . . . Making money is the greatest pleasure in life, but next to winning comes the excitement of losing. In fact, the Americans are perpetually playing at games of chance," declared a writer in *Blackwood's Magazine,* published in Scotland.[9] The spirit of speculation in America was not only equated with economic skill or duty, but primarily with pleasure and excitement in a popular culture that provided the energy needed constantly to renew the speculative spirit.[10]

This narrative of a speculative foundation of the United States was often accompanied by a sense that America was superior to the Old World. The speculative spirit contributed in large part to the daring that made the United States a successful industrial nation—a success that had no geographical bounds, turning speculation into the great world "civilizer."[11] In the euphoric descriptions of speculation, the speculator represented the ideal American individual, who had precisely the pioneer spirit and willingness to take risks that Ross had found lacking in a decadent Europe.

It was not only the myth of a common origin that allowed speculation and national identity to be articulated together in America, but also the specific geographical and cultural makeup of the United States. The boundlessness in quests for imaginary profit and in colonial fantasies that Mackay vividly described became a reality in the vista encountered by the speculator: "The 'magnificent distances' in our country, and its boundless resources, opened a *vista* to the speculator which is not likely to occur again in the history of mankind" (Gibson 1889, 69; emphasis added). The free, unimpeded gaze on geographically and temporally distant—but nonetheless already recognizable possibilities—could be readily inserted into the established vocabulary of speculation, since this vocabulary emphasized the central role of the eye and vision.[12] Whitman's *Democratic Vistas* found a counterpart in George Gibson's speculative vistas, as it were. Despite their differences, these two sets of vistas both show a fascination with the figure of boundlessness.

The image of a country with almost unbounded space resurfaces in Mottram's claim that speculation would fill the empty space in America. It is worth looking more closely at this metaphor, since it makes geographic and economic imagination coincide in a particularly striking way. Mottram also traced the urge to speculate to a yearning for discovery. Speculation made use of unknown fluctuations in price dependent on events in isolated locations: "[T]he slow but sure filling up of the great waste spaces that used to be vacant of everything but wind and sun, and could be left clean out of any calculation whatever" (Mottram 1929, 46). Mottram found irony in the fact that both the emptiness and the "filling up" of these "waste spaces" were "absolutely necessary to any sort of speculative activity." The same metaphor appears a few pages later: "And with the gradual filling up of the world the stabilisation and standardisation seem likely to increase" (50). Speculation was based on but also threatened by "the filling up of the world." The threat to speculation was not only that the world would become homogeneous, but that the open spaces would disappear—spaces that, on their own, had no economic meaning, but at the same time gave impetus to the speculative imagination: "But economic density, the filling up of desirable sites, is sufficient to remove what has been one of the greatest sources of potential speculation" (50). At the latest by the end of the nineteenth century, however, the era of open spaces had given way to a new political self-description in the United States (Hardt and Negri 2000, 167ff.).

3. The Articulation of Crowds and Speculation: The Figure of the Immigrant and the Love of the Unknown

Nearly the same terminology that was used to contrast American individuals with European crowds is found in depictions of the United States as a nation, and its individual citizens, as open to possibilities, daring, and willing to take risks. At first glance, it is surprising that the crowd psychology should have been applied—and not only by critics—to speculation in America. How could language used of decadent Europe also signify the American speculative spirit?

A magazine article written in 1882 linked European crowds to American speculation by pointing to the similarities between the *figures* of the immigrant and of the speculator. The hope for a better future, literally inscribed on the faces in train station crowds, made immigrants resemble small and large speculators. Both immigrants and speculators had varied social backgrounds, and both were seeking a new fortune: "[T]he more ignorant or unsophisticated they may happen to be, the more apprehensive they may feel of the unknown that lies before them" (Anon. 1882, 707). This orientation toward the future, an orientation expressed as concern for the unknown, was shared by the immigrant and the speculator.[13] John Findlay draws the same parallel in his history of gambling in the United States. The American pioneers, who were themselves immigrants, shared many features with gamblers, such as "high expectations, risk taking, opportunism, and movement. . . . Like bettors, pioneers have repeatedly grasped the chance to get something for nothing—to claim free land, to pick up nuggets of gold, to speculate on western real estate. Like bettors, frontiersmen have cherished risks in order to get ahead and establish identity. Like bettors, migrants to new territories have sought to begin again in a setting that made all participants equal at the start" (Findlay 1986, 4). The love of highly individualized risk ("Take your chances!") was not external to the identity of speculator and immigrant, but defined their identity.

In contrast to the early pioneers, who still had enough "waste space" to use for speculation, those who speculated after the land supply had decreased had to project their fantasies onto increasingly rare spaces. Like the immigrants in overflowing train stations and public squares, the speculator could only succeed by fighting against crowds of other speculators. The coarticulation of the discourse of crowd and speculation was a response to the changing American landscape: crowds and speculation had to be rearticulated once the vast open spaces in the United States had been filled, and once the solitary pioneer was forced to coexist with countless other solitary pioneers. The speculator no longer simply had to love risk and discovery, but had to face a crowd of other speculators with exactly the same disposition. In this American context, the notion of crowds assumes a different meaning than in Europe. The American crowd was established in opposition to open spaces, even if these open spaces disappeared when subsequently (over)filled by crowds. The rise of crowds, however, did not mean that the speculative imagination was deprived of all the possibilities formerly enabled by open spaces. Rather, what happened was that the discourse of crowds was recoded as a discourse of possibility—a process that culminated in the contrarian theories of the market that relied on crowd psychology.

The initially clear opposition between the *individual American speculator* and the *decadent European crowd* thus began to break down when the speculator could be compared to an immigrant—a figure who otherwise epitomized the European masses. Crowds could be individualized in the figure of the immigrant who speculated on a new future. Stock exchanges, on the other hand, could become populated by crowds, a phenomenon particularly evident in crowd scenes near and inside exchanges from around this time (see, e.g., Frothingham 1882, 164).

New York provided a unique stage on which crowds and speculation could coexist. In *Sunshine and Shadow in New York*, published in 1868, Matthew Hale Smith concentrates on the simultaneous existence of misery and luxury, and of order and disorder, in New York. In his descriptions of the stock exchange, Smith also relies on these oppositions. He portrays the exchange as being in a wild and noisy state of confusion. The streets near the exchange are overrun by a "motley crowd, who all day long make the neighborhood hideous with their shoutings, yellings and quarellings. The sidewalk is impassable . . . the brokers are pronounced a nuisance" (48). The topos of clogged streets would later recur, for example, in Edward Calahan's account of the invention of the stock ticker.[14] Other accounts from around Smith's time also emphasize the noisy and chaotic atmosphere of Wall Street. For example, one account speaks of a "boisterous overflow of commotion" and a "shouting crowd" (McCarthy 1871, 633). Like Mackay, who had represented crowds as indifferent to stratification, Smith saw crowds as having a leveling effect: "Professional men of all classes and all grades, merchants, retired capitalists, trustees, widows, farmers, try their hand at gaining sudden wealth in Wall Street" (Smith 1868, 48). Speculation was attractive and could spread like an epidemic: "The mania touches all classes. Women and ministers are not exempt" (251).

Were the crowds of speculators in New York the American equivalent of Mackay's financially driven crowds? Unlike Mackay's crowds, the New York crowds did not serve to explore new forms of equality, but were themselves also divided along the lines of a *difference*. The outside of the stock exchange had to be distinguished from the inside of the stock exchange. How were the crowds behind the walls of the exchange described? It is initially surprising that little distinction between inside and outside appears in these descriptions: "Chairs are abandoned, men rush pell-mell into the cock-pit, and crowd, jostle, push, and trample on one another. They scream out their offers to buy and sell. They speak all at once, yelling and screaming like hyenas. The scene is very exciting. Pandaemonium is not wilder, or more disorderly."[15]

Stock traders could easily be confused with members of a mob on the streets. Smith uses a series of verbs expressing sudden and brutal action to capture the raw dynamic on the trading floor: "stamping, yelling, screaming, jumping, sweating, gesticulating, violently shaking their fists in each other's face, talking in a tongue not spoken at Pentecost" (46). Life inside the stock exchange was no more orderly or directed than the crowd scenes that took place in the streets. In fact, the opposite could be true: crowds inside the stock exchange were described as more intensely chaotic than crowds in the streets. These descriptions resisted a simple opposition between the disorder of the streets (crowds) and the order of the stock exchange (professional traders).

It soon became clear, however, that despite first impressions, the disorder inside the exchange was clearly distinct from that outside the exchange. The disorder inside could, *at any time*, be transformed into order: "In the midst of this mad frenzy and *apparent disorder*, every word of which is understood by the initiated, the mallet comes down with a shower of vigorous blows. 'Order! order!' . . . The noise and tempest is hushed in a moment" (48; emphasis added). The stock exchange turned out to be in an *apparent state of disorder*, a state that seemed incomprehensible and chaotic only from the external perspective of the amateur speculator. Disorder thus became a question of observation. The observer had to be in a position to cut through surface appearances in order to decipher how the exchange functioned. To such a professional observer, the chaos of the exchange was no longer threatening. The professional speculator (the "initiated") completely understood "every word" spoken in the "mad frenzy" (48). Because disorder was only a surface phenomenon, it could be stopped at any time. Unlike in front of the exchange, the call for order inside immediately brought quiet. Thus, the professional speculator had an advantage because he knew that a latent order existed beneath the loud cries and the twisted faces. It is only the outsider who is not aware that the seemingly chaotic events on the exchange follow the digital logic of on and off.

In a contribution to *Harper's Magazine*, Samuel Osgood narrated a similar scene: "No visitor would suppose for a moment that any serious business was going on during the shouting gesticulations of the session of the Broker's Board, and the impression given in the Gold room would be that a rampant mob of rival factions had come together in wrath, either to pick each other's pockets or to make a combined onslaught" (Osgood 1867, 618).

The narrator adopts the external perspective of a hypothetical visitor, who is reminded of a criminal mob by the events on the exchange.[16] Osgood, like Smith, reveals that the criminal mob only appears to be chaos: "Yet there is method in madness; and after the noise and smoke are done away, it is seen that a great amount of business has been transacted" (618). Once again, the appearance of chaos hides a wish for order. Important business is conducted in the confusion of the exchange! The noise only conceals the fact that speculators have to work hard.

Smith and Osgood use a formulaic narrative. The stock exchange is first described as chaos from the perspective of an excluded observer. In a second step, there is a change in perspective, which reveals the exchange to be orderly under its chaotic surface.[17] This juxtaposition of two different orders of observation—the external perspective of the visitor, and the internal perspective of the professional trader (and of the narrator)—corresponds to the distinction between inclusion and exclusion. The visitor in the gallery finds himself to be an "included exclusion": he can observe and experience events on the exchange, but he can neither understand nor intervene in them. It is precisely this precarious position of "included exclusion" that makes the peak point of the narrative told by Smith and Osgood clear, namely, what is required for order to arise from disorder is a shift in the perspective of the observer. The discourse of crowds found in Smith and Osgood differs in this important sense from Mackay's, who describes crowds as carnivalesque, all-inclusive spectacles; now, the distinction between inclusion and exclusion is inscribed into the scene. The spectacular confusion of the exchange is only a spectacle to the excluded observer, since he cannot understand what is happening, a lack of understanding that turns into fascination. Order can quickly be found in disorder by anyone who has the information and codes required to decipher gestures on the exchange floor, anyone who knows how financial transactions are conducted.

The scene of this spectacle is described as a space: whether the floor as it is observed by a visitor from the balcony, or the entire United States, it is a stage for speculation. The use of this theatrical metaphor underlines the fact that we are confronted with a process of *audience*-making for speculation. Events on the stage of the stock exchange can be observed by an audience, but this audience cannot play an active role in the performance. Whereas for Mackay, inclusion generates a pull attracting and including everybody in the speculative crowd, the situation has now changed. Although the chaotic events on the exchange floor exert a strong attraction, they do not simply draw in all nearby observers. Rather, the amateur speculator remains excluded from these events by a wall of incomprehension and can only either enjoy or be repulsed by the show.

In the field of finance, however, this kind of audience differentiation could not last long, since the audience in no way remained separate from active speculation. I have earlier discussed the ways in which speculation mutated into an entertaining form of communication that was particularly fascinating to incompetent speculators. The instability of this construct was embedded in the metaphors and in structure of audience narratives, as indicated. In these metaphors and narratives, the boundary between inclusion and exclusion was staged as the distinction between noise and meaning. The implicit reader initially occupied the position of an ignorant observer and was supposed to be astonished at the chaos depicted on the stock exchange floor. This astonishment, however, was only intended to allow the reader to discover a hidden economic meaning. This narrative of speculation thus staged a learning process designed to transform the reader into a speculator *in nuce*. Meaningless speculation provided a fascinating spectacle that, in turn, lent impetus to inclusion. The limits of meaning could also be observed externally, a fact suggesting that meaningful processes took place on the stock exchange. As a result, the pull to inclusion was doubled. On the one hand, the noisy spectacle of the stock exchange served as affective communication that was fascinating on a level preceding meaning. On the other hand, this affectively produced attentiveness offered the "promise of meaning" (Stäheli 2003a), since noise proved to be decodable once the ignorant observer was included.

This chapter began by asking how a positive understanding of speculation came to be articulated in relation to the discourse of crowds. A strangely ambivalent notion of crowds emerged in the United States. Crowds were primarily seen, not to represent a crisis in the feudal order, but simultaneously to promote and threaten democracy. The notion of crowds also has to be connected to immigration in the United States and to the loss of open space. The possibilities offered by unexplored vistas were transformed into the odds of success in a chaotic crowd. Discourses of the crowds were articulated with discourses of individual risk. Like the undiscovered colonies, speculation offered wealth only to those who took risks. Yet, as early descriptions of migration suggest, once the individual became a crowd, open spaces no longer offered the same opportunities. These individual opportunities were replaced by the prospects, and dangers, offered the masses.

The discourse of crowds thus became a discourse of *observing* the crowds. In order to properly understand the odds of success, it became necessary to decipher crowds. This turn to observation helped connect notions of speculation and crowds that initially appeared to be little related. As the accounts given by Osgood and Smith indicate, to an ignorant viewer, the stock exchange appeared almost indistinguishable from a mob on the streets. Crowds of speculators became a spectacle beneath which "serious business" took place (Osgood 1867, 618). Was the discourse of crowds yet another deception that hid the true character of the stock exchange? Or was the strange appearance of speculation inessential to the functioning of the market? These questions came to the forefront in economic and noneconomic debates on speculation at the beginning of the twentieth century.

4. The "Suggestive Market": Crowds and Speculation in Early American Crowd Psychology

> The American mind is highly suggestible.
> —G. T. W. Patrick, "The Psychology of Crazes" (1900)

Crowd psychology began at the point where the previous conceptual model—namely, the dynamics arising from the wish to understand market crowds—left off. For crowd psychology, owing to a massive inclusionary pull, the possibility of drawing a clear distinction between a passive audience and the knowledgeable speculator could no longer readily be maintained. What was emerging was a new, all-encompassing audience, also consisting of professional identities, which could no longer, however, be opposed to an unprofessional audience. Crowd psychology had to abandon the distinction between a professional audience and the crowds external to this audience. It became too obvious that the crowds previously seen as a mere surface covering orderly activity were central to the market. Crowd psychology, however, was not content simply to expose the carnivalesque way in which speculation suspended social hierarchy (as Mackay would have it). Rather, crowd psychologists were interested in the particular nature of the economy and its crowds, and they thus started to engage with the form of functional differentiation. This strange construction of a "mass audience" was seen to have a mysterious dynamic in need of explanation. For crowd psychology, speculation was no longer an economically normal activity entirely distinct from the unusual spectacle of crowds. Crowds pointed to an emerging social phenomenon that could not be reduced to the status of an exception, or to the mistaken observations of the uninitiated.

4.1 The Normalization of Crowds in Boris Sidis's *The Psychology of Suggestion*

Crowd psychology began with a problem of emergence that was difficult to solve: how do normal, rational individuals become an irrational crowd? Gustave Le Bon had always emphasized that crowds could not simply be understood as the average of their component individuals, but had qualities that could not be reduced to those individuals: "The psychological crowd is a provisional being formed of heterogeneous elements, which for a moment are combined, exactly as the cells which constitute a living body form by their reunion a new being which displays characteristics very different from those possessed by each of the cells singly," he asserted. He was fascinated by this "new being" that *suddenly* took shape, and that had a "new body possessing properties quite different from those of the bodies that have served to form it" (Le Bon 1903 [1895], 30). The mechanism Le Bon used to explain the emergence of crowds was suggestion, the only form of communication that went beyond the intentions of rational individuals. Le Bon hoped to explain the dark forces at work in society, but he ironically ended up with a theory that described the market as a perfect example of an emergent phenomenon.

The notion of suggestion became central to crowd psychology at the turn of the twentieth century (Faber 1996). The influence of this notion can be seen particularly in the work of Boris Sidis. In *The Psychology of Suggestion* (1899), Sidis used the notion of suggestion to carry out a psychological analysis of modernity on an individual and social level.[18] Because of his anti-tsarist commitments, Sidis fled Russia and came to the United States, where he studied at Harvard with, among others, William James.[19] Sidis quickly became one of the best-known American psychologists following his efforts to create an experimental basis for crowd psychology.[20] The link between individual and social suggestion examined in *The Psychology of Suggestion* led Sidis to use historical examples that extended well beyond his contemporary political context. While European crowd psychologists like Le Bon relied on the French historian Hippolyte Taine for historical examples, Sidis drew a large amount of his historical material from Mackay. Sidis saw witch mania and the South Sea Bubble as examples of social suggestion. He added to these examples only a few specific "American mental epidemics," outlined in the last section of *The Psychology of Suggestion.*

Le Bon primarily analyzed the crowds, proletarian and democratic, confronting the sovereign aristocratic statesman. Sidis developed another notion of crowds. He emphasized that crowds could not be stratified: crowds were not proletarian, and they did not primarily consist of immigrants. Rather, Sidis argued, mass suggestion and modern society were mutually constitutive: "Social life presupposes suggestion. No society without suggestibility. Man is a social animal, no doubt, but he is social because he is suggestible. . . . Society and mental epidemics are intimately related, for the social gregarious self is the suggestible subconscious self. . . . Society by its nature, by its organization, tends to run in mobs, manias, crazes, and all kinds of mental epidemics" (Sidis 1899, 310–11).

By connecting society and suggestibility in this way, Sidis fundamentally changed the status of mass phenomena. Le Bon saw crowds as a phenomenon closely linked to the collapse of feudal order and the resulting universalization of inclusion. He believed that democracy had led modernity into a state of crisis, from which crowds emerged. Sidis avoided describing crowds in such apocalyptic terms. Instead, he used arguments from anthropology and evolutionary theory to explain why crowds and social epidemics had become unavoidable in modernity.[21]

The anthropological argument made by Sidis presupposed that human beings were inherently suggestible (Sidis 1899, 297). Sidis defined suggestion as the "intrusion into the mind of an idea; met with more or less opposition by the person; accepted uncritically at last; and realized unreflectively, almost automatically" (15). From an anthropological perspective, the uncritical acceptance of suggestion that characterized human beings could no longer be evaluated morally.[22] Instead, human suggestibility became a prerequisite for social interaction. This suggestibility meant, in evolutionary terms, that humans were able to communicate quickly and without an elaborate code. Sidis used the example of animal herds rapidly able to communicate a perceived danger. For example, movements expressing fear were immediately imitated. Sidis emphasized that efficient communication was an evolutionary advantage: "Suggestibility is of vital importance to the group, to society, for it is the only way of rapid communication social brutes can possibly possess" (309). Careful and often extended reflection was replaced by a suggestive communication whose speed almost entirely shut down autonomous judgment.

Sidis explained this process using his model of "disaggregated consciousness." The waking self was typically capable of guiding the subwaking self, since these two dimensions of the self were often intimately linked. It was possible for the two dimensions to separate temporarily in crowds. However, only in mobs did the two dimensions of the self remain separate, causing a pathological condition to arise (297). The boundaries between individual and environment were weakened: "[T]he naked subwaking self alone remains face to face with the external environment" (300). In order for this major division of the self to take place, physical, psychic, and social conditions had to be met. Physically, movements of the individual had to be largely restricted (47); psychically, the individual's attention had to be captivated by a particularly attractive or spectacular object; socially, an atmosphere of "overstrained expectation" had to be created (300), a contagious atmosphere in which mob dynamics rapidly unfolded.

More than Tarde or Le Bon, Sidis made clear the *self-referential* character of the emergent phenomenon represented by mobs:

> The given suggestion reverberates from individual to individual, gathers strength, and becomes so overwhelming as to drive the crowd into a fury of activity, into a frenzy of excitement. . . . Each fulfilled suggestion increases the emotion of the mob in volume and intensity. . . . The mob is like an avalanche: the more it rolls the more menacing and dangerous it grows. . . . In the entranced crowd, in the mob, every one influences and is influenced in his turn; every one suggests and is suggested to.[23]

Sidis saw mobs as a network of individuals who interacted by mutual suggestion. As these reciprocal interactions became more intense and referred to themselves, self-reference became uncontrollable. The effect of this excessive self-reference was described as a fundamentally affective process.

These figures representing a primal scene of emergence were concerned, not only with social order, but also with the dark underside of society—that is, with the world of violent mobs, lynch justice, and religious delusions. Yet this dark underside was not simply chaotic, but also generated an alternative form of order, whose basis could not be found in existing social structures, whether political, religious, or even economic.

For Sidis, crowds represented neither a spectacular exception (Mackay) nor a crisis of modernity (Le Bon). It was precisely modern society that was in need of a mechanism of suggestibility to guide its anonymous course toward blind obedience: "Blind obedience is a social virtue" (311). Thus, suggestibility became even greater in a functionally differentiated society,[24] for in a carefully regulated society, the individual had practically no room to move—a situation that created the ideal conditions for manias and panics. The "demon of the demos" (311) was awakened as soon as something out of the ordinary captured the attention of the constrained and almost motionless individual.[25]

This demon was not produced by excessive democratization, but always already resided in the organization of society. In saying this, Sidis was asserting that a *constitutive* relationship existed between society and the mob. Society could hardly be conceived of without the mobs, at times barely hidden, beneath its surface.[26] If the social was defined by an openness of one person to the suggestion of others, then the formation of crowds and mobs could not be external to the social. This assumption was all the more provocative given the fact that the mob was destructive:

> When, however, it [normal suggestibility] rises to the surface and with the savage fury of a hurricane cripples and maims on its way everything it can destroy, menaces life, and throws social order into the wildest confusion possible, we put it down as mobs. We do not in the least suspect that the awful, destructive, automatic spirit of the mob moves in the bosom of the peaceful crowd, reposes in the heart of the quiet assembly, and slumbers in the breast of the law-abiding citizen. (17)

This insight into the destructive violence of mobs was made more poignant by the fact that normal social life was closely linked to mobs.

Suggestion and suggestibility were not pathological conditions for Sidis, but described the basic way in which society functioned.[27] Suggestion thus became a central concept that *simultaneously* explained the dynamics of the social and of crowds. This dual explanation meant, however, that every social phenomenon was now virtually a crowd, or even mob, phenomenon. The only difference between mobs, crowds, and society was the way in which suggestion was configured: the suggestion essential to the social was escalated in the mob to the point of self-referential short-circuit—that is, to the point at which suggestions mirrored each other with lightning speed. However, this excluded the successful application of already-established efforts to normalize crowds. Crowds were no longer *decadent* or an *exception*, because they, like all other social events, relied on suggestion. Rather than representing an other, crowds escalated the logic of society, and thus embodied the very principle of society itself. Crowds were also not exclusively a *surface appearance* that could be normalized and properly understood only when observed from the right perspective. Certainly, crowd psychology also emphasized the importance of viewing crowds as surface phenomena from the right perspective. This emphasis, however, was not designed to separate crowds from actual social processes, but to study the laws of crowds as social laws, and thus to be able to intervene in these laws.

4.2 Suggestion and Speculation

The notion of suggestion thus made it difficult to distinguish between crowds and public, since both sides of this distinction relied on a mechanism of suggestion. If the two were constituted by the same social logic, and thus could not be distinguished on the basis of this logic, a new basis for distinction had to be created, making crowd psychology attractive for describing and analyzing speculation.[28]

Suggestion allowed economic activities like stock market panics, which had been classified as irrational, to be linked to the normal functioning of economic communication. Sidis proposed a crowd psychology that was more optimistic than Le Bon's. Panics did not have to be seen as decadent, but could be regarded as a normal part of the economy. Precisely because the notion of suggestion lacked moral connotations, and provided a basis for *all* social relations, a strategy had to be developed to control suggestibility. Put another way, the notion of suggestion drew attention to the precarious process of boundary-making between communication in a normal economy and communication in a panicked economy.

Sidis's notion of suggestion opened up a new discursive realm, and it is interesting to ask how excessive suggestive communication was distinguished from normal suggestive communication.[29] The concept of suggestion played an important role in observing and regulating inclusion in stock market trading, helping separate the mass of speculators under the influence of suggestion from the small minority of rational and successful speculators. The two groups did not have to be viewed as essentially different. The popular could thus be described as a specifically economic phenomenon consisting of a disciplined professional cadre and a crowd unsuited for that role.

In the following, I would like to distinguish three aspects of the process by which the concept of suggestion was used to draw, and erase, the boundaries between crowds and a public *within* a public. First, I discuss *rumor*, which addressed an uncontrollable increase of (para)economic communication. Second, I explore the way in which suggestibility and *imitation* were linked. Third, I explore the role of *affectivity* in terms of panic. It is important to note that suggestive economic communication was seen in all three dimensions, in negative terms, to contradict the ideal of rational economic activity. However, these dimensions also point to the difficulties involved in separating suggestion from rational behavior. Speculation could easily be infected, as it were, by suggestion. The three forms of suggestive economic communication I am addressing prove to be popular communication on a structural and functional level, since it is precisely here that creating an audience becomes problematic.

4.3 Rumor

The contested distinction between information and rumor helped create a financial public. From the standpoint of information theory, a rumor is also information, but around 1900, a normative notion of information was opposed to rumor. Information was rational and came into existence transparently. Rumor lacked shape, and it thus failed to provide a firm basis for communication. This distinction proved difficult to maintain because, often, the entire audience for speculation was believed to act on, and spread, rumor. Sidis, like Mackay, was astonished by highly credulous speculators who invested in the most reckless of undertakings, and in the most unbelievable projects: "'Man believes as much as he can,' says Prof. [William] James, but a gregarious man believes whatever is suggested to him" (Sidis 1899, 348). This willingness to believe rumors was contrasted with access to reliable information. The conflict between reliable information and rumor relied on the distinction between speculator and gambler. While the speculator had reliable knowledge, the gambler acted on unverified information, since he relied on "mere chance, impulse, rumor or 'inside information'" (Moore 1921, 39; cf. Dice 1926, 8). This kind of knowledge was not to be trusted: "Rumor is, as a rule, uncertain and untrustworthy" (Clews 1968 [1900], 7).

Sidis viewed the fact that a crowd of speculators was susceptible to rumor as strong evidence for his theory of suggestion.[30] Credulity had an anthropological basis, but turned into nearly arbitrary suggestibility in crowds. According to Sidis, this suggestibility only arose because individuals in a crowd were in close spatial proximity. In economic suggestion, however, rumor increasingly assumed the role of catalyst.[31] Suggestion took place, not only through immediate physical contact, but also through a range of different mass media. For the economist Charles Moore, rumors spread in brochures and newspaper articles could be blamed for the irrationality of the economic audience: "This erroneous opinion . . . is usually the result of unconscious mental suggestion brought about by inspired articles or comments or financial periodicals or from circular letters, or from what they may have heard observed by their acquaintances" (Moore 1921, 47).

Such media exposed the spatially isolated individual to the power of suggestion. Even when alone, the speculator was prone to believe rumors—particularly rumors that confirmed his already existing conjectures: "The 'type' is a 'susceptible' subject for mental suggestion. He is easily swayed or convinced."[32] The speculator was easily impressed by rumor because he lacked the capacity to process information. His reactions were reduced to pure impulse.[33] Rumor was hyperconnective, since it almost automatically and instantaneously generated connectivity.[34] Because the speculator was open to rumor, he could no longer evaluate information rationally. The speculator was barraged with too much information too quickly to be able to develop criteria for selection. Any form of reflective thought hindered communication and negated the opportunity for profit, an opportunity that arose when the speculator possessed rapid and exclusive information. While the classical *homo oeconomicus* still carefully performed a cost-benefit calculation of whether a rumor could be considered information, the suggestive speculator had already long ago reacted and was already confronted with new rumors—rumors he might also help spread.

Hyperconnectivity was not all that transformed rumor into popular speculation. Rumor also came to play this role by means of an implicit understanding of *universal inclusion*. We have already seen that rumor was contrasted with "reliable" or "true" information. However, rumor also functioned based on the assumption that it provided access to information from which one would normally be excluded. Rumor substituted for the inner circles of stock market communication in which small speculators could not participate. The rapid and successful spread of rumor can be attributed to the way in which it refers to a secret—that is, to otherwise unavailable information (Kapferer 1996). The popular and its ideal of universal inclusion functioned in rumor as a dystopia of unrestricted conditions for inclusion. Financial rumors created an alternative form of access that could only be viewed with disapproval by the economic system. The small investor was thus often characterized as naively trusting (Anon. 1882, 719; Harper 1966 [1926], 67; Carrett 1990 [1930], 66; Dice 1926, 281; Bond 1928, 142).

All speculators knew that rumor spread quickly, and thus lost its value. For this reason, speculators had to act quickly on rumor. Rumor provided rapid and unproblematic inclusion to the small speculator by promising access to the information necessary for professional speculation. The widespread criticism of rumor in guides to speculation also focused on this simulated inclusion. Such criticism produced stricter criteria for inclusion in speculation, and thus narrowed access to it. The former broker Henry Clews noted that the beginning speculator should "wait patiently for a proper opportunity, and not rush headlong to purchase on the 'tips' of the delusive rumor mongers" (Clews 1973 [1908], 23). By relying on rumor, the speculator could avoid the strenuous disciplinary mechanisms required for inclusion to speculation: "Young speculators are too impatient and prefer to listen to tips, they become 'slavish' and rely on others thinking for them, they fail to cultivate self-reliance" (20). The popular speculator who based decisions on rumor lacked his own identity, because he relied exclusively on others (Smitley 1933, 116).

Rumor interfered with the structure of the financial audience at a fundamental level by implying that communication could function *without* an individualized and disciplined audience. The destabilized boundaries between audience and outside could be seen in the way rumor undermined techniques of individualization. Financial rumors bypass economic individuality and thus not only compensate for the loss of time involved in reflection but also permit the boundaries of inclusion in speculation to be ignored. (Significantly, in German, rumor [*Gerücht*] is linked etymologically to smell [*Geruch*].) Rumors follow the logic of epidemics, which are not constrained by inclusionary criteria of economic competence and spread uncontrollably, ignoring established boundaries.[35]

From the perspective of the "efficient market hypothesis" (Fama 1970), rumor proved to be a peculiar form of economic communication. On the one hand, it was inefficient, because information transmitted by rumor was neither rational nor transparent. On the other hand, rumor appeared to be extremely efficient. By sacrificing transparent information to speed, rumor eliminated one of the two conditions underlying the efficient market hypothesis. As Sidis had already observed, suggestion provided an evolutionary advantage by allowing for rapid communication in an emergency. Transparent communication, and an autonomous individual who communicated such information, no longer existed. A typical response to this loss could be seen in criticisms faulting the way speculators were manipulated by rumor. According to such criticism, speculators who blindly followed rumor could easily be misled by market actors who spread false information. This suggestibility and dependence on manipulative insiders almost inevitably resulted in losses for the speculator: "This is why the crowd, or the outside public, is nearly always wrong marketwise" (Moore 1921, 109).

Criticism of the role of rumor in speculation thus distinguished between professionals and a suggestible *outside public* that was excluded from the secrets of the market. Informed professionals mistrusted rumor, implying that rumor could be controlled. A professional audience could distinguish between rumor and information, and could even profit by manipulating this distinction. For an observer like Clews, anyone who wanted truly to understand the market had to grasp the distinction between information and rumor.

However, the distinction proved difficult to maintain. Rumor developed its own peculiar dynamic within financial markets. Rumor began as a "small compact thing" but quickly grew to be a "cloud without shape and consistency," Clews explains.[36] Rumors proliferated to the extent of contaminating speculation. The market might react not only to information, but also to rumor.[37] Charles Emery notes that false rumors were occasionally mistaken for true information and subsequently became the basis for action.[38] The stock market was thus no longer able to fulfill its function of critically distinguishing rumor from valid information, but encouraged manipulation of the distinction.[39] The logic of rumor threatened in this way to contaminate the financial market in the same way that, for Sidis, suggestion permeated social life.

Financial rumors were hyperconnective, spreading impulsively and rapidly. This hyperconnectivity was linked to perceptions that rumor was all-inclusive. Even if rumor was ultimately sustained by a secret, this secret had to appear accessible to those it excluded. The success of rumor is attributed to this false access in accounts given, for example, by Clews and Emery. Rumor provided a false sense of all-inclusiveness and thus became a form of popular communication. Like popular communication, rumor was mobile and unstable, a fact that resulted from operating at the boundaries of a system. At these boundaries, rumor could no longer be separated from nonrumor. Continuous vigilance was required to protect economic truth from rumor. Even the market—which, for Emery, was the standard for distinguishing information from rumor—could be contaminated.

4.4. Suggestion and Imitation: The Danger of "Derivative Judgments"

As a mode of communication, rumor rapidly simulated access to exclusive information. However, suggestion not only communicated information, but also relied on a particular means of communicating information. Viewed in terms of suggestion, the way in which market participants acted also provided information (Luhmann's term for this is *Mitteilungshandeln,* or "utterance").

In crowd psychology, efforts had been made to distinguish between suggestion and imitation. Imitation was used to describe the act of copying a given behavior. For Le Bon, the behavior of an individual was imitated by others, and thus spread like a contagion. Gabriel Tarde based his sociology on the "laws of imitation."[40]

The *logic of imitation* becomes particularly clear in comparison to rumor. Rumor was repeated and spread by imitation. However, communication based on rumor did not require imitating the actions of other speculators. Rumor always introduced an outside reference into speculation by creating the suspicion that information was being externally manipulated. The notion of imitation, however, always conceives of speculation as self-referential process. If rumor was not to be trusted, the behavior (and not only the opinions) of others could provide reliable information.[41] One rumor led to another, but not necessarily to a new payment operation. In contrast, useful information could be gained by observing and imitating market participants.[42]

The issue of imitation raised the classic question of creating order on the market. How did uniform action emerge on the market without being derived from higher-level norms? In this process, emphasis was not placed on calculations of cost and benefit that, when correctly applied, would lead all individuals to an identical result. Rather, the collective behavior of a large number of speculators was brought about by suggestibility (Bond 1928, 178). An individual in a suggestible condition was open to almost any external stimulus, and imitated this stimulus without extensive rational consideration. Understanding became a matter of immediately accepting premises for behavior. From this perspective, uniform action arose when market participants imitated each other. As was the case with rumor, imitation relied on suggestibility. However, imitation used a different mode of observation. In communication based on rumor, speculators observed and adopted the opinions of other speculators. Such opinions were mistrusted by the speculator who imitated other speculators. Rather than following potentially deceptive self and external observations, the imitative speculator observed the decisions other speculators made about buying and selling.

The possibility of *imitative speculation* was viewed with skepticism. In his book defending speculation, Edward Dies (1925) argued that speculation functioned best when imitation could be avoided. For Dies, the greatest problem was that small speculators were ruined by imitating powerful, well-informed financiers. This imitation of other speculators was equivalent to loss of reference. Speculators no longer made transactions based on their own knowledge, but derived this knowledge by observing other speculators: "In speculation, as in most other things, one individual derives confidence from another. Such a one purchases or sells, not because he has any particular or accurate information in regard to the state of the demand and supply, but because some one else has done so before" (McCulloch 1825 cited in Jones 1900, 202).

The "derivative judgments" resulting from imitation led to a disastrous "mutual accumulation of error."[43] Mutual imitation distorted the random distribution of economic decisions, and thus corrupted the necessary variety of the market. "They [the public] do not speculate altogether at random; but they act more mischievously and disastrously to themselves than if they did," the great British economist Alfred Marshall said of this imitation (Marshall 1920 cited in J. A. Ross 1938, 59).

Arguments from crowd psychology helped shed light on the way an imitative and homogeneous crowd of speculators came into existence. As president of the New York Stock Exchange, Richard Whitney observed that the great increase in the number of amateur speculators had led to a "form of public opinion in regard to security prices which can only be discussed in terms of mass psychology."[44] A crowd of amateur speculators displayed a form of activity irreducible to randomly distributed economic decisions. The pattern formed by amateur speculators also could not be deduced from the economic rationality of the small speculator. The speculating public became an undifferentiated "emotional mass" that did not produce the microdiversity necessary for the economic system to function.[45] As the economist Irving Fischer observed, the process by which this undifferentiated mass took shape was marked by contagion:

> Were it true that each individual speculator made up his own mind independently of every other as to the future course of events, the errors of some would probably be offset by those of others. But . . . the mistakes of the common herd are usually in the same direction. . . . A chief cause of crises, panics, runs on banks, etc., is that risks are not independently reckoned, but are a matter of imitation. (Fischer cited in Brenner and Brenner 1990, 98)

The peculiar link between individual and action became especially clear during panics. Panics were caused by "groups of men, acting individually, yet in concert" (Collman 1968 [1931], 149). These individual economic subjects did not abide by the rules of the neoclassical market. "It is a political economy of persons, not of the people" (Lloyd 1883, 75). Calculated action was replaced by the herd logic of imitation. Market equilibrium was interrupted by a factor that appeared to be external to the market—namely, the suggestibility of economic subjects.

Arguments about crowds did not simply proceed from the intersection of systemic order and chaotic microdiversity, but raised the problem of an order that could no longer be regulated by the system itself. This way of proceeding endangered, for those friendly to speculation, the essential function of speculation for a globalized economy: the function of forming prices. The discourse of crowds helps us to show how dynamics otherwise dismissed as uneconomic arose within the financial system. Even when used by representatives of a liberal model of the market, crowd psychology thus points to the mostly unarticulated presuppositions of such a model—that is, to the production of an economic subject capable of independent judgment.

Imitative communication also proved to be a mode of popular communication that, in many respects, resembled rumor. Precisely as was the case with rumor, imitation intervened in audience structures, since it bypassed established modes of individualization and competence profiles. Moreover, imitation—like rumor—was an extremely rapid mode of communication, capable of escalating in intensity, and thus of producing unpredictable market phenomena classified as irrational. The difference between operations based on rumor and those based on imitation was that an imitated action was not simply believed in, but actually observed (e.g., the selling of shares). The operation itself thus turned into information. Did he buy—or didn't he?

4.5 Suggestion as Affect and Panic

> Hope, greed, and fear make up the market's eternal paradigm.
> —John Bogle, founder of the Vanguard Group, "Investing Wisely
> in an Era of Greed" (2000)

Suggestion was not limited to cognitive communication and imitation. It reached a high point in affective communication. Markets were represented, against the classical ideal of rationality, as a setting for intense displays of affect, characterized by three primary economic emotions: hope, greed, and fear.[46] An ideal market would be free from these emotions. Rational calculations would not be distorted, interrupted, or even entirely ignored. "The speculator's deadly enemies are: Ignorance, greed, fear and hope," the financier Jesse Livermore says in Edwin Lefèvre's semi-fictive biography of him (Lefèvre 1982 [1923], 286). Lefèvre himself did not believe that a market could exist apart from emotions like hope and fear. These emotions were part of the anthropological constitution of every speculator: "The speculator's chief enemies are always boring from within. It is inseparable from human nature to hope and to fear" (131). Every successful speculator thus had to struggle against his own nature.

However, not all emotions were understood as external to the economy. As could already be seen in Mackay, hope of future profit was a constitutive feature of speculation. The broker William Worthington Fowler (1968 [1880], 448) based speculation on hope, and Henry Emery defined speculation as the "hope of a profit" (1969 [1896], 96). Hope was the emotion underlying greed and fear. A speculator might initially profit from fluctuating prices and from the profits of other speculators. Following this initial success, however, the hope of profit could easily become greed, which a poised speculator had to be able to temper. Greed made the speculator short-sighted, but also encouraged inclusion. Since the world is not ideal, greed often "cherishes the desire and hope of excessive and untoiled-for profit" (Wilson 1906, 27). Fear was also closely linked to hope. The collapse of hope often not only brought a speculator back to reality but also quickly turned into fear. Sidis identifies two phases in speculation—an initial euphoric phase, transmitted by suggestion, which suddenly becomes melancholic depression—constituting a "folie à double forme," or double folly (Sidis 1899, 348–49; cf. 344, 360).

Affective communication on the stock market became problematic when this communication reached the level of collective panic. At this point, as in the crash of 1873, affective communication led to an "age of unrestrained emotions" (Collman 1968 [1931], 103). Panic linked the two previously discussed instances of suggestion (rumor and imitation) to a highly charged form of affective communication. The suddenness with which panic occurred was especially threatening. Unexpected mental turmoil was described as "panic" in the seventeenth century, and the term was already being used in the eighteenth in the sense of "widespread apprehension in relation to financial and commercial matters, leading to hasty measures to secure against possible loss" (*Oxford English Dictionary*). In both contexts, panics were seen to arise when large crowds were set in motion by fear. The mythological point of reference for panic was Pan, the Greek god of shepherds, who could spread fear by playing the flute. A satirical poem published in the *Atlantic Monthly* titled "Pan in Wall Street" narrated Pan's secular rebirth on Wall Street in 1867: a "strange, wild strain / sound high above the modern clamor, above the cries of greed and gain, / The curbstone war, the auction's hammer" (Anon. 1867, 118). In the poem, Pan is driven away by the police, but the commotion persists.

Wall Street saw panic as inexplicable: "[T]he panic, as an abstract thing, constitutes the great enigma; it is still the least understood of any event that rates its time. . . . What is the panic? An answer to this question would be a triumph of discovery" (Collman 1968, 36–37). Since neoclassical economics and popular notions of the economy could not account for the phenomenon, the world of finance turned to crowd psychology to find answers to this enigma. For crowd psychology, panic was a classical case of *contagion*: "Ideas, sentiments, emotions, and beliefs possess in crowds a contagious power as intense as that of microbes. . . . A panic that has seized on a few sheep will soon extend to the whole flock. In the case of men collected in a crowd all emotions are very rapidly contagious, which explains the suddenness of panics" (Le Bon 1903, 143).

A panic offered an ideal case in which the connectivity of communication increased to the point of no longer requiring criteria for inclusion or function. Crowd psychology described the *affectivity* of stock market communication as an even more effective means of suggestion than rumor or imitation. Authors inspired by crowd psychology conceived of this affectivity in primarily physical terms, as an epidemic "apt to be accompanied by great muscular excitability, varying all the way from extreme mobility, such as shouting, jumping and throwing of the arms, to convulsions like those of epilepsy." These movements could be attributed to "congestion and irritation of the motor centers" and produced the "excessive emotion" typical of epidemic outbreaks of affect (Patrick 1900, 287).

In panic communication, the logic of contagion that also structured rumor and imitation became more intense. However, while it was possible to escape rumor by isolating oneself, panic spread in a sudden and unpredictable way. It was because the signs of a panic could never be recognized in advance that panics were perceived as such a great threat. Panics thus contradicted any notion of slow and predictable change—ideas crucial to neoclassical economic thinking: "[A panic] comes without warning. No wisdom, shrewdness or forecast can anticipate or control it. . . . The click of the telegraph, that communicates the changes in Wall Street every five or ten minutes, to all parts of the continent, carries consternation with the intelligence. . . . When a panic comes, it strikes the heavy men of the street, as it strikes others" (Smith 1972 [1873], 548).

Everyone was exposed to a panic, and for this reason, panics had an equalizing and democratizing effect. Social distinctions no longer existed. The equality experienced when collectively facing the abyss of a panic was rhetorically intensified by pathological and epidemiological metaphors. If panic spread in the same way as microbes, even the highest degree of competence could not protect a speculator from being infected. Panic was like an epidemic to which everyone was, as it were, predisposed. Even before the concept was born, stock market panics constituted a form of "risk society," in which the class structure dissolves when faced with ecological risks (see Beck 1992). Likewise, anyone could be seized by panic.

The equality created by stock market panics, however, did not simply correspond to the classical political notion of individual equality. Rather, the equality during panics resulted from processes of individualization and deindividualization, which became evident in the way the outbreak of panics was explained. As suggested above, financial panic communication is based on economic affects, particularly on the hope for future profit. This hope is individual, but also exceeds individuality. To justify the hope of profit, the individual speculator has to see more, and see differently, than other speculators.[47] Overconfident in their own abilities, small speculators trust that market trends will persist ("The trend is your friend").[48]

This combination of trust in the self and trust in the market was of particular importance for descriptions of financially driven crowds. Individual speculators believed that they could evaluate how long prices would continue to rise, and thus how long fellow speculators could be trusted to contribute to this rise in prices. This precarious discursive arrangement of individual overconfidence and reliance on the crowd intelligence of others marked financial crowds from the beginning. Speculators had confidence in themselves and believed they could rely on other speculators to behave like a crowd. A panic, however, signaled the collapse of this precarious structure. Just as excessive trust had previously driven speculation to the skies, growing mistrust now threatened economic rationality. Panic becomes a figure of reversal, where confidence in the self and certainty about others unexpectedly turns into its opposite: "Suspicion, apprehension, and alarm take possession; reflection and sobriety are crowded out; men do and say irrational and unreasoning things; incidents trifling in themselves are exaggerated into undue proportions; all kinds of difficulties are conjured into the imagination." Self-confidence evaporated: "Panics *seem* to come from lack of money, [but] the real difficulty is lack of confidence."[49]

Like the individual who, for Le Bon, lost the capacity for reflexive thought in a crowd, during a panic, speculators lost perspective on the market, that is, the necessary distance from the market, depriving them of their subjectivity. Edward Jones, whose crisis theory was also influenced by crowd psychology, argued that strong emotions paralyzed individual thought: "If the passion of the haste to be rich operates . . . to upset the individual judgment, destroy experience, suppress proper consideration of risk and dishonesty and force economic activity along unwise lines, it goes very far to account for the occurrence of economic crises" (Jones 1900, 207).

Individual economic competence was contrasted with the contagious "passion of the haste to be rich." During a panic, *homo oeconomicus*, the very foundation of neoclassical economy, escaped: "There are today [i.e., in 1883] men proud to tell you that in the moment of frenzy and horror they hunted, rope in hand, for this disciple of self-interest."[50] However, if panics deprive self-confidence of its individual basis, they also paradoxically promote individualization. Using the well-known example of the panic caused by fire in a theater, Elias Canetti describes panic as the dissolution of a crowd within a crowd.[51] Collective panic may break out as fear of the fire spreads from one spectator to another, but each acts individually and tries to flee the building as quickly as possible. Spectators want to save themselves and pay no attention to other spectators. During panics, *individualism itself becomes contagious.*

How were these de/individualizing panics related to the economy? Was a panic an avoidable lapse in economic rationality? Or was the enigma of a panic also an economic enigma? Panics were linked to finance in two ways. On the one hand, panics were described as noneconomic events with economic effects. On the other hand, panics were seen to exist in a constitutive relation with the economy. The first position is evident in the history of panics published in 1931 by Charles Collman, for whom panics represented the "*misuse* of the elaborated machinery of Wall Street."[52] Collman distinguished between this economic machinery and the people who used it. Only people whose behavior was not entirely determined by economic factors could cause panics.[53] Panics could be traced to human error. However, according to Collman, they were not brought about intentionally—for example, by attempts to manipulate the market: "*Men do not make panics deliberately; they are their unconscious agents*" (Collman 1968 [1931]: 280). Panics were instances of noneconomic excess, and were thus to be contrasted with the perfect machinery of the economy (281). This perfection was best maintained by excluding the "mob of camp-followers" from the stock market (273). Collman thus sought to distinguish between panics as a "human event" and an optimally functioning economy (46). It was blindness to economic consequences that led speculators to experience the cataclysmic event of a panic. They were incapable of recognizing the "real economy."

The argument that inclusion of amateur speculators led to panics often appeared after the 1929 stock market crash. For the *New York World*, the 1929 crash was not an "investor's panic" but a "gambler's panic" (Sobel 1988, 377). This argument emphasized the distinction between gambling and speculation in order to exclude panic from speculation. Speculators who abused economic laws caused panics. These panics, however, were not caused by the logic proper to finance. Walter Bagehot also attributed panics to speculation by the wrong people: "At particular times a great many of stupid people have a great deal of stupid money. . . . The blind capital seeks for some one to devour it, and there is plethora; it finds some one, and there is speculation; it is devoured, and there is panic."[54] The best remedy for panics was thus to exclude unqualified speculators and stabilize the professional identity of the speculator. The speculator had to be trained to develop "individual self-confidence" (Jones 1900, 213). In this way, speculators could properly operate the machinery of the economy.[55] This strategy of treating panics as events external to the economy aimed at establishing a clear boundary. A professional cadre of speculators was distinguished from its outside, a mob governed by affect.

Panics, then, arose when forms of inclusion were overextended. Stock speculation had become too popular. The economic machine, a metaphor often used by Collman, tried to save the machinery of Wall Street from its popular failure, that is, from those who were unqualified to operate it. Speculation thus became an act of rational calculation, in which imagination no longer played a part.

However, such efforts to exclude panics from finance as improper speculation, or as misuse of economic machinery, were opposed by positions emphasizing a constitutive relationship between speculation and panics.[56] Panics arose, according to these positions, from an excess of self-confidence. It was difficult to distinguish excessive self-confidence from a healthy amount of self-confidence that would protect the speculator from simply following the views and actions of other speculators. Given this difficulty, many authors proposed another strategy. These authors did not view panics as an illness external to finance, but instead *normalized* panics. Directly challenging the argument that panics were only caused by inexperienced or greedy speculators, Henry Clews insisted that they were not "accidental freaks of the markets" (1973, 105). Panics were unavoidable because they arose from the basic structure of speculation—namely, the love of risk and the pioneer spirit required to pursue this risk.

Crowd theorists such as Sidis and Jones attempted to reduce the unpredictability of panics by viewing them as cyclical. Panics might be unpredictable, but they followed a definite cycle once they had begun.[57] For G. T. W. Patrick a panic was thus not entirely inexplicable, but was simply the inverse of normal speculation: "There is first greed, furnishing the necessary emotional excitement; then imitation; then precipitate, unreasoning action. In the panic, the psychological sequence is the same, except that fear takes the place of greed" (1900, 293). Even by using the fever metaphor, Patrick did not pathologize panics. Rather, the fever metaphor emphasized the cyclical structure of panics. After a panic, the economy would recover. E. J. Dies even saw in panics a daily process of fever and recovery: "Onward the market races to its daily denouement, rising in high fever, falling in violent chills and war-dancing crazily as powerful world forces clash in the battle of wheat" (1925, 6–7).

If panics were to be a functioning part of the economy, they had to have a function. Andrew Mellon emphasized this function by describing panics as a process of economic purification: "It [the panic] will urge rottenness out of the system. . . . Values will be adjusted, and enterprising people will pick up the wrecks from less competent people" (cited in Kindleberger 1996, 154). The distinction between competent and incompetent speculators was linked with purification in the financial system by excluding incompetent small speculators from the stock market. In this sense, panics were treated, so to speak, as the immune system of finance. They purified speculation of the effects that arose when incompetent speculators were included in the economy. In this way, panics supplemented the normal workings of financial inclusion, and they thus became essential to regulating inclusion in speculation. Van Antwerp even saw panics as a "sign of civilization," since they only took place in wealthy countries, providing "checks upon extravagance and inflation" and chastening "the spirit of over-optimism" in civilized economies (1914, 186). This view of panics, however, sharply contrasted with the views of crowd psychologists who saw panics as a "decivilizing influence."[58]

On the one hand, panics were described as the effect of popular inclusion. On the other, they also normalized excessive hopes of profit and kept incompetent speculators away from the market, thus correcting instances of failed inclusion management. In short, the effect of popular inclusion became the means of restricting popular inclusion. In this way, popular inclusion appeared to control itself: excessive inclusion became part of a self-regulating process that helped to reduce overinclusion from within the financial economy.

Many representations of panics were not limited to this self-regulating process, but also displayed a fascination with the *spectacularity* of panics. Dies describes a panic on the wheat market from the perspective of the spectator: "[The] spectator rejoices. He thrills to the stampede. Screaming headlines may have told him the world had gone wheat crazy. And the pit is the outward expression of this madness. There it is before him, teeming, seething, boiling. A mass of milling humanity struggling for attention" (Dies 1925, 6).

A panic was a unique spectacle. By struggling for attention among themselves, speculators unintentionally drew the attention of an audience and thus became entertainment.[59] "In stark fascination the spectator stares into the strained faces below."[60] The panic of 1893 had such a great appeal that the doorkeeper could not control the crowd of visitors to the gallery: "There, under the gorgeous ceiling, they peered down upon a wild spectacle" (Collman 1968, 164). Collman identified *theatricality* as an essence that persisted throughout the history of panics: "Their stageplay has prevailed for one hundred years" (36). In Collman's history of panics, spectators also took pleasure in observing panics from the balcony (105). For these spectators, panics became an aesthetic phenomenon whose surface structure was of great interest: "[M]assing in lines . . . like regiments of an army of beetles . . . the scene presented a surface black with humans" (132). Panics were described, not only as natural events or as epidemics, but also as theatrical. It was difficult to separate panics from the observer who took a horrified pleasure in them. The "surface" of speculation could thus no longer be distinguished from an underlying economic reality, as was the case in efforts to distinguish between the crowds in front of the stock exchange and crowds inside the stock exchange. The hope no longer arose that occupying the right status as observer would make panics transparent. Whoever was part of a panic could no longer reflect on it, and whoever observed a panic from outside took a horrified pleasure in the spectacle.

5. Suggestion and Financial Markets: The Articulation of Audience and Crowd

Whether as rumor, imitation, or panic, suggestions derived their force from the ways in which they negotiated the distinction between audience and crowd. A first strategy for stabilizing this distinction was to assume that only incompetent speculators were susceptible to suggestion. This assumption allowed, in principle, for the existence of an ideal economic public. The forms of suggestion addressed above were articulated, at least in part, in this way. To counteract rumor, pure economic information was required. To counteract imitation, speculators had to develop their own capacities for reflection and judgment. Furthermore, panics were attributed to a "human element" external to the economy. These strategies imply the existence of an ideal and individualized economic public that could properly operate the machinery of Wall Street. In these cases, discourses of suggestion were used to describe a mode of inclusion that extended beyond classical functional criteria. Suggestion radicalized the element of equality in finance. Rumor promised unofficial access to otherwise secret information. Imitation allowed speculators to replace competence (e.g., knowledge of the economy) with short-term observation of other speculators. Panics had an equalizing effect, as the threats of ecological catastrophe and terrorist attacks do today. Even the professional trader could not escape the risk of being infected, as it were, by a panic on the exchange. Suggestion thus became an important technique for universalizing financial inclusion. Critics tried to stabilize the distinctions between the professional elite and the crowd by treating this universalization as illegitimate and harmful. For example, (supposed) access to exclusive information through rumors was criticized as a shortcut to genuine competence. The notion of equality that arose apropos of suggestion was seen to overextend inclusion.

A second argument, influenced by crowd psychology, also began with the universalization of inclusion. However, this argument did not limit the effects of suggestion on crowds and falsely included speculators. What was now at stake was the distinction that set apart financial professionals. Even they were susceptible to suggestion. It thus became difficult to regulate inclusion to speculation based on suggestion. As for Tarde and Sidis, suggestion played an important role in explaining *all* social phenomena. Social relations established in this way thus always faced the danger of excess suggestion. Precisely this danger can be seen in the forms of suggestion discussed in this chapter. Rumor gained momentum to the point at which it began to be entirely self-referential. Moreover, rumor could suddenly become information, despite efforts to maintain clear distinctions between the two. The market treated rumor as true information, and it thus failed as an entity that was supposed to regulate the distinction between false rumors and correct information. The normative concept of information, which today remains central to behavioral economics, began to unravel.

Imitation also undermined the means of regulating inclusion in the stock market. Imitating other speculators was not only seen as a deceptive and unethical way of acting that was external to the stock market but as a threat to an individualistic model of market action. Not only were imitated actions economic operations, but these operations were linked in such a way as to reduce the necessarily diverse range of decisions about the market. Like rumor, imitation spread quickly and became self-referential. One act of imitation referred to another, a process that led to abrupt changes in price, and to panics.

In turn, panics could not be contained within a particular realm. Panics were highly contagious, not least because they were communicated physically, without the intervention of reflection. Self-referentiality reached its zenith during a panic. Suggestion by means of rumor and imitation was now accompanied by affective suggestion, which problematized the crowd psychology that distinguished between market professionals and an irrational crowd. Speculation could not function without trust in economic processes and media, and without hope of profit. The *human element* was no longer external to the machinery of Wall Street, but had become integral to its functioning. However, the changing role of the human element meant that an ideal financial public was no longer marked by lack of emotion. Rather, during panics, normal economic affects were intensified and became uncontrollable. The problem of suggestion could no longer be easily resolved by strict exclusionary policies, since the affects susceptible to suggestion were already to be found in the financial public. The speculator could not be conceived of apart from his or her hopes. Moreover, hope of profit came to define speculation.

I have not aimed to categorize texts according to this schematic distinction between the two ways in which concept of suggestion was used. Rather, each argument about suggestion overlaps with the other. This dynamic does not follow an "either/or" logic, but emerges from struggles to articulate competing forms of economic logic. The individualistic model of financial markets was confronted by a wild logic of contagion, a logic in which individual action lacked reflection, and instead was guided by imitation.

How did these two forms of logic relate to each other? Walter Benjamin suggests a connection by describing participants in modern markets as an audience of consumers and as crowds. "Their [the street crowds that gather around an accident] models are the customers who, each in his private interest, gather at the market around their 'common cause.' In many cases, such gatherings have only a statistical existence" (Benjamin 1973 [1937], 62). However, this kind of statistical crowd has a hybrid character: "They rationalize the accident of the market economy which brings them together in this way as 'fate' in which 'the race' gets together again. In doing so they give free rein to both the herd instinct and to reflective action" (63). Benjamin distinguishes between clients (audience) and crowd by relying on the notion of crowds in Victor Hugo and Baudelaire. On the one hand, Hugo conceives of crowds as an audience: "To him the crowd meant, almost in the ancient sense, the crowd of clients—that is, the masses of his readers and his voters. Hugo was, in a word, no *flâneur*" (66). For Baudelaire, on the other hand, crowds cannot be reduced to a stable collective and exert a magnetic appeal: "The concentration of customers which makes the market, which in turn makes the commodity into a commodity, enhances its attractiveness to the average buyer" (56). "In the words of Guys as quoted by Baudelaire, 'anyone who is capable of being bored in a crowd is a blockhead'" (37). The street crowd becomes an intoxicating spectacle: "The pleasure of being in a crowd is a mysterious expression of the enjoyment of the multiplication of numbers" (58, quoting Baudelaire).

Benjamin was interested in the relationship between the market and crowds, rather than in stock speculation. However, his reflections point to the complex relationship between the logic of an audience and the logic of crowds. Benjamin suggests that the market has a hybrid character, and thus cannot be reduced to the opposition between rational individuals—who are only predisposed to rationality by being isolated—and the herd instinct of incompetent market participants. According to neoclassical economics, the market could ultimately be freed from this herd instinct by establishing an individual economic subject. However, as Benjamin suggests, this economic audience transforms into a reflective crowd that itself becomes a spectacle, and thus broadens inclusion in the market. At the same time, this greater degree of inclusion in the market does not guarantee that the crowd will be successfully individualized as an audience. The techniques of individualization used to establish an audience for finance, and the discourses of crowds that arise when these techniques of individualization fail, cannot be reduced to each other, but instead constantly produce new configurations of the distinction between an audience and its outside.

CHAPTER 5

ALONE AGAINST THE CROWD

THE COMMUNICATIVE TECHNIQUES
OF THE CONTRARIANS

> Human nature in the stock market is going to be the most
> profitable study in the next bull market. The greater the
> number of traders, the more necessary will it be to study and
> to know market psychology and have a market philosophy.
> —Humphrey Neill, *The Art of Contrary Thinking* (1967 [1954])

The vocabulary of crowd psychology—particularly the notion of suggestion—has been used to describe speculation since 1900. The stock exchange has not only been seen as a privileged stage for crowds, but also considered as governed, at heart, by the laws of crowd psychology. A crowd psychology of speculation became plausible and convincing, since it could draw from the vivid crowd scenes concretely taking place on Wall Street. For the financial journalist Hartley Withers (1867–1950), crowds on the stage of the stock exchange were no longer a surface phenomenon that left its inner reality untouched, but now represented the true logic of speculation:

> The Stock Exchange is a mass of men, and their human and inevitably fallible
> sentiments and opinions are a very important factor in the influences which
> combine to settle the prices of securities. Any mass of men is likely to become
> at any moment an excited mob, and may sometimes degenerate into something
> like a herd of stampeding cattle. . . . The Stock Exchange stands in a crowd all
> day, and is *consequently* excitable, and given to moods and exaggerations.[1]

The equation of markets with crowds drew the attention of financial authors, even beyond the peak of crowd psychology. "Is the market really a crowd?"

asked the popular finance journalist and former portfolio manager George Goodman, writing under the pseudonym Adam Smith. He recounted a meeting with the mysterious and successful "Mr. Johnson" of Fidelity Investments. For Mr. Johnson the answer was clear: "*The market is a crowd,* and if you've read Gustave Le Bon's *The Crowd* (1895) you know a crowd is a composite personality" (Smith 1967, 23; emphasis added). In his bestseller *The Money Game,* Smith outlines a crowd psychology of the market. Smith's crowd psychology is not simply a polemic against Wall Street. Rather, crowd psychology has practical applications, since only those who understand the laws of crowds can succeed in the market. Smith's passionate plea is not a curiosity, but represents a popular investment discourse that uses crowd psychology to approach the market. Excerpts from Le Bon's *The Crowd* and Mackay's *Extraordinary Popular Delusions* have been reprinted as classics in anthologies on investment (e.g., Ellis and Vertin 1997). In 2002, Robert Menschel, a senior director at Goldman Sachs, published an anthology titled *Markets, Mobs & Mayhem: A Modern Look at the Madness of Crowds.* Today, crowd psychology remains popular in the academic subdiscipline of behavioral economics (see, e.g., Thaler 1992; Shiller 2000; Shleifer 2000).[2]

When used to describe the market, crowd psychology makes speculation the object of inclusionary and exclusionary techniques. Two discursive possibilities emerge for ensuring that speculation will be rational despite stock market crowds. The first possibility is that an incompetent audience has to be *excluded* from speculation because of the mass hysteria on the stock market (cf. chapter 3.2.2). This position was common in Europe, particularly in Germany, around 1900, but has also been a recurring motif in American writings on speculation. The second possibility (explored in this chapter) is that the idea of a rational financial market with competent actors has to be abandoned. This position characterizes many American discourses on speculation. According to these discourses, the market is no longer rational, but has to be conceived in terms of crowd psychology. Only the speculator who relies on the laws of crowd psychology has a chance to succeed on the market. Suggestion has become so pervasive that no speculator can escape its influence. Crowd psychology, which informs many manuals on speculation, thus paradoxically turns into a discourse of individualization. Since formal inclusion cannot secure an individual economic subject, new techniques of individualization have to be developed. If processes of inclusion are always already processes of individualization (see Introduction), what role does the psychology of crowds play in the new inclusionary apparatus? My argument is that specific techniques were developed to ensure that the speculator did not become part of the crowd. The investment manuals analyzed in this chapter ask the following question: How can I, as the individual speculator, resist crowds and speculate well despite an irrational market?

1. Crowd Psychology as an Instrument of the Contrarians

The contrarians, an investment school that originated in the 1930s, have a strong interest in crowds—and in the question of how the speculator can resist crowds. Contrarians invoke Le Bon and Mackay, and their precursors in the early twentieth century attempted to establish a crowd psychology of speculation. However, the American speculator and financial author Humphrey Neill was the first to establish a crowd psychology of speculation as the basis of an independent investment school. In the 1930s, Neill began to develop the contrarian position in the handbook *Tape Reading and Market Tactics*.[3] In 1954, Neill published *The Art of Contrary Thinking*, a book in which he elaborated a crowd psychology of speculation (Neill 1967). Today, the contrarians (and neo-contrarians) remain an influential investment school. The school counts among its members Robert Menschel, a prestigious financier and trader, and senior director of Goldman Sachs (along with Menschel 2002, see Dreman 1998). Even investment funds, such as Fidelity's Contrafund, are managed in the contrarian spirit.

The contrarians were not interested in a critique of the stock exchange or in an academic theory of speculation. They asked a more practical question: how do I become a successful speculator? Crowd psychology became an instrument that was to help the individual speculator withstand market adversity. The speculator became successful by "beating the market." Masses of speculators were no longer an exception, or a temporary event, but represented the fundamental structure of the market. Crowd psychology no longer analyzed a pathology of the market, but genuinely analyzed the market by linking two different arguments: on the one hand, the speculator required an instrument that would make the market readable; on the other, the speculator had to develop an arsenal of techniques of the self to secure his or her individual identity on an adversarial market. The discourse of crowd psychology available to the speculator was part of a power-knowledge nexus.[4] By observing the market as a crowd, the crowd psychology of speculation created an epistemic object around which particular strategies of speculation were configured. Specific to the position of the contrarian was the way in which the discursive object—the crowd itself (in this case, equal to the market)—no longer became an object of disciplinary and regulatory techniques, but instead served as a foil for developing an ensemble of self-disciplinary techniques, and thus for creating the ideal speculator. This figure of the ideal speculator brought epistemology and self-discipline into a relation of mutual dependence.

1.1 The Market as a Crowd According to the Contrarians

How did the contrarians understand the market as a crowd? It is particularly striking that crowds were not judged by moral or political criteria, but according to whether they were right or wrong: "The crowd is usually wrong" (Neill 1967 [1954], 2). The degree to which the crowd was mistaken could even be theorized as a percentage: "The crowd is always 75% wrong marketwise. Were it otherwise, the market would be unprofitable for the Insiders" (Moore 1921, 113). Errors were not an unfortunate by-product of an otherwise correct market rationality, but part of the normal way in which the market functioned: "The crowd always loses because the crowd is always wrong. It is wrong because it behaves normally," Fred C. Kelly assserted in his book *Why You Win or Lose: The Psychology of Speculation* (Kelly 1962 [1930], 21). James Fraser, Neill's successor, uses similar words in his foreword to that book: "[C]rowds are wrong in themselves simply because they behave normally" (vii). The norm for the crowd is to make mistakes!

Interaction with crowds, and thus with the market, is described as a zero-sum game. Crowds had to be wrong in order for those in the know to profit: "Realize that you are playing the coldest, bitterest game in the world. Almost anything is fair in stock trading. The whole idea is to outsmart the other fellow" (Neill 1967 [1954], 43). The extent to which the contrarians departed from classical notions of rationality is particularly evident in Kelly's psychology of the exchange:

> In short, if everybody were truly intelligent, no one would sell too cheaply or pay too much, and the result would be that the wide swings in prices could not occur. Price ranges would be confined to such narrow limits that no speculator would pay much attention to the market. There wouldn't be a market! Speculation can be worth while only when a few are taking advantage of the stupidity of the many. (Kelly 1962 [1930], 174–75)

Kelly thus established a *necessary* connection between the market and the crowd. The logic of crowds guaranteed that the market would function. Pushed to an extreme, the classical ideal of rationality was absurd. If *everyone* behaved rationally, no one could profit from speculation. An entirely rational market would negate the purpose for which markets existed. If the contrarians scorned the crowd, they therefore did not do so on the basis of political or moral criteria—that might have led to the incompetent mass of speculators being excluded from the market, threatening its liquidity.

Contrarian crowd psychology was implicitly influenced by the investment theory of John Maynard Keynes, whose diagnosis was similar to that of the contrarians, but led him to a radically different conclusion. Keynes also saw that speculators profited at one another's expense: "The actual, private object of the most skilled investment today is to 'beat the gun,' as the Americans so well express it, to outwit the crowd, and to pass the bad, the depreciating, half-crown to the other fellow" (Keynes 1973 [1935], 155). Keynes did not find the close link between the crowd and the market scandalous simply for moral reasons. Rather, he was alarmed that the investor had to accept the irrationality of the economy and could not defeat the "dark forces of time and ignorance." For Keynes, a market that followed the crowd was an epistemological scandal. A successful speculator had to rely on the judgment of the incompetent. This speculator could not simply ignore crowds: "It may profit the wisest to anticipate the mob psychology rather than the real trend of events, and to ape unreason proleptically" (323).

The contrarians followed Keynes's advice and developed a financial "mob psychology" aimed, not in the least at elucidating the operations of the stock market, but rather at beating other speculators. They abandoned the dream of creating a rational market and focused instead on creating a speculator who could resist the crowd without entirely turning away from it.

Contrarians had to separate themselves from the crowd, but also had to rely on the crowd in order to become successful speculators. Crowd psychology did not depict an exterior to the speculating public so much as describe that public to itself. Within this public, the distinction between the speculating public and its exterior could be rearticulated, significantly reconstituting the concept of the popular of the economy. The distinction between speculator and crowd established an unstable difference in the speculating public. The contrarian speculator and other speculators in the crowd could not be distinguished based on what they did. Both kinds of speculator invested in stocks and shares, even if in different amounts, and with different kinds of knowledge. These speculators played the same professional role within the market, an equality that destabilized the underlying structure of economic roles. On an organizational level, membership in the stock exchange was highly exclusive. On a functional level, however, anyone could be a speculator. The classical distinction between professional action and personal experience used to establish many other inclusionary roles could no longer be maintained.[5] However, the contrarians found a new way to differentiate between these roles, emphasizing the distinction between an elite represented by themselves and a broad public equated with the crowd. Initially, the stock market appeared to be the stage for a Hobbesian struggle among speculators. Speculation resembled a "battlefield," on which a few speculators fought successfully (Neill 1967 [1954], 41).

However, this battle was not a symmetrical struggle among independent individuals or groups. Instead a handful of contrarians combatted a crowd that had lost the capacity for judgment, and was thus doomed to failure. The few contrarian speculators did not struggle against one another, but against the crowd—and against their own psyches. This rhetoric of struggle should not be understood as primarily militaristic. Opponents of the contrarians were not militarily but epistemologically defeated, since they failed as observers of the stock market. Lefèvre, who was critical of the idea that speculation was like a battle, pointed at the epistemological dimension of the problem: "I never fight either individuals or speculative cliques. I merely differ in opinion—that is, in my reading of basic conditions" (Lefèvre 1923, 18). The struggle between contrarians and crowd described by Neill was a question of different strategies for observing the market. Neill may have frequently used the term "battlefield," but he was also concerned with properly observing the market, rather than with conquering opponents.

The "social philosophy" of the contrarians could be called pessimistic individualism. The speculator who resisted crowds and maintained the capacity for judgment in adverse circumstances would be rewarded with success on the stock exchange. Before the contrarians had developed this point of view into a doctrine, similar arguments had been made in public debates about speculation early in the twentieth century, when the ideal speculator was described as having the judgment and endurance to oppose the majority: "The ideal speculator, in both economic theory and the popular mind, was one who was not afraid of opposing the public clamor, one who was not stampeded by temporary reverses of fortune."[6]

1.2 The Contrarian as Observer

The contrarian could only become a contrarian by becoming an observer: to stand against the crowd, the contrarian had first to construct it as a discursive object, then to distinguish himself from it. While the typical investor analyzed fundamental data, the contrarian analyzed the mood of the crowd: "Is not human action also fundamental?" (Neill 1967 [1954], 58). For the contrarian, the truth of speculation was reserved for a small elite, and thus excluded a large number of speculators. The contrarian was not interested in the likelihood that a given company would make a profit, but instead asked whether most speculators believed this company would make a profit. The contrarian was always interested in "derivative judgments" (cf. chapter 4.4.4). He was a classic second-order observer who based decisions on the observations of others. The contrarian took the self-referentiality of stock market trading seriously, and abandoned external references such as fundamental data. Instead of relying on economic data, the contrarian observed other observers, and he had to develop a strong individual will to use his observations to make decisions when faced with adversity, as well as when having to join the minority.

This approach is particularly evident in a passage from Keynes's *General Theory of Employment, Interest and Money* (1936), a book often cited by contrarians, in which Keynes compares the stock exchange to a beauty contest in which jurors do not judge participants objectively, but rely on the judgments of other jurors.[7] The contrarian used fundamental data to come to a different conclusion than most speculators, but also had to accept the judgments of these speculators. Only by accepting that these judgments influenced prices could the contrarian beat other speculators. This relationship between speculator and crowd established the dynamic of individualization in the discourse of crowds. Only the speculator who felt superior to the crowd would begin to speculate. However, this illusion on the part of the individual speculator extended to the crowd: "The illusion of everyone playing Wall Street is that he thinks and believes he can beat the 'Game'" (Ora 1908, 159).

The financial crowd was thus characterized by the strange fact that the individual had to adapt to the crowd in order to resist the crowd. Individual speculators defined themselves as superior to the crowd. As Fred Kelly and others argued, it was normal for crowds to observe the market falsely. These observations could only be established as false when seen from the right perspective. Observing false observations ultimately did not create a problem for the speculator. However, the use to which the speculator had to put these observations was more problematic. The contrarian was not only supposed to observe, but also had to speculate—an act that required making decisions he knew to be false, but from which he could profit. Thus, the relationship between the contrarian speculator and the crowd of speculators was more complicated than simple opposition. By joining the crowd for tactical reasons, the contrarian *temporarily* became indistinguishable from his opponent.

In order to separate himself from the crowd, the contrarian had to have a thorough knowledge of it. How can I know that there is a crowd? How can I be certain that I am observing the "real" crowd? The contrarian had to be sure, moreover, that the crowd he was observing did not reside in himself. For Neill, epistemological certainty was linked to epistemological discipline. Since if he only observed the market occasionally, the contrarian risked confusing his own thoughts with those of the crowd, he had to observe the market *continuously* in order to reach "thought-out conclusions," constantly asking himself: "Is this truly a generalized viewpoint, or is it perhaps a composite of my own views which the 'mirror' misleads me to think are those of the 'crowd'?" (Neill 1967 [1954], 160).

1.3 The Rearticulation of the Leader Figure

How did the contrarian speculator establish a stable identity? How did he distinguish himself from the crowd? This can be addressed by showing how the figure of the leader was rearticulated by contrarian thinking. Le Bon did not believe a leader could entirely control crowds. However, in his crowd psychology, he compiled techniques that would allow a leader to manage crowds at least to a certain degree. Le Bon did not aim to educate a rational audience, but to develop techniques for its partial control and seduction: "A knowledge of the psychology of crowds is to-day the last resource of the statesman who wishes not to govern them—that is becoming a very difficult matter—but at any rate not to be too much governed by them" (Le Bon 1903, 21). Crowd psychology was not primarily designed to control crowds, but also to rescue the very possibility of a statesman or leader. The sovereignty of the leader as individual could only be preserved when he was able to control crowds to the point that crowds did not control him. In this way, crowd psychology proved to have the double program of, on the one hand, gaining a degree of control over the crowd, and, on the other, securing the individuality of the leader.

For Le Bon, only the leader was capable of becoming an individual, since he was characterized by a strong will and a capacity for action: "The leaders we speak of are more frequently men of action than thinkers. They are not gifted with keen foresight, nor could they be, as this quality generally conduces to doubt and inactivity" (Le Bon 1903, 134; cf. 136–37). The leader's strong will was, above all, a source of energy—the strength of this will fascinated the members of the crowd, and thus compensated for their lack of decisiveness: "Men gathered in a crowd lose all force of will, and turn instinctively to the person who possesses the quality they lack" (135). In contrast to the psychoanalytic continuation of crowd theory (Freud 2004 [1921]) Le Bon did not claim that the leader was a necessary condition for crowds to arise. Crowds required identical suggestive stimuli, of course, but these could be ideas or shared emotions. It thus made sense for Le Bon to introduce the way in which crowds functioned before, in the second part of his book, discussing the role of the leader. The part of Le Bon's book dedicated to the leader begins: "We are now acquainted with the mental constitution of crowds, and we also know what are the motives capable of making an impression on their mind. It remains to investigate how these motives may be set in action, and by whom they may usefully be turned to practical account" (Le Bon 1903, 133). For Le Bon, irrational crowds could be manipulated by those who understood how they functioned. The leader was thus not the primary principle of integration, as in Freud's psychoanalytic theory of crowds, but a power that directed the application of forces in the crowd toward useful ends.

To use Le Bon's figure of the leader, contrarians had to adjust this figure in important ways. Crowd psychology established a complementary relationship between leader and crowd. The leader had the strong will lacking in the crowd. This also applied to leaders in speculation, but the way the leader controlled the crowd had to be redefined. The speculator whose training included crowd psychology did not try to become a political leader and control crowds. Neither was he interested in using rumor to influence crowds. By definition, the contrarian speculator was isolated and had to make individual decisions against the crowd. He thus preferred to remain invisible, in order not to be imitated by the crowd. If he were too successful, the contrarian would exert too much influence over the crowd and thus lose his exclusive position and fail.[8] Calling this form of speculation "contrarianism" was a performative contradiction.

The contrarians' crowd psychology thus *divided the function of the leader*. The strong-willed leader was *disarticulated* from a position that would allow him to control and manipulate the crowd. From the perspective of the contrarians, crowds were easily influenced. However, the leader no longer used charisma or classical techniques of suggestion to influence the crowd, although even today, charismatic figures exist in finance, such as the star analysts who often play the role of leader in their professional communities (see Knorr Cetina and Bruegger 2000). Nonetheless, the contrarian discourse emphasized that suggestion was *depersonalized*. In this sense, the contrarians were closer to Le Bon himself than to subsequent psychoanalytical extensions of crowd psychology. The financial crowd did not need a figure outside the market to unify the market (cf. Dupuy 1991); instead, the market itself seduced.

How did the market develop this strange power to seduce? Neill argues that successful contrarian speculators and investment stars were not responsible for the attraction exerted by the market. Rather, rates and prices were responsible for it. Crowds were attracted by movements, particularly upward movements, in stock prices (Neill 1967 [1954], 35; cf. Conant 1904, 1). The idea of price movements was to be taken literally. Quickly changing numbers on the ticker tape took on a life of their own and exerted a physiological attraction on speculators. Observing prices may seem an unspectacular way for markets to observe themselves, but it was this form of observation that ultimately made speculation attractive to a wide audience. The amateur speculator bought because he saw "prices going up before his eyes" (Bond 1928, 142; cf. Kelly 1962 [1930], 60). The audience did not understand why prices changed, but could see that shares went up, and could see that an investment not made on the previous day constituted a loss. The audience followed those stocks that had risen in the past, and that were thus seen as likely to rise in the future. This replacement of the leader with moving prices can also be found in current efforts to make crowd psychology useful for technical analysis of the market. Neil A. Costa, a professional trader and the director of Market Masters, a company that markets courses in stock trading, has put this new function of the leader succinctly: "In the case of trading, the crowd leader becomes 'price.' Members of crowds tend to respond only to very obvious changes (such as a market crash), and not slow, subtle changes, such as a bull market slowly making a topping pattern and turning downward" (Costa 2000, n.p.). Amateur speculators are to be distinguished from professional speculators based on the way the two groups observe the market. The professional speculator observes subtle changes in price, while the amateur speculator is deceived by sharp changes in price that are easy to identify.

The intensity and severity with which prices changed became a stimulus for inclusion in the market. Since the amateur speculator was only able to grasp clear changes in prices, he reduced the complexity of the market to a clear signal. The amateur speculator did not have to understand the underlying economic activity, but only had to react to the signal. In this case, inclusion also followed the logic of the spectacle: fluctuations in price had to be severe in order to draw attention. Relativizing the figure of the leader resulted in a peculiar democratization: the speculator who observed changes in price knew that this observation involved signals generated by the crowd of speculators—and not signals from an exclusive leader. Rather than mimicking a leader—who might once have been part of the crowd, but was now quite distant from it—the "market crowd" mimicked itself.[9] The amateur speculator observing movements in price knew that he was a part of these movements in price, and he could thus profit from them if he acted swiftly. Precisely this perception of missed opportunities created in the speculator a desire to join the crowd before it was too late. Stated formally, by establishing prices, markets observed themselves, and this self-observation became the equivalent of a leader (cf. Luhmann 1988, 72ff.).

However, the classical function of the leader could not be entirely transferred to self-observation by means of prices. The second function of the leader was to exert a degree of control over crowds. Sharply changing prices might attract small speculators eager to be included in the stock exchange, but these prices did not function as mechanisms of control. The contrarians displaced these mechanisms of control from the leader to the individual speculator. Crowds no longer had to be controlled, but the individual speculator had to learn to control *himself.* The contrarian had to be positioned *against* crowds without controlling them. By taking this position, the contrarian risked his individuality and autonomy, not least since the classical techniques of individualization available to the leader were not at the disposal of the speculator. The speculator could not rely on approval and affirmation from the crowd, since he operated invisibly. If his investment strategies were known to the crowd, these strategies would be at risk. Contrarianism destroyed itself the moment it became known to a majority. In order to profit from the "stupidity of the many," the contrarian had to avoid becoming one of many. This position was difficult to stabilize with a simple solution. The contrarian speculator had to beat the market without becoming a popular hero. The leader, adapted from crowd psychology, had become an isolated and mostly invisible second-order observer—an observer who made solitary decisions by observing the observations of others.

2. Disciplining the Speculator: "Self-Mastery"

The contrarian had to discipline himself in order to develop an epistemic position in response to the crowds he observed. For this reason, control had to be shifted from the leader in crowd psychology to the contrarian speculator. The contrarian did not aim to control the crowd, but had to control himself in order to observe the market. He had to develop a strong identity as speculator in order to resist the temptations of the market. Speculators had to preserve their position as a neutral observer against the dynamics of the crowd they were observing. Encounters with the crowd were often described as a major test for the contrarian speculator. The real test was "how you behave when the crowd is roaring the other way. . . . The crowd, the elusive Australopithecus, is still largely an unknown, an exercise in mass psychology still not accomplished" (Smith 1967, 41). The relationship between the contrarians and the market is not a competition, but the scene of a possible seduction[10]—a seduction by the crowd against which the contrarian has to position himself. In this way, the contrarian abstained from the comforts of belonging to the majority. Adam Smith argued accordingly that a stable identity was the precondition for successful speculation: *"If you don't know who you are, this is an expensive place to find out"* (1967, 26, 80). Crowds constantly threatened the speculator's identity. Against this threat, contrarian handbooks in the early twentieth century offered techniques by which speculators could create and maintain an identity in adverse market conditions.

Knowledge and discipline intersected in the techniques offered by these handbooks. The contrarian could only be a good observer when he knew how to distance himself from the market. While the scientist could maintain an illusion of objectivity, the contrarian knew that his observations were not only contemplative, but also affected decisions he made when speculating. Correct observations were thus always subordinate to the criterion of economic success. The promise of economic success led the observer to act falsely in order to act correctly at the right moment.

2.1 Controlling Affect in Speculation

One of the basic dichotomies to be found in handbooks on speculation is the opposition between rational thought and irrational emotion. The contrarian speculator thought rationally; other speculators were emotional and easily swayed by the crowd. However, the trained speculator nonetheless experienced tense emotions when confronted with fluctuating prices. In his definition of the contrarian, Neill emphasized absolute control of emotion and impulse. The speculator was to practice "mastery of himself: of his temperament, emotions, and the other variables that go to make up human nature" (Neill 1960 [1931], 1). The idea of complete self-mastery was fundamental to effective speculation. During the nineteenth century, the vocabulary of self-mastery was spread widely in the United States as a popular version of Kantian ethics. For example, the anti-slavery writings of William Ellery Channing use terms similar to those of Neill: "The great purpose of all good education and discipline is, to make a man a Master of Himself, to excite him to act from a principle of his own mind" (Channing cited by Esteve 2003, 9). As Channing emphasized, self-mastery was a disciplinary technique that led to individualization, since the very principles for action had to be found in the innermost realm of the individual. However, the threat to individuality differed in writings on slavery and in discourses on speculation. In writings on slavery, the moral subject had not been allowed to develop an entirely rational way of life. In discourses on speculation, the moral subject was confronted by emotions that threatened its individual autonomy. These emotions were not simply leftovers of an older, less civilized age, but were brought about by the modern institution of the stock market.[11]

Like the contrarians, Frederic Drew Bond argued that emotions played an important role in constituting financial markets. Relying on neoclassical economics, he established desire as a fundamental concept in economics, a concept that dissolved references to labor and goods. Prices did not reflect value in a classical economic sense, but instead reflected the hopes and fears of speculators: "It may seem that the statement that stock prices are merely the resultant of market actions based on hopes and fears of gain and loss, is so plain as to be hardly worth such emphasis" (Bond 1928, 13). Drawing from this assumption that affect determined the logic of the market, he tried to elaborate a program for controlling emotion. In contrast to other writers who gave advice about speculation, however, Bond did not recommend an entirely emotionless approach, which would have been out of line with his presupposition that prices were based on an emotion: the desire for profit. The public speculator was not wrong because he was emotional, but because he followed the wrong affective pattern: "He has hoped when he should fear, and feared when he should hope" (142). Confused emotions arose because the speculator incorrectly observed the market: "He has, in fact, fallen victim to what has well been called the 'innately deceptive appearance of the market'—its apparent proneness to a still further advance when the advance is, in fact, just about over" (142). The small speculator chose the wrong emotion because he lacked the capacity to observe the market correctly. If the small speculator knew how to see beyond the deceptive surface of the market, he would at least lose hope at the right moment. Surface information, when combined with the "nervous strain" of the market, had a powerful effect on suggestible speculators (177).[12]

The contrarians rejected the role Bond assigned to emotion in the economy. Hope and fear were a risk to the speculator at all times. The ideal speculator, according to Thomas Gibson's classic *The Facts about Speculation*, "has been *cleared* of the delusions of hope and the visions of sudden wealth" (Gibson 1965 [1923], 13; emphasis added; cf. Gibson 1907, 16). Because fear was highly contagious, it was considered especially dangerous (Gibson 1965 [1923], 33). For the contrarians, most mistakes in speculation were of a psychological nature (13). Psychology was equated with irrationality and affect, and thus came under general suspicion. This skepticism had two results. On the one hand, crowd psychology became an important way for the contrarian speculator to observe the mistakes made by other speculators. On the other hand, the contrarians imagined an ideal speculator who was depsychologized, and who automatically made decisions.

The contrarians established a radical psychological program intended to give speculators "a complete mastery over . . . impulses, emotions and ambitions under the most heroic tests of human endurance" (Harper 1966 [1926], 106). This turn away from emotion implied that the speculator had to become a machine by bringing everything human under his control. Anything that compromised the objectivity of the contrarian had to be discarded. This need to ensure the objectivity of speculative communication was also reflected in the list of qualities that defined the ideal speculator: "1st, Judgement or knowledge; 2d, Nerve; 3d, Money; 4th, Patience" (Moore 1921, 42). Strikingly, access to money was not the highest priority on this list. The speculator first had to display professional knowledge and the proper psychological constitution (nerve), qualities that would allow his judgment to act as a "pilot" guiding economic decisions (Moore 1921, 43). The contrarians developed a model of the subject in which judgment was based on a stable *and* neutral foundation. The metaphor of balance especially helped the contrarians articulate this relation between stability and neutrality. Just as a scale became stable once both sides were balanced, the speculator had to make stable decisions without personal bias or external influence.

Self-mastery distinguished the speculator as a reflective and autonomous individual who could be contrasted to unstable and unbalanced crowds (Neill 1967 [1954], 54, 10). Rather than thinking, crowds wallowed in emotion and thus became too lethargic to recognize changing market trends at the right time. Only a stable and individualized identity allowed speculators to develop an *awareness of time* that would make them superior to the crowd. Crowds, on the other hand, were bound to the present. They lacked the awareness of time available to contrarian speculators and instead reacted to changes in time in two possible ways. Crowds either reacted impulsively to changes on the market or saw the present atmosphere on the market as unchangeable. The contrarian, as a nonconformist, recognized that this atmosphere could change unannounced and with such speed that crowds would have a delayed reaction (128).

The crowd reacted to its impulses without delay, and thus did not allow an individualized subject to take shape. However, the contrarian *thought*, and thus created a buffer against the immediacy of the impulses guiding crowds. This buffer allowed the contrarian to establish a temporal consciousness. The contrarian developed this consciousness precisely by taking seriously decisions made by the crowd. Crowd psychology became a temporal technique that allowed the contrarian speculator to react in a more reflective way to the market than the crowd. The crowd was the instrument required to make better predictions about the economy (Neill 1967 [1954], 134). The investor trained in crowd psychology had to master a difficult task. He had to adjust to trends established by the crowd, but at the same time maintain a position that allowed him to observe the crowd from outside. The temporality of this privileged external position was of particular importance. Market trends often changed "*before* masses are *consciously observant*" (62; emphasis added). Neill was careful to note that "'The crowd is usually wrong'—at least, in its *timing* of events" (2). The contrarian speculator should not resist crowds entirely, but should only avoid the poor timing these crowds displayed. Crowds invested when prices were high and anxiously sold when prices began to fall. "The crowd is *with* the trends during run-ups and not prone to 'get off' until prices are well down near the lows of the move" (Neill (1960 [1931], 18).

Paradoxically, then, crowds were not always wrong, but were always too early or too late.[13] Neill observed that crowds lacked an awareness of time, and linked this lack of awareness to the physicality and suggestibility of crowds. In turn, he argued that the contrarian was aware of temporal structures because he was able to think. However, developing an awareness of time also cost the contrarian time. It is not a coincidence that, in many theories of crowds, suggestion and impulse were seen as highly accelerated forms of communication. As I have suggested, Sidis conceived of suggestion as a simple but rapid means of communication during a crisis.[14] This speed could no longer be reached when thought interfered with, or even blocked, the transmission of suggestive impulses. Neill had to rely on a second principle of mistimed, and pleasing, affect in order to relativize the speed with which impulsive crowds acted. Because he was reflective, the contrarian speculator acted slowly, but nonetheless discovered trends with greater speed than the crowd. Neill implicitly resolved this paradox of speed by formulating the awareness of time displayed by the speculator as a technique of observation. Crowds reacted to the market in a physical and emotional way, and thus lacked the capacity to observe time and to identify temporal structures. The ability to historicize prices helped the contrarian recognize cycles. The contrarian was thus able to avoid acting like an "average person" who treated these cycles as if they were entirely new (Neill 1967 [1954], 128).

2.2 Techniques of Isolation

One of the most important preconditions for self-mastery was that the speculator had to be isolated. In *Discipline and Punish*, Michel Foucault convincingly argued that the modern prison used techniques of architectural and communicative isolation to produce individual prisoners: "The crowd, a compact mass, a locus of multiple exchanges, individualities merging together, a collective effect, is abolished and replaced by a collection of *separated individualities*" (Foucault 1977, 201; emphasis added). This process of individualization took place in the panopticon, where cells were arranged in a way that would isolate each prisoner.

The contrarians also recommended a strategy of isolation in order to guarantee the individuality of each speculator. Contrarians could not rely on an architectural apparatus to protect speculators from external influences, but instead used a strategy of *communicative isolation*. A speculator should remain distant from other speculators, since these speculators might compromise his economic judgment: "Trade alone! . . . Close your mind to the opinion of others; pay no attention to outside influences. Disregard reports, rumors, and idle boardroom chatter. . . . Be a calm, unpleasant cynic" (Neill 1967 [1954], 44). Contrarian speculators had to turn away from other speculators in order to become individuals. This imperative, however, had to be reconciled with the equally necessary task that individual speculators observe the crowd. These speculators had to protect themselves from the crowd, but also had to observe the crowd carefully. Only from the dynamics of the crowd could the contrarian position emerge. Nonetheless, the risk that a contrarian speculator would be seduced by the crowd made techniques of isolation necessary. Speculators were literally isolated, and thus able to avoid unnecessary communication. Rumors should not reach the speculator, since he might be tempted to take them seriously. Rather than be misled by tips and rumors, the speculator should only be confronted with current prices—even if, as we have seen, abrupt price movements had a power to seduce.

At times it proved difficult for the individual speculator to ignore the rumors circulated by other speculators. To help resist these rumors, the contrarians recommended simple means of self-control. To keep track of his own speculation, and of the market, the speculator should always have a pencil and notebook handy (the very equipment that Max Weber also saw as characteristic of small speculators). This was less to provide the speculator with information than with self-control. Taking notes helped the speculator keep his distance not only from rumors, but from himself: "Use pad-and-pencil since it will occupy your mind and concentrate your attention. Try it; you will not be able to chatter and keep track of trades at the same time" (Neill 1967 [1954], 44). The speculator used writing and other techniques of inscription to establish communicative isolation, to concentrate, and to avoid gossip.

Along with such techniques of self-control based on media, contrarians recommended that the speculator isolate himself from unnecessary communication. Distance from the stock exchange was an advantage, Samuel Armstrong Nelson noted (1964 [1903], 66ff.). The "out-of-towner" had the time and solitude required to weigh investment options carefully, whereas speculators physically present at the stock exchange—especially when it was hectic—were often tempted to follow the crowd. "The outsider who will wisely study values and market conditions and then exercise patience enough for six men will be likely to make money in stocks," Charles Dow, the inventor of the Dow Jones Industrial Average, predicted in 1907 (cited by Wilson 1963, 122). In fact, by keeping his distance, the "out-of-towner" had already proven a degree of self-control: "Staying away from the market place means self-discipline" (Wilson 1963, 122). This was what put the speculator in charge: "The hardest thing to learn in stock trading is to keep the eye *off* the market" (Harper 1966, 94–95).

When the market became too hectic, big players sometimes retreated to resorts like Newport, Rhode Island, or Saratoga Springs in upstate New York. Moving to an idyllic location away from the stock market helped the speculator establish autonomy. At the same time, the fact that the speculator had to move to such a location pointed to the difficulties of establishing individual and autonomous judgment. If the speculator were truly heroic and above suspicion, he would not have to fear that rumors and price movements would tempt him to act impulsively. However, the professional speculator was aware of his shortcomings and thus isolated himself in order to prove he had a strong will.

Excursus: The Desire to Be Near Wall Street

Guides to speculation suggest that speculators achieved self-control through isolation, but this was not only a question of lack of access to speculation. Distance from the stock market meant the risk of exclusion, and thus often caused anxiety for the speculator. In *The Making of a Stockbroker* (1925), a semi-fictive biography that has now become canonical, Edwin Lefèvre presents the life of his protagonist as a narrative of financial inclusion.[15] The protagonist loves his home state of Maine, but leaves the state for a career on the stock exchange: "I loved Maine, all of it—mountains, lakes, rivers, and coast. But I loved it as a place to have my vacation in" (Lefèvre 1925, 22). After studying at Harvard, the protagonist moves to Boston to take a position in a brokerage left vacant by a colleague who is terminally ill. After moving to another brokerage in Boston, the protagonist comes closer to Wall Street. He now has a direct telegraph connection to New York: "I thought that this was like being in actual personal contact with the source of all market wisdom" (43). The distant New York firms became an imaginary object: "To me that mighty firm of brokers represented everything that made Wall Street what it was" (*viif.*). Reports of the stock exchange fascinate the protagonist, a fascination that extends to the way in which these reports were transmitted: "I often sat beside the telegraph operator and watched him send orders over, and saw the reports come back" (43). The protagonist finally decides that the telegraph cannot replace being physically present in New York—namely, in Wall Street, a place "where everybody who expected to be somebody should go in order to work with money for money" (46). The young trader is gradually overcome by the wish to go to New York, until he finally gets a position there. Surprisingly, the protagonist already appears familiar with New York. He is particularly fascinated by the noises he can hear in the city: "I could hear the unbroken hoarse murmur—a blending of ten thousand noises—that is the audible life of the noisiest city in the world, . . . the nerve centre of high finance" (119). New York embodies the market of all markets, and exerts a magnetic attraction on people from across the country. The protagonist experiences no uncertainty when he arrives in New York. On the first day of his arrival, he is interested in the local section of the newspaper. New York has already become his home.

Occasional departures from New York were a sign of failure, as is made particularly clear in *Reminiscences of a Stock Operator*, another fictionalized biography by Lefèvre (1982 [1923]), which also aimed to provide an introduction to stock speculation. The protagonist fails as a speculator and leaves New York for a vacation. The narrator emphasizes the physical distance between the protagonist and Wall Street. However, this physical distance does not allow the protagonist to entirely abandon his identity: "In the spring of 1906 I was in Atlantic City for a short vacation. I was out of stocks and was thinking only of having a change of air and a nice rest" (73). The protagonist maintains he is not interested in the market, but he nonetheless visits a brokerage every day with his friend. According to the protagonist, keeping track of the market in this way is not the same as actively speculating: "It was more force of habit than anything else, for I wasn't doing anything" (73). However, even watching the market leads the protagonist to develop hunches about the market and ultimately to engage in trading. The speculator cannot escape his identity by taking a vacation: "That summer I went to Saratoga Springs. It was supposed to be a vacation for me, but I kept an eye on the market. . . . Of course I watched the market. With me, to look at the quotation board and to read the signs is one process" (79). Pleasure in the spectacular oscillations of the market could not be separated from financial decisions. For the speculator, the media distributing stock quotations were a signal that he had to obey.[16]

Distance from the market thus has two meanings. On the one hand, it is necessary to allow the speculator temporarily to escape the market, and thus to avoid the effects of hyperinclusion. However, the speculator ultimately cannot be indifferent to the market. Such indifference was admitted to be impossible even by writers who recommended "out-of-town" trading. After the invention of the telegraph and the ticker tape, stock prices were present everywhere. Speculators could hardly avoid them. They were not only treated as information, but as a form of entertainment. Watching the market added excitement to the speculator's vacation. Without speculation, the greatest excitement one of Lefèvre's protagonists experiences on his vacation is a stroll on the boardwalk (Lefèvre 1982, 73). On the other hand, distance from the market reduces inclusion. The speculator who is far from the market risks missing opportunities for profit. The Saratoga Springs vacation narrated by Lefèvre ends in disaster. The protagonist fails to escape rumors and ignores tips that would have led to successful trading.[17] The role of isolation is thus inverted. The vacation, recommended to help the speculator achieve self-mastery, is quickly forgotten. The speculator seeks distractions from boredom by exchanging tips.

Physical distance from the market thus played a contradictory role in discourses of speculation. Speculators went to Saratoga Springs to escape Wall Street and to become more effective traders. However, speculators who went to Saratoga Springs also made poor investment decisions. Moreover, for Lefèvre, Saratoga Springs is a stage in the hero's development. Lefèvre's protagonists follow the pattern found in a German novel of education [Erziehungsroman]: "The Saratoga experience was my last haphazard, hit-or-miss operation. . . . I promoted myself to a higher grade in the hard school of speculation. It was a long and difficult step to take" (Lefèvre 1982, 83). The notion of speculation as a "hard school" of *discipline*, and of self-improvement, links contradictory accounts of spatial distance which differ according to the degree to which speculators ultimately succeed in distancing themselves from the market. For Lefèvre, the speculator ultimately fails to achieve physical isolation from the market because he always finds brokerages reporting the most recent stock prices or meets other speculators eager to exchange gossip about the market. These media do not replace physical proximity to Wall Street. It was not enough to be fascinated by the ticker. However, media like the ticker made it more difficult for speculators to escape the stock market long enough to clear their heads. This clarity was often seen as the goal of distancing oneself from the market: "A day in the country, with the market forgotten, or if necessary forcibly ejected from the thoughts, will often enable the trader to return with a clarified mind" (Selden 1912, 114).

The advice to distance oneself from the market repeated—often without success—earlier discourses recommending isolation to fight epidemics. The speculator had to be quarantined in order to come to his senses. For writers like Lefèvre, this rhetoric of discipline was not guaranteed to work for stock exchange communication. Contagion could no longer be contained in a particular space, since a range of media allowed the virus of speculation, as it were, to spread to distant locations. Moreover, isolation from the stock exchange was not equivalent to isolation from an epidemic. Isolation from the stock exchange was always accompanied by the topos of missed opportunity. Popular literature on the stock exchange took for granted that, under normal circumstances, speculators could have profited from these missed opportunities. Speculators were advised in widely differing ways about the spatial dimension of stock speculation. However, this differing advice had one point in common: discipline was linked closely to the spatial position of the speculator. The speculator displayed self-discipline by retreating from the market to the country for a few days, and by acting as a rational individual when directly confronted by a hectic market.

2.3 Techniques of Self-Observation: Self-Criticism as a Mode of Identification

Communicative and spatial isolation do not suffice for establishing a secure identity. It calls for both a strong will and continual self-criticism. In order to understand the crowd, the speculator has to understand himself (Neill 1960 [1931], 157). To be successful, he also needs "pliability," understood as the "ability to change an opinion, the power of revision" (Wolf 1966 [1924], 71). Sticking to "your own opinion, right or wrong" is a sure way to lose money on the stock exchange; the speculator must objectively evaluate his opinions from an "impersonal view point" (Neill 1967 [1954], 52, 64).

Neill does not address the role of self-criticism to the same extent as other psychological techniques for speculation. However, self-criticism plays an important role in other positions on the market developed in a contrarian spirit. Sloan Wilson, who was strongly influenced by Neill, advises: "You will make mistakes. Analyze them and learn something. Also remember that making a profit can be just luck and no skill—analyze all of your transactions." Speculators should react to their successes with composure and avoid taking pride in their abilities: "Pride of opinion and impatience will be your worst enemies."[18] The speculator is not only to criticize his emotions and opinions, but also his transactions. Even successful speculators should ask whether their success can be attributed to luck, or to competent decisions. This self-criticism is implicitly designed to distinguish serious speculation from pure gambling. The "business-like" attitude recommended by Neill resembles the attitude of a strict but fair teacher. Mistakes cannot be avoided but are an opportunity to learn. As soon as the speculator recognizes that an investment was a mistake, he has to be ready to admit to this mistake: "The one thing which retards success more than any other is the unwillingness of many of us to accept losses, cheerfully and quickly, when we realize that we have misjudged the action of the market."[19]

To be self-critical, the speculator has to avoid empathizing with himself, and instead observe himself with a distant, neutral gaze. In order to develop this, he must view his own investments as abstractions. Even when faced with the greatest pressure to allow "his judgment to be swayed by his hopes," he has to keep "his mind in a balanced and unprejudiced condition" (Selden 1912, 71). Introspection allows the speculator to neutralize his psychological and material biases: "Few persons are so introspective as to be able to tell where this bias in favor of their own interests begins and where it leaves off" (73). This psychological approach to the market appeared around 1900, anticipating discourses of self-awareness that emerged in the 1960s. One of the clearest examples of these later discourses can be found in Adam Smith (George J. W. Goodman), who emphasizes that the speculator has to know himself before he trades on the stock market. A successful speculator has to have "a kind of locked-in concentration, an intuition, a feel, nothing that can be schooled. The first thing you have to know is yourself" (Smith 1967, 25). Smith opposes intuition to the rationalism of George C. Selden and other psychologists of the stock exchange who take it for granted that even the most deeply concealed emotions can be controlled.

Self-criticism provides the speculator with techniques to monitor his identity and produce a new, flexible self. The speculator no longer has an external point of reference by which to establish his identity. The absence of such a point of reference is particularly striking when the speculator is compared to other modern figures of inclusion. Laborers can identify with their work (or at least be alienated from their work), consumers with the products they buy and enjoy, and citizens with their nationality. The speculator, however, lacks these external modes of identification.[20] Identifying with a particular investment (e.g., a stock) is seen in guides to speculation as a costly lack of discipline common among beginners. Small investors frequently make the mistake of treating their investments like other consumer products and choose stocks according to their preferences for a given product. In a guide to the stock market titled *The Art of Speculation*, Philip Carret (1990 [1930]) advises speculators not to be influenced by emotion when buying stocks. Every half year, the speculator should evaluate his portfolio without thinking about the original price he paid for a stock. He must give up his identification with a given company and with the stock he has acquired in it. An investment that once made sense may no longer do so under new conditions, and stocks that are held for too long become soiled goods, reminding the speculator of a past he should forget. The ideal, successful speculator thus has to learn from experience and constantly revise his identity without having recourse to an integrating narrative. He is defined by his ability to trade stocks unemotionally, denying himself an identity based on the history of his stock purchases. "The stock doesn't know you own it," Smith points out.[21] The speculator constantly has to revise his identity, becoming an early version of the flexible subject.

3. Flexible Speculators

I have suggested that the contrarian speculator, as a figure of inclusion, cannot be reduced to binary oppositions. The individual contrarian speculator can, of course, be opposed to the remaining crowd of speculators. Crowd psychology's concept of the leader might also suggest that the contrarian is a hero who resisted the impulsiveness displayed by the crowd. However, can the contrarian be a hero when he lacks the charisma to attract followers, or even to win the admiration of an audience? Thomas Kavanagh (1993) argues that the speculator is not a hero. The gambler displays individual skill, or even genius, when gambling. However, the speculator lacks this opportunity for individual expression. Kavanagh already sees a new form of subjectivity in the speculation of John Law and his contemporaries. In contrast to the gambling that took place in Versailles, this kind of speculation was "not an affirmation of individual valor or courage but an absorption of the individual within a larger community of all buyers and sellers, of all the investors and profit takers" (Kavanagh 1993, 96). Rather than display individual courage, speculators paid "constant attention to what others exactly like themselves were doing. . . . The investor gambles not on himself as an individual but on himself as part of that same large number that was to play so crucial a role in the development of probability theory and statistics" (96–97). This notion of the speculator is, however, as incomplete as the notion that the speculator is a hero. The contrarian speculator is an unusual figure of inclusion, driven by contradictory motives. Contrarianism, more than other investment schools, emphasizes that the speculator depends on the crowd. As a result, the contrarian speculator constantly observes the crowds, but is also obliged to discipline himself. Though the speculator exists in a permanent relation to the crowd, he does not become average. Rather, contrarianism links crowd psychology to the heroic individualism of *homo oeconomicus*.

The individualism of the contrarian speculator differs significantly from the individuality displayed by the aristocratic gambler. The contrarian becomes a silent hero who has to resist the temptation of the crowd, but who also receives no admiration for this resistance. He exemplifies the American individualism formulated by Ralph Waldo Emerson: "It is easy in the world to live after the world's opinion; it is easy in solitude to live after our own; but the great man is he who in the midst of the crowd keeps with perfect sweetness the independence of solitude."[22] The contrarian speculator has to live with a flexible, or even damaged, form of individualism, objectionable to Keynes. Such individualism, however, is accepted by the contrarian as a part of daily business. In order to win on the market, the speculator has to adopt the poor judgment of the crowd, even against his own good judgment—and thus has to do without the vanity of those who know how the economy "really" is. The speculator risks losing himself by temporarily adjusting to the crowd and thus has to develop an individuality that is resistant as well as flexible.

The speculator I have described resembles an autonomous artist more than he does the "average man." Facing a volatile object of identification, the speculator is thrown back on himself. He radicalizes self-reference by replacing external objects of identification with imagined success at future speculation. However, this form of subjectivity is unstable precisely because it is constructed on the basis of a fiction, and on the basis of time. The speculator always faces the possibility that self-reference will take a painful turn. "The destruction of business prospects leave[s] the mind confused, bereft of any serious or sufficient purpose, literally, 'aimless,' and hence despondent," the American economist Edward Jones writes of the effects of an economic depression on the speculator (1900, 211), adopting the widespread vocabulary of psychopathology. Like a melancholic, the failed speculator loses his sense of purpose and falls victim to an excess of idle self-reference.

What is introduced here is an important inflection of the heroic figure of the contrarian. In normal cases, the contrarian defines himself by a constitutive disavowal that consists in refusing, at all costs, to be or to become a part of the crowd. In this rejection, the discourse of democratic inclusion is linked in a strange way to a discourse of a relentless struggle against the crowd. Judith Butler's (1997) figure of the melancholic sheds light on this struggle. Butler reads Freud's notion of melancholy as a means of subject constitution. The figure of the melancholic turns back on itself, and cannot mourn, but only incorporate what it rejects as something unspeakable. The melancholic thus experiences a loss that he can neither recognize nor understand. Nonetheless, the melancholic attempts to incorporate what has been rejected. This process creates an "internal civil war" that divides the melancholic subject.

The melancholic speculator should not be seen as a failed version of the ideal speculator. Rather, this failure is a *necessary* part even of the ideal speculator, and of the idealized version of self-reference by which this speculator resists the crowd. The transformation into a melancholic is not a contingency, but always already part of the logic constituting the speculator. The speculator becomes an autonomous, reflective individual only by rejecting the crowd, and thus by reacting to the claims of democratic all-inclusion made by this crowd. However, the crowd creeps back into the identity of the speculator— not only because the speculator is directly "infected" by the crowd spirit, but also because the very capacities of permanent self-observation and self-reflection that allow him a distinct identity as speculator become excessive. Continual self-observation and self-critique make the decision to buy impossible, and cause the speculator to spiral inwardly to such an extent that, in many representations, his body takes on grotesque traits. The speculator, as melancholic, begins to assume the typical features of the crowd described by crowd psychology: he loses his capacity for judgment and his self-discipline, and, like the crowd, is governed by affect. The unsuccessful speculator thus comes to resemble the crowd that the ideal speculator has to reject—but that nonetheless continually reappears in him.

CHAPTER 6

THE EROTICISM OF THE MARKET
AND THE GENDER OF SPECULATION

Wall Street is not a place for a lady to find either a fortune or character.
—Henry Clews, *Fifty Years in Wall Street* (1908)

"Crowds are everywhere distinguished by feminine characteristics," Gustave Le Bon writes laconically (1903, 44). The leader, in contrast, is often a man. Similarly, the "market crowd" is also coded as feminine. How does this code affect the way the speculator is constructed? What happens to the speculator when *he* is opposed to a market described, in feminine terms, as hysterical, volatile, impulsive, emotional, excitable, and inclined to spread rumors? In this chapter, I argue that inclusion in the stock market is based on a "heterosexual matrix,"[1] which largely determines how the speculator is formed as a figure of inclusion.

As with contrarians, a figure of inclusion always accompanies a specific position as observer, allowing the speculator to read the market in a particular way. I argue that this way of reading the market is coded in gender-specific terms. My focus is thus primarily on the discursive means that configure access to the market, and not on the social question of whether women have access to finance.

In the previous chapter, I read the contrarian speculator as being close to the ideal type of a speculator who rejects, but cannot entirely ignore, the crowd. This speculator is constructed according to an individualistic model of *complete self-mastery*. He lacks all emotion, and instead becomes a reflexive observer who speculates with an iron will. Crowd psychology, when articulated with heterogeneous components of classical economic theory, supports the image of a rationally calculating *homo oeconomicus*. At the same time, this *homo oeconomicus* is confronted by an omnipresent logic of crowds that highlights the drama of his situation—a drama neglected in neoclassical theory. Since he cannot ignore the crowds, the contrarian speculator has no choice but to observe them. He uses self-discipline to eliminate the characteristics that threaten to make him indistinguishable from the crowd. In particular, the speculator has to control his emotions, which make him prone to suggestion.

This opposition between strong-willed speculator and seductive crowds is coded in terms of gender. In ideal cases, a feminine market is contrasted to a gender-neutral speculator formed by processes of abstraction.[2] This ideal speculator resembles the *homo oeconomicus* described by Arjo Klamer as "Max U" (maximizer of utility), a figure who lacked any particular quality (Klamer in Ruccio and Amariglio 2003, 82). Many investment guides—particularly guides written by contrarians—describe this process of disembodiment. Speculators are no longer to display emotion or idiosyncrasy, but are instead to make calculated decisions about their investments and to utilize techniques of self-management. Like *homo oeconomicus*, the neutrality of this disembodied ideal speculator is open to the critique, raised in feminist economics, of universalizing masculine subjectivity (Hewitson 1999). David Ruccio and Jack Amariglio (2002) have criticized this critique, claiming it relies on a classical notion of the subject to tell a melodramatic story of disembodiment. *Homo oeconomicus* may lack the body crucial to humanist notions of the subject, but is by no means a disembodied subject.

The melancholic speculator, as we have seen, represents the way in which *homo oeconomicus* has failed to discipline himself. This failure cannot be attributed to chance obstacles, but is intrinsic to the way the speculator is constituted as a subject. The increasingly disembodied speculator is confronted with an affective and physical abyss that, paradoxically, is a result of the attempt to become more abstract. The frequent use of psychopathological metaphors (depression, euphoria, melancholy) to describe the speculator already suggests that this speculator does not entirely lack emotion and is not entirely disembodied. These metaphors point to the limits of efforts to make the speculator a universal and neutral figure.

I. Feminine Allegories: Cynthia Speculation and Lady Credit

In 1933, the former stockbroker Robert Smitley published a book titled *Popular Financial Delusions*, playing on the title of Charles Mackay's *Extraordinary Popular Delusions and the Madness of Crowds*. The book is both an investment guide and a collection of journalistic reflections on the stock exchange. "All the delusions by which investors annually lose billions of dollars are here," the cover avers. "The reader will learn to identify those delusions that seek to lure him from his ultimate aim—the protection of capital and the profit that comes from common sense handling of money." Smitley promised guidance that would enable even the inexperienced speculator to make a profit.

The lure of the market takes on a specific shape for Smitley. There, the speculator encounters Cynthia Speculation, often suggestively called Cyn. Smitley's description of Cyn deserves careful attention:

> She was a vampire incarnate and she led more people astray than the Pied Piper led children. Yet, when she was in her prime, she was so beautiful that no one could resist her. Of charm she had an abundance and she made it known that her admirers never work. She was devilishly intelligent and yes she could never have exercised her charm and lure had she not had at her command a superabundance of credit. It was only when credit was taken from her that she appeared in her true colors. Then it was found that her eyes were hard, her thin lips cruel, and her body a mere empty shell.[3]

Smitley thus depicts speculation as a beautiful and seductive woman who is aware of her allure. Her beautiful face hides a treacherous, calculating intellect, and on closer inspection, her body is an "empty shell," but she promises fantastic wealth without work. She seduces her victims like a vampire and deceives and manipulates her admirers like a *femme fatale*. Like those of a mechanical doll, her movements are entirely calculated. Even cheapskates are seduced by Cyn into making dangerous investments (Smitley 1933, 9).

Smitley was writing a stock market guide purporting to protect ignorant speculators from deception and bias. So what led him to use this highly sexualized allegory, rather than treating speculation as a rational form of communication and the stock exchange as an ideal economic space, free from what he calls a "primitive mob psychology"? Is Cynthia Speculation just the figment of a third-rate author? Cynthia is assisted by Lady Credit. Only with the help of Lady Credit can Cynthia stay beautiful. Credit and speculation are alluring because they make promises about the future. According to John Pocock (1975), credit is based on trust in the future actions of another investor, and thus became a vehicle for the speculative imagination, exemplified by Daniel Defoe. In his journalistic, political, and economic writings,

Defoe engaged with the culture of finance that emerged and prospered during the seventeenth century.[4] Defoe's writings are marked by a deep concern for, but also by a fascination with, the increasingly widespread phenomena of credit and speculation. Defoe and other writers around his time
noted with astonishment that the nature of credit could not be understood.
Credit was unpredictable and unreal, but Defoe nonetheless tried to grasp
its ephemeral nature: "It gives Motion, yet it self cannot be said to Exist; it
creates Forms, yet has itself no Form; it is neither quantity or Quality, it has
no Whereness, or Whenness, Scite, or Habit" (Defoe 2000b, 51). Credit had
the power to create differences without being among those differences, and
without residing in a particular location. The appearance of credit presented
Defoe with the challenge of representing a new form of wealth. This form of
wealth could not be described with the traditional notions of ownership and
referentiality. Wealth became intangible and mobile (Pocock 1975). Material
possessions, such as property, were located in a concrete place, and experienced as part of everyday life. However, credit was a highly fictional notion
of ownership, a notion in which radical change was always possible. The
fortune won with credit could, the following day, become worthless scraps
of paper.

Toward the end of the seventeenth century, the new and ungraspable
phenomenon of credit began to be represented as a feminine figure (Goede
2000; Mulcaire 1999; Sherman 1996).[5] These representations sexualized the
relationship between trust and economic values that were both fictional and
transitory. The borrower's reputation was essential for credit to function properly. Only a good reputation allowed an investor to obtain credit, for credit
depended on the opinions of others, and thus proved to be unstable. For this
reason, credit was often compared to a "flighty young maiden" (Chancellor
1999, 32).

This neglected aspect of Defoe's writings has begun to receive attention
only in recent work on Lady Credit as a gendered allegory. Sandra Sherman
(1996) and Marieke de Goede (2000) have observed the ambivalent structure
of Lady Credit. Lady Credit not only represented monetary fluctuations, like
the goddess Fortuna. She was also a highly sexualized figure. Like Cynthia
Speculation, she aimed to please even those "who have no occasion for her"
(Defoe cited by Sherman 1996, 42) and quickly deserted those for whom she
had done favors.[6] Credit thus became a "bitch-goddess of unpredictability"
(Alasdair MacIntyre cited by Mulcaire 1999, 1033), an unpredictable deity

who could nonetheless be bought, and whose moods were as volatile as the financial markets. She seduced by celebrating contingency—that is, by showing how everything could be otherwise.

The discourse of femininity used to describe credit sheds light on the ways in which the emerging financial sphere was represented. Defoe and his contemporaries lacked the economic vocabulary to describe the unpredictability of finance, and instead had to rely on alternative vocabularies of contingency. The highly fictional and volatile trading on the stock exchange could not be grasped with traditional economic categories—particularly not with notions of causality. Defoe used Lady Credit to make intelligible an otherwise indescribable form of contingency. Credit, in the form of obligations, stocks, or lottery tickets, required an abstract and fictional notion of ownership. This abstract notion was counterbalanced by a discourse of femininity that gave expression to anxieties about, and the allure of, an economy that lacked a material basis. The analogy of femininity allowed early financial markets to be described as scenes of uncontrollable desire and unpredictable change.[7] These markets were seductive, not because they offered endless profit, but because they offered the nearly uncontrollable allure of contingency separated from fixed values.

Did the feminine allegories used to represent credit and speculation weaken the classical model of *homo oeconomicus*? Was *homo oeconomicus*, whose masculinity was linked to ownership and referentiality, threatened by Cynthia Speculation and Lady Credit? A closer reading of these figures draws attention to an important point: neither Cynthia Speculation nor Lady Credit speculate. Speculation did not speculate, but seduced anyone who came within its reach. Even Lady Credit does not use credit, but gives credit to those who treat her well. The female figures were used to represent the *relationship between speculation and the speculator*, or between credit and creditor. It would be premature to confuse speculator with speculation, and to describe the position of the speculator as feminine. The speculator was usually represented as masculine. Female speculators also existed, but, as we shall see, were primarily used to describe pathological or incompetent forms of speculation. The masculine subject position of the speculator was thus not simply a historical coincidence. As part of a gendered code, this masculine subject position was linked to feminine speculation—a link that designated a particular way of being included in finance. Once feminized, speculation could only properly be addressed by a masculine speculator.

The relationship between speculator and speculation was presented as a scene of heterosexual seduction. The masculine speculator was seduced by speculation, and had to protect his interests and his identity in order to beat the market. This inclusionary apparatus was coded in such a way as to place the speculator in a difficult position: the speculator needed credit to speculate well, and not to be seduced, but also had to be willing to take risks at speculation—a willingness that required being captivated to an extent by the market. The speculator was confronted with the epistemological problem of how to engage with economic contingency. How should he handle the mysterious phenomenon of credit, a phenomenon whose essence was transitory and indescribable? Panics and hysteria arose on the market without warning; credit became unavailable just when it was most needed.

Some authors have argued that Lady Credit was used to establish a masculine position from which to control the uncertainties of the market.[8] However, the phenomenon of credit was entirely new, and strategies of controlling this phenomenon had not yet been established. Mastering the market thus did not mean that individual speculators established control over the market. Rather, the speculator had to engage with the new, and unreal, economy, and learn to act in a successful way on the market. Mastering the market meant, above all, that the speculator mastered himself: "Because it is not only the woman, but man's *own lust* which undermines his self-mastery. . . . Lady Credit requires first and foremost a mastering and submitting of the self" (Goede 2000, 67). The masculine speculator had to be seduced in order to begin speculating, but constantly had to control the degree to which he was seduced. On the one hand, the speculator had to be seduced because, as Keynes would later observe, speculation has no rational basis. On the other hand, the speculator had to control the degree to which he was seduced in order to survive on the market.

2. The Impossibility of a Female Speculator: Why Women Should Not Speculate on the Stock Market

Speculation was represented as feminine, while speculators were represented as men—or, to be more precise, the "feminized market" necessarily turned the speculator into a man. This relationship meant that, long after Defoe created Lady Credit, female speculators occupied an impossible place in the discourse of speculation. "Impossible" here does not refer to empirical impossibility but to the representation of the female speculator, a subject position that was made impossible by the hegemonic discursive logic and thus led to descriptions of female speculators as ridiculous, notwithstanding that women have always speculated.

In his widely read and often reprinted book *Fifty Years in Wall Street*, which was based on personal experience, the former trader Henry Clews asks what kind of people are best suited to be speculators. Clews gives a few examples of people who should not speculate, including ignorant amateurs and naïve Sunday School teachers, but these are only a prologue to his discussion of women speculators, to whom he dedicates an entire chapter. It begins: "As speculators, women hitherto have been utter failures" (Clews 1973 [1908], 437).

What was seen as the basis for this inability to speculate? Women, like ignorant male amateur speculators, should have been able to acquire the economic knowledge necessary to speculate. Why was it not possible for women to be trained as speculators? Why would the stock market, the "great civilizer" according to Clews (18), not be able to "civilize" women? Why could women not benefit from the education by "sledgehammer" Clews recommended to other speculators?

Clews asserted that women were too impulsive and too quickly reached conclusions without having done the necessary research. They were "totally unable to take that broad view of the whole question and situation which the speculator has to seize at a glance"; woman was neither "by nature, nor even by the best possible education, qualified to become a speculator."[9]

This inability to add things up and to generalize also led women to overestimate the importance of temporary fluctuations in the market. Women lacked the ability to keep their distance from the market, an ability that defined the successful speculator.[10] This understanding of female speculators was widespread toward the beginning of the twentieth century. Sereno Pratt also believed women belonged to a group of individuals who should never speculate. A woman should instead focus on the security of her investments (Pratt 1921: 90).[11]

Women speculators were targeted with the same charge of parasitism directed against speculation itself, inasmuch as it produced nothing of value and sought only to profit from the labor of others.[12] Women, who had to compensate for their own inadequacy as speculators by relying on others, were "by nature, *parasites as speculators*," Clews claimed (1973 [1908], 437; emphasis added). If both women speculators and speculation itself were parasitic, women were *parasites of parasites*. Moreover, speculation placed a disproportionate strain on women; women speculators got *too close* to speculation.

Like the stock market itself, women were volatile and erratic. Euphoric changes on the market were as inexplicable as a sudden attack of female hysteria. Why should a hysteric be trusted to handle a hysterical market? *Women were not to be excluded from the market because they were foreign to its logic, but because they followed the same logic!* The exclusion of women from the role of speculator was enabled and legitimized by feminizing the market. The result of this was not simply that women were seen as incompetent, but that they were too close to the market, since they shared many of its characteristics.

The political theorist Marieke de Goede views the relationship between subject and object as an epistemological problem. "[T]he objectivity of finance *cannot* be remedied by the inclusion of Lady Credit's qualities into its analyses," she writes. "This is precisely because *objectivity itself* presupposes the masculine asceticism of the scientist" (2000, 73). I argue that this epistemological problem also structured modes of inclusion to finance, and constituted inclusion as a relation of observation. In this way, the epistemological danger that arose from the proximity of women to the market became problematic for the entire inclusionary arrangement. The distinction between speculator and speculation could collapse if the two sides of this distinction began to resemble each other. Game and gambler would become indistinguishable, endangering the inclusionary apparatus, along with the techniques of self-discipline linked to it.[13]

If the distinction between gambler and game could no longer be maintained, not only would observation become indistinguishable from the object being observed, but the very *observability* of the market—which presupposed an observation point, however precarious—would be called into question. It was thus necessary to stabilize the forces surrounding the processes of inclusion and exclusion, not the least of which were affective. Only in this way could finance be constructed as an economic object, and the speculator as an observer.

The ideal speculator inverted the negative image of the female speculator. Where the female speculator was impulsive, the ideal speculator exhibited composure. The ideal speculator contributed stability in a turbulent market. He knew how to control his emotions and could think in terms of abstractions that gave him a "broad view of the whole." The ideal speculator could see past immediate experiences and recognize general market trends: "He must be an

unceasing and intelligent observer of events at large, and a sagacious interpreter of symptoms of the Exchange; his judgement must be sound . . . and he
must possess the calmness and nerve to face unflinchingly whatever emer-
gencies may arise" (Clews 1973 [1908], 208). The ideal speculator combined
the qualities of a medical doctor and a scientific observer. Like a doctor, he
was an "interpreter of symptoms" (Clews); like a scientific observer, he was
calm enough not to be drawn in by his observations. Given these ideal roles,
the socio-epistemological threat posed by the arrival of the female speculator
becomes particularly clear.

3. Woodhull, Claflin & Co.: The Phenomenology
of the Impossibility of Female Speculation

As we have seen, in the stock market, the speculator played not a gender-
neutral role, but a masculine role. This gendering was articulated in two
ways. On the one hand, gender reinforced an inclusionary apparatus within
which the affective side of inclusion was understood as a process of heterosexual seduction. On the other hand, gender was linked to the possibility of
an observational order in which women had to be excluded from the market
to preserve the fragile position of masculine observers. This discursive exclusion of women was reinforced in narratives that contemplated the unimagi-
nable arrival and success of female speculators on the market. A woman
might, against expectations, initially succeed at speculation. However, this
success could not be attributed to her competence: "If women are fortunate
enough to escape being fleeced when they enter Wall Street, it can only be
from extraordinary luck, or from [the] protecting counsel of their brokers,
or from compassionate indulgence shown to them when swamped by their
losses" (Clews 1973, 442). At the beginning of the twentieth century, brokers expressed a similar skepticism about, and dislike of, female clients: "We
do not like women customers, and execute orders from them only when we
cannot . . . refuse them, as they are usually bad speculators and troublesome
clients" (a broker cited by Cowing 1965, 121). Women were seen as impressionable, and as lacking the psychic stamina required for speculation. After
buying stock, they constantly asked their broker for advice.[14]

What arguments were used to prove that women should not speculate?
One strategy consisted in narrating imagined scenes of women speculating
or historical cases of speculation by women to show that such speculation was
absurd. To support his case that women should not speculate and show what

happened when the masculine position of the speculator was usurped by a woman, Clews cited the case of Victoria C. Woodhull and her sister Tennessee ("Tennie") Claflin, who were the first women to open a brokerage firm in New York. The story of Woodhull and Claflin was frequently told during their own time, and continues to be told today, popularity that makes analysis of it valuable beyond the limited context of an investment guide.

In February 1870, Woodhull and Claflin founded a brokerage firm on Wall Street. Woodhull was one of the most prominent feminists of the nineteenth century. In addition to being the first female American stockbroker, she was a spiritualist medium and the first American woman nominated for president. She edited a newspaper that supported women's rights and free love and translated Marx into English (Gabriel 1998; Goldsmith 1998). Why would a socialist found a brokerage? Of course, Woodhull wanted to earn money, not least in order to support her socialist newspaper and to finance her political career. However, these were not her only aims. The founding of Woodhull, Claflin & Co. represents a serious engagement with the principle of openness implied by the universalist rhetoric of the stock exchange. Class, race, gender, and sexuality were not supposed to play a role in determining access to speculation. Nonetheless, until the 1920s, few women owned stocks. Not until 1967 did a woman buy a seat on the New York Stock Exchange (Siebert 2002).[15] Women who owned stocks usually allowed male relatives and friends to manage them (Cowing 1965, 121).[16] Victoria Woodhull was thus aware that establishing a brokerage firm run by women would be provocative. She took the universalist rhetoric of the stock exchange seriously, and tried to show that a "woman, no less than man, can qualify herself for the more onerous occupations of life." Opening a brokerage would entitle Woodhull and her sister to what they saw as "absolute equality." Woodhull recalled that "When I first came to Wall Street not 100 women in the whole of the United States owned stocks or dared to show independence in property ownership. . . . For a woman to consider a financial question was shuddered over as profanity" (interview with Woodhull in the *Wall Street Journal* in 1927 cited by Gabriel 1998, 39).

Strangely, many studies of Woodhull pay little attention to her life as a broker, and thus underestimate the emancipatory potential of this strategy. These approaches contradict the approach taken by Woodhull herself, who believed that speculation offered women an opportunity for emancipation. Toward the beginning of the twentieth century, representatives of the women's movement increasingly thematized speculation as a potential means of emancipation. The English journalist and social critic Olive Malvery wrote of the "enormous possibilities for women in the world of finance" (1906, 43). In the 1930s, Eunice Fullar Barnard, an early feminist and writer for the *North American Review*, also observed the possibilities for women's emancipation in speculation: "Women are at last taking a hand in man's most exciting capitalist game. For the first time they have the interest, the self-assurance, and the entrance fee." For Barnard, women's access to the stock market not only threatened gendered models of inclusion, but raised questions about the traditional priorities of the women's movement. If women succeeded at speculation, and thus gained financial influence, this struggle was more important than the struggle for the right to vote (Chancellor 1999, 205).

Woodhull did not underestimate the provocative effects her brokerage would have on Wall Street. The opening of her firm caused a "commotion only slightly less dramatic than a crash" (Gabriel 1998, 1). On the firm's opening day, more than a hundred police officers were on hand to control the crowds on Broad Street eager to see the two women stockbrokers (191). Newspaper articles about the opening of the firm took an interest in the clothing and appearance of the sisters, and pointed out that the sisters were attractive. It was emphasized that Woodhull and Claflin "knew their business, and that they proposed to take the stand like men" (*The Herald* cited in Gabriel 1998, 2). Described as the "photograph of a business woman—keen, shrewd, whole-souled, masculine in manner and apparently a firm foe of the 'girl of the period' creation. . . . She was very plainly dressed and spoke business in every gesture," Claflin said in an interview: "My mind is my business and I attend to that solely" (43). Both sisters dressed in a way that emphasized their "manly" professionalism. They wore identical banking suits, but the pants to these suits ended three inches above the sisters' ankles (Goldsmith 1998, 193). Woodhull and Claflin caused a good deal of excitement by wearing men's clothing while displaying their bodies in this way.

Accounts of Woodhull and Claflin frequently mention that their brokerage was financed and supported by the industrialist Commodore Cornelius Vanderbilt (1794–1877), one of the richest men in America. Nonetheless, Woodhull, Claflin & Co. was not seen as an enterprise controlled at a distance by Vanderbilt, but as a radically new challenge for the stock exchange. Woodhull's strategy guaranteed her intense publicity. In a letter, she wrote that her goal in entering finance was to gain "the most general and at the same time prominent introduction to the world. . . . There could have been nothing else in a legitimate business line that could have attracted the public notice . . . than the establishment of a banking house by two young women among the 'bulls' and 'bears' of Wall Street" (Woodhull cited by Gabriel 1998, 41).

The Claflin sisters used the public to test the boundaries of financial inclusion. Matthew Hale Smith dedicated a chapter in his book *Bulls and Bears of New York* (1873) titled "Lady Brokers on the Street" to Woodhull, Claflin & Co. Smith did not follow the polemics of other authors and directly warn against the dangers of Woodhull and Claflin speculating. He emphasized that their initial success had ended. The offices of their brokerage were usually empty, and the visitors who occasionally appeared were mostly relatives or women (Smith 1972 [1873], 273, 275). Smith was convinced that the Claflin sisters were not suited to be brokers: "They spend but little time in the office, and when in, seem to be under a high state of nervous excitement" (273). The sisters lacked composure and distance from the market, and thus either avoided their professional duties or were plagued by nervousness. Like members of a crowd, and the market itself, women speculators were characterized by the "female" diseases of nervousness and hysteria (Showalter 1997). Women speculators were not ready to handle the stress of dealing with stocks and were physically unsuited for speculation. The Claflin sisters appeared to be exhausted and had to drink Vichy water to recover. Smith contrasted these emotional states, which oscillated between fatigue and nervousness, with the efforts the Claflin sisters took to dress fashionably and to act courteously: "Of ordinary height, coarse complexion, masculine in manner, dressed in stunning style, these brokers evidently study to make an impression" (274). Feminine qualities, however, were out of place in the context of speculation. They might draw attention, but they were ultimately exposed as lacking depth. Smith concluded in a sober and dismissive tone: "So far the house has done little or nothing" (275). Using a distant style, Smith presented the economic failure of Woodhull and Claflin as unavoidable. This failure was *natural* and *physical*. The sisters failed because the stock exchange was literally the wrong place for women.

For Henry Clews, too, the example of the Claflin sisters proved women were by nature unsuited to speculation—even the "cleverest" women failed on Wall Street (Clews 1973 [1908]: 439). The sisters were only able to found their brokerage with the help of Commodore Vanderbilt, who had consulted them in their capacity of spiritualist mediums. The only successful strategy used by the sisters was the flattery that won the attention and services of the other sex

(441). Woodhull's claim that a "woman, no less than man, can qualify herself for the more onerous occupations of life" contrasted starkly with the turmoil caused by the founding of her brokerage (443). Clews did not analyze the firm's success and failure from a distance, but sought to publicize Woodhull's remarkable career as a self-revealing cautionary tale. In the end, he shows the proper place of female speculation: "Victoria was a better investor than speculator, and her best investment was her last marriage. Women can only become successful speculators in the matrimonial line" (444).

Even authors who saw women as suited to the role of amateur speculators were skeptical about the idea that women could act as brokers. "Could, or would, or should, she line her delicate throat with bell metal, . . . change her tender heart into stone, crush out her human sympathies with the unfortunate and the distressed, and *see* men reduced from affluence to beggary, and profit by it as a broker?" William W. Fowler asked (1968 [1880], 456; emphasis added). The physicality of the woman—represented for Fowler by her subtleness and vulnerability—was confronted by a materialistic description of the world of the stock market in terms of metal and stone to characterize the highly fictive realm of finance. However, Fowler's actual point was that female speculators occupied a position from which they could observe men in a pitiful state—or, rather, that these women saw men in a state they should not see, and thus became voyeurs. The profession of broker, then, was "almost the last one that a woman would aspire to fill" (456). For Fowler, too, the story of the Claflin sisters was a cautionary tale.

Representations imagining the horror of women brokers made the problem of observation underlying the relationship between speculator and market more acute. On the one hand, women continued to lack the distance from the market that would allow them to develop their own economic subjectivity. However, the grotesque features of male speculators could also become visible from the ultimately impossible position of the female broker. Observing these male speculators would do physical and psychic damage to women. Women were thus unsuited to this kind of observation—an observation that would allow them to see men in a state that typically, and necessarily, remained closed to any female perspective. A magazine article titled "A Dangerous Time" reported that a young woman who observed events on the stock exchange from the gallery became upset and commented: "It is one of the saddest things I have ever *seen*" (Anon. 1901, 106; emphasis added). The author of the article explained that the woman had become upset because she

Fig. 2. "How to Manage a Balky Team," *New York Evening Telegraph*, 1870

saw events not meant for her eyes: "There is something profoundly saddening in the spectacle of the mad rush and whirl of a great speculative movement, when men seem to part with their sanity and rush at prospective profits with a kind of unhuman intensity" (106). Speculation had the uncanny power of dehumanizing men and turning them into an irrational crowd, a sight not meant for any female gaze. This exclusion was based on the precarious structure of the observational order. Within this order, it becomes clear how the speculator, while on the path to becoming *homo oeconomicus*, failed to reach a point of complete self-abstraction. The gender-neutral speculator, imagined as rational and emotionless, proved to be driven by an "unhuman intensity" which compromised the rationality that had previously secured the identity of the speculator. The fragility of the observational order was exposed when that order failed to distinguish between rational speculator and hysterical market. Implicitly, this failure conjured up the danger that the gender of the speculator was not only contingent, but also reversible. This was portrayed in a cartoon in the *New York Evening Telegraph* in 1870 that shows the Claflin sisters driving a coach drawn by leading Wall Street figures, caricatured as monstrous bulls and bears with human faces, whom they whip and control, while tiny male speculators crawl on the ground below them (fig. 2).

Assuming a masculine role in this way supplemented, and thus increased, the provocative effects of an already provocative role. Recall that the brokerage firm was, from its beginning, intended to be a public spectacle. Brokerages were a stage on which to rearticulate the economic inclusionary apparatus.[17] A central strategy for this rearticulation was to *mimic* the masculine standards for speculation. This strategy would lead, in Judith Butler's (1999 [1990]) terms, to a travesty of inclusionary roles. By *cross-dressing*, the Claflin sisters played with the meaning of the business suits worn by men.[18] Wearing men's suits was already provocative in itself, but when the sisters shortened their pants to reveal their ankles, they created a true scandal. Moreover, Tennie Claflin even imitated the rhetoric of the professional businessman when she claimed "my mind is my business" (cited by Gabriel 1998, 43). At the same time, the sisters were famous for their roles as spiritualist mediums, and were the editors of a socialist newspaper. Even the location of their brokerage parodied the official business world. The building was on the right street for a brokerage, but had previously been rented by notorious criminals. Woodhull, Claflin & Co. was thus provocative in two ways. On the one hand, the firm was a reminder of the noneconomic origins of speculation, suggested by the idea that the Claflins used their clairvoyant powers as mediums to pick stocks, not only for themselves but for Commodore Vanderbilt.[19] On the other hand, the firm was a reminder that the fortunes won by some speculators were of criminal origin.[20] This classical ideology critique was supplemented by a politics of parody. The Claflin sisters conformed to the masculine rules of business but openly parodied those rules by merging them into a discourse of female sexuality and seduction.[21]

Excursus: The Gender of the Stock Market Crowd

Many analogies exist between the feminization of the market and descriptions of the market as a crowd. The impossibility of women speculators corresponded to the impossibility of the contrarian speculator asserting himself against the "market crowd." Both the figure of the female speculator and that of the market crowd allowed the economic identity of the speculator to be established, but they also threatened this identity. The close relationship between crowd psychology and gender as means of constructing the speculator was no coincidence, as Le Bon's assertion that "[c]rowds are everywhere distinguished by feminine characteristics" suggests. For Le Bon, women, along with children and savages, represented "inferior forms of evolution" characterized by "impulsiveness, irritability, incapacity to reason, the absence of judgment and of the critical spirit, [and]the exaggeration of the sentiments."[22] Because women were impressionable, and lacked a strongly developed sense of individuality, they were also the ideal members of a crowd. In crowd psychology around 1900 and subsequently, this articulation of women and crowds was commonly backed up by references to hypnosis and the exaggerations and erratic behavior of hysterics.

In his best-selling book *The Money Game*, "Adam Smith" explicitly linked the equations *"Market = Crowd"* and *"Market = Woman,"* writing: "The market is a crowd, and if you've read Gustave Le Bon's *The Crowd*, you know a crowd is a composite personality. In fact, a crowd of men acts like a single woman. The mind of a crowd is like a woman's mind. Then if you have observed her a long time, you begin to see little tricks, little nervous movements of the hand when she is being false" (Smith 1967, 23).

The astonishing chain of equivalences created by Smith ran as follows: *group of individual male actors = crowd = market = woman.* Smith's description of the market as a crowd of men underlines the masculine way in which the speculator was coded. The market was constituted, not by rational actors, but by a group of men whose relationship could only be explained by crowd psychology. Smith constructed an interesting mirror relationship between individual and crowd. A group of individual men acting in a particular way evolved into a crowd with the status of a subject with a "composite personality." This composite subject was transformed in respect to women into a *unified* subject lacking subjectivity. Smith contrasts a "crowd of men" to a "single woman" (23). A masculine plurality is opposed to a feminine unity. This unity, however, is always already a crowd and thus an image of the market. Smith opposes unity in the crowd to the crowd within unity. This opposition fits into a pattern I have already noted. Because the market is represented as a woman, women cannot occupy the position of observing the market. Otherwise, the distinction between observer and market would collapse, and the market could no longer be described as an emergent system.

Viewing the market as a woman had consequences for the relationship between investors and the market. Smith cites a conversation he had with the legendary investor "Mr. Johnson":[23]

> The market . . . is like a beautiful woman—endlessly fascinating, endlessly complex, always changing, always mystifying. . . . I know this is no science. It is an art. Now we have computers and all sorts of statistics, but the market is still the same and understanding the market is still no easier. It is personal intuition, sensing patterns of behavior. There is always something unknown, undiscerned. (Smith 1967, 20)

Mr. Johnson characterized the market as a woman precisely because it was opaque and because it resisted comprehension by rational means.

The feminine discourse of the market described everything the rational subject had to repress or avoid: passions, volatility, irrationality, and the power to seduce. (Lefèvre tells of a female speculator who "wished to make some money all by herself, and womanlike dramatised the temptation so attractively that it was irresistible.")[24] This description, however, destabilized the heterosexual matrix by which inclusion in the market was structured. The masculine observer was not only fascinated by the market as woman. To understand the market as woman, he had to develop *intuition*, a talent repeatedly criticized as a genuinely feminine characteristic.

Cases in which women succeeded at speculation were often attributed to female intuition for the market. How uncanny this intuition appeared to contemporaries is evident in the way successful women speculators were associated with the realm of the occult. As the nicknames given women brokers suggest, these women were seen to have supernatural powers. The Claflin sisters were called "bewitching brokers"; Victoria was even described as "Miss Satan," and Hetty Green, probably the most famous woman speculator in America, was known as the "Witch of Wall Street" (Chancellor 1999, 167–68; Sparkes and Moore 1930). The witch metaphor helped explain the otherwise inexplicable success of women speculators. These women succeeded only by irrational means.[25]

The outside to the inclusionary figure of the male speculator was thus an outside and inside at the same time. Although the speculating woman was constitutively exterior to the male speculator, she was also a constituent of the "internal environment" (Luhmann) of the financial system: a market that the participants constructed by their own observations. The speculator was thus, also for Smith, an observer—an observer of the market who ultimately always had to be a good observer of women. This observer had to recognize the signs, such as a movement of the hand, by which she betrayed her deceptiveness. Only the well-versed speculator could properly read the market, the crowd, and women.[26]

4. The Market as Chance

To this point, I have suggested that the similarity between the market and the impossible position of women speculators was seen as a constant danger to the distinction between speculator and market. However, this similarity was also enthusiastically received by some writers, who asked whether this close-ness demonstrated that women were particularly suited to the position of the speculator.

Writing in the 1870s, William Fowler argued that since both the market and women were driven by hopes, they were thus suited to each other. The thrill of speculation could be compared to the nervous energy displayed by women: "Speculation derives its food from excitement, and women often feed on excitement. Speculation comes from fancy, and women are much given to fancy," he asserted. "There are no more eager and venturesome gamblers at [the world-famous Casino in] Baden Baden, in Germany, than women, and there are no more eager and venturesome speculators in stocks, than women."[27] Nonetheless, speculation by women remained, as described above, a travesty. Women were typically infected with a desire to speculate by men, and speculated as men. Women might have an affinity to the market, but they had to pose as men to become individualized speculators.

Fowler expressed his appreciation for a club of women speculators in Saratoga whose members did not lose their nerve when stock prices rapidly fell: "Instead of going into hysterics or sitting down and have a good cry, they went manfully, or rather womanfully, to work and raised money" (Fowler 1968 [1880], 451). The role of the female speculator was cause for confusion. Women speculators did not immediately act like hysterics, but like men—a confusion Fowler tried to correct by emphasizing that the women behaved "womanfully" rather than "manfully." The identity of the woman speculator remained unstable, and gave way to crisis when women speculators reacted to the market as a crowd: "One can easily imagine the effect produced by several hundred women interested in stocks, being present at a panic and giving way with feminine impulsiveness to the feelings of the hour" (456). The impulsive-ness of women speculators mirrored the impulsiveness of the market. Fowler struggled to reconcile two nearly irreconcilable premises. On the one hand, women resembled the market and thus had a natural talent for speculation. On the other hand, women lacked distance from the market and thus specu-lated with the same degree of irrationality that the market itself displayed. This lack of distance was particularly evident in the way women speculators identified with their stocks, and even called these stocks their "loves" (451).[28] Women speculators thus displayed the fatal lack of discipline noted in the pre-vious chapter. The ideal speculator was not supposed to identify with external objects. The metaphor of the hysterical female speculator was the feminized version of the failed male speculator—a speculator who was no longer able to exercise self-control. This failed speculator threatened to become an indistinguishable element of the deindividualized and hysterical crowd.

The extent to which the position of women speculators was controversial can be seen in investment guides and other writings on the market addressed to a professional audience of female speculators, and often written by women. These writings, in line with the emancipatory discourse of Victoria Woodhull, viewed the market as a potential source of empowerment for women. While writing the articles on the plight of the London poor collected in her book *The Soul Market* (1907), the Anglo-Indian journalist and performer Olive Malvery became interested in the way the stock market functioned. She appears to have shared the belief, held by many male authors, that women were largely unsuited for speculation, but she differed from these male authors in an important way. An author like Clews argued that, from an anthropological point of view, women were unsuited for speculation. Malvery maintained instead in a 1906 article titled "Women and the Money Market" that a better "business education" would create "enormous possibilities for women in the financial world" (Malvery 1906, 43).

Malvery is particularly interesting in our context not only because she viewed the inclusion of women in speculation as emancipatory, but also because she addressed the aversion women displayed for the stock market as dull. Rather than studying columns of stock prices, women occupied themselves with designing ornaments and with other luxurious pleasures. However, Malvery asserted that speculation could be a pleasant recreation, as enjoyable as it was useful: "There is a most astonishing interest in financial matters, which no woman can possibly realise till she has dealt with them personally" (44):

My own conviction is that if women, instead of learning to play the piano very badly, and insulting Nature with paintings which have no excuse for existence, would study commercial and financial affairs, they would find their power and influence increase thousandfold. . . . There is extraordinary pleasure to be derived from seeing your tiny capital grow pound by pound. . . . A woman who has once tasted of the sweetness of this experience will find more excitement and joy in reading the financial columns in her daily paper and her evening journal, and watching the fluctuations of the money markets, than she would in gossiping with her neighbours and wasting her time looking enviously into shop windows at things which she cannot, or ought not to, afford to buy. (45)

In this passage, the classical demand for inclusion was extended to include the pleasure of speculation—a pleasure that, for women, was superior to other kinds of entertainment. Speculation was thus represented as a popular form of communication that connected the demand for inclusion to the pleasure of inclusion.[29]

Discourses of emancipation were also prevalent in the United States shortly before the 1929 stock market crash.[30] Eunice Fuller Barnard maintained that an increasingly large number of women took part in speculation. Barnard estimated that a few companies, and a third of all stocks, were owned by women (Barnard 1929, 406). Like Malvery, Barnard argued that women lacked the proper knowledge of speculation. However, Barnard also believed that women were eager to learn about the market. She noted the common impression that women had a "maternal attitude . . . toward their stock investments," and thus overwhelmed stockbrokers with questions (410). Aside from this maternal attitude, Barnard observed no differences between male and female speculators. Speculation was a one-time chance for women: "If they become intelligent players, and if to any extent they should win financial power, they would probably in our economic society, as a matter of pragmatic fact, do more to raise the level of the common respect for women as a class than all the hard-fought suffrage campaigns" (410). Inclusion in speculation made it possible that a time would come when women "financially became people" (406). Barnard foregrounded the argument that speculation gave women a chance to become visible as individuals within speculation, and thus gave them a chance for emancipation. This classical argument for emancipation focused not on the pleasure women could experience as speculators, but on the opportunities they could win from inclusion in the financial world. For Barnard, once women speculators had gained the right knowledge, they would be indistinguishable from male speculators.

Neither Malvery nor Barnard saw male and female speculators as fundamentally different. The only disadvantage facing women speculators was that they had been included late in finance, and thus lacked knowledge of the market. However, other writers referred to the advantage female speculators had over male speculators. This advantage was linked to characteristics that had feminine connotations. In a 1931 investment guide written for women, Hazel

Zimmerman emphasized the role intuition played in speculation: "Intuition . . . when it is developed by consistent use and strengthened by a knowledge of facts . . . is a woman's most valuable asset. It becomes, in its developed stage, a market sense which men will tell you they have long envied."[31] As we have seen above, intuition was promoted from time to time as a virtue for speculators in investment guides for men. However, intuition could only play a prominent role once discourses on speculation were coded in gender-specific terms. Efforts to establish women as legitimate, talented speculators relied on the same discourse used to exclude women from speculation. The emphasis on intuition to establish a legitimate position as a speculator proved to be an effective tactic, since "intuition" was a highly contested concept. Unlike other characteristics seen as feminine, such as impressionability or hysteria, intuition was highly ambivalent. Intuition tried to grasp the moment that distinguished the talented investor from the merely industrious investor. Zimmerman's investment guide praised intuition as one of the seven virtues for speculation—and thus distinguished itself from investment guides written for men. However, this guide also recognized the danger of intuition. To avert this danger, Zimmerman subjected intuition to a strategy of rational control. The woman speculator had to use intuition consistently and temper intuition with factual knowledge. On the same page on which women were advised to use intuition, Zimmerman was careful to maintain that"[t]here is no place for sentiment in investment" (Zimmerman 1931, 15). However, Zimmerman did not ask to what extent intuition was guided by emotion.

This chapter has followed two premises. The first is that the relation between speculator and market is one of observation. The second is that this relation of observation was coded in gender-specific terms. This premise has led me to ask how a gender-specific code emerged, and what function gender-specific language had.

It is striking that feminized metaphors and allegories were not used to represent a specific subject position, but to represent elusive abstractions of speculation and credit. Only these abstractions were represented as genuinely feminine by the enigmatic figures of Cynthia Speculation and Lady Credit. Feminine metaphors, used as finance became increasingly differentiated, had the advantage of being strongly linked to contingency. Women were portrayed as volatile and irrational, and as having the power to seduce, all of which also applied to the stock market. Speculation did not obey rational laws. Rather, it was a social realm that appeared to be based on fictionality, and that constantly surprised its actors by changing inexplicably. Discourse connoting that the market was feminine succeeded because it offered ways of describing contingency.

However, this description of the market did not mean that finance became a privileged realm for women. Although an increasing number of female speculators appeared, economic theorists saw finance as the preserve of *homo oeconomicus*, gendered as male, although obliged to refer to a constitutive feminized exterior in order to function. The speculator had to develop techniques to encounter a volatile market with composure and allow himself to be seduced by it only to the extent that it was in his interest to do so. An erotic, gendered discourse structured the relation between market and individual speculator.

This highly gendered and sexualized relation between speculator and market had important consequences for the position women occupied as speculators. Popular texts on the stock exchange written before 1900 reasoned that the woman speculator was an absurdity. The invective against women speculators cannot be attributed to the misogyny of individual authors (although it certainly existed), but has to be seen as part of the constraints structuring a gender-specific inclusionary apparatus. In addition to creating unwelcome competitors for men, the inclusion of women in finance endangered the organization of the market. Women speculators threatened the distinction between the market as an object of observation, and the speculator as observing subject. Or rather, what was at stake was the *distance* that first made this distinction possible. The epistemology of the market thus immediately became a problem of communication in finance. If women could occupy the position of speculator, then speculation and speculator—or game and gambler—threatened to become indistinguishable. A gendered inclusionary apparatus provided an extremely sensitive arrangement within which the market first became readable. The woman speculator marked the imaginary collapse of the observational order within which the speculator was constructed in 1900.

Woodhull understood the political and strategic significance of the fact that this inclusionary structure was fragile. The existence of women speculators was even more unthinkable than the existence of women voters. Precisely for this reason, women founding a brokerage was an immense provocation. Woodhull began a countermovement against the heterosexual code by which inclusion in finance was organized. When the limited universalism of market discourse became apparent, women became thinkable as market subjects. Inclusion in speculation thus also became a political opportunity linked to a new economic identity. At the same time, the discourse of seduction became more intense, and could thus be used to comprehend the irrationality of the market—an irrationality located in the speculator's affective "attachment" to the process of inclusion. The heterosexual discourse of seduction and mastery suggested that the speculator's relation to the market could be controlled, a notion Woodhull and Claflin parodied to great public effect. The sisters staged inclusion as a pleasurable act and celebrated the pleasure of inclusion by playing with gender identities. In this carnivalesque celebration of inclusion, crossing boundaries between the audience and its outside gained a uniquely spectacular potential. We are again confronted with the logic of the popular: the process of establishing boundaries between an audience and its outside, which in this case took a particularly interesting form. On the one hand, it became obvious that the construction of the audience was based on a gendered order of observation. On the other hand, this outside (as was already the case for the contrarians) was an internal outside. The feminine represented not the absolutely uneconomic as an outside, but rather those aspects of the economy that were difficult to grasp for the established vocabularies, aspects such as the ephemeral and hysterical economic force of speculation.

Three possible forms of inclusionary politics arose from this configuration of the popular of the economy. First, *a classical discourse of emancipation*, represented by Barnard (1929), saw an opportunity to make women visible by including them in finance. This position tried to integrate itself into the existing arrangement of gendered inclusion and took no interest in the verbal construction of the speculator. From our perspective, the next two positions are of greater interest. These positions tried to rearticulate existing inclusionary relations by paying close attention to the popular structure of these relations. The *spectacular travesty* staged by Woodhull celebrated the pleasure of speculation. Malvery knew that the arrangement of inclusion in finance was in itself not appealing to women. She thus imagined speculation as a pleasurable and entertaining practice that was also useful, and that women could justify to their husbands. A third strategy was introduced by Fowler and Zimmerman, who saw a particular *chance for speculation* in the proximity between women and the feminine discourse of the market. Proximity to the market, according to this argument, also increased the chances of understanding the market. Fowler and Zimmerman differed clearly in the way they understood these chances. Fowler saw proximity to the market primarily as a danger, because women lacked the necessary individuality. This danger also existed for Zimmerman, but she hoped to articulate classical male techniques of individualization with female intuition, which made the market more understandable.

Classical emancipation, spectacular travesty, and *tactical rearticulation* designate the three possible ways in which the politics of a gendered inclusionary apparatus were elaborated. The latter two positions displayed a common awareness that the classical figure of the speculator was fragile and based their tactics on this precarious status. They can hardly be understood without the logic of the popular, since they did not simply view relations of inclusion as a question of access. Rather these rearticulations asked how an established audience, once constructed, related to its outside, and how inclusion became attractive.

Part III

Media

CHAPTER 7

THE RHYTHM OF THE MARKET

Oh, the ticker, oh, the ticker,
How it makes me long to dicker
With the fascinating tape.
Oh, the ticker, oh, the ticker,
How I yearn to get rich quicker,
And from penury escape.
Oh, the ticker, oh, the ticker,
How it sometimes makes me sicker
Than a dope-bewildered ape.
Oh, the ticker, oh, the ticker,
How it makes my wise friends snicker
When they see me wear the crape.
Oh, the ticker, oh, the ticker,
How my senses reel and flicker
When it hits me in the nape.
Oh, the ticker, oh, the ticker,
When it makes the coin come thicker
How I glow and grasp and gape.
Oh, the ticker, oh, the ticker,
How my jaded nerves get slicker
When I'm winner on the tape.

—Susie M. Best, "A Song of the Ticker" (1910)

In the 1860s, dense, noisy crowds often gathered at the New York Gold Exchange, where the messengers of brokerage firms fought their way through a mob of speculators to get the latest quotations.[1] To help control these crowds, the manager of the Gold Exchange, Samuel Spahr Laws (1824–1921), devised the Laws Gold Indicator, a forerunner of the ticket-tape

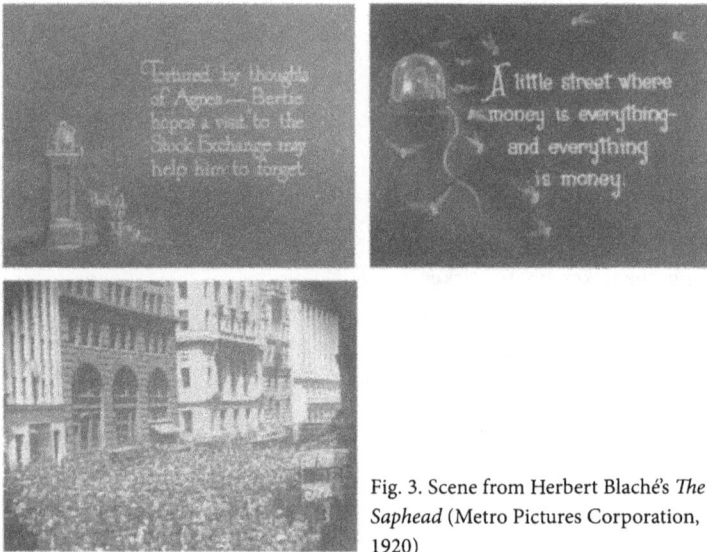

Fig. 3. Scene from Herbert Blaché's *The Saphead* (Metro Pictures Corporation, 1920)

machine, which used large numbers to display the current price of gold. One side of the Gold Indicator faced the street, while the other side was only visible to the traders in the Gold Exchange (Standage 1998, 174; Oslin 1999, 192). Although professional and lay audiences were kept apart spatially, they had access to the same information. However, this technical solution was only partially successful, since the Gold Indicator pushed the noise and disorder of the crowd from the Gold Exchange to the surrounding streets, and thus simply shifted the problem.

In the spring of 1867, E. A. Calahan (1838–1912), the telegraphist who invented the first ticker-tape machine, sought shelter from the rain under the entrance to the Gold Exchange, but found it "a most undesirable refuge. . . . I was simply whirled into the street [by the crowd]" (Calahan 1901, 256). "I naturally thought that much of this noise and confusion might be dispensed with and that the prices might be furnished through some system of telegraphy which would not require the employment of skilled operators" (256), thus avoiding "the congestion of business . . . largely caused by the brokers and their clerks struggling to secure the latest quotations made on the floor" (Calahan cited in Hotchkiss 1965 [1905], 433).

The ticker-tape machine promised to make information about the stock exchange independent of the location at which transactions took place, thus

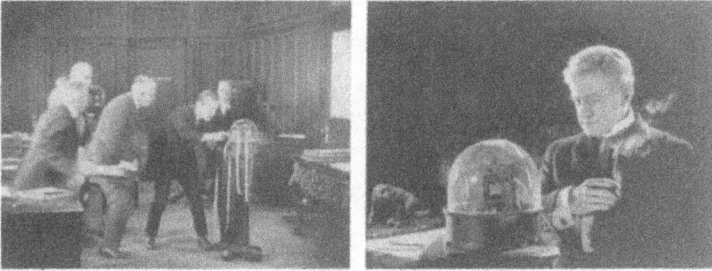

Fig. 4. Scene from Herbert Blaché's *The Saphead* (Metro Pictures Corporation, 1920)

bypassing the "congestion of business" that arose with crowds. Of course, the ticker—which owed its name to the noise it made—could by no means be described as a quiet device. Calahan was not too happy about this name: "The name 'ticker' was given to this instrument by a lounger in a broker's office and for some reason was adopted by the public. The different companies advertising their 'tickers' in the windows of barrooms and restaurants served to endorse this *meaningless* and *most inappropriate* name" (Calahan 1901, 236; emphasis added).

Not least because of its decorativeness, the ticker-tape machine became a symbol of speculation. In Herbert Blaché's silent film *The Saphead* (1920), a ticker not only adorns the intertitles, but plays an important role in the opening scenes, which stage a contrast between the ticker and crowds on the street. The camera shifts from a scene of Wall Street filled with crowds to the office of the tycoon Nicholas Van Alstyne. A glimpse into Van Alstyne's office reveals a ticker enthroned on its own podium. The difference between these two worlds is highlighted by the position of the camera. The crowd on the street is filmed from a bird's-eye view, while the office scene focuses more closely on individual faces and on the ticker (figs. 3 and 4).

In these scenes from the movie, the economic subject appears to be formed by overcoming the disorderly crowd (although a reference to the latter can perhaps be detected in the entanglement of the ticker tape on the floor of Van Alstyne's office). A 1937 cover of *Fortune* magazine (fig. 5) would translate the ticker tape into a decorative ornamental structure.

The ticker was conceptualized in contrast to the crowd and associated with the individualized capitalist financier, making it appear to be exclusively the medium of a small financial elite. However, the ticker quickly became popular

Fig. 5. Antonio Petrucelli, *Fortune* cover, June 1937

and could be found in any brokerage firm or bucket shop. It continued what the two-sided display of the Gold Indicator had started. On the one hand, the ticker became an accessory required by the financial elite and by the economic system. On the other hand, it became a medium popularizing speculation outside the stock exchange.

This doubling will structure the course of my argument. After situating the ticker, in theoretical terms as a medium of dissemination (7.1), I briefly outline a history of the ticker (7.2). I then attend to the "inner function" the ticker had for the economic system, a function already present in Calahan's dream of a disembodied and rapid transfer of information (7.3). However, the ticker was not only an instrument used to increase efficiency and inclusion, but an object that drew a considerable amount of public attention. The ticker fascinated novice speculators (7.4).

I. Media of Dissemination and Mediality

Media of dissemination make communication largely independent of contexts of interaction and create, within a system, an anonymous audience not restricted to physical co-presence (Luhmann 1997a, 202ff.). Although it only implicitly addresses the role of media in a theory of inclusion, Luhmann's account highlights the significance media of dissemination have within processes of differentiation: "Media of dissemination determine and extend the circle of recipients for a piece of information" (202).[2] By promoting the universalization of the public, media of dissemination thus play a significant role for the popular. Social strata previously excluded from the stock market can be reached and potentially included. The size and universality of the public are seen as capable of being increased, implying a nonaudience that can only be transformed into an audience by the use of a new medium.

Stock traders' clubs and other such organizations were spatially located and closed to a large number of people (Welles 1975), for whom the "magical" ticker-tape machine opened up a previously exclusive social realm (Sobel 1977, 30). My thesis is based on the premise that the ticker, as a medium of dissemination, not only increased the *chances* of being included in stock exchange communication, but also shaped *modes of inclusion* by drawing attention to itself as a medium.[3]

The concept of inclusion and exclusion in systems theory will be my starting point for analyzing the role media of dissemination play in processes of inclusion (Luhmann 1997a; Stichweh 1988, 1997). Particularly fruitful for such an analysis is the theory of communication on which this concept of inclusion and exclusion is based. Inclusion takes for granted that one can be observed in terms of the distinction between information and utterance, and thus be addressed (Stichweh 1997, 1, 11). Only those who can be envisioned as the addressees of information and utterance can be included. Observers always use specific media of dissemination and these media structure in advance the group considered as potentially to be included. To be included means having access to the corresponding media of dissemination, and having the corresponding competence to use these media. Functional systems construct addresses specific to a system and oriented toward the rationality of that system. Moreover, these systems also construct a "media subject" marked by its relationship to a particular medium of dissemination (whether a reader of scientific publications, an observer of fine art, or a voter who fills out a ballot).[4]

Media of dissemination allow functional systems to detach their mode of inclusion from the criterion of simultaneous spatial presence characterizing systems of interaction, and instead to regulate inclusion primarily by means of competences specific to functional systems. In this sense, media of dissemination promote, by mostly invisible means, the differentiation of functional systems. However, these media not only passively enable such processes of differentiation, but also come into the foreground themselves. What does it mean for processes of inclusion when the normally invisible medium of dissemination loses its auxiliary role and acts as a medium with its own logic? What happens when the bibliophile takes an interest in the typography of a publication even before examining its contents, or when the possibility of electronic payment media becomes more exciting than the payment function of these media?[5] Could the fact that these media are observed *as media* even become a stimulus (or deterrent) for inclusion not necessarily in line with functional differentiation?

We can understand the role of these media for processes of inclusion if we distinguish between the way the aspect of *information* is related to the aspect of utterance. There are at least two types of this relation relevant to a theory of inclusion: *accessibility* and *mediality*. If the aspect of *accessibility* is foregrounded, questions arise as to what information is accessible, and as to the people for whom this information is—or should be—accessible. At stake in these questions is whether media of dissemination create new chances of inclusion, and for whom such chances arise. My analysis will show that the ticker-tape machine was described around the time of its invention as a medium that increased accessibility to current information about the stock market. This accessibility eliminated the need to be physically present in the stock exchange in order to be included in speculation. The medium was thus represented as a *means* of efficiently disseminating economic information, and of making speculation accessible to an anonymous public. Accessibility thus means that information becomes redundant—that is, information is simultaneously accessible at several locations and thus reaches an anonymous public.[6]

If the aspect of *mediality* is foregrounded, it does not matter *that* information become accessible to an addressee. Instead, what matters is *how* this information becomes accessible. While the medium previously remained invisible, it now comes to the foreground by virtue of its own logic. Beyond the task of efficiently spreading information, the medium of dissemination becomes interesting on its own terms. This relation, when compared to the model of accessibility, decisively weakens the dimension of information in favor of communication. Access to information is no longer as important as the relationship to media of dissemination, and as the visibility of these media.[7] What the notion of mediality refers to is precisely the mode in which the medium becomes visible and intervenes. Such an approach draws from German media theory that accounts for mediality as something that goes beyond classical notions of means and end; mediality is the a priori that precedes, but simultaneously interferes with, the capacity for transmission (Gumbrecht and Pfeiffer 1988; Tholen 1999, 2002).[8] My analysis will ask in what ways the ticker communicated current stock quotations, and what traces the medium left in this process of communication. In early allusions to the ticker, *mediality* was an important topos for describing the ways in which it became a medium capable of attracting inclusion. Mediality played an important role for the popular by allowing the economy to be seen and experienced in a noneconomic way by a lay audience. These experiences were possible because economic operations could now be translated into the rhythm of the ticker—a rhythm accessible to everyone.

The two roles media of dissemination played for processes of inclusion link two questions often analyzed separately, and assigned to separate disciplines. The problem of the communicability and accessibility of information is an object of classical media sociology and communication studies. By contrast, modes of communication and mediality are often problems in media theory and cultural studies. In what follows, I indicate how problems in both surfaced apropos of the ticker, and how these problems were in turn linked to each other. Both dimensions maintain a strong connection to the thesis that media of dissemination both constitute functional systems and structure a public. The expansion of media technologies, and the resulting increase in chances for access, universalized and generalized the stock-trading public. Access to information about the stock exchange was, in principle, no longer restricted to membership in an organization (the stock exchange) or by criteria foreign to the functional system. The dimension of mediality emphasizes, however, that the specific ways in which a medium functioned in the process of communication left nonfunctional "traces" that were viewed as relevant to inclusion.

2. The Ticker as Telegraph and Printer

As we have seen, in 1867, E. A. Calahan developed the first ticker-tape machine that would make current stock quotations accessible outside the stock exchange (Calahan 1901; Hotchkiss 1965; Dyer and Martin 1929; Oslin 1999; Preda 2003). "A stock ticker is a mechanical device which prints on a tape stock quotations as they are sent over the telegraph wires from the Stock Exchange," Charles A. Dice noted in a widely read book (1926, 50). It thus combined two existing media of dissemination: printing and telegraphy.[9]

Telegraphy first made it possible to send messages electronically, and thus independently of established "physical" carriers such as messengers and railroads. A worldwide telegraph communication network was established, allowing communication with even the most distant points to take place in real time. Not without reason, telegraphy has been called the "Victorian Internet" (Standage 1998). Telegraphy already displayed a few of the basic features of the Internet, inasmuch as it was an interactive medium that shaped a worldwide communicative network. A "revolution in communication" accompanied telegraphy. Spatial boundaries became increasingly irrelevant once communication was freed from its physical substrate. The telegraph opened up possibilities for communication that had not previously been thinkable and proved to be of great importance for the establishment of global functional systems. It was seen as a medium of "universal communication" that would lead to a "communion" of societies worldwide.[10]

Beginning in the middle of the nineteenth century, telegraphy allowed current prices on the New York Stock Exchange to be shared with smaller stock exchanges without a noticeable delay. Most important, the stock exchanges in New York and Philadelphia were linked. Local variations in price were increasingly eliminated. This early form of communicating prices by telegraph required that the addressee be determined precisely. Like communication by letter, telegraphy was a form of *point-to-point* communication that required addresses for both sender and receiver. With the stock ticker, the structure of this communication changed. *Point-to-point* communication was replaced by an indeterminate, and ultimately anonymous, circle of addressees.[11] By mechanically replicating information, the stock ticker became one of the first real-time mass media.

The stock ticker was a machine with two cylinders for printing current stock quotations attached to a telegraph network (fig. 6).[12] One cylinder printed letters on a strip of tape and the other printed numbers. Separate

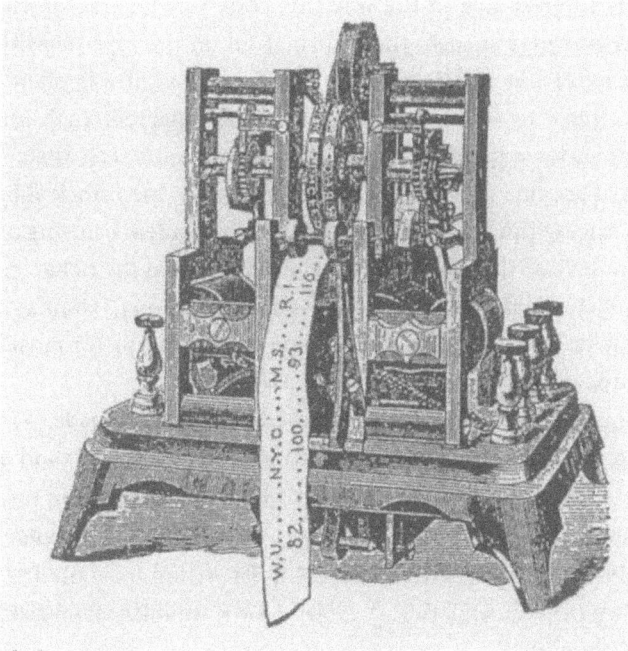

Fig. 6. Edward Calahan's stock ticker (1901, 237)

wires powered each cylinder, while a third wire powered the mechanism used for "inking the wheels" and for feeding the tape (Calahan 1901, 236).[13]

Figure 6 shows a roll of printed tape emerging from the ticker. Stocks were identified by an abbreviation at most three letters in length, under which the price was listed. Normally, a hundred shares of a given stock were bundled and sold together. In later models, when several hundred shares of a stock were sold, a corresponding number was placed before the abbreviation. The ticker communicated prices in a way that led speculation to become highly standardized. Every communication of price was an event that combined the abbreviation for a stock, the price of the stock, and the volume traded. The restrictive code used for standardization, however, by no means excluded a variety of meanings, as a frequently cited saying by a Boston speculator reveals: "The letters and figures used in the language of the tape . . . are very few, but they spell ruin in ninety-nine million ways" (Dyer and Marin 1929, 1).

The communication disseminated by the ticker relied on a standardized code, and was thus extremely susceptible to technical interference, particularly interference in the way this code was written on the tape. In contrast to everyday speech, the information on the tape had little redundancy. If a letter was missing or not clearly printed, it was often no longer possible to know to which stock a given price referred. Such interference became a long-term problem, since early tickers often lost their "rhythm." As a result, it became difficult or even impossible to map stock abbreviations to current prices. Thomas Edison resolved this problem by using a mechanical "unison device" that ensured that the cylinders in the ticker would print simultaneously (Hotchkiss 1965, 435, Oslin 1999, 193, Thomas 1989, 74). This quickly proved a success and became the prototype for most later tickers (Oslin 1999, 193).

From the time the ticker was introduced, efforts were made to improve its capacities to print and transmit information. The first ticker could only strike the tape 210 times per minute and thus inevitably fell behind on reporting current stock prices when the market was very active (Oslin 1999, 314). This delay was particularly upsetting because quick action was required when the market was especially dynamic. A delay of a few minutes could cause massive losses at speculation.[14]

The ticker functioned more rapidly, not only with technical improvements, but also with more efficient organization of communication processes internal to the stock exchange (Preda 2003). The current prices at which shares of stock were being sold had to be transmitted as quickly as possible to a central "station," from which the information was broadcast to stock tickers across the United States (and later also in Europe). During the initial period when tickers were used on the New York Stock Exchange, the latest prices were collected by messenger boys and sent by telegraph to a central station at 18 New Street, from which they were transmitted to tickers across the country (Dyer and Martin 1929, 6). Subsequently, efforts were made to reduce these delays by organizing the channels of communication within the NYSE as efficiently as possible. The central station was also moved to a location within the exchange. George Leffler describes how the channels of communication within the exchange were made more efficient in the 1950s (Leffler 1957, 182–83). Stock exchange employees called "reporters" noted the sale prices on a small piece of paper. This paper was placed in a red wooden container (a "widget") and sent through pneumatic tubes to the "ticker traffic room" on the fifth floor of the NYSE. The newly arrived reports were examined and placed on a conveyor belt. A telegraph operator then typed the new prices, and thus set the procedure for a "mechanical transmission" in motion. Only at this point did the prices appear on the ticker tape. In the 1950s, this process created delays that ranged from thirty seconds to two minutes (191). On the exchange, every delay was of the greatest importance for trading and was thus indicated on "tape delay indicators."

Despite this mild delay in the transmission of current prices, the ticker fundamentally changed financial communication. It could take a long time for stock prices to appear in media such as newspapers.[15] In contrast to these media, the ticker dramatically increased the speed of written economic communication, and thus became a success—first in the United States and later in Europe.[16]

3. Inclusion and Accessibility: The Generalization of Inclusion

The ticker introduced far-reaching changes in the way media were used to speculate. These changes, however, had less to do with the device's technological sophistication than with the innovative way it used and combined existing technologies. Before the invention of the ticker, telegraphy was already in use in stock speculation, but it was given a new purpose by the ticker. Stock prices transmitted in nearly real time by telegraph were linked to the display of these prices on the ticker tape. Since this communication was *continuous*, the ticker made the financial market a phenomenon outsiders could experience in an almost "immediate" way, without being present at the stock exchange. Stock prices were reported a day late (and under constant suspicion of manipulation!) by newspapers, but occurred almost simultaneously at the variety of places where a ticker could be found. The prices reported with a delay by newspapers were useless when compared to the prices reported by the ticker (Neill 1960 [1931], 26). In what follows, I examine the three dimensions of communication based on the ticker mentioned above: real time, display, and continuity.

The ticker transformed a spatial order founded on representation into a temporally organized order founded on simultaneity.[17] Speculative communication no longer required spatial presence. This implied a crucial shift from space to time. What became important was the speed of the ticker medium, doing without the "congestions of business" which Calahan complained about. Moreover, this increase in efficiency did not come at the cost of excluding a wide audience.[18] Issues of spatial organization, such as congested entryways or streets, no longer posed communication problems that would significantly affect profits or losses in speculation. In 1922, James Meeker emphasized the "uncanny swiftness and accuracy of the American stock ticker system."[19] The speed of the ticker was particularly astonishing to visitors from foreign countries.[20]

The ticker was not only characterized by its speed, but also by the fact that this speed served to *continually represent* the market. The central position occupied by the ticker was linked to the specific structure of finance communication: "The workings of the new financial economy existed discursively, to be accessed on the page and recreated imaginatively in the mind of the investor" (Ingrassia 1998, 6). Payment operations, like the price making on the stock exchange, were largely invisible and abstract. For precisely this reason, the medium that could represent these operations and prices gained a particular significance. Only the strip of ticker tape allowed financial communication to be observed remotely. The ticker machine became the basis for global economic connectivity; interactions formerly bound to the space of a specific setting became part of a globally operating functional system. This is a necessary condition for financial markets: "All you have is a ticker tape recording market actions, and a certain number of board rooms all over the country with people watching this movement" (Smith 1967, 44). The visibility of these operations ensured that the resulting communication would be experienced as a continuous stream of information. For its contemporaries, the ticker thus became a reliable "seismograph" or "barometer" (cf. Moore 1921, 68). Everyone had access to current information on stock prices (Meeker 1922, 64).

This open access contrasted starkly with communication on the stock exchange before the telegraph was introduced, when American stock exchanges were highly exclusive and guarded their information carefully. Until the middle of the nineteenth century, for example, the Philadelphia stock exchange—the oldest exchange in the United States—imposed a strict code that forbade members to leave the building and return during trading. Anyone who even took the account books paid a double penalty. Until 1872, it was also impossible for an "outsider" to learn current prices (Duguid 1901, 218). Once differentiated from other kinds of trading conducted on the street, the stock exchange became an exclusive organization resembling a club (Welles 1975; Stringham 2002). As the conflicts over bucket shops show, a long struggle over the ownership of prices took place between 1870 and 1900 (see chapter 2.5). The main controversy between the bucket shops, stock exchanges, and communication companies was the degree to which information "produced" by the stock exchange was public. Disclosing prices posed a significant challenge to the stock exchange as an organization. The stock exchange had only become an exclusive space after a difficult struggle in which communication was detached from the disordered transactions on the streets and in coffeehouses and localized within the stock exchange building (Sobel 1970). Once caught in the expanding communication network of telegraphy, the stock exchange faced the threat of losing its own space, and thus its exclusivity. The ticker endangered the clear boundaries established by giving the stock market its own building and rules (Duguid 1901, 218). Chances to participate in stock trading now extended well beyond the exclusive space within the stock exchange—a space regulated by clear rules for membership, and by the requirement of physical presence.

Nonetheless, around 1900, handbooks on the stock exchange mostly welcomed the way in which the ticker extended the chances for inclusion beyond this exclusive space.[21] It is striking that this expanded access to finance communication was described with a political rhetoric of *democratization* that celebrated increased accessibility as a uniquely democratic achievement: "nothing could be more democratic in principle than the way the business is conducted nowadays," one commenter wrote in 1914.[22] Even the small speculator had a means of learning about current prices, and thus of making his own decisions. In this way, he became an individual speculator. The real-time display of prices offered speculators the advantage of being able to check the value of their investments at any time: "He [the stockholder] knows the price of his holdings every hour of the day. He is exposed to no fraud, and at the mercy of no rumor and unscrupulous dealer. The ticker gives him instantaneous quotations" (Van Antwerp 1914, 22). The stockholder thus became "altogether independent" (22), not least from unreliable sources of information and from deception by rumors.

This argument not only rearticulated the economy by establishing parallels to the emancipated democratic subject, but also found a positive function for "democratic speculation" beyond the individual. The medium was not only seen as an invisible means of dissemination, but also as having the effect of creating transparency. The ticker *made* the economy *more transparent*. The display of prices on the ticker tape was praised as a way of protecting speculators from the "non-economic" and "non-transparent" manipulation of prices: "The ticker is essential to publicity and offers the very protection which the Stock Exchange seeks to extend. Speculation was never so unscrupulous and wrongdoing never so abundant as in the days before this instrument was invented" (162). Van Antwerp emphasized that this rising inclusion was not a side effect, but also structured finance communication in a new way. The large number of anonymous and independent speculators made speculation more transparent, since dishonest individual financiers would have greater difficulties manipulating the market. E. H. H. Simmons argued along similar lines in a speech he gave at the Detroit Exchange. One of the strengths of the stock exchange, according to Simmons, was that transactions took place openly:

> It is one of the important functions of a stock exchange to give the fullest publicity to all the transactions which occur upon it. In this country, the perfection of the stock ticker system permits of the almost instantaneous printing of all open market transactions on the New York Stock Exchange in every part of the country. If there is anything irregular or peculiar in these transactions, the whole nation is informed of the matter at once. (Simmons 1927, 53; see also 57, 281)

The entire country became an audience of critics who could follow every transaction without delay. Transactions on the stock exchange were not tainted by secrets; manipulators had no chance to succeed. Millions of eyes watched over events on the market and ensured these events were legitimate.

To be sure, a great deal of skepticism about the ticker also existed. The loss of the stock exchange's exclusive, clublike status was mourned. Criticism was also directed at the lack of competence shown by amateur speculators. Nonetheless, most handbooks on the stock exchange quickly came to view the ticker as an essential medium for the stock market. The ticker was crucial to the promise of universal inclusion into the stock market, and it became a medium creating transparency. In this sense, ticker-based communication was fully in line with the requirements of a functionally differentiated stock market.

"Ticker friendly" discourse called for techniques of communication that would implement the universal inclusion demanded in self-descriptions of the economic system—demands not restricted by criteria external to function, such as class or gender (Harper 1966, 69; Clews 1973). This process did not unfold according to a dynamic in which unfit economic subjects were emancipated, as would be expected in a political discourse of democratization. Rather, openness already appeared to be inscribed from the beginning

in the technique of communication represented by the ticker, which extended
the audience in a way that could only be prevented by elaborate, and often
unsuccessful, efforts at regulation (such as the efforts the Chicago Board of
Trade made against the bucket shops offering it competition). Many proponents of the ticker had no disagreements with the open communication this
technology created. At most, problems might arise from the technological
shortcomings of early tickers, but not from the process of universal inclusion itself. Rather, this process was represented as conforming to a program
of functional differentiation. Moreover, establishing a "democratic" mode of
inclusion resolved problems of *impure* connections in economic communication. For example, this expanded inclusion ensured that rumor would not
be mixed with information about prices, since the ticker did not transmit
rumor.[23] Proponents of the ticker viewed manipulation of the stock market,
and other deceptive forms of speculation, as opposed to this new mode of
democratic inclusion. The "democratically open" economic system created by
the ticker would purify economic communication.

Discussion of the ticker as a means of disseminating information thus
linked three dimensions that are also important for media of digital communication existing today. The ticker increased the *speed* of financial communication, not only as a *point-to-point* medium (such as telegraphy), but
as a medium with an anonymous circle of addressees. This speed was linked
to the *continuity* of ticker communication. The market appeared as an endless stream of characters restricted by the code of the ticker. The ticker thus
closely followed the imperative of the economic system by only connecting
one payment event to another, and by not combining different types of communication. This exclusively economic connectivity was represented by the
ticker code, which was limited to stock abbreviations, volume, and price. By
restricting speed and continuity, the ticker code increased inclusion. Financial communication could now be observed anywhere (speed), not only as a
report of selected past events, but as a reliable "seismograph" of the market
(continuity). The market existed everywhere, and chances to access it thus
increased drastically. Because the ticker was fast and continuous, prices
remained current for a short time only, after which they were of purely historical interest.[24] The discourse of democratization connected the expansion
of inclusion enabled by the ticker to the claims of all-inclusiveness made by
the economic system. The exclusive boundaries of the stock exchange were
torn down, and the speculator became an abstraction. From the perspective of

ticker proponents, inclusion and information augmented each other: "democratization" was understood, not as something foreign to the financial realm, but as a genuinely economic logic that made prices more transparent and created greater liquidity.

4. Inclusion and Mediality: The Visibility of the Ticker

The history of the ticker cannot simply be reduced to a narrative of progress about the increasing differentiation of the economic system. The ticker was not only a medium of *dissemination* that relayed information more efficiently than older media, but was also a *medium* of dissemination that itself came to the foreground. The history of the ticker illustrates how a device used to disseminate information became visible and began to fascinate observers. Once observed as a spectacular mode of communication, the ticker became interesting to a non-economic audience. In the previous section, ticker communication was viewed from the perspective of accessibility, which implied the construction of a rational addressee capable of processing information. However, if one focuses on the medium, it becomes important to ask how the addressee is affected by the means ofutterance.[25] This perspective, in turn, implies the construction of an addressee who, as a subject, was fascinated by the medium of dissemination. In fact, fascination can become so intense that the subject faces the danger of being drawn in by the medium. The ticker was by no means a neutral medium, but instead generated a spectacle of its own. When "dematerialized" ticker communication replaced physical interaction (i.e., the transmission of new prices by messengers), this transformation was treated as a sensational event and attracted a great deal of public attention. Early reports of the ticker tape even reverted to the vocabulary of conjuring up spirits in order to grasp the unfamiliar and nearly incomprehensible visibility of stock prices. Thus, precisely the ability to make the transmission of prices invisible became spectacular.

The prices that appeared, disembodied, on the tape were observed by a crowd gathered around the ticker (Hotchkiss 1965, 433). In a report based on his experiences as a stock messenger, Charlie Tilghman described the reaction to the first ticker-tape machine in Cincinnati in 1871. Once it was set up, "bankers, brokers, and business men were invited to see the *new wonder* of printing by electricity. A crowd came and I operated the transmitter, sending out stock quotations. It created quite a lot of *excitement* and talk" (Tilghman 1961; emphasis added). Attention was not only directed toward the information transmitted by the medium, but toward the functioning and possibilities of the medium itself.[26] Fascination with the stock market was derived, above all, from the experience of a new medium.

The ticker facilitated inclusion by eliminating the spatial restraints on financial communication and by democratizing access to the market. However, the public became interested not only in the information the ticker disseminated, but in the ticker as a material device. The ticker, *as* a medium of dissemination, increased inclusion. Sources from the early twentieth century describe the ticker as a medium that "advertised" for the stock exchange:

> One of the most powerful stimuli to stock market gambling on the part of the outside public is the *easy and pleasant access* to the market provided by the stock ticker and the comfortable board rooms of brokerage houses. . . . The feverish and exciting atmosphere *created by these devices* . . . kindles and magnifies the urge for gambling. In addition, the best *advertising medium* which the pool operator has . . . is the ticker. (Clark Evans [1934] cited by Cowing 1965, 124–25; emphasis added)

The means of utterance specific to the ticker also caught the attention of Europeans who observed the stock exchanges in America—perhaps because the ticker was introduced in Europe later than in the United States. The German economist Adolf Weber explicitly attributed Americans' enthusiasm for speculation to the ticker. A culture of competition existed in the United States, but it was also important to observe "*the way in which prices are shared with the public.* . . . This continuous public quotation of prices often causes new orders to be relayed practically from the street to the stock exchange during its operation."[27] Like Clark Evans, Richard Lewinsohn and Franz Pick saw the ticker as encouraging the public at large to gamble on the stock market: "To a greater extent than the press and the radio, the mechanical and textless coverage of the stock exchange, widespread only in America, advertises for gambling. . . . When the stock exchange is open, the ticker makes America into an enormous gambling hall" (Lewinsohn and Pick 1933, 82).

The ticker made it evident that inclusion did not only presuppose media of dissemination working in the background. Observing the means by which these media of dissemination communicated increased inclusion.[28] The ticker created a "feverish atmosphere" (Evans) and thus had an effect that went beyond simply increasing the possibilities for access. Reports of the excitement on the stock exchange not only described this atmosphere, but performatively established it. This effect did not primarily arise from the uttered information, but from the means of utterance. The ticker was not only a tech-nological means of disseminating current stock prices with greater speed. Rather, fascination with the ticker was directed toward the fact that it was *possible* to disseminate information with such great speed: "The speed of the ticker *in itself* stimulates a desire to speculate."[29]

The significance of this fascination to a theory of inclusion is particu-larly evident in documents that relate the encounters novices have with the medium of the ticker. These documents reveal that the ticker and the ticker tape generated attention not least by disseminating *unintelligible* informa-tion. Because it was impossible to decipher information about the stock market, novices focused purely on the symbols, endless strips of tape, and fading noise produced by the ticker. The figure of the novice allowed many introductions to the stock exchange to describe, in a deliberately one-sided way, stock market communication as based on the ticker. These descriptions focused on the relationship between the media apparatus and the newcomer to the market:

> On entering he immediately finds himself in a large room filled with the noise of ringing telephones and clicking telegraph instruments. Small groups of men are watching a large blackboard covering a whole side of the room. A ticker in the center near the blackboard is printing symbols on a narrow tape that is eagerly watched by one or two young men who write quotations upon the board. . . . Some men in the room seem quite excited, others are calm; many men are smoking; some are reading the day's telegrams on a bulletin board. . . . The whole thing is a *mystery, a confusion, unintelligible.* (Dice 1926; emphasis added)

Initiation to stock exchange communication is thus presented as a *multimedia* event. The newcomer was confronted by a media network ranging from the well-known technology of writing on the blackboard to the telephone and stock ticker.[30] These media were not only a visual spectacle, but were also audible. The ringing telephone and the endless clattering of the ticker filled the room.

For the novice, encountering the stock ticker was thus mysterious. The ticker was not only a new medium, but also confronted the novice, as an observer, with accompanying processes of individualization. The novice did not understand the information relayed by the ticker, but could observe others who presumably understood this information. The uninitiated, on the other hand, could only observe meaningless symbols: "[T]he tape means little—it

Fig. 7. The stock ticker in its glass case

is simply a confusion of hieroglyphics and figures" (Neill 1960 [1931], 8). The newcomer who was to be included to this communication found his situation paradoxical. He could observe that the attention of other speculators was drawn to a variety of media, but he could not know what meaning processes were taking place. Based on the tense atmosphere in the ticker room, the novice expected a high concentration of meaning, but only encountered the noise produced by different media. The novice experienced the boundaries between inclusion and exclusion, and thus also experienced an intermediate stage in the process of individualization.

The newcomer could not be seduced to inclusion by meaningful stock exchange communication, since, in this case, he would already have had to be included in the system.[31] Rather, a moment arose that was logically prior to, but could only be described in terms of, meaning. This moment surfaced with the noise made by the medium of utterance.[32] The rhythm of the ticker highlighted the mediality of a medium used to communicate meaning—a mediality that had a fascinating, but at times irritating, effect. The noise made by the medium of the ticker was not only called to mind by its name, but also by its design. To dampen the noise it made, the ticker was often covered by a glass case (see fig. 7). Covering the ticker in this way had the effect of staging it as an exhibition of its mediality.

The process of inclusion itself gradually created a distance from this moment of fascination that preceded meaning. The meaning of the confused symbols eventually came to be grasped, and the attention dedicated in this way to the medium was replaced by understanding, in the sense Luhmann gives this term. Luhmann's concept of understanding has a formal structure that prevents excessive hermeneutic demands from being placed on the novice. The correct meaning does not have to be understood, but *a* distinction has to be made between information and utterance (Luhmann 1995). This presupposes that such a distinction between noisy utterance and information can be drawn. Making this distinction required generating a level of attention and fascination that led (or seduced) the novice to distinguish between information and utterance. The world of the ticker room, described by Dice as unintelligible *confusion*, became distinguishable over the course of the inclusionary process. Precisely the capacity to make distinctions helped slowly to resolve the mysteries of the communication taking place in the ticker room: "But after he has made a few visits the confused whole begins to fall into its parts."[33] Confusion was replaced by the act of making distinctions, an act that led to the creation of meaning. Once understanding arose, however, the noise made by the medium did not entirely disappear. This noise itself continued to be decoded. Even speculators who had successfully been included established a particular relationship to the medium. Stories were told of speculators who, before looking at the ticker tape, deduced current market tendencies simply from the noise the ticker made: "[W]hen the market was breaking he could tell it with his eyes closed just by listening to the ticker" (Schwed 1940, 157). The rising and falling sounds of the ticker—sounds with their own beat and volume—acted as indicators of the current situation on the market. The rhythm of the ticker not only linked individuals to the market, but gave rise to a collectivity experienced as immediate. Robert Lacour-Gayet pointed out this collective power of the ticker: "Each vibration of the 'ticker' corresponds to an identical vibration in the hearts of millions of individuals who are united across space in the same wish or in the same disillusionment" (1929, 174). The noise of the ticker united America into a "community of feeling." Such all-inclusiveness had also been envisioned by Walt Whitman with the notion of sentimental democracy.[34] The ticker made possible a mode of inclusion that not only individualized economic individuals, but also produced an overarching sentiment. This affectivity became the basis on which individuals could develop and pursue interests.

As a medium of communication, the ticker reveals that processes of inclusion cannot be thought to rely entirely on processes of meaning. Attention also has to be paid to the way these processes of a meaning give rise to fascination. Hans-Ulrich Gumbrecht speaks of a necessarily anti-hermeneutic moment in the fascination experienced by spectators at a football game in America—a moment he calls the "production of presence." In team sports, this moment arises primarily by the creation of a *spatial* presence in which an event gains tactile proximity: "'[P]roducing presence' means to put things into reach so that they can be touched" (Gumbrecht 1998, 522). The ticker followed a similar logic, but did not produce bodily presence. Nonetheless, a particular form of presence did exist, which was devoted to the medium rather than to the body.[35] Presence effects arose when speed and noise were connected. As a real-time medium, the ticker promised immediate participation in events on the stock exchange. Gabriel Tarde had noted that an anonymous audience only became an audience when everyone knew that everyone else had access to the same information at the same time (Tarde 1989 [1898]). The noise made by the ticker allowed this simultaneity to be experienced physically. An emphasis on physicality could also be found in metaphors describing the ticker. The novelist Robert Grant represented the ticker as functioning with a pulse that could no longer be escaped, and that even affected outsiders. The ticker "plays its spasmodic tune in some conspicuous recess adjacent to the stream of life that comes and goes. It is, indeed, a monument well adapted to mark the temper of the age" (Grant 1884, 607).

Precisely the role of the ticker as a medium of presence was seen as unsettling and dangerous. The irresistible attraction of the ticker became a topos. This attraction, which overshadowed or even suspended all other activity, is best illustrated by the figure of the businessman who had caught "the fever of the ticker" (Carret 1990, 4). This "media-pathological" notion of "tickeritis" (Harper 1966, 11) viewed the relationship to the medium of the ticker as a disease.[36] The individual developed a strong attraction to the ticker, to the extent that escaping this medium was no longer possible: "He would not miss being present to hear the music of the ticker even if his wife's funeral were the same day" (Smitley 1933, 115). The ticker had the effect of overshadowing every other form of communication. In a report on speculation, New York Governor Hughes's Committee on Speculation in Securities and Commodities spoke of a strange "lure of the ticker" (MacDougall 1936, 122; New York [State] Committee on Speculation in Securities and Commodities 1910). The fascination mentioned above was described with a psychopathological vocabulary as an addiction and disease. The ticker stood for everything to which critics of speculation objected, but, at the same time, functioned as the symbol of a new global economy. Henry Harper asserted in 1926 that the ticker produced *hypnotic effects* "similar to that which one feels after standing for a considerable time intently watching the water as it flows over the Niagara Falls."[37] Looking into the depths of Niagara Falls, however, was not without danger. Observers could lose their balance and plummet to death on the rocks. The hypnotic effect of the ticker was, moreover, only a preliminary stage of the hysteria it induced: "[E]xperience proves that anyone whose reasoning faculties become confounded is apt to be affected by some form of hysteria, and will frequently do the opposite of what he would do under normal conditions" (13).

The ticker was entangled in discourse of hypnosis and hysteria proceeding from the way it functioned. The information communicated by the ticker might shock or exhilarate, but this information did not hypnotize. Rather, hypnotic effects were caused by the continuous and regular means of utterance. As the ticker tape slid rapidly before the eyes of the speculator, the figures on the tape might blur. The noise of the ticker only came to an end when the ticker suddenly paused. At this point, the market came to a standstill and the subject emerged from the hypnosis induced by the ticker.

The ticker, then, represented a paradox. While acting as an instrument that rationalized stock trading, it was also an apparatus that hypnotized the speculating subject—and thus deprived the speculator of rationality. At stake in this paradox was the success of inclusion by means of the ticker. The new stock-trading public developed a strong connection to the medium and to speculation, but it also faced the danger of losing its economic rationality. Critics contemporary to Calahan responded to this combination of irrationality and rationality by trying to draw technological boundaries: "The record of the chattering little machine can drive a man suddenly to the very verge of insanity with joy or despair . . . but if there be blame for that, it attaches to the American spirit of speculation and not to the ingenious mechanism which reads and registers the beating of the financial pulse" (anonymous source cited by Standage 1998, 176)

The speculative impulse had to be disassociated from tickers, which were a neutral technology, often praised as "almost perfect technical devices" (Hill

1975 [1904], 438). Drawing this boundary proved, however, to be difficult. The ticker's hypnotic effects were intrinsic to its functioning—or, more precisely, its perfect functioning. It was thus pathological precisely because of its effectiveness. Before the invention of the ticker, relaying stock prices had depended on the speed with which the broker acted. The ticker increased the speed with which information was disseminated, but this had unexpected side effects. The ticker was too fast, and the attentive observer could no longer avoid hearing its invasive noise. The "congestion of business" on the stock exchange was replaced by the hypnotic daze that overcame speculators in bucket shops and brokerage firms, leading them to act in abnormal ways. Hysterical speculators were financially irrational, Harper noted with concern in *The Psychology of Speculation* (1966 [1926], 13).

5. The Relationship Between Accessibility and Mediality

The ticker proved relevant to inclusion and exclusion in two ways. On the one hand, it was an important medium for expanding the *accessibility* of financial information. On the other hand, the *mediality* of the ticker came to the foreground. In terms of accessibility, the ticker created a relationship in which information and utterance were seen as increasing each other. Reproducing information made this information redundant, and in turn led to an expanded circle of addressees. Discourse primarily concerned with the accessibility of information represented the ticker as an efficient medium. This medium was characterized, above all, by a combination of three features. First, the ticker increased the *speed* of financial communication, which ceased to be restricted to a given space. As an early form of a (nearly) real-time medium, the ticker made the same current prices available at a variety of locations. Second, the ticker linked this real-time communication to a *continuous* mode of communication by reporting all transactions while the stock exchange was open. Third, stock trading was *represented* outside the stock exchange. A standardized system of symbols made the "pure" market open to experience. In combination, these three features are particularly important for a theory of inclusion. Wherever a licensed ticker was connected to the telegraph network, current stock prices could be observed, and speculation took place on this basis. The ticker was thus incorporated into an ideal of universal and general inclusion that characterized functional systems. Moreover, the ticker allowed the inclusion of traders who would have otherwise been excluded from receiving current information.

As the discourse of economic democratization emphasized, the ticker supplied financial information regardless of class, gender, and ethnicity. In this respect, it was a wholly modern medium.

Countless forms of media analysis oriented toward the social sciences accept this story of the ticker. By contrast, I seek to discover not only how the ticker increased the efficiency of finance, but also what the visibility of the medium meant for the process of inclusion. Focusing on the aspect of communication has meant shifting attention away from content—in this case, financial information—and asking instead how that content was disseminated and became relevant to inclusion. The term "ticker" refers to the loud sounds the device made, rather than to what it disseminated, and an analysis focusing on content would tend to ignore this noise. Unless the noise made by the ticker interfered with the function of dissemination, it would be seen as an unimportant side effect.

I have proposed, instead, to take the mediality of the ticker seriously. This mediality did not only play a decisive role in perceptions and representations of stock trading. Discussions about the new means of communication made clear that inclusion arose not only through access to financial communication, but through the inclusionary effects produced independently by the *mode* of utterance. The ticker became an *advertising medium* for what it represented—and for itself. This doubling also helps explain the ambivalent role mediality played in questions of accessibility. As a medium, the ticker advertised the stock exchange, and thus made the stock exchange interesting. In this way, the fascinating effects of the ticker reinforced the process of expanding accessibility. The apparatus did not accomplish this "effective advertising" either by using slogans, or by elaborately staging events on the stock market. This effective advertising also did not present stock trading in a generally understandable way. The ticker was a nearly "ascetic" medium, strictly confined to placing abbreviations and numbers in a sequence. Exclusively representing payment operations was intended to optimize understanding, but these operations were, however, unintelligible to the uninitiated. Speculators instead directed their attention and interest toward the ticker as a medium. This attention can be seen in descriptions of the ticker as a "magical device," or as creating a mysterious atmosphere.

In time, the ticker took on an autonomous function and no longer merely played the subordinate role of disseminating information. This independence is indicated by the emphasis on the noise made by the ticker and the public's intoxication with it, among other things. Furthermore, the spasmodic rhythm and hypnotic powers of the ticker were described using pathological metaphors and the ticker was celebrated as uncanny. What the ticker had made possible was now at risk, not because the numbers on the ticker tape might be falsified, but because the medium of communication itself intervened in the process. Dazed, the reader of the ticker tape became absorbed by the medium to such an extent that he risked losing the ability to process rational and transparent information—an ability his heightened attention was supposed to guarantee. This medium thus *uttered* itself, often to the point of becoming the dominant piece of information.

6. Disciplining the Ticker Reader

> "Tape Reading: 'The science of determining from the
> tape the immediate trend of prices. It is judging from
> what appears on the tape *now* [emphasis added], what
> is likely to be shown in five minutes or more.'"
> —Richard Wyckoff, *Studies in Tape Reading* (1910)

The danger of being dazed by the ticker was counteracted by a "hermeneutics of speculation." Carefully refined techniques of observation were used to contain fascination with the ticker, at least to the point at which the mysteries of the ticker tape could be unlocked. In what follows, I examine this double fascination with the ticker and the ticker tape by distinguishing between hermeneutics of the ticker and its mediality—a mediality based on presence rather than on meaning.[38] These can by no means be separated. As I maintain, their intersection—and confusion—created the effect of fascination particular to the ticker. This exemplary discussion of the ticker is, at the same time, meant to be a tile in a larger mosaic representing a media archaeology of seduction. Nonetheless, my analysis aims to understand how communication specific to a functional system continually reinforced open universality by introducing new means of popular inclusion.

Reading the ticker tape, as discussions of hypnosis by the ticker indicate, was by no means free of risk. The reader of the tape not only faced the danger of becoming addicted to the process, but could also lose his financial judgment. The ticker had a power to seduce. Precisely for this reason, any observational apparatus closely linked to the speculator as a figure of inclusion is of particular interest. How was the speculator to handle the ticker as a medium that posed dangers to, but was also essential for, his activities? How could the danger of being seduced by the tape be reduced?

Such questions were raised in guides to tape reading, which constituted a specialist literature and were not written for the amateur who occasionally read the ticker at a brokerage firm.[39] Tape reading was not reduced to simply observing the tape—if this kind of innocent reading can even be said to exist—but became the explicit foundation on which to create a method for speculation. Professional tape reading increasingly faced a tension between the fascination exerted by the tape and the necessity of calmly reasoning about speculation. Underlying these efforts to elaborate a professional method for reading the tape was an important theoretical question: how was the moment at which presence was produced (i.e., the presence of stock exchange operations) connected to a "hermeneutic of speculation" (i.e., observations of stock exchange operations)?

Richard Wyckoff began his now frequently cited classic on tape reading, published under the pseudonym "Rollo Tape," by reflecting on the problem of the speculative imagination. Like many other tape readers, Wyckoff presupposed "that in some way the market momentarily indicates its own immediate future; that these indications are accurately recorded on the tape; therefore he who can interpret what is imprinted on the narrow paper ribbon has within his reach unlimited wealth" (Wyckoff 1910, 5). The ticker tape was especially interesting to speculators, since it not only recorded what had happened or what was happening on the stock exchange, but also gave the trained reader insight into the future. This specific kind of reading was described as "market instinct," which was nothing other than "the ability to interpret with a reasonable degree of accuracy the true meaning and significance of price movements and volume changes and their relationships. If the term 'market instinct' has any meaning whatever, it may be considered as a popular equivalent for 'intelligent tape reading'" (Wolf 1966 [1924], 47).

Whoever knew how to read the tape could also predict the future of the market. Reading the tape thus became a mode of speculative imagination that presented itself as scientific. Although the tape revealed the future of the market, not everyone could understand this future. Only those who had the competence required to read the tape could unlock the true meaning in the confusion of symbols. The temporal structure of the market, as written on the tape, thus came to be of great interest. The ticker acted as an augur of the market. The true meaning of the tape did not arise when the symbols had been properly decoded, but only when those symbols were read as symbols of the future. The truth of the tape was the future of the market. This future was used to measure a tape reader's competence. A successful interpreter of the stock exchange would be rewarded with fantastic wealth, while misreadings could be punished by ruin and exclusion from the system.

The hermeneutics of the tape was confronted with two challenges. On the one hand, one was supposed not only to know how to read symbols of the past, but even to recognize traces of the future in these symbols.[40] On the other hand, such a speculative imagination directed at the future was liable to drift easily out of control. In order to manage this tension, reading the tape required exceptional discipline: "The power to drill himself into the right mental attitude; to stifle his emotion, fear, anxiety, elation, recklessness, to train his mind into obedience so that it recognized but one master—the tape—these, if possessed, would be as valuable in shaping the result as natural ability, or what is called the sixth sense in trading" (Wyckoff 1910, 7).

Reading the tape required an attitude that was almost entirely disinterested and dispassionate. What had to be excluded was any emotion aroused by looking into an imaginary future, since it might impair the objective reading of the tape. The tape reader thus had to exclude such emotion. The truth about the future of the market was already inscribed in the tape (and only had to be decoded). An emotional reading would thus jeopardize the value the tape had as truth.

The tape reader faced a classical communication problem: how could the truth of the tape be communicated without losing its nature as truth in the process of communication? Put another way: every distinction the tape reader could make threatened the truth of the tape, but without making distinctions, he could not understand this truth. The hermeneutics of the tape, then, turned out to be an illusionary effort to reverse the situation of the newcomer described above. The layperson saw communication as fascinating noise because he could only observe this communication as an utterance lacking decipherable information. However, the hermeneutics of the tape tried to exclude any aspect of communication as an utterance—and thus to exclude the mediality of communication. The tape was pure information, but this pure information was distorted with every attempted utterance. To remedy this situation, it was not only advisable to control and exclude emotion. These remedies were designed to promote complete submission to the tape. The tape was an absolute ruler—a tyrant (Wyckoff 1910, 8)—and tolerated no other rulers (such as rumor or the news ticker). The financier Jesse Livermore, for example, regularly studied the tape in order to discipline, and improve on, the talent he had for observation: "[T]he tape does not concern itself with the why and wherefore. It doesn't go into explanations. Your business with the tape is now—not to-morrow. The reason can wait" (Lefèvre 1982, 11).

This claim of absolute rule was primarily directed toward excluding other media. The newspaper, the dominant medium of the day, was too unreliable to be a good complement to the ticker. On the one hand, the newspaper was too slow. Relying on information in the newspaper would always lead one to intervene too late in the market. On the other hand, and not less important, the newspaper article had a narrative structure that was inferior to the ticker. The trained reader not only learned actual prices and volume traded from the symbols on the ticker, but treated these symbols as a real-time news organ: "Everything from a foreign war to the passing of a dividend; from Supreme Court decision to the ravages of the boll weevil is reflected primarily upon the tape" (Wyckoff 1910, 11). Ticker communication was precise because it did not rely on other media, but *immediately* recorded data: "but the ticker records *immediately* the transactions of those who know the facts" (Dice 1926, 281; emphasis added). Unlike other forms of telegraphy, ticker communication required no operators to decode and transmit messages to the audience on the side of the receiver (cf. Calahan 1901). As a result, ticker communication had an even greater immediacy. The intervention of a "human medium" could corrupt data in ways ranging from simple errors to manipulation and the selective transmission of important information. The ticker thus became a medium that directly confronted its audience with codes—codes that held information not only on current prices, but on events across the world.

The ticker not only set free the speculative imagination of the tape reader. Prior to speculation based on meaning, the tape reader was fascinated by the immediate effects of the ticker. Precisely because the tape narrated no stories, the ticker could claim to present pure data. Anything that distorted the technical neutrality of the ticker data was an obstacle to successfully reading the tape. The ticker reader thus had "no ear for rumors, gossip, tips, newspaper opinions, or stories" (Dice 1926, 282). He had to truly isolate himself to protect the neutrality of the tape from other influences, and from his own uncontrollable emotions—a task that included not taking part in the production of rumors. These recommendations were designed, not only to sanitize communication, but also to ensure that the tape reader did not discard an interpretation he had already made and abandon a decision to buy or sell: "[D]o anything but join in the idle, unintelligent gossip in a broker's board room."[41]

However, continuous information about the market had the disadvantage of being transient. The ticker tape occupied a position between speech and writing. Like speech, the ticker tape was not usually archived. Nonetheless, ticker communication was recorded on a tape often thrown away the same evening, and thus had a greater permanence than oral communication. Ticker readers were advised to take old tapes home. Studying these tapes at night would help them improve their reading techniques: "Those who have not time to study at least five hours a day the tape should try to get the tape to take it home" (Wyckoff 1910, 84). At home, the entire apparatus should perfectly simulate a ticker found in a brokerage office: "One should buy an automatic reel, so the tape can run across one's desk just as though it were coming from the ticker" (84). Ultimately, however, the tape confronted the ticker reader with too much information for making the market visible. For this reason, the ticker reader was advised to write down the most important information. "If you wish to 'see' market-action develop before your eyes, I suggest that you adopt the use of pad and pencil. Many of us find it difficult to concentrate." In this way, the tape reader could further improve his ability to observe. Moreover, writing down information gave the tape reader "a commanding grasp of the action" (Neill 1960 [1931], 43).

However, to further process information from the ticker, the ticker reader had to use the medium of writing carefully. Not every kind of writing was suited to reproduce the precision of the data on the tape. The tape reader should not rely on mechanical aids such as tables or charts which were incompatible with tape reading: "The full tape cannot be charted. The tape does tell the story."[42] Any interference with the *immediacy* and *totality* of the information on the tape was dangerous, and jeopardized the general and distant perspective on the market the tape had first made possible.[43] The tape reader himself became an *automaton*, and thus also became an extension of the ticker: "The Tape Reader evolves himself into an automaton which takes note of a situation, weighs it, decides upon a course and gives an order. There is no quickening of the pulse, no nerves, no hopes or fears. The result produces neither elation nor depression. There is equation before, during and after the trade" (16).

Of particular interest here, the word "equation" not only implies that the tape reader is part of a mathematical formula, but signals his composure. The tape reader is nothing other than the embodiment of an equation that will lead to a decision about trading. Even rational reflection is not allowed to be an obstacle. Once made, a decision has to be carried out mechanically: "The trader must train himself into a kind of double personality. In forming his judgements and making his decisions he must employ to the utmost all the intellectual powers which he possesses. Having reached a decision, however, and given his order, he straightaway should become more or less of a machine and conduct the technical details appertaining to the trade without any emotion whatever" (Wolf 1966, 98).

The transformation of the ticker reader into an automaton ideally led to the spatial isolation of the ticker reader. In an isolated, quiet room, rather than in a noisy brokerage office, the ticker reader could concentrate entirely on the tape: "A tiny room with a ticker, a desk and private telephone connection with his broker's office are all the facilities required. The work requires such a delicate balance of the faculties that the slightest influence either way may throw the results against the trader. . . . Silence is a much needed lubricant to the Tape Reader's mind" (Wyckoff 1910, 18).

The ideal tape reader stood in clear contrast to the popular speculator who followed the crowd. The profession of this ideal tape reader was anything but glamorous. The luxurious furnishings in the broker's office, the feverish exchange of new rumors, and the shared excitement in front of the ticker were all factors that could impair success at reading the ticker. However, the figure of the disciplined tape reader is not to be placed fully outside discourses of the crowd. Rather, the reading apparatus contained forms of discipline that have to be understood as techniques of communication whose meaning only emerged against the background provided by discourses of crowds. Recall that in the discourse of the crowd, the crowd subject was distinguished by three important dimensions. First, the subject was open to almost any kind of *suggestion*. Second, the subject's behavior was not based on rational and independent decisions, but on the *imitation* of others. Third, the crowd psyche often arose by means of *physical and affective* proximity. Only when the crowd had been constructed as a discursive object could a field of intervention open up for the disciplinary techniques used to create a successful tape reader. The tape reader had to be protected from any kind of suggestion, and thus should not be led astray by rumors and reports in the press. This reader had to rely on his own judgment and isolate himself to the greatest extent possible from other speculators. Moreover, the ideal of the tape reader was to reach a disembodied form of existence free from affect. This form of existence made it possible for the tape reader, who now resembled an automaton, to take decisions rationally. Every emotion was seen as potentially interfering with the tape reader's precarious essential equilibrium (Wyckoff 1910, 25). What did the process of reading the tape look like? What hermeneutic directives were given to the tape reader? The observational apparatus that made possible a corresponding set of reading practices can be outlined against the background of my previous claims. In ideal cases, the ticker reader occupied an ascetically arranged room—a space protected from the outside world. This room was, however, linked to the "market" by a ticker and a telephone. Only a small group of professional speculators could afford their own ticker, however. Speculators who did business in the ticker room of a broker thus had to make every effort not to be distracted by the noise and the constant rumors. This notion of the tape reader, in turn, presupposed a psychologically coherent personality. Ideally, the tape reader was an autonomous individual capable of entirely controlling his emotions. He experienced "no fear, no anxiety or ambition. When a Tape Reader has his emotions well in hand, he will play as though the game were dominoes. When anything interferes with this attitude it should be eliminated," Wyckoff insisted (166).

Only in this way was the tape reader in a position to devote the necessary attention to the tape, and, in the act of reading it, to submit to the rule of the tape. The tape reader directed his attention entirely to observing the symbols of the market. If properly read, the market would provide advice on the basis of which to trade. The tape reader might follow and read the tape with complete attention, but he could not develop a "deep hermeneutic." Rather, he had to be satisfied with what he saw on the tape: the symbols for stocks being sold, current prices, and volume traded. Noticeably absent was the question of an "actor." Knowing who sold a large number of stocks ultimately meant no longer reading the tape (Neill 1960 [1931], 9). Reading the tape thus proved to be an ideal mode of observation that detached communication specific to functional systems from interactions in which reference to an actor was, for the most part, essential. The question of an utterer, obscured by the anonymity of events on the market, became irrelevant. Tape reading, then, developed as a hermeneutic that did not ask about motives behind payment operations, but took these payment operations themselves seriously. With Foucault (1972), it is possible to speak of a "monumental" rather than a "documentary" way of reading. Tape reading was exclusively interested in regularities, and in the frequency with which communication occurred as an event.

By concentrating on the way regularities changed, the tape reader was able to decipher symbols that pointed to reversals in market trends or in the price of a particular stock. The tape listed the price of stock bought and sold, and the amount of stock bought and sold. The ticker reader now observed the way prices and amounts evolved, and could immediately recognize whether the supply of a stock was too high, or whether the demand for a stock was too low. The ticker tape represented, in written form, the axiom of supply and demand: "The force of supply is always matched against that of demand" (Dice 1926, 286). The law of supply and demand provided the background against which the ticker reader interpreted figures on the tape (cf. Wyckoff 1910, 83). The tape reader was not interested in the premise that individual companies had an intrinsic value, but instead paid attention exclusively to the connection between payment events. This interest also helps explain why the ticker reader was not allowed to be distracted by other information—particularly information in narrative form. The tape presented a market resembling the neoclassical ideal of an economy based on the law of supply and demand.

However, the ticker reader not only had to read the stock prices presented on the tape but also had to identify the "critical point" that signaled whether he should enter or withdraw from the market. This decision could not be derived from a particular rule. The tape reader had recourse to no "system" or other mechanism, but ultimately had to rely on an *intuition* developed by endlessly observing the phenomena of supply and demand.[44] Wyckoff used the analogy of traffic on the streets to illustrate this intuitive judgment on the part of the tape reader: "When you cross a street where the traffic is heavy, do you stop to consult a set of rules showing when to run ahead of a trolley car or when not to dodge a wagon? No. You take a look at both ways and at the proper moment you walk across. Your mind may be on something else but your judgement tells you when to start and how fast to walk. That is the attitude of the trained Tape Reader" (128).

Mastering the law of supply and demand could not be translated into a particular set of rules. Decisions thus had to be made on the basis of *intuitive judgment*—judgment that could not be reduced to processing economic rules. For some authors, this intuition became the basis of rational calculation: "Reasoning rests upon the ultimate basis of immediate and intuitive judgements" (Nelson 1964, 158).

In the struggles over the distinction between gambling and speculation, functionalization had made speculation a lubricant for the law of supply and demand. Speculation oscillated between economic rationality and an irrational other in a way that was difficult to define, but relied on an intuition that could sense how the market was inclined to act. This intuition only came to the experienced trader. The trader even used intuition to escape temporarily from the dictates of the tape: "He can feel the shadow of coming events *before* they are manifested on the tape" (Wolf 1924, 96; emphasis added). The shadows of future events hinted that the tape reader should give up his attachment to the present in order to figuratively and literally *sense* the future. The contrarians, who were also interested in tape reading, had tried to gain consciousness of time through reflexivity. According to the concrete instructions he was given about tape reading, the speculator now had to rely on a feeling.[45]

Intuitive judgment occupied a strange position in the observational apparatus of the ticker reader, who aimed to develop a form of subjectivity in which the mind controlled all emotion. Although, he should be in control of himself, he had to become an automaton that submitted to the tape, blindly carrying out its orders. Intuition mediated between the contradictory demands of self-control and total submission. Intuitive judgment appeared to resolve this paradox. It did not rest on the secure use of rational calculation, but required an "intuitive eye" or "second sight" (Neill 1960 [1931], 1) that would recognize the meaning of the figures on the tape simply by looking at them. To develop this special kind of sight, the tape reader had to exercise absolute self-mastery, and concentrate entirely on the tape. Emphasis on sight allowed the tape reader to be connected to the ideal speculator, who was defined by his forward-looking gaze. It was this form of unconscious judgment, based on perception, that linked market participants. After all, they aimed "to make money by exercising speculative, intuitive judgement" (Neill 1960 [1931], 9).

Intuition made possible, and even necessary, that which was denied to the speculator without emotion and body. Only through intuition could the "'feel' of the tape" be established (Neill 1960 [1931], 12). Intuitive judgment bypassed the self-reflexive loops of the rational and autonomous individual, and instead created a direct mimetic relationship (cf. Taussig 1993) between the tape and the psychic system of the tape reader. The feel for the tape "sends a definite signal to our brains when important action takes place" (Neill 1960 [1931], 30). As a quicker way to process information, intuition thus ideally complemented the imperative that stock exchange operations take place with great speed.

Too much self-reflection required too much time for a speculator to operate efficiently on the market. The inclinations of the market had to be sensed intuitively in order to be internalized. Presumably, the ideal ticker reader would be connected to the telegraph wires leading to the ticker and receive electrical impulses directly to his brain.

Intuitive observation of the ticker brings us back to our discussion of the hypnotic effects the ticker had, and of the way the tape was observed. The ticker reader had to place himself in a state similar to hypnosis in order to see the commands given on the tape, and had to recover his individuality to the extent that he could subordinate himself to these commands. For this task, the tape reader relied on absolute self-mastery. This paradox of tape reading by no means went unnoticed by critics of speculation, who expressed skepticism about the nature of tape reading, which was seen as "very light reading indeed. There seems so little to read. The tape readers will refer to their 'trading instinct'" (Schwed 1940, 157).

The ticker reader had a short time to make interpretations, and, if possible, arrive at a clear judgment. Moreover, he could not simply arrive at a judgment, but had to use this judgment to make decisions about buying and selling stock. In this case, it once again became important that the tape reader not view himself as a master of interpretation, but understand the tape only to the extent of knowing what action to take. The tape reader was not a captain who gave orders, but an engineer who followed, without hesitation, the exact orders given by the tape (Wyckoff 1910, 60). Following these orders included not hesitating once a clear interpretation had been made, but instead immediately communicating the corresponding instructions to the broker: "The appearance of a definite indication should be immediately followed by an order" (60). Hesitation would only jeopardize the time saved by the tape over other media. The connection between observation, interpretation, and operations on the stock exchange was also clear in the way the communications devices in the solitary office of the tape reader were arranged. The ticker was to be placed as close as possible to the telephone used to relay orders to the broker: "Every step means delay" (27).

7. The "Passionate Attachment" of the Tape Reader

Acting like an automaton, when combined with market intuition, brought the speculator to the limits of his identity. The speculator was paralyzed, and gave up his individual judgment: "[T]he public speculator when in the market is a bewildered man. His attitude towards the market can probably best be described as that of a man not yet fully awake . . . [and] as a man on the edge of a cliff who wants to get away and who cannot. The man's personality is temporarily shaken or at least disturbed and *he acts in a condition of intense suggestibility*" (Bond 1928, 177).

The speculator found the precipice represented by the market simultaneously attractive and repulsive. The dramatic situation of the man on the edge of the cliff again represented a subjectivity divided between mechanical submission and empowerment. The small speculator was ultimately in a classical *double bind*. Either he fell from the cliff, and thus brought about the downfall of the inclusion process, or he was absorbed by—and had to devote himself entirely to—the market. In both cases, the speculator would lose, at least if success were measured by the mode of the autonomous individual. The paradoxical moment Judith Butler locates before and in the process of making a subject appeared, in this case, when the speculator was "temporarily shaken." The fictive premise of an already existing individual began to collapse. "Attachment" was formed in a contradictory way, as if "it" already sensed that only submission would bring the man on the cliff to speak as a speculating subject. This "attachment" to intelligible communication arose as a "condition of intense suggestibility," that is, as the condition of an almost unconditional openness to the other. The speculating subject was open to any kind of communication about speculation and developed an addiction to information presented by the news ticker, or in the "more pure" form of the stock ticker. A constant flow of information, and thus of suggestion, confronted a potential speculator who was *over-suggestible*. This nearly hypnotic undecidability shook the foundations underlying the economic identity of the speculator, and thus revealed the affectivity of inclusion in finance. Like the individual who, in Sidis's account, was immobilized as part of a crowd, the speculator became paralyzed and lost his economic rationality. However, the speculator was also exposed to a "passionate expectation of the law" (Butler 1997, 129). This expectation was not always structured according to an economic subject. Rather, subjection had to follow a grammatically incorrect procedure and presupposed an "attachment" that came before the subject (102).

To be sure, the moment of expectation described by Frederic Bond as over-suggestibility also existed for the professional speculator. However, a web of subtle disciplinary techniques was designed to prevent the professional speculator from being lost to excessive suggestion, and thus from taking a false step that would lead him to fall from the cliff into a communicative abyss. Bond distinguished between the popular speculator and the professional speculator based on the degree of discipline they showed: "But, unless, when under severe strain, he is able to conquer his latent suggestibility, he simply cannot succeed in the stock market" (Bond 1928, 177). This idea implied that the "over-suggestibility" attractive to the popular investor could be controlled, and that the process of inclusion ultimately ended with an "entirely" disciplined subject. Such a perspective failed to see that, structurally, the professional speculator also had the concentration and "passionate expectation" required to decode the ticker symbols.

Discourses of suggestion and suggestibility were thus especially revealing. Literature on suggestion written around 1900 identified the "becoming machine" of human beings as a characteristic of suggestions and hypnosis (see, e.g., the writings of Paul Janet). The notion of suggestion was a reaction to the crisis experienced by the discourses of individuality. Suggestion did not proceed rationally, but took byways. The Russian psychoneurologist Vladimir Bechterew maintained, for example, that suggestion did not "enter by force through the main door of logical persuasion, but, so to speak, by the back stairs that bypass the 'I' of individual consciousness and will" (cited by Loewenfeld 1901, 39).

Such a back stairway would also allow the speculator to take faster and more immediate decisions. The ticker reader was hypnotized, not primarily by the information on the tape, but by the experience of a presence separate from meaning. The symbols on the tape were indecipherable to the newcomer and fascinating to speculators, who listened with excitement to the clicking of the ticker. Both cases involved the repetition of monotonous sounds, movements, or markings. Precisely these means were identified as techniques of hypnosis (cf. Loewenfeld 1901, 96ff.). This fascination with the tape made it possible to resolve the circle of subjectivation: How to interpellate someone who does not yet speculate as a speculator? A speculator could become a speculator by the thrills of the medium—and not the content—of speculation.

8. The Self-Extinction of the Subject Speculator

"'Subjection' signifies the process of becoming subordinated by power as well as the process of becoming a subject," Judith Butler asserts. In Butler's sense, tape reading can be seen as a process of subjection.[46] Only by submitting to the tape did the tape reader create an identity. It might at first be surprising, however, to see that this submission was accompanied by a strong expression of individuality. Richard Wyckoff emphasized that, as for any other pursuit, "the amount of I WILL" was what determined success or failure at tape reading (1910, 7). This was paradoxical, given that the process of complete submission to the tape ruled out individual acts of will. Precisely this paradoxical logic of subjection confronted the tape reader, however. He ultimately had *to will to have no will*. The strong will exercised by the tape reader was founded on the expectation that he would undergo a radical process of extinction.

The ideal tape reader would have direct access to information on the tape, and was thus ultimately a subject of information. Willing himself to quash anything that would interfere with the process of subjection, he had to conform entirely to the tape—but without entirely surrendering his individuality. He "appeared to be in a *trance* while his mental processes were being worked out" (Wyckoff 1910, 7), but never entirely went into a trance. He only *appeared*, to the external observer, to be in this state, which disguised rationally evolving investment decisions. Absolute submission allowed the self to emerge in its purity precisely in the moment of self-extinction. This self, however, was embodied in mimicry. By submitting to the tape and becoming a "transparent" medium, the reader made the tape speak.[47]

In his novel *The Cost* (1904), David Graham Phillips strikingly represented the fatal process by which, in this paradoxical form of subjectivity, individuality was subordinated to the medium of the tape. At the end of the book, the successful speculator and financier Dumont finds himself trapped. His reputation has been destroyed by the collapse of his marriage, and his enemies have organized a conspiracy against him. Dumont appears to lie defeated on the floor. The news ticker announces his death, causing an enormous financial crisis:

> As that last word jerked letter by letter from under the printing wheel the floor of the Stock Exchange became the rapids of a human Niagara. By messenger, by telegraph, by telephone, holders of National Woolens and other industrials, in the financial district, in all parts of the country, across the sea, poured in their selling orders upon the frenzied brokers. And all these forces of hysteria and panic, projected into that narrow, roofed-in space, made of it a chaos of contending demons. . . . [A]nd all the Dumont stocks bent, broke, went smashing down, down, down, everyone struggling to unload. (Phillips 1904, 327–28)

Panic is represented not least as a media event. Media ranging from messengers to the telegraph are activated by the last word of the news ticker, setting in motion a "human Niagara" (Henry Harper would use the same metaphor) of global communication.

The flood of news in the newspapers is not to be trusted, however—truth is only to be found in the numbers and symbols of the stock ticker. Thus, it is no surprise that the reports of Dumont's death turn out to be wrong. Moreover, as a ruined man, treated with disrespect even by the elevator boy, he has prepared his retaliation. He may be dying as a public man, but this social death also turns him into an ideal speculator, disembedded from the social word. He sits alone in his room "among the piled-up coils of ticker-tape" (Phillips 1904, 395). Meanwhile, the crowd on the stock exchange is frantic: "Reason fled, and self-control. The veneer of civilization was torn away to the last shred; and men, turned brute again, gave themselves up to the elemental passion of the brute" (396).

The collapse of civilization in the turmoil on the stock exchange parallels events in Dumont's isolated room, where the distinction between the speculating subject and the medium of the ticker increasingly dissolves: "The floor near his lounge was littered with the snake-like coils of the ticker-tape. They rose almost to his knees as he sat and through telephone and ticker drank in the massacre of his making, glutted himself with the joy of the vengeance he was taking" (396). Dumont reads the ticker tape accurately. His rivals have been driven to ruin. But it is the ticker tape that rules. All that remains of Dumont, whose body is already half covered by the tape, is a desire for the tape and the pleasure of revenge.

It can hardly be decided which scene has a more horrifying effect. On the stock exchange, the panicked crowds of what were once speculators lose their subjectivity to the tune of the frenetic functioning of the media apparatus. In his room, Dumont abandons himself to the ticker tape and to the apocalyptic story it tells. In merging with the tape in a setting not open to view from outside, Dumont should be an ideal economic subject. He is undisturbed by external influences, and is spatially distant from the stock exchange. As prescribed by guides to reading the ticker tape, he concentrates entirely on the tape. Admittedly, he fails to observe another basic principle often repeated in this literature: he does not control his emotions, but takes delight in the horrifying spectacle brought about by his business strategies.

In this final scene, the paradox exemplified by the ticker taper presents itself most clearly: By appealing to his passions, the tape seduces its reader and transforms him into a dispassionate, transparent automaton, who submits entirely to the ticker (and thus speaks for the market). This impossible juxtaposition of extreme affectivity and extreme rationality is staged as an unsettling spectacle closed to uninitiated bystanders. Dumont's wife Pauline risks a glimpse into his room, but immediately closes the door in order to "shut from view that spectacle of a hungry monster at its banquet of living flesh" (397).[48] What is left of Dumont after his submission to the tape is only grotesque bodily mass, lacking any subjectivity. The tape, repeatedly described as a snake, not only buries Dumont, but *coils* around him: "In his struggles the tape had wound round and round his legs, his arms, his neck. It lay in a curling, coiling mat, like a serpent's head, upon his throat, where his hands clutched the collar of his pajamas" (399).

EPILOGUE

The death of the speculator at the hands of the ticker tape symbolized the uncanny combination of economic subjectivity and mediality. The ticker, the medium that reliably represented the life and pulse of the market even in times of crisis, strangled the once-successful speculator. Dumont's fate reveals two motifs that have been of great importance to this study: the unstable figure of the speculator and the mediality of financial communication.

The speculator was seen as a privileged manifestation of *homo oeconomicus*. More than the laborer, the entrepreneur, or even the consumer, the speculator was thought to be the figure of economic inclusion closest to the model of *homo oeconomicus*, but also as its greatest challenge. The speculator was considered to a large extent free of the disruptive materiality of goods and labor, making him an exemplary second-order observer. The speculator increased his economic rationality because he was able to do without the intervention of unwanted references to the "real" economy. In fact, he had to do without these unwanted references, since they would interfere with his differential calculations.

This study has challenged the "official" view of the speculator and stock speculation by focusing on the noneconomic aspect of speculation. My analysis of self-descriptions and external descriptions has aimed to show how these figures of inclusion could be installed, and how aporias arose within such figures. In this way, my analysis has been directed against the functionalistic understandings of economic identities that characterize theories offered by

neoclassicism, Marxism, and even systems theory. The figure of the speculator cannot be unquestioningly derived from the functioning of the financial
economy, or from a predetermined economic rationality. Formulating this
figure of inclusion was a process fraught with indeterminacies, aporias, and
conflicts. An economization of this figure had to take place—a task accomplished, for example, by strategies of semantic functionalization. Speculation
had to become a form of economic communication, and the speculator had
to be separated from the gambler. This economization could not entirely succeed. The identity of the speculator remained precarious.

The speculator was thus denied a complete identity by an exterior that
could not be integrated. Likewise, the operations of finance were similarly
affected by an outside. This study has tried to show that figures of inclusion
and the operations of a functional system required specific procedures, technologies of communication, and discourses in order to become differentiated.
The definition of the economy was not simply a given and was not reproduced
in the connection of economic operations alone. Rather, it had to be constantly produced, and protected from impurities. For this reason, self-descriptions and external descriptions of speculation have played an important role
in my analysis. Only the performativity of these descriptions made an operation economic.[1] Semantic conflicts, then, were not only harmless appearances
on the surface of a "solid" economy. As indicated, for example, by my discussion of the way futures trading was regulated, these semantic conflicts could
also play a decisive role in establishing the connectivity of economic communication. In this way, semantic conflicts created a horizon for what could
be thought and said about the economy. The boundaries of this horizon were
by no means given, and could thus become the object of renewed semantic
conflict.

My analysis has used the notion of the popular to grasp this situation.
Stock speculation was not confronted by this as a problem encountered in
an incomprehensible environment. It was not simply a PR challenge for stock
exchanges and brokers, but a more deeply rooted problem, since it was always
already embedded in the operations that constituted finance—whether in the
form of the communicative mechanisms of thrill and suspense, of the erotici-
zation of economic communication, or of the media that produced moments
of "immediacy." These noneconomic factors played a constitutive role in stock
trading. Only they allowed finance to do justice to its claims of universality by
addressing, and fascinating, an outside that was still to be included. Starting

with these economic impurities has allowed me to complicate oversimpli-fied notions of the "economization of society." My interests are not directed toward the way discourses of speculation spread in a variety of social fields. To be sure, the model of a speculator who was flexible and prepared to take risks may have been highly appealing in other social realms. However, the notion of "economization" presupposes a pure economic logic. The popular brings precisely the heterogeneity of this economic logic into view. A "contamination of the economic" precedes every "economization."

This book has examined the popular side of the financial economy by focusing on three problems: the distinction between gambling and specula-tion, the description of the market as a "market crowd," and the mediality of stock exchange communication represented by the ticker. In all three fields, ideal notions of the economic were confronted by a moment of the popular that was both necessary and disruptive.

Ideally, speculation was meant to be understood as a form of economic communication free of any elements that resembled gambling. This ideal could be reached, for example, by an outright struggle against gambling in speculation, or by the economization and annexation of gambling in the calculations of neoclassical economic actors. Efforts to drive elements of gambling out of speculation led to a paradox of purification. These efforts increased the fictionality of finance, and thus created what appeared to be, strangely enough, a nearly aesthetic desire for fiction at the heart of finance. The logic of suspense and the experience of thrills were deeply inscribed in the basic structure of stock market activity.

Even the ideal notion of the solitary and heroic speculator could not escape the logic of the popular. The contrarian represented, in nearly ideal form, the type of speculator who relied only on himself, and who turned away from the money-hungry "market crowds" not called to speculate. Who, if not the contrarian, could practice the ideals set out for speculators in self-descrip-tions of finance? The contrarian emerged as an elite cynic who aimed to guard himself from "market crowds," but who also needed them. In the contrarian, the popular—defined by distinguishing between the public of stock market professionals and its exterior—took a particularly interesting turn. Contrari-anism greatly weakened, if not entirely suspended, the distinction between the public of professional stock traders and its exterior. Anyone could be a speculator! However, this distinction was now emphasized in the inclusivity of stock trading. The contrarian, who initially appeared to represent the ideal speculator, had to develop elaborate techniques of self-control. The popular also introduced an existential uncertainty, since the contrarian never knew whether he was still himself or whether he had been subsumed by the crowd. The uncertainty of the contrarian also points to the fragile way in which the speculator was constituted. His economic subjectivity had to be continually reestablished in ways that were both arduous and incomplete.

Finally, the mediality of finance represented a third way in which the popular challenged ideal notions of the economy. Ideally, the economy was imagined as a sphere that might require a variety of media, but that was not affected by these media. From this perspective, media such as the telegraph or the stock ticker were simply means to economic efficiency and did not interfere with economic communication. These media might, by the dissemination they performed, make speculation popular in a quantitative sense—a popularity that remained external to stock trading. Yet the ticker not only disseminated information but also revealed the specific mediality of stock exchange communication. The mediality of ticker communication itself became of interest, whether as the dizzying speed with which new information was relayed or as the hypnotic noise of the medium and the experience of "economic immediacy." The experience of presence brought about by the ticker had somatic effects even on those who lacked economic competence. In this case, moment of the popular also could not be attributed to an external contingency. Rather, the medium of the ticker perfected speculation by accelerating this communication and thus making it accessible, largely independent of location, to a wide public. Significantly, the very medium that perfected the financial economy developed a noneconomic power to fascinate.

As used in the title of this book, the phrase "spectacular speculation" refers to this overflowing of the noneconomic into financial operations. The three fields I have examined—gambling, crowds, and media—were historically affected by this overflow in different ways. Gambling incorporated thrills and suspense into economic operations, transforming and "mutating" them into entertainment. The stock exchange became a stage for a crowd that appeared as a spectacle to the uninitiated observer. Finally, the ticker exerted a fascination as a device of "economic immediacy."

Taking the spectacular structure of stock speculation seriously in no way means reducing it entirely to a spectacle. To resolve the tension in the speculation one-sidedly in that way would be to miss precisely the entanglement that is of interest in this book, either opposing speculation to a spectacle exterior to it, and thus perpetuating the struggle for economic purity, or announcing and laconically observing the dissolution of the economy into a spectacle. In contrast, the notion of a popular of the economy suggested here feeds on precisely this irresolvable tension and seeks to highlight the ruptures that emerge in this spectacular structure.

NOTES

INTRODUCTION

1. "[N]o reader of sentiment and imagination can be entertained or interested by a detail of transactions such as these, which admit no warmth, no colouring, no embellishment, a detail of which only serves to exhibit an inanimate picture of tasteless vice and mean degeneracy," Tobias Smollett wrote (cited by Mackay 1980 [1841–52], 74).

2. Seeking to give an account of popular culture—an endeavor that would be characteristic of British cultural studies over a hundred years later—Mackay foregrounds the "people" and their fate—but soberly and with no intention of glorifying them. "The intrigues of unworthy courtiers to gain the favour of still more unworthy kings, or the records of murderous battles and sieges, have been dilated on, and told over and over again . . . ; while the circumstances which have most deeply affected the morals and welfare of the people have been passed over with but slight notice, as dry and dull, capable of neither warmth nor colouring," he complains (74).

3. Thomas Mortimer (1801 [1761]) was one of the earliest English financial advisors; for the American context of interest here, see Nelson 1964 (1903); Wyckhof 1910; Carrett 1990 (1930). A good example of the moral critique of gambling is Frothingham 1882. An example of popular representations of stock speculation in literature is the play *Henrietta*, filmed under the title *The Lamb* in 1910 and later as *The Saphead* (Herbert Blaché, 1920) with Buster Keaton. See also Charles Dudley Warner's novel *A Little Journey in the World* (1969 [1889]) and Theodore Dreiser's *The Financier* (1912), one of the most outstanding examples of the American financial novel. For more on the motif of finance in American novels, see Westbrook 1980 and the everyday history of Wall Street by Steve Fraser (2005); a more general history of Wall Street is in Geisst 1997.

4. Not until the nineteenth century was it possible to establish the fledgling new modes of speculation that emerged in the early modern era as legitimate (Goux 1997; 2000), and it thus became necessary to come up with new economic self-descriptions and external descriptions no longer exclusively based on the discourse of production, exchange, and labor. Thomas Mortimer feared offending the good taste of his readers by depicting the daily uproar of the London stock exchange: "I am to apologize for letting anything so very low appear in print" (1801, 14).

5. An essay on the stock market from 1850 begins, e.g., "stock-jobbing, comparatively speaking, is scarcely known in the United States" (Anon. 1850, 252).

6. Financial speculation is situated in a singularly fraught network of economic abstraction and popular spectacle. The gambling association is still apparent today in terms such as "casino capitalism" (Strange 1986).

7. J. A. Ross 1938; Cowing 1965. These figures should be viewed with caution. Charles Morris (1999, 72) begins with a substantially lower count of active speculators, estimating that there were 1.5 to 2 million shareholders in the United States in 1920, of whom only 600,000 actively speculated on the margin.

8. On the concept of "everyday economics," which emphasizes the heterogeneity of economic knowledge, see Ruccio and Amariglio 2003.

9. See Van Antwerp 1914 for an important introduction to the stock market addressed to a wide audience; on handbooks, see ibid., fn. 2. Periodicals under consideration include *North American Review, The Century: A Popular Quarterly, Harper's,* and *Outlook*.

10. Important texts on the psychology of speculation were written by George C. Selden (1996 [1912]) and Henry Howard Harper (1966 [1926]).

11. For a complementary perspective, see the microsociological works of Karin Knorr Cetina and Alex Preda (Knorr Cetina and Bruegger 2000, 2002; Preda 2001).

12. For a genealogical perspective on finance, see Goede 2002, 2004, 2005.

13. The term "speculator" does not imply a moral or political critique. I adopt the English usage from the time period under consideration and make no distinction between speculator and investor (cf. Chamberlain and Hay 1931).

14. Cf. Gumbrecht 1997 for an exemplary analysis of how binary social and cultural codes are constituted and deconstructed.

15. On deconstruction as a form of reading constantly in danger of becoming a method, see Derrida 1989.

16. One of the limits of deconstruction for social theory can be found here. Social theory cannot discard the task of developing new concepts and analytical strategies even if it is aware of how they can be deconstructed.

17. See Foucault 1978 (1976). An introduction to discourse analysis is not possible here. Foucault's *Archaeology of Knowledge* (1972) and the discourse theory of Laclau and Mouffe (1985) are particularly important for the understanding of discourse theory represented by this study.

18. See Stäheli 1999b for a preliminary sketch of the relationship between cultural studies and systems theory, as well as the overviews in Johnson 1986–87, Hartley 2003, Turner 2003, and Storey 2001. Hall 1981 designates the popular as a territory where the distinction "the people / not of the people" is contested. For the concept of the popular, also see Fiske 1987, Frow 1995, Grossberg 1992, Grossberg, Nelson, and Treichler 1992, Shiach 1989, and Williams 1983 (1976). Overviews from the German-speaking perspective can be found in Hügel 2001 and Winter 2001.

19. See Hall 1981 and especially Fiske 1987 and 1989. For a critical discussion of the popular in cultural studies, see Stäheli 1999b, 2004c, 2004d, and 2005.

20. See Fiske 1989, with critique in Stäheli 2004d. "Unfortunately, it's difficult to discover what the cult studs themselves think about the parallel world of market populism. For all its generalized hostility to business and frequent discussions of 'late capitalism,' cultural studies have failed almost completely to produce close analysis of the daily life of business," Thomas Frank writes bitingly (2000, 290–91).

21. "If 'people's capitalism' did not liberate the people, it nevertheless 'loosed' many individuals into a life somewhat less constrained, less puritanically regulated, less strictly imposed than it had been three or four decades before," Stuart Hall asserts apropos of Thatcherism (1988, 215).

22. "The problem is that Thatcherism articulated this popular desire to the 'free market' and the very powerful idea of 'freedom,'" Hall says (1988, 278). Cf. Frank 2000 for an analysis of the "market populism" of the so-called new economy.

23. Hall 1988, 215. For an overview of this discussion, see McGuigan 1992, 39–40.

24. Max Weber 2000b (1894), 367. Weber's *Schriften zur Börse* (Stock Market Writings) were aimed at a lay readership.

25. Foucault 1991; Dean 1999. On the concept of problematization as an alternative to the classical history of ideas, see Foucault 2001 (1983), 115 (in 1996 German trans.). Problematization examines the discursive and nondiscursive practices shaping something (e.g., schizophrenia).

26. This paragraph is based on Stäheli 2002a.

27. Cf. Stäheli 2002a, 119.

28. Phenomenologically, these two dimensions can rarely be separated. Most forms of hyperconnectivity also function as affective communication. A conceptual division between hyperconnectivity and affectivity is nonetheless helpful. The former cites forms within processes of communication. The latter relies on a noncommunicative capacity for attachment.

29. Symbiotic mechanisms are configurations of social systems that "make it possible for them to activate and direct organic resources" (Luhmann 1974, 100). Luhmann argues that specific functional systems are linked to a particular symbiotic mechanism (111). In this context, the system serving as a reference point for affective communication remains unspecified.

30. Lieb 2001, 34, follows Spangenberg 1993 by arguing that in mass media, "the qualities produced in communication are in the position to fascinate on a psychic level."

31. See also Weingart 1999 and Shaviro 1993.

32. Spangenberg 1993, 82; Lieb 2001, 41. This concept of popular capitalism also follows so-called new economic sociology. It is not a matter of embedding the economy in social or cultural relations (see, e.g., Granovetter 1985), but of examining noneconomic processes and elements immanent in the economy.

CHAPTER I

1. The ambivalence of speculation resurfaces in Jane Austen's *Mansfield Park*. The choice of game already makes this term undecidable. Mrs. Grant cannot decide

between a game of skill (whist) and the "democratic" game of chance (speculation). She is reassured that speculation is more enjoyable, and that there is no simpler game (chapter 25). Cf. Holway 1992, 106, on the ambiguity of speculation in Austen.

2. John A. Hobson, whose book *Imperialism* (1902) was one of the most important reference points for Lenin's theory of imperialism, formulated an almost identical argument for the gambler. He accounted for the popularity of gambling on the basis of the monotonous regime of modern daily life, into which gambling introduced an element "of the unexpected, the hazardous, the disorderly" (Hobson 1906, 6).

3. One of the central presuppositions of the "efficient market hypothesis" is that prices adequately reflect all available information (for criticism of this hypothesis, see Shiller 2000, 171).

4. Van Antwerp 1914, 6–7, drawing on Denslow 1888, 107.

5. Merrill 1938, 560. This conception of the stock exchange is of course not undisputed. Along with Merrill's essay, the *American Journal of Sociology* published a commentary contradicting this assessment of the stock exchange: "At any rate, the stock-exchange operators and the speculating public are far from being representatives of the typical *Homo Oeconomicus*; the fact that well-informed American scholars (and similarly J. M. Keynes in his latest book) tend to assign him this position is in itself a significant indication of substantial changes either in the structure of capitalism or at least in the outlook of intelligentsia in the present phase of financial history" (Melchior Palyi in Merrill 1938, 576).

6. On the observation-theoretical conception of markets, see Luhmann 1988; Baecker 1988. On the system-theoretical analysis of speculation, see Baecker 1999; Piel 2003.

7. "Today the bourse has become the market of all markets [*der Markt aller Märkte*], the center of all big business life. The knowledge of all leading business personalities is distilled in their view on the bourse.... Its prices are the barometer for the entire national and international life of business" (Gustav Schmoller, *Grundriß*, 2: 488–89, cited in von Reibnitz 1912 103).

8. Welles 1975. "The activities of the Exchange ... are among the farthest removed of all those in our culture from the simple commercial transactions of a precapitalist society.... Their activities are couched in a universe of discourse that is unintelligible to the layman," Francis Merrill observes (1938, 568). Max Weber also emphasized the club character of the American and English stock exchanges (Weber 2000c [1894], 326–27).

9. On the connection between contingency and mass culture, see Makropoulos 2003.

10. See Gally 1955–56; Connolly 1983.

11. Baecker 2002 emphasizes that the economy is constituted by observing its own realm of possibilities. In our case, the distinction between speculation and gambling is one of the central means by which finance observes itself. Moreover, the same distinction becomes more significant for external observers of the economy.

12. These discursive dislocations produce instances of undecidability about the meaning of a specific concept. Cf. Ernesto Laclau's concept of the political (Laclau 1990). For the inscription of the political in systems theory, see Stäheli 2000b.

13. To a large extent, I am following Ernest MacDougall's definition: "Gambling is a betting or wagering, by agreement between two or more persons, whereby the money, property or other thing of value of one or more of the parties to agreement becomes the property of the other party or parties to the agreement, without legal consideration, upon happening of an uncertain, future event designated for the purpose" (MacDougall 1936, 22). Bodie, Kane, and Marcus 2003 defines gambling in terms of its relation to a future contingency, i.e., as "to bet or wager on an uncertain outcome." See Ganßmann 2002 on gambling from the position of social theory.

14. Luhmann 1988, 47. Christoph Deutschmann (1999, 71) asserts that a shortage of goods is created by a reported scarcity of money.

15. This dissociation from a discourse of scarce goods was already highlighted as a characteristic of gambling in the middle of the nineteenth century: "Any mode of operating upon prices that cannot have that tendency [i.e., distribution of goods] is gambling" (Laylor 1852, 83).

16. "[Gambling] involves simply sterile transfers of money or goods between individuals, creating no new money or goods. Although it creates no output, gambling does nevertheless absorb time and resources. When pursued beyond the limits of recreation, where the main purpose after all is to kill time, gambling subtracts from the national income" (Samuelson 1976, 425).

17. In film theory, suspense refers to how expectations are intensely elevated on the basis of clear and restricted alternatives (Borringo 1980; Prieto-Pablos 1998). It is not possible for anything to happen. Rather, only one option will be realized from a limited set of possibilities. Admittedly, the suspense in gambling is not the same as in the thriller. To a large extent, gambling lacks signals that anticipate a particular outcome. Gamblers often compensate for this lack of anticipation by constructing (private) mythologies—e.g., lucky numbers.

18. Of course, a more precise analysis has to differentiate between types of gambling. The situation described here is modeled on a card game in which the ante lies on the table and waits for a "receiver." In the lottery, the suspense mechanism is no longer built into the individual operation. The gambler instead receives a lottery ticket.

19. Cf. Gumbrecht 2004 on the concept of presence.

20. The concept of the mutant arises in evolutionary theory and is also a favorite motif in science fiction. A mutant is distinguished by a highly developed feature or capability. In the film *X-Men* (Brian Singer, 2000), the main roles are played by benign mutants whose genetic code has been altered by the x-factor. Through this alteration, the mutants acquire telekinetic and telepathic capabilities.

21. Piel 2003, 25.

22. Baecker 1999, 297. With reference to C. J. Fuchs 1891 (commodity futures), Emery 1969, 116, speaks of the "price forming power" of speculation.

23. In this way, a mode of payment based on anticipation becomes operationally effective: "Accordingly, financial markets operate with payments that anticipate their own reproduction by other payments" (Baecker 1988, 281).

24. The Italian word *speculare* appears as early as the fifteenth century, but not yet in reference to economic interactions. It means, generally, "to spy out," "to examine," and "to observe." Only at the end of the eighteenth century is the term "speculation" used as an economic concept. At this point, it is drawn into a lexical field influenced by neighboring concepts such as "adventure," "gambling," and "vice" (*Oxford English Dictionary*).

25. Following Baudrillard, Konstanze Piel speaks of the "virtualization" (*Virtualisierung*) of stock trading by speculation (Piel 2003, 40ff.).

26. This is not to say that money plays an unproblematic role as a medium of interaction. Rather, conflicts arise around what can be considered money, and the extent to which detaching a medium from its reference (e.g., gold) destroys the medium itself.

27. Reith 1999, 58. This passion—nearing obsession—for gambling was in no way restricted to England, but could also be seen, for example, in France during John Law's speculative undertakings: "The pernicious love of gambling diffused itself through society and bore all public and nearly all private virtue before it" (Mackay 1980 [1841/52]: 24). Today, the strong connection between gambling culture and enthusiasm for speculation is also emphasized. For example, the differing popularity of speculation in Germany and Hong Kong has been explained by the lack of a gambling culture in the former (Fuhrmans/Mungan 1999).

28. Defoe cited in Crump 2003 (1874), 11. For a discussion of Defoe's writings on speculation, see esp. Ingrassia 1998.

29. Cf. my remarks on the figure of "Lady Credit" in chapter 6.1. See Kintzelé 1986 on the modern logic of credit.

30. Similarly, an anonymous English text from 1720 warned about how credit would pollute money as a medium of circulation, but could at least be of passing use: "'Tis certain, that 'till we have a greater Plenty of Money, Trade and all other Business must be assisted with Paper Credit" (cited in Bolla 1989, 113).

31. Cf. the prevalence of this motif in theories of market manipulation still readily advanced today.

32. See Luhmann 1991 on the distinction between danger and risk. A subject is passively exposed to dangers, while calculable risks are attributed to a subject as originator.

33. Findlay 1986, 4, 51. Tocqueville emphatically describes this connection between democracy and contingency: "Those who live in the midst of democratic fluctuations have always before their eyes the image of chance; and they end by liking all undertakings in which chance plays a part" (cited ibid., 3).

34. For a description of the Amsterdam stock exchange in the seventeenth century, see Vega 1957 (1688) .

35. On sleeplessness in descriptions of the speculator, see Stäheli 2002a, 110–11.

36. Excessive speed is also linked to speculation in an article in *Blackwood's Magazine*: "Never has a nation lived faster in every sense; and their very distractions take the form of speculations and business enterprise" (Anon. 1882, 723).

37. Smith 1868, 48–49. See also Smith's description of a pastor addicted to financial news: "The business transformed the man. His face became haggard; his eyes dilated; his hair dishevelled; he could not sleep; he bought all editions of the papers; got up nights to buy extras; chased the boys round the corner for the latest news; was early at the stock market, and among the last to leave the Fifth Avenue Hotel at night when the board closes its late session" (251).

38. Cf. Verdicchio 2006 on vampirism in films that deal with the stock market.

39. Anon. 1884, 629. The futures trader was also seen as a parasite (Cowing 1965, 5).

40. Early forms of financial speculation were understood to disrupt the economy and the political community, "to deracinate value from a material basis, to disengage and disrupt order, to introduce profound and widespread volatility in socioeconomic life" (Holway 1992, 111).

41. For Simmel, value could only be constructed by sacrifice and renunciation: "Within the economic sphere, this process develops in such a way that the content of the sacrifice or renunciation that is interposed between man and the object of his demand is, at the same time, the object of someone else's demand. (Simmel 2004, 77–8). The speculator was criticized as no longer capable of this renunciation excluding any kind of immediacy (cf. Rieusset-Lamarié 1992, 158). In texts friendly to speculation, the capacity to keep one's distance became a financial criterion: "They are the men, and the women, too, . . . who are content to go without present income from an investment, provided it promises large rewards in the future. I call them conservative because the gambling element of chance does not control their operation" (Ives 1888, 559).

42. Nelson 1964 [1903], 21; Wolf 1966 [1924], 68–69. This stance on contingency was also of great importance in the history of science. The theory of probability was developed on the basis of games of chance. This cannot be addressed here, but see, e.g., Hacking 1990; Bernstein 1998; Reith 1999.

43. Simmel 2000a [1895], 230. Elsewhere, Simmel compares the gambler to an alpinist, emphasizing the tension that could lead to the disintegration of the gambler's identity: "An alpinist would be indignant if one wanted to compare him or her to a gambler. And yet both wish to place their existence at risk as a purely subjective excitation and gratification. Frequently the gambler does not look for material profit but the excitement of risk and the gripping combination of the cold-bloodedness and passion of one's own skill and the incalculability of fate" (2000b [1911], 221). In this comparison, the production of tension also increases affect.

44. While gambling, the gambler is reduced to emotions, becoming a "self-absorbed emotionalist" (Hobson 1906, 8). Hobson cites W. D. MacKenzie, who claims that a bet involves neither reason nor will, but exclusively the emotions.

45. On the role of contingency in mass culture, see Makropoulos 2003.

46. The phrase "mask of business" also appears elsewhere in the same issue of *The Century* (Anon. 1884, 627).

CHAPTER 2

1. The terms " proponent" and "opponent" of speculation are used here to simplify.

2. The American economic writer Charles Conant, an influential supporter of extending U.S. markets, maintained that gambling was "destructive to the morals and pockets of young men, and cannot be too severely censured" (Conant 1904, 85). This harsh verdict was supported by the argument that gambling was not subject to the laws of supply and demand.

3. Luhmann 2000, 137–38, emphasizes that the function of a system is always constructed by an observer performing either a self- or external observation.

4. See Neal and Youngelson 1988 on the role myths and rituals play in the stock market. Functional myths legitimate both the stock exchange itself and aspects of stock trading that might otherwise seem irrational.

5. See Fabian 1990, 174. With this distinction, proponents of speculation could recapitulate the classic critique of gambling. In contrast to speculation, gambling was morally reprehensible because it was unproductive (e.g., see Martin 1919, 76).

6. See chapter 4 on strategies of inclusion and exclusion and on mass psychology.

7. Cf. Goux 1997 and 2000 for an analysis of the role Proudhon played in the speculation paradigm.

8. Comments on Proudhon are restricted to the enthusiasm displayed for speculation in his *Manuel du spéculateur à la Bourse* (Stock Exchange Speculator's Manual), believed to have been written with an unnamed coauthor. Proudhon's aversion to any form of monetary exchange—an aversion consistently ridiculed by Marx—cannot be discussed here.

9. Marieke de Goede (2004, 203) shows in a reading of Charles O. Hardy's *Risk and Risk-Bearing* (1927) how speculation became a matter of risk management. For Hardy, the speculator is also distinguished from the gambler by a visionary function. Only the speculator can recognize future market needs.

10. E. H. H. Simmons, president of the NYSE, made a similar distinction: "Both processes [gambling and speculation] involve the assumption of risks in the hope of making profits. But the risks assumed in speculation are the inherent risks attending the ownership of property. They are not risks artificially trumped out or created, but already existing in the nature of things" (1927: 48). Simmons also distinguished between necessary and artificial risks. Necessary risks were anchored in the order of things. With a double gesture, Simmons was able to found contingency on a noncontingent ground. He pointed to the way contingency and noncontingency depended on property relations, and subsequently naturalized these property relations ("the nature of things").

11. In a similar vein, Ralph H. Mottram writes: "From the earliest shadow of its present form speculation has always meant the taking of risk in order to exorcise, circumvent, and nullify risk" (Mottram 1929, 20).

12. Carret 1990 [1930], 12. For a discourse analysis of the market's truth function, see Tellmann 2003.

13. It is possible to speak of a "cynical market," following Oscar Wilde's definition, in act 3 of *Lady Windermere's Fan* (1892), of a cynic as "[a] man who knows the price of everything and the value of nothing."

14. Conant 1904, 116; emphasis added. On the logic of the supplement, see also Derrida 1976 (1967), 244ff. (in 1983 German trans.).

15. André Dessot, "Faut-il éliminer les petits porteurs?" (Should Small Shareholders Be Eliminated?), *Le Monde*, 1989, cited by Rieusset-Lemarié 1992, 148. New communications technologies offered by online brokers opened the financial markets to a wide public. These technologies led to deregulation and acceleration of speculation, but also brought about a crisis in the regime of inclusion: "On the one hand, it is necessary to have contagious networks because of the transaction speed they make possible and the extension of the market. On the other hand, a contagious network is, by definition, a 'user-friendly network,' that is, for the most part indiscriminately open to a huge number of market participants" (Rieusset-Lemarié 1992, 151).

16. As a point of contrast from the 1930s, see the explicit call for a politics of exclusion by the German law professor Heinrich Göppert (1930).

17. Weber 2000a, 573. This argument also shows how greatly perspectives on speculation differed in Germany and the United States. At the end of the nineteenth century in Germany, speculation was still mistrusted as an illegitimate practice. Though moralistic literature criticizing speculation also existed in the United States, speculation was used as an almost euphoric national self-description.

18. Parker cited by Cowing 1965, 107. On the legal and human right to speculation, see also Hill 1975 (1904), 398: "Speculation is inherent in the human constitution, and men have a legal and moral right to speculate, provided they do so reasonably, intelligently and at their own risks."

19. In an overview of discussions about the economy, Frank Fayant (1909, 32) also emphasized the "broadness of the market," a broadness that again depended on the number of speculators.

20. Lewinsohn and Pick 1933, 14.

21. Ibid., 64. Lenin also observed that speculation became a highly inclusive form of communication when stock values decreased. At least in the self-understanding of the actors, this decrease in value ultimately undermined the distinction between capital and labor. With shares of stock, even the worker felt like a small capitalist: "The 'democratisation' of the ownership of shares, from which the bourgeois sophists and opportunist so-called 'Social-Democrats' expect (or say that they expect) the 'democratisation of capital,' the strengthening of the role and significance of small-scale production, etc., is, in fact, one of the ways of increasing the power of the financial oligarchy. Incidentally, this is why, in the more advanced, or in the older and more 'experienced' capitalist countries, the law allows the issue of shares of smaller denomination. . . . [T]he magnates of German finance look with an envious eye at Britain, where the issue of one-pound shares (= 20 marks, about 10 rubles) is permitted. Siemens, one of the biggest industrialists and 'financial kings' in Germany, told

the Reichstag on June 7, 1900 that 'the one-pound share is the basis of British imperialism'" (Lenin 1999 [1917], 59–60).

22. This politics could already be seen in the way John Law's Banque Générale aimed for the greatest possible distribution of shares to investors: "It is our intent to allow the greatest possible number of our subjects to participate in the transactions of the company, and in the earnings it is granted. In order that everyone can participate in this way, we shall divide the stock in shares of 500 livres" quoted in Lewinsohn and Pick 1933, 64).

23. Stock prices are democratically arrived at inasmuch as they "reflect what people think the stock is worth or what they think it may be worth at some time in the future" (James Wood 1966, 104).

24. Carret 1990 (1930), 9; cf. Moore 1921. A blurb from *Esquire* magazine on the Wiley Investment Classics reprint praises Carret's book as a "genuine rarity" containing "timeless insights." It is striking that, in the literature on investment handbooks, classics are seen as up to date.

25. Gibson 1907, 17; emphasis added. In a similar vein, the well-known financier Jesse Livermore wrote: "Speculation is a business. It is neither guesswork nor gamble. It is hard work and plenty of it" (cited in Wilson 1963, 124).

26. Clashing worldviews also became evident at this point. The neo-Kantian Friedrich Albert Lange (cited in Fayant 1909, 30) saw in speculation the possibility for a "more solid and real character to business." Speculation was also seen in euphoric terms as tearing down all boundaries to individual action.

27. Warner 1969 (1889), 37. Daniel Defoe, who regarded the distinction between gambling and speculation as unimportant, questioned the fictional nature of the financial system in the early eighteenth century (see Sherman 1996), but critics only came to see futures trading as artificially heightening its fictionality in the late nineteenth century.

28. Warner 1969 (1889), 37. Warner resumed his critique of futures in the novel he wrote with Mark Twain, *The Gilded Age*. In one passage, they caricature the attention given to futures as a waste of the present. The out-of-luck speculator Colonel Beriah Sellers first criticizes women for being trapped in the present, only to be parodied by his wife for living in a dematerialized future: "'You dear women live right in the present all the time—but a man, why a man lives'—'In the future, Beriah? But don't we live in the future most too much, Beriah? We do somehow seem to manage to live on next year's crop of corn and potatoes as a general thing while this year is still dragging along, but sometimes it's not a robust diet—Beriah'" (Twain and Warner 1915 [1873], 1: 266).

29. Because of its virtual character, futures trading was defined as an elaborate undertaking: "[A sale] by a party who does not have the grain and does not expect to have it and does not want to have it, selling to a party who does not want the grain, does not expect to get it, and does not intend to get it, and in fact, does not get it" (Clifford Thorne in Michaels 1987, 66). Max Weber's definition of stock speculation also covers futures trading: "[O]n the exchanges, a deal is struck over a set of goods that

are not present, and often 'in transit' somewhere, or often yet-to-be-produced; and it takes place between a buyer who usually does not himself wish to 'own' those goods (in any regular fashion) but who wishes—if possible before he receives them and pays for them—to pass them along for a profit" (Weber 2000c [1894], 309–10)

30. Thomas Gibson emphasized precisely this point, distinguishing gambling from speculation on the basis of the "mechanical devices" used in gambling (Gibson 1907, 6).

31. In the middle of the nineteenth century, economists such as Calvin Colton read this process of abstraction as a sign of "cultural sophistication" (Harding 1993, 212).

32. This paradox of purification should not be understood as a linear temporal progression. The expulsion—or at least the containment—of thrills did not precede concerns about fictionalization. Rather, both arguments appeared at the same time.

33. See also Stäheli 2004f on the similar process of fictionalization in discourses following the collapse of the so-called new economy.

34. *Kirkpatrick & Lyons v. Bonsall*, 72 Pa. 155, 158 (1872), cited in Stout 1999, 717. The Stock Exchange Act of 1934 was also influenced by fears that speculation could produce false prices (Stout 1999, 729).

35. *Irwin v. Williar*, 110 US 499 (1884), 508, 4 Sup. Ct. Rep. 160, cited in MacDougall 1936, 72. In his biography of Bernard Baruch, James Grant argues that strong measures were taken against gambling on the stock exchange around 1900 (Grant 1983, 79–80 [in 1999 German trans.]). Fictive transactions prohibited during this time are allowed today, but conversely some forms of manipulation prohibited today were allowed in 1900.

36. *Clews v. Jamieson*, 182 US 461 (1901): "Contracts for the future delivery of merchandise or stock are not void, whether such property is in existence in the hands of the seller or to be subsequently acquired. On their face these transactions are legal, and the law does not, in the absence of proof, presume that the parties are gambling. The proof must show that there was a mutual understanding that the transaction was to be a mere settlement of differences; in other words, a mere wagering contract."

37. Cf. the discussion of the problematic legal distinction between the permissible act of "offset" futures trading and the prohibited act of "settling differences" in Stout 1999, 720–21.

38. *Irwin v. Williar*, 110 US 499 (1884), 508, 4 Sup. Ct. Rep. 160, cited in MacDougall 1936, 72; emphasis added. For Judge Job Barnard of the U.S. District Court for the District of Columbia (Supreme Court of the District of Columbia), the criterion for the legitimacy of futures trading was likewise the exchange of real goods: "Nothing passes between the parties beyond the money from loser to winner, and nothing else was intended to pass. This is a mere bet—a gamble. But where the actual delivery is made of the goods contracted to be sold and received, the transaction becomes a commercial one" (Barnard cited in Dies 1925, 42).

39. See the argument in Goede 2004, 202, that legal intervention made it urgently necessary for speculation to be separated from gambling.

40. See the history of bucket shops in Fabian 1990. Contemporary criticism of bucket shops is thoroughly documented in Hill 1975 (1904).

41. Fabian 1990, 192; quoted words within the quotation are from Hill 1975 (1904), 43, and Patton 1900.

42. On the ticker, see chapter 7.

43. In this sense, bucket shops turned out to be precursors of modern-day online brokerages, which also offer the small investor the opportunity for high-speed trading in real time.

44. Francis Merrill (1938, 566) suggested that the existence of bucket shops created problems for the stock exchange, since the public easily confused speculation with gambling in bucket shops. Cf. also Cowing 1965.

45. Petrażycki 1906, 58.

46. Ibid., 47. "It has often been remarked that the average man is an optimist regarding his own enterprise and a pessimist regarding those of others," G. C. Selden observed in his classic *Psychology of the Stock Market* (1996 [1912], 29). See also Odean and Barber 2001; Odean and Gervais 2001.

47. Harper 1966, 69. The speculator "enters 'the game' . . . with eyes open, and the cards all faced up on the table" (91). Everyone had the same chances because everyone had the same information. The idea of an efficient market could be represented by the metaphor of gambling.

48. Following the success of his book, Goodman went on to moderate several television shows on business, work for which he even won an Emmy award. For affirmative use of the gambling metaphor, see also, e.g., Gordon 1999, 17.

49. Schelling cited in Smith 1967, 12.

50. In no way do I want to claim that speculation has been exclusively defined as gambling since the 1960s. There continues to be conflict over the boundaries between gambling and speculation. "We want people interested in wealth-building, not gamblers," the electronic broker Ronald Shear emphasized in a report on day traders (Der Hovanesian 2001, 151). In my analysis, Smith does not represent a new hegemonic model, but a popular and provocative way of dispensing with the distinction between gambling and speculation.

PART II. CROWDS: INTRODUCTION

1. Baruch cited in Sobel 1988, 367. See also the contemporary historian Frederick Lewis Allen on the euphoria of speculation preceding the 1929 crash (Allen 1931, 315).

2. MacClelland 1989 traces theorizing about crowd psychology back to Plato and the origin of political thought. Crowds were directly linked to the universalization of inclusionary regimes, and following the introduction of universal male suffrage by the French Revolution, their mentality came to be seen as a problem. On crowd psychology in nineteenth-century France, see Barrows 1981.

CHAPTER 3

1. After the collapse of the so-called new economy of the 1990s, the founder and former chairman of the Vanguard Group, John Bogle, who popularized index-fund investing as opposed to stock picking, asserted that the current financial market was simply another chapter of Mackay's *Extraordinary Popular Delusions* (Bogle 2000, 134). For other references to Mackay as our contemporary, see Savage 1996, *The Economist*, no. 343 (1997): R4–R5, and Evans 2002. Mackay's book has also been recommended for managers (MacCallum 2001).

2. *Extraordinary Popular Delusions* was reprinted by MetroBooks in 2002 with Baruch's 1932 foreword (Baruch 2002).

3. Recent popular and economic reception of Mackay thus presumes a continuity between contemporary and historical forms of speculation. This presumption of continuity can also be found in many new editions of other classic speculation handbooks. Financial markets function more rapidly, the sums of money involved have become greater, and financial products and techniques have become more complicated. Speculation is nonetheless seen as unchanged. This argument is mainly supported anthropologically (emotions like fear and hope remain the same), and can be linked to the fundamental lack of foundation for finance in the nineteenth century.

4. See Minton 1975; Murphy 1997; Chancellor 1999; Tvede 2001.

5. See Carswell 1961; Garber 2000.

6. Nineteenth-century American accounts often mention these three major cases of speculation in Europe, sometimes using the same language as Mackay; see, e.g., Hooper 1876 on Tulipomania and Colton 1845 on Law's Mississippi scheme and the South Sea Bubble, who suggests that the history of American "commercial delusions" still has to be written (345).

7. Mackay 1980 [1841–52], xvii.

8. Luhmann sees the differentiation of the three meaning dimensions as a historical process (1995, 86). Only with the establishment of writing can these dimensions be clearly separated and identified individually. Precisely these divisions can also be observed in crowd psychology. Furthermore, an analysis in terms of meaning dimensions reveals the ways in which the modernity of crowds is represented.

9. Deutschmann 1999. Cf. Gabriel Tarde's (1989 [1898]) classification of crowds on the basis of functionally determined themes.

10. Debord 2006 (1967) emphasizes that the spectacular consists precisely in this link between collective spectacle and individual spectator.

11. This striking connection between individualization and deindividualization reappears in subsequent investment theory as regards overconfidence in speculation (Odean and Gervais 2001). Crowds form when everyone believes they are more rational, and more individual, than the crowd. Individualism becomes contagious, so to speak.

12. Cf. Norberg 2003; Preda 2001. See also esp. Jones 1900, 216, who suggests that focusing exclusively on the economy is pathological.

13. See the similar account of Tulipomania in the Netherlands in Mackay 1980 (1841–52), 94.

14. The social dimension of meaning addresses the problem of organizing the relation between ego and alter ego (Luhmann 1995, 8off.).

15. Bagehot 1931 [1873], 35.

16. With this potential for contagion, theorizing about speculation anticipated one of the central points in debates about the risk society. In these debates, it was also assumed that in modern societies, risk no longer recognized class boundaries, but had gone beyond social status and class (cf. Beck 1992). Mackay speaks, e.g., of the "inordinate thirst of gain that had afflicted all ranks of society" (1980 [1841–52], 55).

17. Mackay does not use the metaphor of contagion in chapters on speculation, but mainly in his account of the crusades. He described emotions, primarily enthusiasm and fear, as contagious.

18. Cf. Stallybrass and White 1986, especially in relation to Bakhtin's model of the carnivalesque.

19. Not all notions of crowds were marked by this indifference to stratification. Cf. Brantlinger 1996, who proceeds from the assumption that crowd psychology saw crowds as proletarian. Financial crowd psychology nonetheless showed an indifference to class distinctions.

20. Mackay 1980 [1841–52], 15. Apropos of this mass self-referentiality, Gabriel Tarde later noted the aimless pleasure "loving crowds" at festivals took in their own existence (1989 [1898], 58).

21. Cf. Sloterdijk 2000, who incisively observes that crowds are communities of hearing.

22. The weather can be seen as an equivalent to pathology in such discourse, as is particularly evident in Mackay's example of a sudden, unexpected storm (1980 [1841–52], 2).

23. See Catalogue of Prints and Drawings in the British Museum, Div. I, Political and Personal Satires, vol. 2 (London, 1873), 541–43.

24. I discuss this process in chapter 7, focusing particularly on handbooks for reading the ticker tape, which provided exemplary techniques for controlling the speculative imagination.

25. This articulation of fictionality and universal inclusion did not first appear in Mackay. Daniel Defoe had already foregrounded the fictionality of speculation, and had also emphasized that it was contagious. See chapter 1.2.

CHAPTER 4

1. Anon. 1877. Mackay's Extraordinary Popular Delusions was being actively discussed in the United States only a few years after it was published there. For a thorough American review of the book in that era, see Anon. 1863a, which, however, moralizes about Mackay's descriptions of crowds and contrasts the pursuit of money with immaterial wealth (93).

2. On crowds in nineteenth-century American literature, see Mills 1986, 76, who writes that "in the America they knew, democratic men acting as a crowd were time and again a danger to the freedom and independence of democratic man."

3. "To Peters, Lincoln, James Fenimore Cooper, and many other Whigs and conservative Democrats in the antebellum period, mobs were evidence of an unstable public opinion that had to be properly guided" (Bush 1991, 13).

4. *Chicago Tribune*, May 6, 1886, cited in Leach 1994, 210.

5. I am following the account of Ross given by Raymond J. Wilson 1968, 96ff.

6. Gibson 1889, 67; Mottram 1929, 35. A similar formulation can be found in Simmons (1927, 59), who argued that the United States, more than any other country, owed its existence to speculation: "If it had not been for the financial speculations of Queen Isabella of Spain . . . Christopher Columbus could not have obtained the ships in which he sailed to discover the new western world." Cf. Noble 1933, 40, who also traced the existence of the United States to speculation by Columbus.

7. The British historian and Liberal politician James Bryce argued in his study *The American Commonwealth* that although speculation had European roots, it was more widespread and more competently practiced in America (Bryce 1895 [1888], 656).

8. In the United States, everyone speculated, and everything became an object of speculation, the French economist Michel Chevalier observed (1961 [1836]).

9. Anon. 1882, 721; emphasis added. Charles Albert Collman speaks of "the great financial arena, in which America's capital pits itself against the world" in his book *Our Mysterious Panics, 1830–1930* (1968 [1931], 3).

10. "The American people are regarded by foreigners as the greatest of all speculators," Henry Emery wrote (1969 [1896], 7).

11. See Nobel 1933, 40; Clews 1973 [1908], 18. "The members of the Stock Exchange are, through the power of electricity, in closer sympathy with the great heart of civilized humanity than all the missionaries and philanthropic societies in the world. They are the great cosmopolitans of the age," Henry Clews asserted (15).

12. The boundless vista described by Gibson was connected to the speed with which new possibilities could not only be seen, but also realized: "A new world waiting to be made, with no native or local civilised institutions, too big, too suddenly discovered, too vital in its possibilities to be fashioned within the slowly formed restrictions that its present possessor's ancestors left behind when they quitted small, already partially exhausted and rigorously partitioned Europe" (Mottram 1929, 27).

13. "The human mind is more interested in the unknown than in the known. . . . This is also true marketwise," William Moore says, e.g., in *Wall Street: Its Mysteries Revealed* (1921, 110).

14. See Sobel 1970 and Wood 1966, 94, on stock trading in the streets. The street market only lost importance when the telephone was introduced on the stock exchange in 1897 (Wood 1966, 95).

15. Smith 1868, 4. For a first outline of the argument here, see Stäheli 2003a.

16. Osgood 1867 thus anticipated the connection between mobs and criminality that would later be seen as typical by crowd psychologists.

17. This narrative structure was often employed. In his *Drama of Money Making*, Hubert A. Meredith (1931) argued that internal order was not apparent from the perspective of the outsider (cf. Stäheli 2003a). This opposition has not lost its power

even today. A commercial for the online broker Datek titled "The Wall" (1999) contrasted the chaos in front of the exchange with the chaos on the exchange floor (Stäheli 2008).

18. Cf. the social psychology of Edward Ross (1929 [1908]), which was strongly influenced by Tarde, and the "constructive" crowd theory of Gerald Stanley Lee, which became one of the bases for the newly emerging field of public relations (Bush 1991).

19. See the short biographical note on Sidis in the *Atlantic Monthly* 94 (December 1922): 36.

20. Sidis also experimented with hypnosis.

21. For Le Bon (1903 [1895]), crowds represented a lower evolutionary level of society, and Tarde (1989 [1898], 49) similarly asserted that the crowd and the family were archaic social forms. However, Sidis emphasized the evolutionary advantages of crowds.

22. Cf. the controversy over the pathological significance of hypnosis between Charcot and the Nancy School. Sidis follows a line of thought closely resembling that of the Nancy School, which saw the state of hypnosis not as abnormal, but as a universal anthropological characteristic (see Leach 1992).

23. Sidis 1899, 303. See Ross (1929 [1908], 43) for a similar argument. In his social psychology, Edward Ross found the phenomenon of "multiplied suggestion" to be characteristic of crowds. Ross relied primarily on Tarde, but was also influenced by Sidis.

24. Sidis (1899, 311) did not speak of functional differentiation, but of a society with differentiated religious, political, and economic institutions.

25. Sidis linked "fixation of the attention" to constrained physical movement (1899, 45) and spoke of a "limitation of voluntary movements" (47), observing: "If anything gives us a strong sense of our individuality, it is surely our voluntary movements" (299).

26. Cf. the close relationship between the social and suggestion in Tarde. According to Tarde, suggestion could not be excluded from a society primarily constituted by imitation: "The social like the hypnotic state is only a form of dream, a dream of command and a dream of action. Both the somnambulist and the social man are possessed by the illusion that their ideas, all of which have been suggested to them, are spontaneous" (Tarde 1903 [1890], 77).

27. The notion of suggestion occupied the position that in later social theories would be occupied by notions of action and communication.

28. In a chapter titled "Financial Crazes," Sidis analyzes speculation in terms of his theory of suggestion (Sidis 1899, 343ff.), but he hardly goes beyond summarizing the descriptions of Tulipomania in the Netherlands, John Law's Mississippi scheme in France, and the South Sea scandal in England found in Mackay. Sidis does not develop an analysis of speculative manias based on crowd psychology, but is often content to graft his notion of suggestion onto the descriptions by Mackay.

29. This approach avoids simply examining, as would a history of ideas, the influence Sidis had on economic theories and manuals. The notion of suggestion was mostly linked by implication to crowd psychology, and it is not surprising that it was used imprecisely.

30. See the analysis of rumor in terms of media theory in Kapferer 1990 and discussion of this in Rötzer 1996.

31. Through "suggestion at a distance" (*suggestion à la distance*), it is possible to be part of a crowd even without immediate physical contact, Tarde observes (1989 [1898], 34).

32. Moore 1921, 109. Moore emphasized this point: "Man is naturally disposed to listen to suggestions or accept advice agreeable to his inclination, wishes or interests, regardless of their source or their soundness" (50).

33. See also chapter 7.7 on suggestibility and the stock ticker.

34. This emphasis on the impulsiveness of rumor already existed at the end of the nineteenth century. For example, the financier in Robert Grant's novel *An Average Man* reacts immediately to rumor: "He acted at once" (1884, 608).

35. The mathematician Harald Günzel cited in Neubauer 1998, 215. On the link between popular capitalism and vampirism as epidemic communication, see Stäheli 2004f.

36. Clews 1968 [1900], 7. Cf. Kapferer 1990 on the problematic distinction between rumor and information.

37. Harper 1966 (1926), 11. Even today, behaviorist financial theory has to distinguish between information and noise on a normative basis (see Thaler 1992; Black 1986).

38. Emery (1969 [1896], 177. Conant (1904, 97) also emphasized that on the stock exchange, rumor could replace information.

39. See Tellmann (1999, 2003) on the argument that the market itself became a standard of truth.

40. Le Bon 1903, 144; Tarde 1903 (1890). Imitation interacted with suggestion in a mutually supportive way. Emory Bogardus (1920, 117) spoke of a "suggestion-imitation phenomenon": "Suggestion is the initiating part and imitation is the resulting phase. Suggestion is the process whereby an idea or mode of action is presented to the mind and accepted more or less uncritically. Imitation is the process of copying an idea or mode of action and carrying it out more or less immediately in a relatively unchanged form." Bogardus distinguished between presenting and accepting an idea, and copying an idea. Luhmann (1995, 147–49) would see this distinction as a difference between understanding communication and accepting communication. For Luhmann, accepting communication means changing one's own premises for behavior.

41. This argument later became important for contrarian investors, particularly in relation to the tape reader, who provided information rather than spread rumor about the market.

42. In his classic study *Mass Persuasion: The Social Psychology of a War Bond Drive*, Robert Merton mentions the rationale provided by a small investor for his

decision to buy bonds: "We felt that others had been impressed and bought a bond. And the fact that so many people felt the same way made me feel right—that I was in the right channel" (Merton 1946, 56).

43. Jones 1900, 202. On the behavior of small investors and the accumulation of errors, see also, e.g., Odean 1998; Odean and Gervais 2001.

44. Whitney cited in J. A. Ross 1938, 92. See also Whitney's address to the Illinois Chamber of Commerce (1930, 120). Whitney became famous for his stock purchases during the crash of 1929. In 1931, he became president of the NYSE. Whitney vehemently defended governmental regulation of the exchange: "The exchange is a perfect institution" (Gordon 1999, 238). However, he and his brokerage not only made a number of poor investments but also embezzled large amounts of money. In 1938, the bankruptcy resulting from these poor investments and the crimes committed by Whitney were exposed. Gordon (248) describes Whitney as the "most famous felon" produced by Wall Street.

45. J. A. Ross 1938, 159; cf. Luhmann 1997b. Whitman's sentimental notion of democracy resurfaced as a danger in the "emotional mass" of speculators.

46. Hope, fear, and greed were often mentioned together. These emotions were readily used to justify a crowd psychology of the market. Adam Smith speaks, e.g., of "hope, fear, greed, ambition" as states that cannot be grasped by rational analysis (1967, 13). Humphrey Neill lists a number of emotions that must be accounted for in a theory of speculation: "habit, custom, imitation, contagion, fear, emotion, greed, hope, credulity, susceptibility, irritability, pride-of-opinion, wishful thinking, impulsiveness, conceit" (1967, 10).

47. The small speculator was often described as optimistic and trusting under normal market conditions. This speculator was almost always bullish, and rarely speculated on falling prices. During the 1920s, the atmosphere on the market was described in precisely these optimistic terms: "Good feeling was contagious and pervasive . . . , and the little five- or ten-share traders were close kin emotionally to those who dealt in thousand-share blocks" (R. T. Patterson cited in Klingaman 1989, 31). On the general role of trust in financial markets, see Pixley 2004.

48. See Odean and Gervais 2001. Cf. also Petrażycki 1906 on overconfidence, discussed in chapter 2 above.

49. Van Antwerp 1914, 183, 211. Panic was sometimes seen as the antithesis of speculation: "[I]f they [gamblers] could only foresee the precise date when distrust shall take the place of confidence, timidity follow boldness, and panic crush speculation" (Carpenter 1883, 80).

50. Lloyd 1883, 78. Panics played on fear of the unknown, and thus led to impulsive behavior that could spread from the "brain" of one speculator to the "brains of other fellow men" (Moore 1921, 111).

51. Canetti 1984 (1960). Cf. Theodor Geiger (1967 [1926]), who argued that panics were not best understood in terms of crowd dynamics, since one individual acted against another.

52. Collman 1968 (1931), 280; emphasis added. For Collman, Wall Street was "the most powerful machine in an age of machines" (4) a machine whose primary purpose was "money making" (21).

53. Ibid., 277. Like Collman, Alex J. Wilson argued that human nature played a large role in causing panics: "Human nature rather than the share market must therefore be blamed for the manias and delirious gambling" (1906, 26). Wilson did not compare the economy to a machine, but contrasted human nature to the market.

54. Bagehot cited in Gibson 1907, 32. "While the participation of speculators in the market increases the chances of an intelligent forecast of coming events, it also affords the opportunity for panic influence," Emery pointed out (1969 [1896], 122).

55. "A merchant must not only have confidence in those around him, but also in himself" (quoted apropos of the 1857 crisis in Jones 1900, 213).

56. "The market contains, in both senses of the word, panic as a contagion. Panics are impeded by the market but also contained within it" (Dupuy 1991, 70).

57. Cf. Collman 1968, 38. For Collman, a panic represented the end of a cycle. A panic destroyed unrealistic hopes and dreams. After the panic, however, speculators experienced renewed hopes for permanently growing profit.

58. Patrick 1900, 290. "The mind of society . . . is an imitative, unreflective, half-hypnotic, half-barbaric mind . . . in times of crazes, epidemics and social cataclysms, . . . causing disastrous relapses to a lower plane of civilization" (294).

59. This theatrical dimension was reinforced by the fact that panics could take place in a theater as well as on the stock market: "Anyone who has ever witnessed a panic in a theatre or auditorium, or in the stock market, need not be told that under such circumstances men are but little saner than cattle" (Harper 1966 [1926], 83).

60. Dies 1925, 6. However, since it was confined to business hours on the exchange, and its beginning and end were theatrically ordered by the sound of a gong, the spectacle of panic described by Dies was controllable. At the end of the session, the visitor reluctantly left the exchange: "[It] has been an exciting day, a day in a world set apart—a day in the world of wheat" (7). Panics only fascinated within this separate space. Embedded in a narrative of initiation, like descriptions of crowds on the exchange above, panics were qualified relative to an observer and thus predictable.

CHAPTER 5

1. Withers 1910, 22; emphasis added. Cf. the description of the NYSE by the travel writer Colin Ross: "One sees waving arms and gesticulating hands. Mad cries rise from the pit. The people in the pit have been crushed into a repulsive mass, an intricate knot of struggling bodies. The pit has become a morass. The cries have become howls. . . . What happens below is no longer only about bread and corn. The figures that fly from mouth to mouth no longer have anything to do with however many thousands of bushels of wheat. These figures are empty, imaginary numbers in a game of blind chance, a wheat roulette" (Colin Ross cited by Adolph Weber 1933, 271).

2. For references to crowd psychology in investment literature, see Dines 1996; Connors and Hayward 1995; Ellis 2002.

3. Neill 1960 (1931). Representatives of the contrarian position include James Fraser (an investment fund manager and successor to Humphrey Neill), Sloan Wilson, Fred Kelly, Robert Smitley, "Adam Smith," and John Magee.

4. This examination of crowd psychology and speculation can be connected to work on governmentality that studies technologies of exerting power at a distance (Dean 1999).

5. Science is another exception in which the classical distribution of audience and professional roles does not exist (Stichweh 1988). However, unlike the economic system, the science system does not constantly try to rearticulate distinctions between these roles.

6. Cowing 1965, 109, referring to *Public Papers of Charles E. Hughes* (n.p., 1910), 308–10.

7. Keynes's comparison implicitly feminized the stock exchange. On the feminization of the stock exchange, see chapter 6.

8. "No, our numbers have not grown in the past half-century, nor in the centuries since the Dutch began to tiptoe and to stamped through their tulip craze. That is as it should be: Different drummers cannot by definition beat their tom-toms in unison, and a 'herd of individualists' is a contradiction in terms. Contrarians are a permanent minority, comfortable only in articulate opposition to the placidly received wisdom or panicked self-delusion of the majority" (Safire in Menschel 2002, xi). In this context, Safire cited Mackay's *Extraordinary Popular Delusions*, which he and Menschel had venerated during their student years (Menschel 2002, xii).

9. So-called noise traders follow precisely this logic (Black 1986).

10. In chapter 6, I examine the ways in which the relationship between market and speculator are sexualized.

11. The stock market has often been described as hysterical (see chapter 6).

12. Bond reached a dead end in his analysis, however, because he could not reconcile the risks of suggestion with a desiring speculator modeled after the neoclassical subject. Even under the most difficult conditions, the speculator had to conquer his suggestibility (Bond 1928, 177). However, Bond did not address how the speculator could conquer suggestibility without undermining the role his hopes and fears were to play as the basis of the market.

13. A writer in the magazine *The World's Work* observed that the good speculator "is in close enough contact with the market to act before the outside public can act" (Anon. 1920, 230).

14. See the discussion of hypnosis and suggestibility in chapter 4.4.1.

15. To correct distorted public impressions of trading on Wall Street during the 1920s, Lefèvre tells the story of John K. Wing of Kuhn, Loeb & Co. in *The Making of a Stockbroker* (1925).

16. The immediate effects of the media representing share prices are discussed in detail in chapter 7 of this book.

17. The vacation is a topos of trauma that appears often in popular autobiographical and biographical writings about the stock exchange. In his book *One Up on Wall Street*, the collapse of the stock market hangs over a trip to Ireland that Fidelity Investments' famous fund manager Peter Lynch takes in the fall of 1987: "I was thinking about Dow Jones and not about Blarney, even at the moment I kissed Blarney's stone. . . . That night at Doyle, I couldn't have told you what sort of seafood meal I ate. It's impossible to distinguish cod from shrimp when your mutual fund has lost the equivalent of the GNP of a small, seagoing nation" (Lynch 1989, 11–12). Being away from the market was also linked to missed opportunity. In this case, Lynch had missed the opportunity to limit his investment losses during the October 1987 crash.

18. Wilson 1963, 125.

19. Neill cited by Wilson 1963, 126. Here Neill touches on a theme that is also important for investment psychology today. Small investors tend to keep stocks they should sell, refusing to admit that they have made a poor decision and unrealistically hoping that their stocks will rise in value again. See Odean and Gervais 2001. Selden 1912, 118, makes a similar point: "The successful trader gradually learns to study his own psychological characteristics and to allow to some extent for his customary errors of judgment."

20. The following is based on Stäheli 2003b.

21. Smith 1967, 81. Cf. Somers 1994 on the way narration can be used to construct identity.

22. Emerson 1997 (1841) cited by Menschel 2002, 181. Ross 1897 also contrasts Emersonian individualism with the crowd: "We must hold always to a sage Emersonian individualism, that . . . shall brace men to stand against the rush of the mass" (298).

CHAPTER 6

1. Judith Butler (1999 [1990], 145) uses the term "heterosexual matrix" to describe a concept of gender in which the human body is rendered socially uniform and meaningful only through heterosexuality. At times, in Butler's writings, this matrix appears to encompass all other discourses. My argument does not presuppose the discursive unity of the heterosexual matrix, but uses this matrix as a principle to regulate modes of inclusion according to functional systems. Cf. Pasero and Weinbach 2003.

2. Cf. Warner 1992 and Stäheli 2002a on processes of abstraction.

3. Smitley 1933, 8–9.

4. The public debt that arose in the seventeenth century led to a number of speculative ventures, to which the spread of credit is linked (Chancellor 1999, 50–51; Dickson 1993).

5. For a characterization of the Bank of England and the South Sea Company as "Ladies" with the charm of a new lover, who are given the "utmost Adoration," see Milner 1720, 34, 36.

6. In *Sober Advice from Horace*, Alexander Pope represented speculation with Fufidia, a calculating figure who acts like a whore (Pope cited by Nicholson 1994: 165):

"Fufidia thrives in Money, Land and Stocks: / For Int'rest, ten per cent. her constant rate is; / Her Body? Hopeful heirs may have it gratis. / She turns her very sister to a Job, / And, in the Happy minute, picks your Fob." At the same time, Defoe represented credit as a virgin. Like virginity, creditworthiness could not be restored once lost (Sherman 1996, 43).

7. Only recent work on Lady Credit has recognized that this discourse was innovative, and should not simply be seen as the corruption of masculine ideals (cf. Mulcaire 1999).

8. A similar constellation of masculine and feminine positions can be seen in descriptions of the market as hysterical. Hysteria on the market was a feminized illness that could only be controlled by a masculine speculator (cf. Mackie 1997, 131).

9. Clews 1973 (1908), 444. It was also taken for granted that women did not understand the economy.

10. Cf. a similar characterization of women speculators in Lewinsohn and Pick (1933, 39). Lewinsohn and Pick encountered problems in their efforts to compare female speculators to male speculators. Even the male speculator had characteristics that were "the basis for all speculation," including "belief, superstition, and a quantum of hysteria." However, he compensated for these irrational characteristics by an "inclination to systematize."

11. Pratt 1921, 209, established four levels of investment according to risk. He recommended that women not go beyond the first, and most secure, level. Women thus remained distant from the pure speculation that took place on the fourth level, since this speculation was focused on future profit rather than protecting a secure investment.

12. Cf. the criticisms of gambling and speculation discussed in chapter 1.3.

13. Russell 2000, 485, notes that a similar configuration of male and female roles can be found in discourses on gambling. Gambling itself plays the feminine role of seducer, while gamblers are often men. Russell suggests that when this distinction between gambling and gambler collapses, women come to be seen as particularly dangerous.

14. Frederic Bond also mentions the impatience of women speculators, and accounts for this impatience by claiming that women had not learned to live with taking risks: "Not that women cannot speculate well. . . . But the enormous majority of women, having been used to protection, take losses in a manner so distressed and so distressing to the broker that it is practically a fixed rule in the Street, not to handle their accounts" (Bond 1928, 173). Cf. Klingaman 1990, 70, on the topos of the female speculator as a difficult client.

15. It is difficult to find reliable statistics on the percentage of women who participated in speculation. James Ross (1938, 95) cited a 1914 issue of the *Wall Street Journal* in which the first efforts were made to count the number of women speculators. According to Ross, this issue estimated that 15 percent of speculators in the United States were women. Cowing 1965, 119, referring to Wendt 1941, estimated that in 1933, women constituted 20 percent of stock holders. Klingaman 1990, 6,

also estimates that in 1928 and 1929, 20 percent of speculators were women. Beginning in the 1920s, the number of women speculators increased greatly. As a result, brokerages reserved separate rooms for female clients. However, these statistics are open to debate. An investment guide for women written during the 1930s estimated that 51 percent of stock assets were controlled by women. For this estimate to make sense, the 20 to 25 percent of woman speculators would have had to own an above-average amount of stock.

16. In this approach to managing stocks, America differed from England and France, where women brokers already existed at the end of the eighteenth century.

17. Cf. Frisken 2000 on Woodhull as a public figure.

18. The motif of cross-dressing on the stock exchange also appears in *The Speculator*, a novel by Olive Malvery (1908), whose heroine disguises herself as a dandyish Italian broker.

19. The sisters worked as spiritualist mediums for Vanderbilt, who often consulted them in this capacity before he made decisions about speculation. Matthew Hale Smith (1972 [1873], 276) suggested that the Claflin sisters might regularly use clairvoyance at their brokerage firm to pick stocks.

20. Not only the address of Woodhull, Claflin & Co. was a reminder of these criminal origins. *Claflin's Weekly*, the newspaper published by the Claflin sisters, regularly exposed fraudulent speculation.

21. Woodhull, Claflin & Co. closed after two years. Woodhull had to devote her efforts to becoming a presidential candidate. She and her sister disappeared from the stock exchange as quickly as they had appeared on it. This rapid disappearance further undermined the ideal of the stockbroker who dedicated his entire life to speculation and could no longer escape its attractions.

22. Le Bon 1903 (1895), 40. Le Bon also wrote that "like women," a crowd "goes at once to extremes" (56).

23. "Mr. Johnson" was Edward Crosby Johnson, the owner of Fidelity Investments (Nocera 1994, 48).

24. Lefèvre 1982 (1923), 202.

25. Chancellor 1999, 167, cites a description of the amateur speculator who is "befooled, bewitched and bedeviled by what he hears in the market."

26. Distinguishing between the positions of female reader and male author, Huyssen 1986 argues that mass culture was conceived of as a woman in the nineteenth century. As is the case in *Madame Bovary*, nineteenth-century women tended to be passive readers of bad literature, whereas the role of writer of genius was a male preserve. A main criticism of women readers was that they developed a pathological addiction to reading, and a male observer of the market might similarly become addicted to the latest stock quotations. Speculation thus strikingly inverted the relationship between female reader and male author. The female market "wrote" the economy, as it were, through its activity, functioning as the author of the tragedy (although unconscious of that role, of course, not being an individual, but a crowd). The male speculator was a distant observer and reader of the market, whose activity was often difficult to decode,

not to speak of being highly contagious, making a sovereign reader necessary if it was to be properly understood.

27. Fowler 1968 [1880], 448–49. An article on gambling used similar terms to describe the passion women had for gambling: "The most ardent and persistent game- sters are women. Both the young and the old, the comely and the ill-favored, hazard everything in order to gratify this taste, and usually succeed in gratifying it to the full. To the young, who deny themselves no sensual delight, this furnishes an additional pleasure, while the old who can no longer practise the degrading vices which they love, find in gaming a fresh and unfailing excitement" (Anon. 1863b, 306).

28. "Women are drawn to the stock exchange by its capriciousness, and often gam- ble on a stock because the name of this stock—like the name of a *haute couture* fashion designer—appeals to them, and promises to bring them luck" (Lewinsohn and Pick 1933, 38).

29. "Many women who play the stock market read the daily listing of quotations with an unusual and almost sexual excitement" (Lewinsohn and Pick 1933, 38).

30. Cf. Ross 1938, 95, for articles on women and speculation written during the 1920s.

31. Zimmerman 1931, 15. Intuition continues to be seen as an advantage for women investors today. A German investment manual titled *Frauen sind die besseren Anleger* (Women Are Better Investors) claims that women are better prepared to spec- ulate than men: "As a rule, they [women] are ready to find a balance between informa- tion and intuition, a balance that makes them less vulnerable to the classic traps on the trading floor" (cited by Stroczan 2002, 66).

CHAPTER 7

1. A shorter version of 7.1 through 7.5 appeared in the *Zeitschrift für Soziologie* (Stäheli 2004e).

2. Luhmann 1995, 161, similarly points out that media of dissemination have resulted in "an immense extension of the scope of the communicative process."

3. Like that of writing, the effect of the stock ticker cannot simply be explained by an "increase in the number of addressees" (Luhmann 1997a, 269). Luhmann mentions that writing brought about a "new order of time and of culture." My task will be to ask what qualitative effects are to be attributed to the stock ticker.

4. Tarde 1989 (1898) presciently observed the close link between the way in which new media of dissemination like the telegraph were established and the way in which different audiences arose. For Tarde, members of an audience could, despite spatial distance, simultaneously understand information spread by modern media of dissem- ination. Anonymous audiences were a paradigmatically modern phenomenon. These audiences were no longer the copresent audiences, subject to spatial restrictions, he had described as crowds (Stäheli 2004e).

5. Media of dissemination do not necessarily have to be charged with positive affects. For example, new media of dissemination can also inspire fear when they

foreground their own role as media. In my analysis, I focus mainly on media of dissemination charged with positive affects.

6. As my analysis will show, the ticker was mainly watched collectively by small audiences—though a few financiers had their own tickers. In this sense, the ticker closely resembled forms of dissemination like cinema, which also required that a partial audience occasionally gather at a particular place and time.

7. In connection with Gilgenmann (1997), I rely on the premise that techniques of communication and media of dissemination constitute utterances as an aspect of communication. I thus internally shift Luhmann's notion of communication. An utterance is not only determined by reference to an actor. Rather, my interest is in the way an utterance comes into existence, and in which media (techniques) are used to bring this utterance into existence. For a more extensive treatment of this shift, see Stäheli 2001.

8. The problem of mediality poses itself in the mode by which a communication is uttered: it is not only a transmission, but it inserts a gap into the very process of communication. Mediality interrupts the smooth functioning of communication; it marks the "unintended and unintentional aspects of media in contrast to the contents these media transmit." The medium itself leaves a trace in the process of communication that cannot be entirely grasped hermeneutically (Tholen 2002, 42, in connection to Sybille Krämer). This trace of the medium, which often appears in seemingly negligible details, is what I want to pursue.

9. The success story of the ticker points to the close connection between telegraphy and events on the stock market. Toward the end of the nineteenth century, more than half of all messages sent by telegraph consisted of stock market communication (Chancellor 1999, 166). Wall Street changed visibly. It went from being a place where the exchange was based on interaction to being the site of a communicative network. Before telegraph lines were installed underground, Wall Street was surrounded by countless telegraph poles. The telegraph wires are said to have formed such a thick web that not even a sparrow could fly through them (Thomas 1989 [1967], 63).

10. Czitrom 1982, emphasizing that this notion of a unified world finds a counterpart in Christian theology.

11. Cf. Field 1998. The Trans-Lux display allowed information from the ticker to be projected. This information thus became immediately visible, and messengers were no longer needed to transfer the newest information from the tape to a board in the "customer room" of a brokerage.

12. The stock ticker used the same series circuit technology as the telegraph: "The wire ran from the floor of the exchange to the nearest broker's office, through an electromagnet in the ticker machine, and then on to the next office. . . . The start of a trade message was a break in the circuit (start pulse) which caused the ticker mechanism to start spinning. The following sequence of marks and spaces caused the mechanism to select a particular character on its wheel and a hammer struck the paper strip against it" (www.baudot.net/docs/harvey--mark-and-space.pdf, accessed June 18, 2012).

13. Calahan 1901, 236. Early tickers were powered by batteries, which had to be filled with acid twice a week, and the battery acid often ate away at the clothes of employees (Hotchkiss 1965, 435).

14. When the stock market crashed in October 1929, the NYSE ticker was delayed by 147 minutes during the afternoon: "All over the nation Americans hovered over ticker tapes, stunned by the realization that the prices they were seeing were substantially behind the actual floor transactions" (Thomas 1989, 229).

15. The first lists of stock prices already existed in England toward the end of the seventeenth century (Neal 1987, 99).

16. In the United States, ticker service was provided by the New York Quotation Company and Western Union's Gold Exchange Service. In 1874, 116 tickers outside New York were already included in the network (Field 1998, 167). Preda 2003 claims that 23,000 offices in the United States had a ticker in 1905. By the end of the 1930s, there were 3,722 NYSE tickers, 650 Trans-Lux displays, and 5,650 similar devices (Loeb 1996 [1935], 281). Stock quotations were received not only in brokerage firms but in bucket shops and even restaurants. The ticker was introduced in London only a few years after coming into use in the United States (Meeker 1922, 435).

17. See Luhmann 1993, Stichweh 1998, and Werber 1998 on spatiality and functional differentiation.

18. By contrast, in the political system, the participation of the public has a legitimizing function, although it complicates decision making.

19. Meeker 1922, 64. See also Sconce 2000 on descriptions of "haunted media" using metaphors of the uncanny and the spectral.

20. The French economist Paul Leroy-Beaulieu recommended that a similar system be introduced on the French stock exchange (Van Antwerp 1914, 163).

21. The precursor of the *Wall Street Journal* was called *Ticker*.

22. Van Antwerp 1914, 162. The stock exchange was described as even more democratic than the political system, since everyone had a chance for success, regardless of birth. Henry Harper, who wrote one of the first books on stock market psychology, called the stock exchange "one of the fairest and most open games ever played; a game in which every participant, man or woman, rich or poor, old or young, has an equal chance" (Harper 1966, 69). This argument was revived in stronger form during the so-called new economy of the 1990s (see Frank 2000).23. Dice 1926, 282. "The palpitant voice of the ticker never records fluctuations of the heart, only of the stock-market" in Elizabeth Cavazza's short story "When Angry, Count a Hundred" (1892, 599).

24. In the science system, a real-time medium would not have the same meaning for a theory of inclusion. Scientific publications are, or should be, relevant after their publication dates.

25. See Massumi 1996 and Stäheli 2003a on media and affectivity.

26. There was similar fascination with the cinematic apparatus when it was originally introduced; see, e.g., Metz 1977.

27. Adolf Weber 1933, 288; emphasis added. Although Max Weber hardly mentions the ticker in his writings on the stock exchange, he describes the use of a device

resembling the Gold Indicator, a precursor of the ticker, in transactions "in American saloons, where electrically controlled indicators display . . . rates on the exchanges on an hourly basis and patrons bet . . . on the direction in which the indicator will move" (Weber 2000b [1894], 359; trans. modified).

28. Stock speculation was criticized as a "game" that increasingly attracted incompetent speculators, whose fervor focused entirely on the medium itself, since they were unable to grasp the "reality" of the prices displayed on the ticker.

29. Lewinsohn and Pick 1933, 83; emphasis added. Cf. Sconce 2000 on the topos of the uncanny in descriptions of new media.

30. Although the ticker portrayed stock trading nearly in real time, it was a one-way medium and could not be used to take orders to buy or sell stock, which had to be done telegraphically. The blackboard made the latest prices and volumes reported by the ticker visible to the audience of the bucket shop or brokerage firm.

31. Althusser's (1977) theory of interpellation has to struggle with a similar paradox, since only a subject that has already been interpellated can at all understand an interpellation.

32. See Stäheli 2003a on the role noise plays in processes of economic inclusion.

33. Dice 1926, 43. "To the uninitiated, the tape appears to be a meaningless jumble of letters and figures. But the broker and regular habitué of the Street soon learn to read it at sight" (Pratt 1921, 184).

34. See chapter 4.1.

35. For the connection between media and presence effects, see also Fohrmann, Schütte, and Voßkamp 2001.

36. Reading the stock prices listed in the paper was at times also described as pathological, and can be connected in this way to criticism of the addiction to reading (e.g., Anon. 1882, 715).

37. On the notion of an explicit connection between a stock boom and hypnosis, see Patrick 1900.

38. Cf. Gumbrecht 2004, who speaks of an oscillation between meaning and nonmeaning.

39. See, e.g., Wyckoff 1910 and Neill (1960 [1931]).

40. On speculation as the self-adjustment of society to the probable, see chapter 2.1.2 above.

41. Neill 1960 [1931], 44. The tape reader isolated and individualized himself through his mode of reading, which demanded great concentration and made communication with others impossible. Cf. chapter 5.2 above.

42. Wyckoff 1910, 137. Preda's (2003) assertion that reading the ticker tape was professionalized by chart analysis should thus be approached with caution. Chart analysis rests on the assumption that conclusions drawn from the past can be used for the future. The tape reader, however, relied exclusively on signs of the future detected in the continuous flow of the present.

43. Even Neill, who left room for at least a basic form of writing, emphasized that this writing had a primarily disciplinary effect. Reading the ticker required great

concentration. Writing down information from the ticker helped the ticker reader develop this concentration, along with his abilities as an observer.

44. See chapter 6 above on intuition as an element in the feminization of the market.

45. The notion of intuition also played an important role in philosophical discussions around the turn of the twentieth century. Bergson 1999 (1903) argued that intuition played a role in constituting cognition. The world could only be grasped through intuition. For Bergson, intuition was also marked by a temporal dimension. Only through intuition could real time (as opposed to mathematical time) be grasped. Intuition thus became a means of "nonconceptual cognition."

46. Butler 1997, 2.

47. Victoria Woodhull saw the connection between acting as a spiritualist medium and speaking for herself as essential. On spiritualism and emancipation, see Sconce 2000 and Stäheli 2003c.

48. Denying the female gaze is crucial for inclusion in the gendered observational apparatus in which Dumont is embedded.

EPILOGUE

1. Self-descriptions were retroactively constitutive, deferring what had been observed; see Stäheli 2000b, 184ff.

REFERENCES

Abt, Vicki, James F. Smith, and Eugene M. Christiansen. 1985. *The Business of Risk: Commercial Gambling in Mainstream America*. Lawrence: University Press of Kansas.

Agger, Ben. 1989. *Fast Capitalism: A Critical Theory of Significance*. Champaign: University of Illinois Press.

Allen, Frederick Lewis. 1931. *Only Yesterday: An Informal History of the Nineteen-Twenties*. New York: Blue Ribbon Books.

Althusser, Louis. 1977. *For Marx*. Translated by Ben Brewster. London: Verso.

Angas, Lawrence. 1936. *Investment for Appreciation: Forecasting Movements in Security Prices*. New York: Somerset.

Anonymous. 1850. "Stock Markets." *United States Democratic Review* 27, no. 147 (September): 252–62.

———. 1863a. "Review: Charles Mackay, Popular Delusions." *North American Review* 96, no. 198 (January): 87–110.

———. 1863b. "Gamesters and Gaming-Houses." *Westminster Review* in *The Living Age* 78, no. 1002 (August): 305–316.

———. 1867. "Pan in Wall Street." *Atlantic Monthly* 19, no. 111 (January): 118–19.

———. 1870. "Punchinello in Wall Street." *Punchinello* 1, no. 8 (May 21): 117.

———. 1877. "New Books." *Scribner's Monthly* 13, no. 4 (February): 571.

———. 1882. "Romance in Business." *The Living Age* 152, no. 1970 (March 25): 707–24.

———. 1884. "Business Gambling." *The Century: A Popular Quarterly* 28, no. 4 (August): 627–29.

———. 1901. "A Dangerous Time." *The Outlook* 68 (2): 105–6.

———. 1920. "The Investment Tortoise and the Speculative Hare: Distinction Between Legitimate Speculation and Stock Gambling." *World's Work* 39, no. 3 (January): 230–31.

Baecker, Dirk. 1988. *Information und Risiko in der Marktwirtschaft*. Frankfurt am Main: Suhrkamp.

———. 1999. "Die Preisbildung an der Börse." *Soziale Systeme* 5 (2): 287–312.

———. 2002. "Die Form der Zahlung." In *Die gesellschaftliche Macht des Geldes*, edited by Christoph Deutschmann. Special issue of *Leviathan* 21: 73–82. Wiesbaden: Westdeutscher Verlag.

Bagehot, Walter 1931 (1873). *Lombard Street: A Description of the Money Market.* London: John Murray.

Barnard, Eunice F. 1929. "Ladies of the Ticker." *North American Review* (Spring): 405–10.

Barrows, Susanna. 1981. *Distorting Mirrors: Visions of the Crowd in Late Nineteenth Century France.* New Haven: Yale University Press.

Baruch, Bernard. 2002 (1932). "Introduction to Extraordinary Popular Delusions and the Madness of Crowds by Charles Mackay." In *Markets, Mobs, and Mayhem: A Modern Look at the Madness of Crowds,* edited by Robert Menschel, 37–38. Hoboken, NJ: John Wiley & Sons.

Beck, Ulrich. 1992. *Risk Society: Towards a New Modernity.* Translated by Mark Ritter. London: Sage Publications.

Benjamin, Walter. 1973 (1937). *Charles Baudelaire: A Lyric Poet in the Era of High Capitalism.* Translated by Harry Zohn. London: NLB.

Bergson, Henri. 1999 (1903). *An Introduction to Metaphysics.* Translated by T. E. Hulme. Indianapolis: Hackett.

Bernstein, Peter. 1998. *Against the Gods: The Remarkable Story of Risk.* New York: John Wiley & Sons.

Best, Susie M. 1910. "A Song of the Ticker." *Ticker* 6, no. 6: 247.

Bigelow, Gordon. 1998. "Technologies of Debt: Bank, Finance and the Subject of Economic Thought." *New Orleans Review* 24, no. 2: 14–22.

Black, Fischer. 1986. "Noise." *Journal of Finance* 41, no. 3: 529–43.

Blanchot, Maurice. 1982. *The Space of Literature.* Translated by Ann Smock. Lincoln: University of Nebraska Press.

Bodie, Zvi, Alex Kane, and Alan Marcus. 2003. *Investments.* Chicago: McGraw-Hill.

Bogardus, Emory. 1920. "Suggestion-Imitation Phenomena." *Essentials of Social Psychology* 6: 117–36.

Bogle, John C. 2000. "Investing Wisely in an Era of Greed." *Fortune,* October 2: 124–29.

Bolla, Peter de. 1989. *The Discourse of the Sublime: Readings in History, Aesthetics and the Subject.* Oxford: Basil Blackwell.

Bond, Frederic D. 1928. *Stock Movements and Speculation.* New York: Appleton.

Borringo, Heinz-Lothar. 1980. *Spannung in Text und Film: Spannung und Suspense als Textverarbeitungskategorien.* Düsseldorf: Pädagogischer Verlag Schwann.

Boyle, James E. 1921. *Speculation and the Chicago Board of Trade.* New York: Macmillan.

Brantlinger, Patrick. 1996. *Fictions of State: Culture and Credit in Britain 1694–1994.* Ithaca, NY: Cornell University Press.

Breithaupt, Fritz. 1998. "Money as a Medium of Communication and Money as Individuation." *New Orleans Review* 24, no. 2: 23–29.

Brenner, Reuven, and Gabrielle Brenner. 1990. *Gambling and Speculation: A Theory, a History, and a Future of Some Human Decisions.* Cambridge: Cambridge University Press.

Bruyn, Frans de. 2000. "Reading *Het groote tafereel der dwaasheid*: An Emblem Book of the Folly of Speculation in the Bubble Year 1720." *Eighteenth-Century Life* 24, no. 2: 1–42.

Bryce, James. 1895 (1888). *The American Commonwealth*. Vol. 2. New York: Macmillan.

Bush, Gregory. 1991. *Lord of Attention: Gerald Stanley Lee and the Crowd Metaphor in Industrializing America*. Amherst: University of Massachusetts Press.

Butler, Judith. 1997. *"Excitable Speech": A Politics of the Performative*. New York: Routledge.

———. 1999 (1990). *Gender Trouble: Feminism and the Subversion of Identity*. New York: Routledge.

Butler, Samuel. 1903. *The Way of All Flesh*. London: Grant Richards.

Caillois, Roger. 1961. *Man, Play, and Games*. Translated by Meyer Barash. New York: Free Press of Glencoe.

Calahan, Edward A. 1901. "The Evolution of the Stock Ticker." *Electrical World and Engineer* 37, no. 6: 236–38.

Canetti, Elias. 1984 (1960). *Crowds and Power*. Translated by Carol Stewart. New York: Farrar Straus Giroux.

Carey, John. 1992. *The Intellectuals and the Mass*. London: Faber & Faber.

Carpenter, Frank D. 1883. "Boomtown." *Atlantic Monthly* 52, no. 309: 76–84.

Carret, Philip L. 1990 (1930). *The Art of Speculation*. New York: John Wiley & Sons.

Carswell, John. 1961. *The South Sea Bubble*. London: Cresset Press.

Cavazza, Elizabeth. 1892. "When Angry, Count a Hundred." *The Century* 44, no. 4: 597–602.

Chancellor, Edward. 1999. *Devil Take the Hindmost: A History of Financial Speculation*. London: Macmillan.

Chamberlain, Lawrence, and William W. Hay. 1931. *Investment and Speculation: Studies of Modern Movements and Basic Principles*. New York: Henry Holt.

Chevalier, Michel. 1961 (1836). *Society, Manners and Politics in the United States: Being a Series of Letters on North America*. Boston: Weeks, Jordan. Originally published as *Lettres sur l'Amérique du Nord* (Paris: C. Gosselin, 1836).

Clews, Henry. 1968 (1900). *The Wall Street Point of View*. New York: Greenwood Press.

———. 1973 (1908). *Fifty Years in Wall Street*. New York: New York Times.

Collman, Charles A. 1968 (1931). *Our Mysterious Panics, 1830–1930*. New York: Greenwood Press.

Colton, Calvin. 1845. "'Commercial Delusions'—Speculations." *American Whig Review* 2, no. 4: 341–57.

Conant, Charles A. 1904. *Wall Street and the Country: A Study of Recent Financial Tendencies*. New York: G. P. Putnam's Sons.

Connolly, William E. 1983. *The Terms of Political Discourse*. Princeton: Princeton University Press.

Connors, Laurence A., and Blake E. Hayward. 1995. *Investment Secrets of Hedge Fund*

Managers: Exploiting the Herd Mentality of the Financial Markets. New York: McGraw-Hill.

Costa, Neil A. 2000. "The Temple of Boom." Presentation at the Australian Technical Analysts Association, Sydney. www.marketmasters.com.au/46.0.html (accessed May 25, 2012).

Cowing, Cedric B. 1965. *Populists, Plungers, and Progressives: A Social History of Stock and Commodity Speculation, 1890–1936.* Princeton: Princeton University Press.

Crump, Arthur. 2003 (1874). *The Theory of Stock Exchange Speculation.* London: Longmans Green.

Czitrom, Daniel J. 1982. *Media and the American Mind: From Morse to McLuhan.* Chapel Hill: University of North Carolina Press.

Dean, Mitchell. 1999. *Governmentality, Power and Rule in Modern Society.* London: Sage.

Debord, Guy. 2006 (1967). *The Society of the Spectacle.* Translated by Donald Nicholson-Smith. New York: Zone Books. Originally published as *La société du spectacle* (Paris: Buchet-Chastel, 1967).

Defoe, Daniel. 2000a (1719). "The Anatomy of Exchange Alley." In *Political and Economic Writings of Daniel Defoe*, edited by W. R. Owens and P. N. Furbank, vol. 6: *Finance*, edited by John McVeagh, 129–56. London: Pickering & Chatto.

———. 2000b (1710). "An Essay upon Publick Credit." In *Political and Economic Writings of Daniel Defoe*, edited by W. R. Owens and P. N. Furbank, vol. 6: *Finance*, edited by John McVeagh, 49–62. London: Pickering & Chatto.

———. 2000c (1701). "The Villainy of Stock-Jobbers Detected, and the Causes of the Late Run upon the Bank and Bankers Discovered and Considered." In *Political and Economic Writings of Daniel Defoe,* edited by W. R. Owens and P. N. Furbank, vol. 6: *Finance,* edited by John McVeagh, 33–47. London: Pickering & Chatto.

Denslow, Van Buren. 1888. *Principles of the Economic Philosophy of Society, Government and Industry.* New York: Cassell.

Der Hovanesian, Mara. 2001. "The Rabbi of Day-Trading." *Business Week*, December 4: 150–52.

Derrida, Jacques. 1976 (1967). *Of Grammatology.* Translated by Gayatri Chakravorty Spivak. Baltimore: Johns Hopkins University Press.

———. 1989. "Some Statements and Truisms about Neologisms, Newisms, Postisms, Parasitisms, and Other Small Seismisms." In *The States of Theory*, edited by David Carroll, 63–94. New York: Columbia University Press.

Desan, Philippe. 1993. *L'imaginaire économique de la Renaissance.* Mont-de-Marsan: Éditions Interuniversitaires.

Deutschmann, Christoph. 1999. *Die Verheißung des absoluten Reichtums: Zur religiösen Natur des Kapitalismus.* Frankfurt am Main: Campus.

Dice, Charles A. 1926. *The Stock Market.* New York: McGraw-Hill.

Dies, Edward J. 1925. *The Wheat Pit.* Chicago: Argyle Press.

Dickson, Peter G. M. 1993. *The Financial Revolution in England: A Study in the Development of Public Credit, 1688–1756*. Aldershot: Gregg Revivals.

Dines, James. 1996. *How Investors Can Make Money Using Mass Psychology: A Guide to Your Relationship with Money*. Belvedere, CA: James Dines.

Dreiser, Theodore. 1912. *The Financier*. New York: Boni & Liveright.

Dreman, David N. 1998. *Contrarian Investment Strategies: The Next Generation; Beat the Market by Going Against the Crowd*. New York: Simon & Schuster.

Duguid, Charles. 1901. *The Story of the Stock Exchange: Its History and Position*. London: Grant Richards.

Dunstan, Roger 1997. *Gambling in California*. California Research Bureau, California State Library. www.library.ca.gov/CRB/97/03/crb97003.html (accessed May 25, 2012).

Dupuy, Jean-Pierre. 1991. *La panique*. Paris: Delagrange.

Dusaulx, Jean. 1779. *De la passion du jeu, depuis les temps anciens jusqu'à nos jours*. Paris: l'imprimerie de Monsieur.

Dyer, Frank L., and Thomas C. Martin. 1929. *Edison: His Life and Inventions*. New York: Harper and Brothers.

Ellis, Charles D. 2002. *Winning the Loser's Game: Timeless Strategies for Successful Investing*. New York: McGraw-Hill.

Ellis, Charles D., and James R. Vertin. 1997. *The Investor's Anthology: Original Ideas from the Industry's Greatest Minds*. New York: John Wiley & Sons.

Emerson, Ralph W. 1997 (1841). "Self-Reliance." In *Anthology of American Literature*, edited by George L. McMichael, 863–66. Upper Saddle River, NJ: Prentice Hall.

Emery, Henry C. 1969 (1896). "Speculation on the Stock and Product Exchanges in the United States." PhD diss., Columbia University. New York: Greenwood.

Esteve, Mary. 2003. *The Aesthetics of the Crowd in American Literature*. Cambridge: Cambridge University Press.

Ettema, James, and Charles Whitney. 1994. *Audience Making: How the Media Create the Audience*. London: Sage.

Evans, Jules. 2002. "We're Forever Blowing Bubbles." *Euromoney* 33, no. 402: 6–7.

Faber, D. P. 1996. "Suggestion: Metaphor and Meaning." *Journal of the History of the Behavioral Sciences* 32, no. 1: 16–29.

Fabian, Ann V. 1990. *Card Sharps, Dream Books, and Bucket Shops: Gambling in 19th-Century America*. Ithaca, NY: Cornell University Press.

Fama, Eugene. 1970. "Efficient Capital Markets: A Review of Theory and Empirical Work." *Journal of Finance* 25, no. 2: 383–417.

Fayant, Frank H. 1909. *Some Thoughts on Speculation*. New York.

Field, Alexander J. 1998. "The Telegraphic Transmission of Financial Asset Prices and Orders to Trade: Implications for Economic Growth, Trading Volume, and Securities Market Regulation." *Research in Economic History* 18: 145–84.

Findlay, John M. 1986. *People of Chance: Gambling in American Society from Jamestown to Las Vegas*. New York: Oxford University Press.

Findlay, M. C., and E. E. Williams. 2000. "A Fresh Look at the Efficient Market

Hypothesis: How the Intellectual History of Finance Encouraged a Real 'Fraud-on-the-Market.'" *Journal of Post Keynesian Economics* 23, no. 2: 181–99.

Fisher, Irving. 1924. "Useful and Harmful Speculation." In *Readings in Risk and Risk-Bearing*, edited by Charles O. Hardy, 346–49. Chicago: University of Chicago Press.

Fiske, John. 1987. *Television Culture*. London: Methuen.

———. 1989. *Understanding Popular Culture*. London: Methuen.

Fohrmann, Jürgen, Andrea Schütte, and Wilhelm Voßkamp, eds. 2001. *Medien der Präsenz: Museum, Bildung und Wissenschaft im 19. Jahrhundert*. Cologne: DuMont.

Foucault, Michel. 1972. *The Archaeology of Knowledge*. Translated by A. M. Sheridan Smith. New York: Pantheon Books.

———. 1977. *Discipline and Punish: The Birth of the Prison*. Translated by Alan Sheridan. New York: Vintage Books.

———. 1978 (1976). *The History of Sexuality, Vol. 1: An Introduction*. Translated by Robert Hurley. New York: Vintage Books.

———. 1991. "Governmentality." In *The Foucault Effect: Studies in Governmentality*, edited by Graham Burchell, Colin Gordon, and Peter Miller, 73–86. London: London University Press.

———. 2001 [1983]. *Discourse and Truth: The Problematization of Parrhesia*. Edited by Joseph Pearson. Los Angeles: Semiotext(e).

Fowler, William W. 1968 (1880). *Twenty Years of Inside Life in Wall Street; or, Revelations of the Personal Experience of Speculator*. New York: Greenwood Press.

Frank, Thomas. 2000. *One Market Under God: Extreme Capitalism, Market Populism, and the End of Economic Democracy*. New York: Doubleday.

Fraser, Steve. 2005. *Every Man a Speculator: A History of Wall Street in American Life*. New York: Harper Collins.

Freud, Sigmund. 2004 (1921). *Mass Psychology and Analysis of the "I."* In *Mass Psychology and Other Writings*, translated by J. A. Underwood. New York: Penguin Books.

Frisken, Amanda. 2000. "Sex in Politics: Victoria Woodhull as an American Public Woman, 1870–1876." *Journal of Women's History* 12, no. 1: 89–111.

Frothingham, O. B. 1882. "The Ethics of Gambling." *North American Review*: 162–75.

Frow, John. 1995. *Cultural Studies and Cultural Value*. Oxford: Clarendon Press.

Fuchs, Carl Johannes. 1891. *Der Waren-Terminhandel, seine Technik und volkswirtschaftliche Bedeutung*. Leipzig: Duncker & Humblot. Offprint of *Schmollers Jahrbuch für Gesetzgebung* 15, no. 1.

Fuchs, Peter. 1992. *Die Erreichbarkeit der Gesellschaft*. Frankfurt am Main: Suhrkamp.

Fuchs, Peter, and Andreas Göbel, eds. 1994. *Der Mensch—das Medium der Gesellschaft?* Frankfurt am Main: Suhrkamp.

Fuhrmans, Vanessa, and Christina Mungan. 1999. "What Happened? It's All in Their Heads: Different Markets Have Different Psychologies." *Wall Street Journal*, April 26, R5.

Gabriel, Mary. 1998. *Notorious Victoria: The Life of Victoria Woodhull, Uncensored.* Chapel Hill, NC: Algonquin Books of Chapel Hill.

Gally, W. B. 1955–56. "Essentially Contested Concepts." *Proceedings of the Aristotelian Society* 56: 167–98.

Ganßmann, Heiner. 2002. "Das Geldspiel." In *Die gesellschaftliche Macht des Geldes*, edited by Christoph Deutschmann. Special issue of *Leviathan* 21: 21–46. Wiesbaden: Westdeutscher Verlag.

Garber, Peter. 2000. *Famous First Bubbles.* Cambridge, MA: MIT Press.

Gatens, Moira. 1996. *Imaginary Bodies: Ethics, Power and Corporeality.* London: Routledge.

Geiger, Theodor. 1967 (1926). *Die Masse und ihre Aktion: Ein Beitrag zur Soziologie der Revolutionen.* Stuttgart: Ferdinand Enke.

Geisst, Charles R. 1997. *Wall Street: A History.* Oxford: Oxford University Press.

Gibson, George R. 1889. *The Stock Exchanges of London, Paris and New York.* New York: G. P. Putnam's Sons.

Gibson, Thomas. 1907. *Cycles of Speculation.* New York: Moody.

———. 1965 (1923). *The Facts About Speculation.* Wells, VT: Fraser.

Gilgenmann, Klaus. 1997. "Kommunikation—ein Reißverschlußmodell." *Soziale Systeme* 3, no. 1: 33–56.

Ginneken, Jaap van. 1992. *Crowds, Psychology and Politics, 1871–1899.* New York: Cambridge University Press.

Gladden, Washington. 1884. "Three Dangers." *The Century: A Popular Quarterly* 28, no. 4 (August): 620–27.

Goede, Marieke de. 2000. "Mastering Lady Credit: Discourses of Financial Crisis in Historical Perspective." *International Feminist Journal of Politics* 2, no. 1: 58–81.

———. 2004. "Repoliticising Financial Risk." *Economy and Society* 33, no. 2: 197–217.

———. 2005. *Virtue, Fortune, and Faith: A Genealogy of Finance.* Minneapolis: University of Minnesota Press.

Goldsmith, Barbara. 1998. *Other Powers: The Age of Suffrage, Spiritualism, and the Scandalous Victoria Woodhull.* New York: Knopf.

Göppert, Heinrich. 1930. *Börse und Publikum.* Berlin: Julius Springer.

Gordon, John. 1999. *The Great Game: The Emergence of Wall Street as a World Power, 1653–2000.* New York: Scribner.

Goux, Jean-Joseph. 1997. "Values and Speculations: The Stock-Exchange Paradigm." *Cultural Values: Journal of the Institute for Cultural Research* 1, no. 2 (October): 159–77.

———. 2000. *Frivolité de la valeur: Essai sur l'imaginaire du capitalisme.* Paris: Blusson.

Granovetter, Mark. 1985. "Economic Action and Social Structure: The Problem of Embeddedness." *American Journal of Sociology* 91, no. 2–3: 481–510.

Grant, James. 1983. *Bernard M. Baruch: The Adventures of a Wall Street Legend* (New York: Simon & Schuster.

Grant, Robert. 1883. *An Average Man*. Boston: Houghton Mifflin.

———. 1884. "An Average Man." *The Century: A Popular Quarterly* 27, no. 4 (February): 606–14.

Grossberg, Lawrence. 1992. *We Gotta Get Out of This Place: Popular Conservatism and Postmodernism in Contemporary America*. London: Routledge.

Grossberg, Lawrence, Cary Nelson, and Paula A. Treichler. 1992. *Cultural Studies*. London: Routledge.

Gumbrecht, Hans-Ulrich. 1997. *In 1926: Living at the Edge of Time*. Cambridge, MA: Harvard University Press.

———. 1998. "Epiphany of Form." In *Mimesis und Simulation*, edited by Andreas Kablitz and Gerhard Neumann, 517–40. Freiburg: Rombach.

———. 2004. *Production of Presence: What Meaning Cannot Convey*. Stanford: Stanford University Press.

Gumbrecht, Hans-Ulrich, and K. Ludwig Pfeiffer, eds. 1988. *Die Materialität der Kommunikation*. Frankfurt am Main: Suhrkamp.

Hacking, Ian. 1990. *The Taming of Chance*. Cambridge, MA: Cambridge University Press.

Hadley, Arthur T. 1897. *Economics: An Account of the Relations Between Private Property and Public Welfare*. New York: G. P. Putnam's Sons.

Hall, Stuart. 1981. "Notes on Deconstructing the 'Popular.'" In *People's History and Socialist Theory*, edited by Raphael Samuel, 227–40. Boston: Routledge & Kegan Paul.

———. 1988. *The Hard Road to Renewal: Thatcherism and the Crisis of the Left*. London: Verso.

Harding, Brian. 1993. "Transatlantic Views of Speculation and Value, 1820–1860." *Historical Research* 66, no. 160: 209–21.

Hardt, Michael, and Antonio Negri. 2000. *Empire*. Cambridge, MA: Harvard University Press.

Hardy, Charles O. 1927. *Risk and Risk-Bearing*. Chicago: University of Chicago Press.

Harper, Henry H. 1966 (1926). *The Psychology of Speculation: The Human Element in Stock Market Transactions*. Wells, VT: Fraser.

Hartley, John. 2003. *A Short History of Cultural Studies*. London: Sage.

Headley, Joel Tyler. 1971 (1873). *The Great Riots of New York, 1712 to 1873, Including a Full and Complete Account of the Four Days' Draft Riot of 1863*. New York: Dover.

Hennessy, Elizabeth. 2001. *Coffee House to Cyber Market: 200 Years of the London Stock Exchange*. London: Ebury Press.

Hewitson, Gillian J. 1999. *Feminist Economics: Interrogating the Masculinity of Rational Choice Man*. Cheltenham, UK: Edward Elgar.

Hill, John, Jr. 1975 (1904). *Gold Bricks of Speculation: A Study of Speculation and Its Counterfeits, and an Exposé of the Methods of Bucketshops and "Get-Rich-Quick" Swindles*. New York: Arno Press.

Hobson, John A. 1906. "The Ethics of Gambling." In *Betting and Gambling: A National Evil*, edited by Seebohm B. Rowntree, 1–11. London: Macmillan.

Hochfelder, D. N.d. "Partners in Crime. The Telegraph Industry, Finance Capitalism, and Organized Gambling, 1870–1920." MS. IEEE History Center, Rutgers
University.

Holway, Tatjana. 1992. "The Game of Speculation: Economics and Representation."
Dickens Quarterly 9, no. 3: 103–14.

Hooper, William R. 1876. "The Tulip Mania." *Harper's New Monthly* 52, no. 311
(April): 743–46.

Hotchkiss, H. L. 1965 (1905). "The Stock Ticker." In *The New York Stock Exchange*,
edited by Edmund C. Stedman, 430–35. New York: Greenwood Press.

Hubbard, George H. 1888. "The Economics of Speculation." *New Englander and Yale
Review* 49, no. 220 (July): 1–11.

Hügel, Hans-Otto. 2001. "Nicht identifizieren—Spannungen aushalten! Zur Wort-
und Begriffsgeschichte von 'populär.'" In *Das Populäre in der Musik des 20. Jahr-
hunderts: Wesenszüge und Erscheinungsformen*, edited by Claudia Bullerjahn and
Hans-Joachim Erwe, 11–38. Hildesheim: Georg Olms.

Hutter, Michael, and Gunther Teubner. 1994. "Der Gesellschaft fette Beute. *Homo
juridicus* und *homo oeconomicus* als kommunikationserhaltende Fiktionen." In
Der Mensch—das Medium der Gesellschaft? edited by Peter Fuchs and Andreas
Göbel, 110–45. Frankfurt am Main: Suhrkamp.

Huyssen, Andreas. 1986. "Mass Culture as Woman: Modernism's Other." In *Studies
in Entertainment: Critical Approaches to Mass Culture*, edited by Tania Modleski,
188–208. Bloomington: Indiana University Press.

Ingrassia, Catherine. 1998. *Authorship, Commerce, and Gender in Early Eighteenth-
Century England: A Culture of Paper Credit*. Cambridge: Cambridge University
Press.

Ives, Brayton. 1888. "Wall Street as Economic Factor." *North American Review* 147, no.
384 (November): 554–72.

Jackson, Kevin. 1995. *The Oxford Book of Money*. Oxford: Oxford University Press.

Jevons, William. 1871. *The Theory of Political Economy*. London: Macmillan.

Johnson, Richard. 1986–87. "What Is Cultural Studies Anyway?" *Social Text* 16:
38–80.

Jones, Edward D. 1900. *Economic Crises*. New York: Macmillan.

Kapferer, Jean-Noel. 1990. *Rumors: The World's Oldest Media*. Translated by Bruce
Fink. New Brunswick, NJ: Transaction Publishers.

Kavanagh, Thomas M. 1993. *Enlightenment and the Shadows of Chance: The Novel and
the Culture of Gambling in Eighteenth-Century France*. Baltimore: Johns Hopkins
University Press.

Kelly, Fred C. 1962 (1930). *Why You Win or Lose: The Psychology of Speculation*. New
York: Houghton Mifflin.

Keynes, John M. 1971 (1930). *The Collected Writings of John Maynard Keynes*, vol. 6:
The Applied Theory of Money. London: Macmillan.

———. 1973 (1935). *The Collected Writings of John Maynard Keynes*, vol. 7: *The General
Theory of Employment, Interest, and Money*. London: Macmillan.

Kindleberger, Charles P. 1996. *Manias, Panics and Crashes: A History of Financial Crises*. New York: John Wiley & Sons.

Kintzelé, Jeff. 1986. "La logique du crédit comme logique de la modernité." *Revue de l'Institut de Sociologie* 3 (4): 139–51.

Klingaman, William K. 1989. *1929: The Year of the Great Crash*. New York: Harper & Row.

Knorr Cetina, Karin D., and Urs Bruegger. 2000. "The Market as an Object of Attachment: Exploring Postsocial Relations in Financial Markets." *Canadian Journal of Sociology* 25 (2): 141–68.

———. 2002. "Global Microstructures: The Virtual Societies of Financial Markets." *American Journal of Sociology* 107, no. 4: 905–50.

Kristeva, Julia. 1982. *Powers of Horror: An Essay in Abjection*. Translated by Leon S. Roudiez. New York: Columbia University Press.

Laclau, Ernesto. 1990. *New Reflections on the Revolution of Our Time*. London: Verso.

Laclau, Ernesto, and Chantal Mouffe. 1985. *Hegemony and Socialist Strategy: Towards a Radical Democratic Politics*. Translated by Winston Moore and Paul Cammack. London: Verso.

Lacour-Gayet, Robert. 1929. "La Spéculation en Amérique." *Revue de Paris* 36, no. 9 (May): 158–75.

Lawrence, Joseph. 1929. *Wall Street and Washington*. Princeton: Princeton University Press.

Laylor, John. 1852. *Money and Morals: A Book for the Times*. London: John Chapman.

Leach, Eugene E. 1986. "Mastering the Crowd: Collective Behaviour and Mass Society in American Social Thought, 1917–1939." *American Studies* 27, no. 1: 99–114.

———. 1992. "'Mental Epidemics': Crowd Psychology and American Culture, 1890–1940." *American Studies* 33: 5–29.

———. 1994. "Chaining the Tiger—The Mob Stigma and the Working Class, 1863–1894." *Labor History* 35, no. 2: 187–215.

Le Bon, Gustave. 1903 (1895). *The Crowd: A Study of the Popular Mind*. London: T. Fisher Unwin.

Lefèvre, Edwin 1925. *The Making of a Stockbroker*. New York: George H. Doran. A biography of John K. Wing.

———. 1982 (1923). *Reminiscences of a Stock Operator*. Burlington, VT: Fraser. A novel based on the life of Jesse Livermore.

Leffler, George L. 1957 *The Stock Market*. New York: Ronald Press.

Lenin, Vladimir I. 1999 (1917). *Imperialism, the Highest Stage of Capitalism*. Chippendale, Australia: Resistance Books.

Lewinsohn, Richard, and Franz Pick. 1933. *Sinn und Unsinn der Börse*. Berlin: Fischer.

Lieb, Claudia. 2001. "Gemütserregungskunst: Der Grenzfall Unterhaltung in funktionalistischen Medientheorien." In *a/effektive Kommunikation: Unterhaltung und Werbung*, edited by Siegfried J. Schmidt, Joachim Westerbarkey, and Guido Zurstiege, 25–52. Beiträge zur Kommunikationstheorie 19. Münster: Lit-Verlag.

Link-Heer, Ursula. 1999. "Nervosität und Moderne." In *Konzepte der Moderne*, edited by Gerhart von Graevenitz, 102–19. Germanistische Symposien, Berichtsbände 20. Stuttgart: Metzler.

Lloyd, Henry D. 1883. "The Political Economy of Seventy-Three Million Dollars." *Atlantic Monthly* 50, no. 297 (July): 69–81.

Loeb, Gerald M. 1996 (1935). *The Battle for Investment Survival*. New York: John Wiley & Sons.

Loewenfeld, Leopold.1901. *Der Hypnotismus: Handbuch der Lehre von der Hypnose und der Suggestion mit besonderer Berücksichtigung ihrer Bedeutung für Medicin und Rechtspflege*. Wiesbaden: J. F. Bergmann.

Luhmann, Niklas. 1974. "Symbiotische Mechanismen." In *Gewaltverhältnisse und die Ohnmacht der Kritik*, edited by Otthein Rammstedt, 107–31. Frankfurt am Main: Suhrkamp.

———. 1988. *Die Wirtschaft der Gesellschaft*. Frankfurt am Main: Suhrkamp.

———. 1991. *Soziologie des Risikos*. Berlin: Walter de Gruyter.

———. 1993. "Gleichzeitigkeit und Synchronisation. In *Soziologische Aufklärung*, vol. 5, edited by Niklas Luhmann, 95–130. Opladen: Westdeutscher Verlag.

———. 1995. *Social Systems*. Translated by John Bednarz Jr., with Dirk Baecker. Stanford: Stanford University Press.

———. 1997a. *Die Gesellschaft der Gesellschaft*. Frankfurt am Main: Suhrkamp. Translated by Rhodes Barrett as *Theory of Society* (Stanford: Stanford University Press, 2012–).

———. 1997b. "Selbstorganisation und Mikrodiversität: Zur Wissenssoziologie des neuzeitlichen Individualismus." *Soziale Systeme* 3, no. 1: 23–33.

———. 2000. *Art as a Social System*. Translated by Eva M. Knodt. Stanford: Stanford University Press.

———. 2002. *Die Politik der Gesellschaft*. Frankfurt am Main: Suhrkamp.

Lynch, Peter. 1989. *One Up on Wall Street: How to Use What You Already Know to Make Money in the Market*. New York: Simon & Schuster.

MacCallum, John. 2001. "Stock Market Trouble: Five Books for Executives." *Ivey Business Journal* 65, no. 3 (January–February): 45–47.

MacClelland, John. 1989. *The Crowd and the Mob: From Plato to Canetti*. London: Unwin Hyman.

MacDougall, Ernest D. 1936. *Speculation and Gambling*. Boston: Stratford.

Mackay, Charles. 1980 (1841–52). *Extraordinary Popular Delusions, and the Madness of Crowds*. New York: Three Rivers Press. Reprint with foreword by Bernard Baruch (Boston: L. C. Page, 1932; New York: MetroBooks, 2002).

Mackie, Erin.1997. *Market à la Mode: Fashion, Commodity, and Gender in The Tatler and The Spectator*. Baltimore: Johns Hopkins University Press.

Makropoulos, Michael. 2003. "Massenkultur als Kontingenzkultur: Artifizielle Wirklichkeiten zwischen Technisierung, Ökonomisierung und Ästhetisierung." In . . . *lautloses irren—ways of worldmaking, too* . . . , edited by Harm Lux, 153–71. Berlin: Verlag der Kunst.

Malvery, Olive C. 1906. "Women and the Money Market." *Lady's Realm*, November 21: 41–45.

———. 1907. *The Soul Market*. New York: McClure, Phillips.

———. 1908. *The Speculator*. London: T. Werner Laurie. A novel.

Marshall, Alfred. 1920. *Industry and Trade: A Study of Industrial Technique and Business Organization, and of Their Influences on the Conditions of Various Classes and Nations*. London: Macmillan.

Martin, Edward Sanford. 1908. *In a New Century*. New York: Scribner.

Martin, H. S. 1919. *The New York Stock Exchange: A Discussion of the Business Done: Its Relation to Other Business, to Investment, Speculation and Gambling: The Safeguards Provided by the Exchange and the Means Taken to Improve the Character of Speculation*. New York: F. E. Fitch.

Massumi, Brian. 1996. "The Autonomy of Affect." In *Deleuze: A Critical Reader*, edited by Paul Patton, 217–39. Oxford: Blackwell.

McCarthy, Justin. 1871. "Lady Judith." *The Galaxy* 11, no. 5 (May): 623–41.

McCoy, Drew R. 1980. *The Exclusive Republic*. Chapel Hill: University of North Carolina Press.

McCulloch, John R. 1825. *Principles of Economics*. Edinburgh: W. and C. Tait.

McGuigan, Jim. 1992. *Cultural Populism*. London: Routledge.

McVey, Frank. 1901. "Speculation." *The Current Encyclopedia* 1, no. 1 (July): 138–40.

Meeker, James E. 1922. *The Work of the Stock Exchange*. New York: Ronald Press.

Menschel, Robert, ed. 2002. *Markets, Mobs & Mayhem: A Modern Look at the Madness of Crowds*. Hoboken, NJ: John Wiley & Sons.

Meredith, Hubert A. 1931. *The Drama of Money Making: Tragedy and Comedy of the London Stock Exchange*. London: Sampson Low, Marston.

Merrill, Francis E. 1938. "The Stock Exchange and Social Control." *American Journal of Sociology* 43, no. 4: 560–77.

Merrill, Francis E., and Carroll D. Clark. 1934. "The Money Market as a Special Public." *American Journal of Sociology* 39, no. 5: 626–36.

Merton, Robert K. 1946. *Mass Persuasion: The Social Psychology of a War Bond Drive*. New York: Harper & Brothers.

Metz, Christian. 1977. "'Trucage' and Film." *Critical Inquiry* 3, no. 4: 657–75.

Michaels, Walter Benn. 1987. *The Gold Standard and the Logic of Naturalism: American Literature at the Turn of the Century*. Berkeley: University of California Press.

Miller, Perry. 1982. *The New England Mind: The Seventeenth Century*. Cambridge, MA: Harvard University Press.

Mills, Nicolaus. 1986. *The Crowd in American Literature*. Baton Rouge: Louisiana State University Press.

Milner, James. 1720. *A visit to the South-Sea Company and the Bank: in a letter to a friend, concerning the late proposals for the payment of the nation's debts. The second edition, to which is added a second letter, occasion'd by what has past since, in relation to the South-Sea Company's bargain*. London: J. Roberts and A. Dodd.

Minton, Robert. 1975. *John Law, The Father of Paper Money*. New York: Association Press.

Moore, William C. 1921. *Wall Street: Its Mysteries Revealed—Its Secrets Exposed*. New York: Moore William.

Morris, Charles R. 1999. *Money, Greed and Risk: Why Financial Crises and Crashes Happen*. New York: Times Business.

Mortimer, Thomas. 1801 (1761). *Every Man His Own Broker, or, A Guide to the Stock Exchange*. London: W. J. and J. Richardson.

Mottram, Ralph H. 1929. *A History of Financial Speculation*. Boston: Little, Brown.

Mulcaire, Terry. 1999. "Public Credit; or, the Feminization of Virtue in the Marketplace." *PMLA* 114 (October): 1029–42.

Munro, Rolland. 1997. "Ideas of Difference: Stability, Social Spaces and Labour of Division." In *Ideas of Difference: Social Spaces and the Labour of Division*, edited by Kevin Hetherington and Rolland Munro, 3–24. Oxford: Blackwell.

Murphy, Anthony E. 1997. *John Law: Economic Theorist and Policy-Maker*. London: Oxford University Press.

Neal, Arthur G., and Helen L. Youngelson. 1988. "The Folklore of Wall Street: Gamesmanship, Gurus, and the Myth-Making Process." *Journal of American Culture* 11, no. 1: 55–62.

Neal, Larry. 1987. "The Integration and Efficiency of the London and Amsterdam Stock Markets in the Eighteenth Century." *Journal of Economic History* 47, no. 1: 97–115.

Neill, Humphrey B. 1950. *The Inside Story of the Stock Exchange: A Fascinating Saga of the World's Greatest Money Market Place*. New York: Forbes.

———. 1960 (1931). *Tape Reading and Market Tactics: The Three Steps to Successful Stock Trading*. Burlington, VT: Fraser.

———. 1967 (1954). *The Art of Contrary Thinking*. 4th enlarged ed. Caldwell, ID: Caxton Printers.

Nelson, Samuel Armstrong. 1964 (1903). *The ABC of Stock Speculation*. Wells, VT: Fraser.

Neubauer, Hans-Joachim. 1998. *Fama: Eine Geschichte des Gerüchts*. Berlin: Berlin Verlag. Translated by Christian Braun as *The Rumour—A Cultural History* (London: Free Association Books, 1999).

New York (State) Committee on Speculation in Securities and Commodities. 1910. *Report of Governor Hughes' Committee on Speculation in Securities and Commodities, June 7, 1909*. Albany, NY: J. B. Lyon, Printers, 1910. www.archive.org/details/reportofgovernoroonewyuoft (accessed August 22, 2012).

Nicholson, Colin. 1994. *Writing and the Rise of Finance: Capital Satires of the Early Eighteenth Century*. Cambridge: Cambridge University Press.

Nobel, H. G. 1933. *The Stock Exchange: Its Economic Function*. New York: Harper & Brothers.

Nocera, Joseph. 1994. *A Piece of the Action: How the Middle Class Joined the Money*. New York: Simon & Schuster.

Norberg, Peter. 2003. "Re-enchanting Financial Markets: Community, Myth and Morality." *SSE Working Papers in Business Administration*. Stockholm. http://swoba.hhs.se/hastba/papers/hastba2003_015.pdf (accessed June 18, 2012).

Odean, Terrance. 1998. "Are Investors Reluctant to Realize their Losses?" *Journal of Finance* 53, no. 5: 1775–98.

Odean, Terrance, and Brad M. Barber. 2001. "Boys Will Be Boys: Gender, Overconfidence and Common Stock Investment." *Quarterly Journal of Economics* 116, no. 1: 261–92.

Odean, Terrance, and Simon Gervais. 2001. "Learning to be Overconfident." *Review of Financial Studies* 14, no. 1: 1–27.

Ora, Reyam N. 1908. "Speculitis." *The Ticket* 2, no. 4: 159–61.

Osgood, Samuel. 1867. "A Money Article." *Harper's Magazine* 34, no. 203 (April): 615–21.

Oslin, George P. 1999 (1979). *The Story of Telecommunications*. Macon, GA: Mercer University Press.

Parisi, Luciana, and Tiziana Terranova. 2001. "A Matter of Affect: Digital Images and the Cybernetic Re-wiring of Vision." *Parallax* 7, no. 4: 122–27.

Pasero, Ursula, and Christine Weinbach, eds. 2003. *Frauen, Männer, Gender Trouble: Systemtheoretische Essays*. Frankfurt am Main: Suhrkamp.

Patrick, G. T. W. 1900. "The Psychology of Crazes." *Popular Science Monthly* 18: 285–94.

Patton, Thomas. 1900. "The Bucket Shop Speculation." *Munsey's Magazine* 24: 68.

Petrażycki, Leon. 1906. *Aktienwesen und Spekulation: Eine ökonomische und rechtspsychologische Untersuchung*. Berlin: H. W. Müller.

Phillips, David G. 1904. *The Cost*. Indianapolis: Bobbs-Merrill.

Piel, Konstanze. 2003. *Ökonomie des Nichtwissens: Aktienhype und Vertrauenskrise im Neuen Markt*. Frankfurt am Main: Campus.

Pixley, Jocelyn. 2004. *Emotions in Finance: Distrust and Uncertainty in Global Markets*. Cambridge: Cambridge University Press.

Pocock, John G. A. 1975. *The Machiavellian Moment: Florentine Political Thought and the Atlantic Republican Tradition*. Princeton: Princeton University Press.

Pratt, Sereno S. 1921 (1903). *The Work of Wall Street: An Account of the Functions, Methods and History of the New York Money and Stock Markets*. New York: D. Appleton.

Preda, Alex. 2001. "The Rise of the Popular Investor: Financial Knowledge and Investing in England and France, 1840–1880." *Sociological Quarterly* 42, no. 2: 205–32.

———. 2003. "On Ticks and Tapes: Financial Knowledge, Communicative Practices, and Information Technologies on 19th Century Financial Markets." MS.

Prieto-Pablos, J. A. 1998. "The Paradox of Suspense." *Poetics* 26, no. 2: 99–113.

Proudhon, Pierre-Joseph. 1857 (1854). *Manuel du spéculateur à la Bourse*. 5th ed. Paris: Garnier frères.

Reibnitz, Kurt von. 1912. *Die New Yorker Fondsbörse*. Jena: Gustav Fischer.

Reith, Gerda. 1999. *The Age of Chance: Gambling in Western Culture*. New York: Routledge.

Rieusset-Lemarié, Isabelle. 1992. *Une fin de siècle épidémique*. Arles: Actes Sud.

Ross, Edward A. 1897. *The Mob Mind*. New York: D. Appleton.

———. 1929 (1908). *Social Psychology: An Outline and Source Book*. New York: Macmillan.

Ross, James A. 1938. *Speculation, Stock Prices and Industrial Fluctuations*. New York: Ronald Press.

Rötzer, Florian. 1996. "Gerüchte—das älteste Massenmedium." *Telepolis*. www.heise.de/tp/r4/artikel/2/2042/1.html (accessed May 25, 2012).

Ruccio, David, and Jack Amariglio. 2003. *Postmodern Moments in Modern Economics*. Princeton: Princeton University Press.

Russell, Gillian. 2000. "Faro's Daughters: Female Gamesters, Politics, and the Discourse of Finance in 1970s Britain." *Eighteenth-Century Studies* 33, no. 4: 481–504.

Samuelson, Paul A. 1976. *Economics*. New York: McGraw-Hill.

Savage, Terry. 1996. "Tulips Redux?" Review of *Extraordinary Popular Delusions and the Madness of Crowds* and *Confusion de confusiones* by Charles Mackay and José de la Vega, introduction by Martin S. Fridson. *Barron's* 76, no. 16 (April 15): B54.

Schwed, Fred, Jr. 1940. *Where are the Customer's Yachts? or, A Good Hard Look at Wall Street*. New York: Simon & Schuster.

Sconce, Jeffrey. 2000. *Haunted Media: Electronic Presence from Telegraphy to Television*. Durham, NC: Duke University Press.

Selden, George C. 1996 (1912). *Psychology of the Stock Market*. Burlington, VT: Fraser.

Seligman, Edwin. 1905. *Principles of Economics*. London/Bombay: Longmans, Green, and Co.

Serres, Michel. 2007 (1980). *The Parasite*. Translated by Lawrence R. Schehr. Minneapolis: University of Minnesota Press.

Shaviro, Steven. 1993. *The Cinematic Body*. Minneapolis: University of Minnesota Press.

Shell, Marc. 1999. "The Issue of Representation." In *The New Economic Criticism: Studies at the Intersection of Literature and Economics*, edited by Martha Woodmansee and Mark Osteen, 53–74. London: Routledge.

Sherman, Sandra. 1996. *Finance and Fictionality in the Early Eighteenth Century: Accounting for Defoe*. Cambridge: Cambridge University Press.

Shiach, Morag. 1989. *Discourse on Popular Culture: Class, Gender and History in Cultural Analysis, 1730 to the Present*. Cambridge: Polity Press.

Shiller, Robert. 2000. *Irrational Exuberance*. Princeton, NJ: Princeton University Press.

Shleifer, Andrei. 2000. *Inefficient Markets: An Introduction to Behavioral Finance*. Oxford: Oxford University Press.

Showalter, Elaine. 1997. *Hystories: Hysterical Epidemics and Modern Culture*. New York: Columbia University Press.

Sidis, Boris. 1899. *The Psychology of Suggestion: A Research into the Subconscious Nature of Man and Society.* New York: D. Appleton.

Siebert, Muriel. 2002. *Changing Rules: Adventures of a Wall Street Maverick.* New York: Simon & Schuster.

Simmel, Georg. 2000a (1895). "The Adventure." Translated by David Kettler. In *Simmel on Culture,* edited by David Frisby and Mike Featherstone, 221–32. London: Sage.

———. 2000b (1911). "The Alpine Journey." Translated by Sam Whimster. In *Simmel on Culture,* edited by David Frisby and Mike Featherstone, 219–21. London: Sage.

———. 2004 (1901). *The Philosophy of Money.* Translated by David Frisby. London: Routledge.

Simmons, E. H. H. 1927. *Modern Capitalism, and Other Addresses.* New York: n.p.

Sloterdijk, Peter. 2000. *Die Verachtung der Massen: Versuch über Kulturkämpfe in der modernen Gesellschaft.* Frankfurt am Main: Suhrkamp.

Smith, Adam [George J. W. Goodman]. 1967. *The Money Game.* New York: Random House.

Smith, Matthew H. 1868. *Sunshine and Shadow in New York.* Hartford, CT: J. B. Burr.

———. 1972 (1873). *Bulls and Bears of New York.* New York: Books for Libraries Press.

Smitley, Robert L. 1933. *Popular Financial Delusions.* Philadelphia: Roland Swain.

Sobel, Robert E. 1970. *The Curbstone Brokers: The Origins of the American Stock Exchange.* London: Macmillan.

———. 1977. *Inside Wall Street: Continuity and Change in the Financial District.* New York: Norton.

———. 1988. *Panic on Wall Street: A Classic History of America's Financial Disasters with a New Exploration of the Crash of 1987.* New York: Truman Talley Books.

Somers, Margaret. 1994. "The Narrative Constitution of Identity: A Relational and Network Approach." *Theory and Society* 23, no. 5: 605–49.

Spangenberg, Peter. 1993. "Stabilität und Entgrenzung von Wirklichkeiten. System-theoretische Überlegungen zu Funktion und Leistung der Massenmedien." In *Literaturwissenschaft und Systemtheorie: Positionen, Kontroversen, Perspektiven,* edited by Siegfried J. Schmidt, 66–100. Opladen: Westdeutscher Verlag.

Sparkes, Boylden, and Samuel T. Moore. 1930. *Hetty Green: A Woman Who Loved Money.* New York: Doubleday, Doran.

Stäheli, Urs. 1999a. "Diskursanalytische Hegemonietheorie: Ernesto Laclau und Chantal Mouffe." In *Politische Theorien der Gegenwart,* edited by André Brodocz and Gary Schaal, 143–66. Opladen: Leske & Budrich.

———. 1999b. "Das Populäre zwischen Cultural Studies und Systemtheorie." In *Politik des Vergnügens: Zur Diskussion der Populärkultur in den Cultural Studies,* edited by Udo Göttlich and Rainer Winter, 321–37. Cologne: Von Halem.

———. 2000a. "Die Kontingenz des Globalen Populären." *Soziale Systeme* 6, no. 1: 85–111.

———. 2000b. *Sinnzusammenbrüche: Eine dekonstruktive Lektüre von Niklas Luhmanns Systemtheorie.* Weilerswist: Velbrück Wissenschaft.

———. 2001. "Schreibhandeln: Doppelte Kontingenz und Normalisierung." *kultuR-Revolution, Zeitschrift für angewandte Diskurstheorie* 43: 76–82.

———. 2002a. "Fatal Attraction: Popular Modes of Inclusion in the Economic System." In *Inclusion/Exclusion and Socio-Cultural Identities*, edited by Urs Stäheli and Rudolf Stichweh. Special issue of *Soziale Systeme* 8, no. 1: 110–23.

———. 2002b. "Die Wiederholbarkeit des Populären." In *Archivprozesse: Die Kommunikation der Aufbewahrung*, edited by Hedwig Pompe and Leander Scholz, 73–83. Cologne: DuMont.

———. 2003a. "Financial Noise: Inclusion and the Promise of Meaning." *Soziale Systeme* 9, no. 2: 244–56.

———. 2003b. "Der melancholische Spekulant." In *Kapitalismus oder Barbarei?* Special issue of *Merkur* 57, nos. 9–10: 957–63.

———. 2003c. "134—Who Is at the Key? Zur Utopie der Geschlechterindifferenz." In *Frauen, Männer, Gender Trouble: Systemtheoretische Essays*, edited by Ursula Pasero and Christine Weinbach, 186–216. Frankfurt am Main: Suhrkamp.

———. 2003d. "The Popular in the Political System." *Cultural Studies* 17, no. 2: 275–99.

———. 2004a. "Börsenschwindel." In *Politik und Verbrechen III: Das Schwindelerregende*, edited by Carl Hegemann and the Volksbühne am Rosa-Luxemburg-Platz, 120–28. Berlin: Alexander

———. 2004b. "Competing Figures of the Limit." In *Laclau: A Critical Reader*, edited by Simon Critchley and Oliver Marchart, 226–40. London: Routledge.

———. 2004c. "Das Populäre in der Systemtheorie." In *Luhmann und die Kulturtheorie*, edited by Günter Burkart and Gunter Runkel, 169–88. Frankfurt am Main: Suhrkamp.

———. 2004d. "Subversive Praktiken? Cultural Studies und Globalisierung." In *Doing Culture: Neue Positionen zum Verhältnis von Kultur und sozialer Praxis*, edited by Karl Hörning and Julia Reuter, 154–68. Bielefeld: transcript.

———. 2004e. "Der Takt der Börse: Inklusionseffekte von Verbreitungsmedien am Fallbeispiel des Börsen-Tickers." *Zeitschrift für Soziologie* 33, no. 3: 245–63.

———. 2004f. "Der Verrat des Kapitalismus: Fiktionalisierung und Finanzspekulation." In *Freund, Feind und Verrat*, edited by Torsten Hahn and Erhardt Schüttpelz, 238–51. Cologne: DuMont.

———. 2005. "Das Populäre als Unterscheidung: Eine theoretische Skizze." In *Popularisierung und Popularität*, edited by Gereon Blaseio, Hedwig Pompe, and Jens Ruchatz, 146–67. Cologne: DuMont.

———. 2008. "'Watching the Market': Visual Representations of Financial Economy in Advertisements." In *Economic Representations—Academic and Everyday*, edited by David Ruccio, 242–56. New York: Routledge.

Stallybrass, Peter, and Allon White. 1986. *The Politics and Poetics of Transgression*. London: Methuen.

Standage, Tom. 1998. *The Victorian Internet: The Remarkable Story of the Telegraph and the Nineteenth Century's On-line Pioneers*. New York: Walker.

Stichweh, Rudolf. 1988. "Inklusion in Funktionssysteme moderner Gesellschaft." In

Differenzierung und Verselbständigung: Zur Entwicklung gesellschaftlicher Teil-systeme, edited by Renate Mayntz, Bernd Rosewitz, and Uwe Schimank, 261–93. Frankfurt am Main: Campus.

———. 1997. "Inklusion/Exklusion, funktionale Differenzierung und die Theorie der Weltgesellschaft." *Soziale Systeme* 3, no. 1: 123–36.

———. 1998. "Raum, Region und Stadt in der Systemtheorie." *Soziale Systeme* 4, no. 2: 341–58.

Storey, John. 2001. *Cultural Theory and Popular Culture: An Introduction*. Harlow, UK: Pearson.

Stout, Lynn A. 1999. "Why the Law Hates Speculators: Regulation and Private Order-ing in the Market for OTC Derivatives." *Duke Law Journal* 48, no. 4: 701–86.

Strange, Susan. 1986. *Casino Capitalism*. Oxford: B. Blackwell.

Stringham, E. 2002. "The Emergence of the London Stock Exchange as a Self-Policing Club." *Journal of Private Enterprise* 17, no. 2: 1–9.

Stroczan, Katherine. 2002. *Der schlafende DAX, oder, Das Behagen in der Unkultur: Die Börse, der Wahn und das Begehren*. Berlin: Wagenbach.

Tarde, Gabriel. 1903 (1890). *The Laws of Imitation*. Translated by Elsie Clews Parsons. New York: Henry Holt.

———. 1968 (1890). *Penal Philosophy*. Translated by Rapelje Howell. Montclair, NJ: Smith.

———. 1989 (1898). *L'opinion et la foule*. Paris: Presses universitaires de France.

Taussig, Michael T. 1993. *Mimesis and Alterity: A Particular History of the Senses*. New York: Routledge.

Tellmann, Ute. 1999. "Markt als Dispositiv?" Diss., Bielefeld.

———. 2003. "The Truth of the Market." *Distinktion* 7: 49–63.

Thaler, Richard. 1992. *The Winner's Curse: Paradoxes and Anomalies of Economic Life*. New York: Free Press.

Tholen, Georg C. 1999. "Überschneidungen: Konturen einer Theorie der Medialität." In *Konfigurationen: Zwischen Kunst und Medien*, edited by Sigrid Schade and Georg C. Tholen, 15–35. Munich: Wilhelm Fink.

———. 2002. *Die Zäsur der Medien*. Frankfurt am Main: Suhrkamp.

Thomas, Dana L. 1989 (1967). *The Plungers and the Peacocks: An Update of the Classic History of the Stock Market*. New York: William Morrow.

Thomas, W.I. 1901. "The Gaming Instinct." *American Journal of Sociology* 6, no. 6: 750–63.

Tilghman, Charlie R. 1961. "Telegraph History: Some Early Days of Western Union's Stock Ticker Service 1817–1910." *Western Union Technical Review* 15, no. 2 (April). http://massis.lcs.mit.edu/archives/history/stock.ticker (accessed August, 8, 2012).

Turner, Graeme. 2003. *British Cultural Studies: An Introduction*. London: Routledge.

Tvede, Lars. 2001. *Business Cycles: From John Law to the Internet Crash*. London: Routledge.

Twain, Mark, and Charles D. Warner. 1915 (1873). *The Gilded Age*. New York: Harper & Brothers.

Van Antwerp, William C. 1914. *The Stock Exchange from Within*. New York: Doubleday, Page.

Vega, José de la. 1957 (1688). *Confusion de confusiones*. Boston: Harvard Graduate School of Business Administration

Verdicchio, Dirk. 2006. "Vampires, Werewolves, and Brokers: Monsters at Wall Street." MS.

Vethake, Henry. 1838. *The Principles of Political Economy*. Philadelphia: P. H. Nicklin & T. Johnson.

Vogl, Joseph. 2002. *Kalkül und Leidenschaft: Poetik des ökonomischen Menschen*. Munich: Sequenzia.

W. 1834. "Mobs." *New England Magazine* 7, no. 6 (December): 471–78.

Walker, D. A. 2000. "La relation entre la Bourse au XIX siècle et la modèle de Léon Walras d'un marché organisé." In *Les traditions économiques françaises 1848–1939*, edited by Pierre Dockès, Ludovic Frobert, Gérard Klotz, Jean-Pierre Potier, and André Tiran. Paris: CNRS Éditions.

Walras, Léon. 2005 (1880). "The Stock Exchange: Speculation and *agiotage*." In *Studies in Applied Economics: Theory of the Production of Social Wealth*, vol. 2, translated by Jan van Daal, 321–52. New York: Routledge.

Warner, Charles D. 1969 (1889). *A Little Journey in the World*. New York: Johnson Reprint.

Warner, Michael. 1992. "The Mass Public and the Mass Subject." In *Habermas and the Public Sphere*, edited by Craig Calhoun, 377–401. Cambridge, MA: MIT Press.

Warshow, Robert I. 1929. *The Story of Wall Street*. New York: Blue Ribbon Books.

Weber, Adolf. 1933. *Geld, Banken, Börsen*. Leipzig: Quelle & Meyer.

Weber, Max. 2000a (1895). "Börsenwesen. (Die Vorschläge der Börsenenquetekommission.)" In *Max Weber Gesamtausgabe*, edited by Horst Baier, M. Rainer Lepsius, Wolfgang J. Mommsen, Wolfgang Schluchter, and Johannes Winckelmann, § 1, vol. 5.2, *Börsenwesen: Schriften und Reden 1893–1898*, edited by Knut Borchardt with Cornelia Meyer-Stoll, 558–90. Tübingen: Mohr.

———. 2000b (1894). "Commerce on the Stock and Commodity Exchanges." Translated by Steven Lestition. *Theory and Society* 29, no. 3: 339–71. Originally published as "Die Börse II: Der Börsenverkehr," in *Max Weber Gesamtausgabe*, ed. Horst Baier, M. Rainer Lepsius, Wolfgang J. Mommsen, Wolfgang Schluchter, and Johannes Winckelmann, § 1, vol. 5.2, *Börsenwesen: Schriften und Reden 1893–1898*, edited by Knut Borchardt with Cornelia Meyer-Stoll, 619–57. Tübingen: Mohr, 2000.

———. 2000c (1894). "Stock and Commodity Exchanges." Translated by Steven Lestition. *Theory and Society* 29, no. 3: 305–38. Originally published as "Die Börse I: Zweck und äußere Organisation der Börsen," in *Max Weber Gesamtausgabe*, ed. Horst Baier, M. Rainer Lepsius, Wolfgang J. Mommsen, Wolfgang Schluchter, and Johannes Winckelmann, § 1, vol. 5.1, *Börsenwesen: Schriften und Reden 1893–1898*, edited by Knut Borchardt with Cornelia Meyer-Stoll, 135–74. Tübingen: Mohr, 1999.

Weingart, Brigitte. 1999. "Faszinationsanalyse." *Verstärker* 4, no. 4. www.culture.hu-berlin.de/verstaerker/vs004/weingart.html (accessed May 25, 2012).

Weld, Walter E. 1938. *The Technique of Speculative Investment*. New York: Barron's.

Welles, Chris. 1975. *The Last Days of the Club*. New York: Dutton.

Wendt, Paul F. 1941. "The Classification and Financial Experience of the Customers of a Typical New York Stock Exchange Firm from 1933–1938." Thesis, Marysville, TN.

Werber, Niels. 1998. "Raum und Technik: Zur medientheoretischen Problematik in Luhmanns Theorie der Gesellschaft." *Soziale Systeme* 4, no. 1: 219–32.

Westbrook, Wayne. 1980. *Wall Street and the American Novel*. New York: New York University Press.

Weyler, Karen A. 1996. "A Speculating Spirit: Trade, Speculation, and Gambling in Early American Fiction." *Early American Literature* 31, no. 2: 207–42.

White, Harrison. 1981. "Where Do Markets Come From?" *American Journal of Sociology* 87, no. 3: 517–47.

Whitman, Walt. 1982 (1871). *Complete Poetry and Collected Prose*. New York: Library of America.

Whitney, Richard. 1930. "Speculation—Address delivered before the Illinois Chamber of Commerce." Unpublished lecture, Chicago

Williams, Raymond. 1962. *Culture and Society, 1780–1950*. Harmondsworth, UK: Penguin Books.

———. 1986 (1976). *Keywords: A Vocabulary of Culture and Society*. London: Fontana.

Wilson, Alex J. 1906. "Stock Exchange Gambling." In *Betting and Gambling: A National Evil*, edited by B. Seebohm Rowntree. New York: Macmillan.

Wilson, Raymond J. 1968. *In Quest of Community: Social Philosophy in the United States, 1860–1920*. New York: John Wiley & Sons.

Wilson, Sloan J. 1963. *The Speculator and the Stock Market*. New Jersey: Investor's Library.

Winter, Rainer. 2001. *Die Kunst des Eigensinns: Cultural Studies als Kritik der Macht*. Weilerswist: Velbrück.

Withers, Hartley. 1910. *Stocks and Shares*. New York: Dutton.

Wolf, H. J. 1966 (1924). *Studies in Stock Speculation*. Burlington, VT: Fraser.

Wood, Gordon, ed. 1971. *The Rising Glory of America, 1760–1820*. New York: Braziller.

Wood, James P. 1966. *What's the Market? The Story of Stock Exchanges*. New York: Duell, Sloan & Pearce.

Wood, Sarah. 1801. *Dorval; or the Speculator*. Portsmouth, NH: Nutting & Whitelock.

Wyckoff, Richard [Rollo Tape, pseud.]. 1910. *Studies in Tape Reading: A 1910 Classic on Tape Reading & Stock Market Tactics*. New York: Ticker Publishing.

Yamada, Louise. 1998. *Market Magic: Riding the Greatest Bull Market of the Century*. New York: John Wiley & Sons.

Zimmerman, Hazel. 1931. *Do's and Dont's for the Woman Investor*. San Francisco: self-published.

INDEX

abstraction, 2–3, 7, 20–21, 45–47, 54,
    69–70, 167, 175, 178, 191, 211, 253n31;
    relationship to spectacularity, 3, 70,
    71–72, 81, 91
Abt, V., 33
addiction, 36–37, 82–83, 102, 218
affectivity, 15, 62–63, 72, 112, 113, 125, 157–
    61, 216–18, 226–27, 229, 233–35, 249n44;
    as communication, 12, 13–14, 90, 135–42,
    144, 245nn28,29; fear, 135–36, 140,
    158–59, 255n3, 256n17, 260n46, 262n12;
    hope, 135, 137–38, 141, 144, 158–59, 167,
    188, 255n3, 260n46, 261n57, 262n12,
    263n19; melancholic speculators, 135–36,
    170, 172; pleasure, 14, 16, 19, 27, 35, 36,
    41, 50, 54, 55, 65, 66, 69, 81–83, 85–86,
    87–88, 91–92, 115, 142, 189–90, 193;
    and women, 185, 187. See also Hysteria;
    Panic; Thrill
Agger, B., 36
Allen, F. L., 254n1
Althusser, I., 269n31
Amariglio, J., 172, 244n6
Angas, L., 64
audience, 15–16, 95–96, 112, 113–14, 121,
    122–23, 262n5, 267n6; as anonymous,
    201, 204, 211, 217, 266n4; vs.
    nonaudience, 9–11, 12, 108, 130–31,
    142–45, 193–94, 201
Austen, J., 19, 245n1

Baecker, D., 27, 28, 246nn6,11, 247nn22,23
Bagehot, W., 103, 139
Baldwin, J. M., 113
Barber, B. M., 254n46
Barnard, E. F., 181, 190, 193
Barnard, J., 253n38
Baron, R., 99
Barrows, S., 254n2

Baruch, B. M., 95, 98
Baudelaire, C., 144–45
Baudrillard, J., 12, 248n25
Bechterew, V., 232
Beck, U., 137, 256n16
Benjamin, W., 26, 144, 145
Bergson, H., 270n45
Bernstein, P., 249n42
Best, S. M., 197
Bigelow, G., 21
Blaché, H., 198, 199, 243n3
Black, F., 259n37, 262n9
Blanchot, M., 14
Bodie, Z., 247n13
Bogardus, E., 259n40
Bogle, J., 135, 255n1
Bond, F. D., 37, 130, 132, 155, 158–59, 231–32,
    262n12, 264n14
Borringo, H.-L., 247n17
boundary conflicts, 3, 13, 14, 25, 74, 238,
    244n18, 254n50
boundlessness, 100–101, 102, 108, 115–16
Boyle, J. E., 75, 77
Brantlinger, P., 256n19
Bruegger, U., 155
Brush, M. C., 55
Bruyn, F. de, 106
Bryce, J., 257n7
bucket shops, 73, 75–81, 88–89, 200, 208–9,
    211, 219, 254nn40,43, 268n16, 269n30
Bush, G., 112, 257n3
Butler, J., 170, 185, 231, 232–33, 263n1
Butler, S., 64

Caillois, R., 33
Calahan, E. A., 118, 198–99, 200, 204, 205,
    207, 218, 224
Canetti, E., 138–39
capitalism, 12, 21, 30, 33, 36–37, 48–48,

171, 172–73, 175–76, 178, 182, 186–87, 188, 191–92, 193–94, 262n7, 265n26; free competition in, 20, 46, 47; ideal markets, 3, 20–21, 51–54, 57, 58, 67, 76, 86–87, 135; liquidity of, 12, 58, 62, 63, 66, 150, 212; popularity of, 4–7, 9, 23, 53, 58–61, 65, 66, 72, 80, 86, 89, 226, 245n22; regulation of, 43, 52, 53, 58, 59–60, 72–75, 77, 78–79, 80, 86, 89, 96, 149, 211, 238, 253n39, 260n44; as self-correcting, 49; as self-referential, 20–21, 22–23, 27, 28–29

Marshall, A., 133
Martin, E. S., 37, 42, 47
Martin, H. S., 250n5
Martin, T. C., 36, 204, 205, 206
Marx, Karl, 238, 250n8
McCarthy, J., 118
McCulloch, J. R., 61, 133
McVey, F., 64
media of dissemination, 13, 201–3, 209, 212, 213, 266nn2–5, 267nn6,7,9
Meeker, E., 40, 48, 50, 208, 268nn16,19
Meeker, J. E., 207–8
Mellon, A., 141
Menschel, R., 147, 148, 262n8
Meredith, H. A., 257n17
Merrill, F. E., 246nn4,8, 254n44
Merton, R. K., 259n42
Metz, C., 268n26
Michaels, W. B., 68, 69
microdiversity, 10, 134
Mill, J. S., 82
Miller, P., 40
Mills, N., 256n2
Milner, J., 263n5
Mississippi scheme, 99, 104, 106, 107, 168, 255n6, 258n28
modernity, 19, 124, 126, 246n2
money as medium, 21, 24–26, 29–30, 31, 33, 34, 37–38, 40, 41, 59–60, 248n26
Moore, W. C., 65, 128, 129, 131, 149, 159, 208, 252n24, 257n13, 259n32, 260n50
morality, 1, 2, 4, 22, 23, 26, 31, 35, 36, 37, 39, 42, 44, 45, 61, 62–63, 82, 83, 85, 113, 149, 150, 243n3, 251n17
Morris, C. R., 244n6
Mortimer, T., 243nn3,4
Mottram, R. H., 48–49, 50, 115, 116, 250n11, 257n12
Mouffe, C., 244n17

Mulcaire, T., 174, 264n7
Mungan, C., 248n27
Munro, R., 89

Neal, A. G., 250n4, 268n15
Negri, A., 116
Neill, H. B., 146, 148, 149, 151, 152, 153, 155, 158, 160, 161, 162, 166, 167, 207, 215, 225, 227, 229, 260n46, 262n3, 263n19, 269nn39,40,43
Nelson, C., 244n18
Nelson, S. A., 70, 162, 228, 243n3, 249n42
neoclassical economics, 3, 20, 24, 45, 81–82, 83, 85, 91–92, 136, 138, 145, 158, 172, 238, 239, 262n12
Nicholson, C., 29
Noble, H. G., 257n6
Nocera, J., 265n23
Norberg, P., 255n12
number of speculators, 4, 5–6, 8–9, 55–56, 57, 58–63, 84, 133, 139–40, 146, 210, 244n6, 251nn15,19, 252n22

observation, 28, 73, 100, 119–20, 133, 155, 161, 178–79, 183–84, 187, 191, 192, 193, 224; as second-order, 21, 22–23, 27, 72, 152–53, 156–57, 237; self-observation, 45, 53, 133, 156, 166–68, 170
Odean, T., 254n46, 255n11, 260nn43,48, 263n19
Ora, R. N., 152
Osgood, S., 120, 122, 257n16
Oslin, G. P., 198, 204, 206
overconfidence, 13, 65, 84, 255n11, 260n48

Paddock, A., 67
Palyi, Melchior, 246n4
panic, 10, 70, 126, 127, 128, 134, 136–42, 143–44, 176, 188, 233–34, 260nn49–51, 261nn53,54,56,57,59,60
paradox of purification, 24, 71–72, 239, 253n32
parasitism, 31, 37, 44, 45, 51, 56, 64, 80, 83, 177
Parisi, L., 13
Parker, C., 57–58
Parsons, T., 13
Pasero, U., 263n1
Patrick, G. T. W., 122, 137, 140, 261n58, 269n37
Patterson, R. T., 260n47

The authorized representative in the EU for product safety and compliance is:
Mare Nostrum Group
B.V Doelen 72
4831 GR Breda
The Netherlands

www.ingramcontent.com/pod-product-compliance
Lightning Source LLC
Chambersburg PA
CBHW031405270326
41929CB00010BA/1331